Russia's new politics

The management of a postcommunist society

Stephen White

CAMBRIDGE
UNIVERSITY PRESS

PUBLISHED BY THE PRESS SYNDICATE OF THE UNIVERSITY OF CAMBRIDGE
The Pitt Building, Trumpington Street, Cambridge, United Kingdom

CAMBRIDGE UNIVERSITY PRESS
The Edinburgh Building, Cambridge CB2 2RU, UK http://www.cup.cam.ac.uk
40 West 20th Street, New York NY 10011–4211, USA   http://www.cup.org
10 Stamford Road, Oakleigh, Melbourne 3166, Australia

First published 2000

Printed in the United Kingdom at the University Press, Cambridge

Typeset in Plantin 10/12 pt   [CE]

A catalogue record for this book is available from the British Library

Library of Congress cataloguing in publication data

Russia's new politics : the management of a postcommunist society /
Stephen White.
    p.   cm.
Includes bibliographical references (p.   ) and index.
ISBN 0 521 58319 5 (hard). – ISBN 0 521 58737 9 (pbk.)
1. Russia (Federation) – Politics and government – 1991–
2. Russia (Federation) – Social conditions – 1991–
3. Post-communism – Russia (Federation)   I. Title.
JN6695.W48   2000
320.947′09′49 – dc21   99–31474   CIP

ISBN 0 521 58319 5 hardback
ISBN 0 521 58737 9 paperback

Contents

Plates

Figures

Tables

Preface

This book began life as 'Mrs Simpson', after a restaurant in Washington that bears the name of the American wife of the British king who abdicated in the 1930s. But it has its origins in a study I published in 1990 called *Gorbachev in Power*, which soon became *Gorbachev and After*, and then, in 1993, *After Gorbachev*. There was another revision, in 1994; but as its publisher, Michael Holdsworth, remarked at this point, 'We really need a new book, don't we?' This book is my response, and an attempt to provide for the postcommunist 1990s the kind of study that *Gorbachev in Power* sought to provide for the last years of Soviet rule.

The central focus of this book is Russia in the 1990s, although I am less persuaded than other scholars that there was a decisive break in 1991 and there is accordingly a good deal in earlier chapters on the years of Soviet rule and particularly the reforms that took place under the leadership of Mikhail Gorbachev. Equally, it is more than a study of politics: the changes that have taken place since 1991 have embraced the entire range of public policy, and there are chapters here on the economy, on a changing society, on values and beliefs, and on foreign policy. It is, of course, 'too soon to say' how the postcommunist 1990s will be considered within the wider context of Russian history, and the still wider context of the changes that have taken place throughout the formerly communist world. In a final chapter, nonetheless, I have offered some reflections on a series of changes that had taken Russia well beyond communist rule by the late 1990s, if less clearly to the kind of balance between leadership and accountability within a framework of law that has generally been agreed to constitute a democracy.

This is a very different book in another sense, in that it reflects the enormous advances that have taken place in what we know about the late Soviet system and in the opportunities that are available to investigate its successor. I have been able to draw, for instance, upon a mass of survey evidence, including some polls that were conducted for myself and colleagues. I have tried to keep up with a flood of memoir literature, in books, newspapers, and journals. All kinds of archival sources are now available, including the Centre for the Study of Contemporary Documentation in Moscow, which is based upon the records that were held by the General Department of the CPSU Central Committee up to its dissolution in 1991. It has become possible to interview leading officials at many levels, both about the present and the Soviet past, and to act (as I did in 1995 and 1996) as an official election observer. Equally, it has become much easier to work with Russian colleagues, in my own case with the Institute of Sociology of the Academy of Sciences. It is, of course, as important as it has ever been to take account of the printed press, of translation and abstracting journals, and of electronic sources of information, and to visit the country (and not just its capital) as often as possible.

In preparing this book, accordingly, there are many people I must thank and many others who will I hope be satisfied with a more general acknowledgement. Within my own department I have had the privilege of working with William Miller in a substantial survey-based investigation of postcommunist Europe, including Russia, and with Sarah Oates, first as a research assistant and then as a colleague, who made a particular contribution to the sections of this book that depend upon computing and urged me from the outset to 'write another book like *Russia Goes Dry*'. Jeanette Berrie, Avril Johnston, and Eileen Doherty offered expert secretarial support, including the preparation of graphics. I have drawn at some points on a Leverhulme-funded project on spatial aspects of electoral behaviour that I have been conducting with Matthew Wyman, now of the University of Keele, as well as Sarah Oates and Ian McAllister of the Australian National University. I have also drawn on research conducted with Evan Mawdsley of Glasgow's Department of Modern History for an ESRC-funded study of the political elite in the Soviet period; and upon another ESRC-funded study, of the implications for Russia and other former Soviet republics of the expansion of NATO and the European Union, which I have begun to undertake in association with John Löwenhardt of the Institute of Central and East European Studies at Glasgow as well as Margot Light of the London School of Economics (who was kind enough to read my chapter in this book on foreign policy). One of the most welcome consequences of the changes that have taken place in the formerly communist world is the way that they have brought together complementary groups of scholars in different institutions with a variety of backgrounds; this has led in my own case to a series of collaborative studies with Richard Rose of Strathclyde University, who has led the way internationally in bringing the postcommunist countries within the parameters of comparative politics.

Elsewhere, it is a pleasure once again to acknowledge the assistance I have had from Olga Kryshtanovskaya and her colleagues at the Institute of Sociology in Moscow; and to thank colleagues elsewhere in Britain for helping to alert me to publications of which I might have been unaware, including Martin Dewhirst and David Wedgwood Benn. In Glasgow University Library, Tania Konn and Ada Boddy have helped to maintain the kind of research collection without which a book of this kind could not be seriously contemplated, and responded to a series of more specific inquiries. Michael Holdsworth and John Haslam, at Cambridge University Press, encouraged my progress without yielding to impatience and welcomed the suggestion that I make use of photographs and other illustrations; this book was Michael's idea, and with their assistance it has been published with despatch as well as professionalism. I would like to dedicate this book, finally, to my eleven-year-old son Alexander: he wanted to see his name in a book, and he read some of the chapters – readers may guess which ones – with great approval.

Finally, a note on conventions. For the transliteration of Russian I have based myself upon the scheme used by *Europe–Asia Studies*, but where other forms are familiar to an English-language reader I have preferred them (thus Alexander rather than Aleksandr, Yeltsin rather than Yel'tsin, Lebed rather than Lebed', Archangel rather than Arkhangel'sk). Citations are given in full when they first occur in each chapter, and thereafter in a shortened form. Placenames are particularly difficult, given that so many of them have changed; but as a general rule I have preferred the name that prevailed at the time to which the discussion refers (so it was Leningrad until 1990, and thereafter St Petersburg; although Leningrad region still remains, as does Sverdlovsk region). Russians, as well as Western scholars, will hope that there is less instability in these matters in the future than there has been in the recent past.

1   From Brezhnev to Yeltsin

In early 1982 Leonid Brezhnev was apparently at the height of his powers. General secretary of the ruling Communist Party since October 1964 and, since 1977, chairman of the Presidium of the Supreme Soviet or head of state, he had presided over a steady rise in living standards at home and an expansion of Soviet influence throughout the wider world. Under Brezhnev's leadership gross national product had doubled between 1960 and 1970 and more than trebled by 1980. Industrial production had more than quadrupled. Agricultural production had increased more modestly (in 1981 and 1982 the harvests were so poor that the figures were simply suppressed), but the real incomes of ordinary citizens had more than doubled over the two decades and the wages paid to collective farmers had increased more than four times. Nor was this simply statistics. By the end of Brezhnev's administration three times as many Soviet citizens had acquired a higher education; there were more hospital beds, more cars, and many more colour televisions. And despite the disappointments in agriculture, for which climatic conditions were at least partly responsible, there had been considerable improvements in the Soviet diet. The consumption of meat, fish, and fruit per head of population was up by about half, while the consumption of potatoes and bread, the staples of earlier years, had fallen back considerably.[1]

By the early 1980s, in parallel with these domestic changes, the USSR had begun to acquire an international influence that accorded rather more closely with the country's enormous territory, population, and natural resources. Forced to back down in humiliating circumstances in the Cuban missile crisis of 1962, the USSR had since acquired a strategic capability that gave it an approximate parity with the USA by the end of the decade. The Soviet Union had one of the world's largest armies and one of its largest navies, and it dominated the Warsaw Treaty Organisation, which was one of the world's most important military alliances. It was the centre of one of the world's largest trading blocs, the Council for Mutual Economic Assistance, and was a founding member of the United Nations, where it occupied a permanent seat in the Security Council. The USSR's status as a superpower had been confirmed by a series of agreements with its capitalist rival, the United States, particularly SALT I in 1972 and its unratified successor, SALT II, in 1979. And it was represented much more widely in international affairs: the USSR had diplomatic relations with 144 foreign states by the early 1970s, twice as many as in the early 1960s; it took part in the work of over 400 international organisations, and was a signatory to more than 7,000 international treaties or conventions.[2] The Soviet Union was 'one of the greatest world powers', the official history of Soviet foreign policy could boast by the early 1980s, 'without whose participation not a single international problem can be resolved'.[3] This was an exaggeration, but a pardonable one.

Leonid Brezhnev, the symbol of this developing military and politico-economic might, had increasingly become the central element in the political system that underpinned it. Originally, in 1964, a 'collective leadership', it had become a leadership 'headed by comrade L. I. Brezhnev' by the early 1970s. In 1973, in a further sign of his increasing dominance, Brezhnev's name was listed first among the members of the Politburo even though KGB chairman Yuri Andropov had joined and should, on alphabetical principles, have displaced him. The general secretary made his own contribution to these developments, complaining whenever he thought he was being neglected by the newspapers (it was 'as if I don't exist', he told *Pravda* in 1975),[4] and taking 'organisational measures' to ensure that his public addresses were welcomed with sufficient enthusiasm.[5] By 1976, at its 25th Congress, Brezhnev had become the party's 'universally acclaimed leader' and *vozhd'* (chief), a term previously used to describe Stalin; there was 'stormy, prolonged applause' when it was announced that he had been re-elected to the Central Committee, and a standing ovation when Brezhnev himself announced that he had once again been elected general secretary.[6] He became a Marshal of the Soviet Union later the same year, and a bronze bust was unveiled in his birthplace;[7] an official biography, published in December, declared the general secretary an 'inspiring example of selfless service to the socialist motherland [and] to the ideals of scientific communism'.[8]

In 1977 Brezhnev consolidated his position by adding the largely ceremonial chairmanship of the Presidium of the USSR Supreme Soviet, or collective presidency, at the same time as the dominant position of the Communist Party was itself being acknowledged in Article 6 of the new constitution. He took receipt of the Gold Medal of Karl Marx, the highest award of the Academy of Sciences, for his 'outstanding contribution to the development of Marxist-Leninist theory';[9] in 1978 he added the Order of Victory for his 'great contribution' to the success of the Soviet people and their armed forces in the Great Patriotic War,[10] and then in 1979 the Lenin Prize for Literature for memoirs that had been written for him by an assistant who himself received the Order of Lenin a few days later.[11] At the 26th Party Congress in 1981 Brezhnev was hailed as an 'outstanding political leader and statesman', a 'true continuer of Lenin's great cause', and an 'ardent fighter for peace and communism';[12] his speech was punctuated seventy-eight times by 'applause', forty times by 'prolonged applause', and eight times by 'stormy, prolonged applause',[13] and there were shouts of 'hurrah' when it was announced that he had unanimously been re-elected to the Central Committee.[14] Unprecedentedly, the whole Politburo and Secretariat, Brezhnev included, were re-elected without change; Brezhnev's son Yuri, a first deputy minister of foreign trade, became a candidate member of the Central Committee at the same time, and so too did his son-in-law Yuri Churbanov, a first deputy minister of internal affairs.

Brezhnev's seventy-fifth birthday, in December 1981, brought these tributes to a new pitch of intensity. Seven of *Pravda*'s eight pages on 19 December were wholly or partly devoted to the event, and tributes continued to appear in the central press throughout the following week. Brezhnev himself attended a ceremony in the Kremlin where he was invested with a series of distinctions by the leaders of the East European communist states, who had come to Moscow for the occasion. The Soviet awards, which he had himself to authorise as head of state, included a seventh Order of Lenin and a fourth Hero of the Soviet Union citation. Mikhail Suslov, a few years his senior, remarked at the conferment of these distinctions that seventy-five was regarded in the Soviet Union as no more than the 'beginning of middle age'.[15] Brezhnev's life was turned into a film, *Story of a Communist*; his wartime exploits in the Caucasus, little noted at the time, were presented as all but the decisive turning point in the struggle against the Nazis; his memoirs became the subject of a play, a popular song, and a full-scale oratorio. He had already accumulated more state awards than all previous Soviet leaders taken together, and more military distinctions than Marshal Zhukov, who had saved Leningrad and liberated Berlin;[16] when he died, more than 200 decorations followed his coffin to the grave.[17] Even a modest poem, 'To the German Komsomol', written when he was seventeen, received front-page treatment when it appeared in *Pravda* in May 1982.

Brezhnev's personal and political powers, nonetheless, were clearly

Plate 1.1   Statues of Leonid Brezhnev in the Tret'yakov Gallery sculpture park, Moscow

failing. According to subsequent accounts, he began to suffer serious ill-health at the end of the 1960s and in January 1976 was clinically dead for a short time following a stroke.[18] For two months he was unable to work, as his speech and writing had been impaired, and thereafter he was constantly surrounded by doctors, with a fully equipped ambulance following his car on trips abroad. His speech became slurred, his breathing laboured, his concentration limited; visiting Baku in one of his last public appearances, he startled his audience by referring repeatedly to 'Afghanistan' instead of 'Azerbaijan' (he had been reading the wrong speech); visiting Prague, he read out some pages twice and asked for a translation when the Czech party leader ended his welcoming address with a passage in Russian (there was a 'deathly silence in the hall').[19] Newspapers did what they could to conceal Brezhnev's physical decline by using a much earlier photograph, adding new medals as they were awarded.[20] But there was no disguising his condition from immediate colleagues, to whom, indeed, he had twice suggested resignation;[21] Politburo meetings, which used to take several hours, dwindled to fifteen or twenty minutes,[22] and public occasions, however formal, left a 'pitiful impression'.[23] Among the wider public unkind anecdotes were already circulating: his eyebrows, in one of these, were 'Stalin's moustache at a higher level'; in yet another, he was to have an operation to enlarge his chest to accommodate the medals he had been awarded (even his son-in-law had to concede that this fondness for decorations was one of the general secretary's weaknesses[24]).

Perhaps most serious of all, Brezhnev's grip on affairs of state became increasingly infirm. The death of Suslov, in January 1982, seems in retrospect to have been crucial. One of the Politburo's oldest and longest-serving members with acknowledged authority in both ideology and foreign affairs, Suslov had served as kingmaker in 1964, declining the general secretaryship for himself and backing Brezhnev for the position, and then becoming the 'second person in the party' towards the end of his period of rule.[25] With Suslov gone, the Brezhnev leadership began to disintegrate rapidly. At the end of the same month the death was reported of Semen Tsvigun, first deputy chairman of the KGB and the husband of the younger sister of Brezhnev's wife; rumour suggested it was a case of suicide precipitated by his impending arrest on corruption charges.[26] At the beginning of March 1982 came the arrest of 'Boris the gypsy' and other figures from the world of circus entertainment on charges of bribery and currency speculation; all were close friends of Brezhnev's daughter Galina and their arrest showed that the general secretary's authority was no longer sufficient to protect them.[27] Later the same month the head of the trade union organisation, Alexei

Shibaev, was replaced amid reports that he had diverted union funds to build dachas for his relatives and friends, and led a disreputable private life; in April, the procurator general announced that a former fisheries minister had been executed for a caviare fraud.[28]

Still more significantly, in May 1982 a plenary session of the CPSU Central Committee took place at which Brezhnev was unable to secure the election of his 'faithful Sancho Panza',[29] Konstantin Chernenko, to the powerful position of Central Committee secretary with responsibility for ideology that had become vacant with the death of Suslov. In a development widely seen as significant both at home and abroad it was the head of the KGB, Yuri Andropov, who was successful, apparently with the support of the armed forces lobby. Another Brezhnev associate lost his position when in July 1982 the Krasnodar first secretary, Sergei Medunov, was summarily dismissed (he had extracted bribes on a massive scale but deflected all criticism by entertaining investigators to a variety of forms of hospitality including a 'rest home' where they were provided with sexual services); later still came the arrest of the manager of Moscow's most famous food store and his wife, both of whom were close associates of Brezhnev's daughter.[30] All of this suggested that Brezhnev's political authority as well as physical health were in decline, and reports circulating in the West suggested that it had already been decided he would retain the largely ceremonial state presidency, allowing another figure to be elected to the more demanding post of party leader. Brezhnev, in the event, anticipated any changes of this kind by dying suddenly on the morning of 10 November 1982, his health undermined by a two-hour stint in the reviewing box at the anniversary parade in Red Square three days earlier. *Pravda*'s obituary mourned the passing of a 'continuer of the cause of Lenin, a fervent patriot, an outstanding revolutionary and struggler for peace and communism, [and] an outstanding political and government leader of the contemporary era'.[31]

It had widely been expected that a decent interval would elapse before a successor was named as general secretary, and indeed that a prolonged succession struggle might ensue. On 11 November, however, it was announced that Andropov was to chair the committee making arrangements for Brezhnev's funeral, and the following day it was announced that an emergency meeting of the Central Committee had elected him to the vacant general secretaryship. Andropov's main rival for the succession, Konstantin Chernenko, had the task of proposing his candidacy to the Central Committee, where it was accepted unanimously. Brezhnev was buried on 15 November, Andropov making the funeral oration, and a week later the new general secretary made his first speech as party leader to the Central Committee, a brief but effective review of

Soviet foreign and domestic policy.[32] In May 1983 it became known that Andropov had succeeded Brezhnev as chairman of the Defence Council, which had ultimate authority in military and security matters, and in June he was elected to the chairmanship of the Supreme Soviet Presidium, thus concentrating in his hands after only seven months the same combination of posts that Brezhnev had taken almost thirteen years to accumulate. A series of changes in the membership of the Politburo and Secretariat, and at lower levels of the party and state, had meanwhile begun to put in place a coalition of reform-minded technocrats who might be expected to support both the new general secretary and the policies he intended to promote.

Andropov's own health, however, was far from certain. He was an elderly man (already sixty-eight when he assumed the party leadership) with a history of heart trouble, and there were rumours of incapacity from almost the outset of his period of office. The 'Brezhnev mafia' continued to lose influence, but Andropov's rival for the general secretaryship, Konstantin Chernenko, remained prominent, making the opening speech at the June 1983 Central Committee plenum and chairing the Politburo in his absence. Andropov's effective authority in fact lasted for only a few months: he was last seen in public in August 1983 and then failed to attend the anniversary parade in Red Square on 7 November and the Central Committee and Supreme Soviet meetings that took place a few weeks later. It became known that he was receiving kidney dialysis treatment at the Central Committee hospital near Moscow and that Mikhail Gorbachev, the youngest member of the Politburo and apparently the one most closely attuned to the general secretary's own thinking, was maintaining links between him and other members of the leadership.[33] A series of 'interviews', and an address that was circulated to the Central Committee plenum he was unable to attend, suggested that Andropov's intellectual powers were largely unimpaired; and further changes in the Politburo and Secretariat at the December 1983 plenum indicated that his control over the most important of all the powers of a party leader, that of patronage, was scarcely diminished. Nonetheless, explanations in terms of 'colds' began to wear thin, and it was not entirely unexpected when on 11 February 1984 the central press reported that the general secretary had died two days earlier after a 'long illness'.[34] Once again the party leadership was plunged into the search for a successor.

As before, there were two principal contenders: Chernenko, whose political fortunes had revived with Andropov's illness, and Gorbachev, who was evidently Andropov's own favoured candidate for the succession.[35] Chernenko was named on 10 February to head the funeral committee, which appeared to suggest he was all but certain to secure the nomination; but the formal choice took some time to arrange because of the divisions within the leadership that it reflected, with a 'Brezhnevite' faction supporting Chernenko and composed for the most part of long-serving members of the leadership like Prime Minister Nikolai Tikhonov, Kazakh party leader Dinmukhamed Kunaev, and Moscow party secretary Viktor Grishin, and an 'Andropovite' faction consisting of the younger, more reform-minded members who had joined or advanced within the leadership under the late general secretary, including Vitalii Vorotnikov, who headed the government of the Russian republic, the Azerbaijani first secretary Geidar Aliev, and Gorbachev himself.[36] The choice fell finally on Chernenko, partly, it appears, because of his seniority and experience, and partly because a Gorbachev leadership would have been likely to last rather a long time: Gorbachev was just fifty-two and had been a full member of the Politburo for less than four years.

At all events, on 13 February 1984, four days after Andropov had died, another extraordinary meeting of the Central Committee took place at which Chernenko, proposed by Tikhonov, was elected unanimously to the vacant general secretaryship.[37] It emerged subsequently that Gorbachev had also addressed the plenum,[38] and unofficial reports suggested that he had been installed as a *de facto* second secretary with a power of veto, on behalf of the younger 'Andropovite' faction, over leadership decisions.[39] Gorbachev's greater prominence was apparent in, for example, his more advanced placing in the line-up of leaders beside Andropov's coffin, in the ranking he received in pre-election speeches and on other formal party and state occasions. In turn it indicated that the Chernenko leadership was a relatively evenly balanced coalition, containing both supporters of the late party leader's reforming policies and those who believed they had been pressed too far. These sharp internal divisions were sufficient in themselves to slow down the momentum of reform, quite apart from what the new general secretary might have wished, and they persisted throughout his period of office as neither side could allow the other to gain a decisive advantage by adding to their supporters in the Politburo or Secretariat.

The chairmanship of the Supreme Soviet Presidium and of the Defence Council, as well as the party leadership, had become vacant on Andropov's death. It became known later in February 1984 that Chernenko had also assumed the chairmanship of the Defence Council, and in April 1984, on Gorbachev's nomination, the first session of the newly elected Supreme Soviet elected him to the chairmanship of its Presidium, which made him the *de facto* head of state.[40] Chernenko was nevertheless, at seventy-two, the oldest general secretary ever to have assumed office, and he had a history of lung disease that caused difficulty in breathing. Perhaps inevitably, it was regarded as a transitional general secretaryship from the outset. Two regular Central Committee plenums were held during Chernenko's period of office: the first, in April 1984, was devoted to the work of the soviets and educational reform, and the second dealt with land improvement. Neither made any change in the membership of the Politburo or Secretariat or even in the membership of the Central Committee itself, and neither could be said to have initiated any major departure in public policy (the educational reforms, which were of some importance, had been launched the previous year). There was equally little success when efforts were made to develop the significance of Chernenko's service in the border guards in the early 1930s ('there could be no personality cult', it has been pointed out, 'in the absence of a personality'); nor could much be made of his undistinguished war record.[41] A series of missed engagements suggested that Chernenko's health was already deteriorating, and official spokesmen had to admit that the recently elected general secretary was suffering from a serious cold, or perhaps worse.

Chernenko was last seen in public at the end of December 1984. He failed to meet the Greek prime minister Papandreou on his visit to Moscow in February 1985, and failed to deliver the customary eve-of-poll address to the Soviet people in the republican and local elections later the same month. Although he was shown voting on television on 24 February and was pictured in the central press receiving his deputy's credentials a week later,[42] rumours of the general secretary's physical incapacity were strengthened rather than dispelled by his evident ill-health. Finally, on the evening of 10 March 1985, he died, the medical bulletin recording that he had expired as a result of heart failure following a deterioration in the working of his lungs and liver.[43] The next day, with unprecedented speed, an extraordinary session of the Central Committee elected Mikhail Gorbachev as its third general secretary in three and a half years; he was proposed by the veteran foreign minister Andrei Gromyko in an eloquent speech that had the support of the Andropovite faction within the leadership and of the regional first secretaries, who were 'increasingly determined not to let the Politburo manoeuvre another old, sick, or weak person into the top position again'.[44] Gorbachev, who had just celebrated his fifty-fourth birthday, was still the youngest member of the Politburo and apparently in robust good health, which was in itself a considerable change. As one of the earliest jokes put it: 'What support does Gorbachev have in the Kremlin?' Answer: 'None – he walks unaided.'[45]

A changing policy agenda

Gorbachev began his acceptance speech by paying tribute to Chernenko as a 'true Leninist and outstanding figure of the CPSU and the Soviet state'.[46] Although he was later concerned to emphasise the decisive break that had occurred with his election and still more with the April 1985 Central Committee plenum at which his programme was first set out, there was in fact a good deal of continuity between the policy agenda that had been established by Andropov and Chernenko and the agenda that Gorbachev came to promote over the years that followed. The decisive break had arguably taken place under Andropov, whose security background tended to obscure his earlier exposure to the East European reform experience while Soviet ambassador to Hungary in the mid-1950s and a penetrating, somewhat puritanical intellect that was completely at odds with the complacency and corruption of the later Brezhnev era.[47] Even Chernenko, despite his background in propaganda and party administration and his career links with Brezhnev, had a number of special priorities that associated him with broadly 'liberal' opinion in the leadership context of the time, among them an interest in letters from the public, an emphasis upon the consumer sector of the economy, and a commitment to détente.[48] There were, in fact, a number of elements in common throughout the reorientation of policy that took place between the death of Andropov and the accession of Gorbachev, although the reformist impetus un-doubtedly slackened under Chernenko and acquired a new scope and impetus under Gorbachev.

One element in that reorientation of policy was leadership renewal, which had already begun in the last months of Brezhnev's term of office but which was now pursued with especial urgency. At the November 1982 meeting of the Central Committee, just ten days after Andropov's election as general secretary, Nikolai Ryzhkov, an experienced manager who had been working in the state planning office, joined the leadership as a member of the Secretariat.[49] Further changes took place in June 1983 when the Leningrad party leader Grigorii Romanov moved to Moscow to become another new member of the Secretariat, and Vitalii Vorotnikov, who had been banished to Cuba as Soviet ambassador by Brezhnev, became a candidate member of the Politburo (and shortly afterwards prime minister of the Russian Republic).[50] The December 1983 Central Committee plenum, the last under Andropov's leadership, saw Vorotnikov consolidate his rapid advance by becoming a full member of the Politburo, and Yegor Ligachev, who had been first secretary in Tomsk, became a Central Committee secretary with responsibility for appointments and the supervision of lower-level party bodies.[51] There were no changes in the party's leading bodies under Chernenko's rather shorter general secretaryship, apart from the loss that inevitably occurred with the death of Defence Minister Ustinov;[52] the change that had occurred since the death of Brezhnev, however, was already a far-reaching one. In the Politburo that had been elected in March 1981 all but three of its fourteen full members had been born before the revolution, and the average age was over seventy. Arvid Pel'she, born in 1899, had joined the Communist Party during the First World War and had taken part himself in the October revolution. In the Politburo that Gorbachev inherited in March 1985, by contrast, just five of its ten full members were of prerevolutionary origin, and four (including Gorbachev himself) were in their fifties or early sixties, alarmingly young by recent Soviet standards. At least as notable, it had become a leadership of much greater technical and managerial competence. Vorotnikov, for instance, was a qualified aviation engineer who had spent the early part of his career in a Kuibyshev factory; Ryzhkov, before coming to Gosplan, had been the successful director of the Uralmash engineering works in Sverdlovsk; Ligachev was an engineering graduate; and the new KGB head, Viktor Chebrikov, also an engineer, had a background in industrial management as well as party work in Ukraine.[53]

A further priority, associated particularly with Andropov, was social discipline. In part this meant a firm and sustained campaign against the bribery and corruption that had increasingly disfigured the later Brezhnev years. The late general secretary's family and friends were among the first to feel the effects of the new policy. In December 1982, just a month after Andropov's accession, Interior Minister Nikolai Shchelokov was dismissed from his position:[54] a close associate of Brezhnev's from Dnepropetrovsk days, he had enjoyed considerable opportunities for enrichment as head of Soviet law enforcement, acquiring a fleet of foreign cars, a photographer, a cook, and a 'masseuse' as well as rare books from public library collections.[55] Shchelokov was replaced as interior minister by Vitalii Fedorchuk, an experienced KGB career officer and a trusted Andropov associate, and in June Shchelokov and another Brezhnev crony, the former Krasnodar first secretary Medunov, were dismissed from the Central Committee for 'mistakes in their work'.[56] Although his family reportedly celebrated Chernenko's election with an all-night party, Shchelokov continued to lose favour, suffering the humiliation of expulsion from the party and losing his military rank in November 1984 for 'abuse of position for personal gain and conduct discrediting the military title of General of the Soviet

Union';[57] his wife had already committed suicide, his son – who had speculated in foreign cars – was dismissed from the bureau of the Komsomol, and he took his own life early the following year.[58]

Brezhnev's own family was also affected. His daughter Galina and her husband Churbanov were banished to Murmansk; Churbanov lost his post as first deputy interior minister in December 1984 and then his position on the Central Committee,[59] and in December 1988 he was given twelve years' imprisonment for bribe-taking on a large scale and stripped of his state honours.[60] Brezhnev's son Yuri also lost his ministerial post and his Central Committee membership, and his secretary was sentenced to nine years' imprisonment for bribe-taking;[61] Brezhnev's books – nearly 3 million copies – were withdrawn from public sale,[62] and his widow was forced to return his decorations to public custody (his Order of Victory had meanwhile been rescinded).[63] The city of Brezhnev, formerly Naberezhnye Chelny, reverted to its original name in 1988; so too did Brezhnev Square in Moscow, and the Brezhnev – formerly Cherry Tree – district in the capital (unkind humorists suggested that the Brezhnevs would soon become 'Cherry tree family').[64] Brezhnev, according to opinion polls, was already more unpopular than Stalin; the very name, his grandson told a Moscow weekly, had 'become a curse'.[65] The campaign against corruption may have owed something to Andropov's own asceticism: he lived modestly and refrained from any attempts to promote the careers of his own children, although his son Igor became a prominent member of the diplomatic service. More important, perhaps, was the concern of both Andropov and his successor that corruption, if allowed to go unchecked, might reduce the effectiveness of party control and ultimately compromise the regime itself, as had clearly happened in Poland in the late 1970s and early 1980s.

The other side of the post-Brezhnev leadership's campaign of social discipline, which also continued under Chernenko, was an attempt to strengthen discipline in the workplace and law and order in the wider society. One of the first clear signs of this new direction in official policy was the series of raids that the police began to make in early 1983 on shops, public baths, and even underground stations in order to find out which of those present had taken time off work without permission. There was certainly some room for improvement. An official report in late 1982 found that of every 100 workers surveyed, an average of 30 were absent 'for personal reasons' at any given moment, in most cases to go shopping or visit the doctor. Another investigation in 800 Moscow enterprises found that in some cases no more than 10 per cent of the workforce were still at their places during the last hour of the shift.[66] A further series of decrees on 'socialist labour discipline' sought to reduce poor-quality workmanship, alcoholism, and absenteeism at the workplace,[67] and the positive example of Alexei Stakhanov was again held up for emulation, nearly fifty years after his record-breaking exploits in the Donbass coalmines[68] (rather later, in 1988, it was revealed that the champion miner had been transferred to office work, turned to drink, and died a lonely and disillusioned man[69]).

In terms of politics the Andropov period saw no liberalisation, despite early and perhaps inspired reports that the new general secretary spoke English, and liked jazz and modern Western literature. There was an open attack, for instance, upon 'alien' and 'decadent' trends in the arts, particularly at the Central Committee meeting in June 1983 that was devoted to this subject, and there were sharply worded attacks upon the Soviet film industry (which had begun to explore some contemporary social issues) and upon the independent-minded literary journal *Novyi mir*.[70] Direct dialling facilities with the outside world were ended, apparently at Andropov's behest, in September 1982,[71] and postal and customs regulations became more stringent.[72] Steps were also taken against a number of prominent dissidents. The writer Georgii Vladimov, author of *Faithful Ruslan*, a novel about a guard-dog at a prison camp, was compelled to emigrate in early 1983 and deprived of his Soviet citizenship, and the historian Roy Medvedev, untouched for many years, was called to the procurator general's office and warned that if he did not give up his 'anti-Soviet activities' he would face criminal proceedings.[73] The theatre director Yuri Lyubimov and the historian Mikhail Geller, both resident abroad, also lost their citizenship,[74] and the number of Jews allowed to emigrate, another normally reliable barometer of liberalism, fell sharply from up to 50,000 a year in the late 1970s to 2,700 in 1982, 1,300 in 1983, and only 896 in 1984.[75]

The immediate post-Brezhnev period, however, saw no reversion to hard-line Stalinism. Dissidents and oppositionists, certainly, were harshly treated, but for those who were content to advance their objectives within the system there was a greater emphasis than before upon consultation and accountability. For the first time in modern Soviet history, for instance, reports began to appear in *Pravda* of the subjects that had been discussed at the weekly meetings of the Politburo.[76] Attempts were also made to revive the Khrushchevian practice of meeting members of the public face to face at home or in their workplace. Andropov made a symbolic gesture of some importance by visiting the Ordzhonikidze machine tool factory at the end of January 1983 for an extended and frankly worded exchange with its workforce; Chernenko made a less remarkable visit to the 'Hammer and Sickle' metallurgical plant in April 1984.[77] The rights of ordinary workers at their workplace were also strengthened, at least on paper, by a law on labour collectives, adopted in June 1983 after an extended public discussion, which gave workforce meetings greater rights in relation to management and the appointment of leading personnel, but which also required them to take more responsibility for poor workmanship and shirking.[78] The annual plan and budget, for the first time ever, were submitted to the All-Union Council of Trade Unions for its consideration in late 1984.[79]

In public life more generally there was a greater emphasis upon openness and publicity, or what soon became widely known as *glasnost'*. One indication of this rather different approach was the decision, at the June 1983 Central Committee plenum, to establish a national public opinion centre;[80] another was the revival of the Khrushchevian practice of publishing the full proceedings of Central Committee meetings, at least in this instance.[81] And there was a continuing emphasis, throughout the period, upon the need to take account of the concerns of ordinary citizens, particularly in the form of letters to party and state bodies and to the press. The harsher penalties that were imposed upon bribery and corruption were reported to have been prompted by communications of this kind, and the strengthening of law and order was similarly presented as a response to pressure from citizens in Gorky, who had complained that they were afraid to walk the city streets at night.[82] Difficult though it was to assess such matters precisely, these new emphases in public policy appeared to have been well received by the Soviet public: according to an unpublished opinion poll that was reported in the Western press, fully 87 per cent of those who were asked took a 'positive' view of the first three months of the new regime and by implication of post-Brezhnev changes more generally.[83]

Still more fundamentally, there was a reconsideration in the Andropov and Chernenko periods of the official ideology from which the regime still claimed to derive its right to rule. One of the most important contributions was Andropov's article on 'The teaching of Karl Marx and some questions of socialist construction in the USSR', which appeared in the party theoretical journal *Kommunist*. Its sober and realistic tone marked off the post-Brezhnev era from the optimism of Khrushchev, and equally from Brezhnev's somewhat complacent notion of 'developed socialism'; it was, in effect, the 'first public criticism by a ruling leader of the party's general line'.[84] There was a need, Andropov insisted, to understand the stage of development that had been reached in the USSR, and to avoid setting targets that would be impossible to achieve. The Soviet Union, he emphasised, was only at the beginning of the long

Plate 1.2   Com-mu-nism (*Soviet Weekly*, August 1991)

historical stage of developed socialism; there should be no exaggeration of their closeness to the ultimate goal of full communism, and there should be a proper acknowledgement of the difficulties that lay ahead.[85] Andropov's speech at the June 1983 Central Committee plenum, which dealt extensively with the revisions that would be required in the Party Programme, noted similarly that there were elements of 'isolation from reality' in the existing text, adopted in 1961, and which had notoriously promised that a communist society would 'in the main' be established by 1980. It was vital, Andropov had already insisted, to take proper account of the situation that actually existed, and to avoid 'ready-made solutions'.[86]

Chernenko, who became chairman of the commission preparing a new Programme at the same time as he became party leader, took the same practical and unheroic approach. Addressing the commission in April 1984, he reminded the participants that developed socialism would be a 'historically protracted' period and urged them to concentrate their attention upon the complicated tasks that still remained rather than upon what Lenin had called the 'distant, beautiful, and rosy future'.[87] These emphases in turn became the basis for a developing specialist literature which acknowledged, more openly than ever before, that socialism had not necessarily resolved complex issues such as environmental conservation, the nationality question, or gender inequalities. Still more provocatively, it was suggested that Soviet-type societies contained 'contradictions' based upon the different interests of the various groups of which they were composed, and that these could lead to 'serious collisions' of the kind that had occurred in Poland in the early 1980s unless far-reaching democratic reforms were instituted.[88] The debate was suspended in 1984 but two years later it was one of those to which Gorbachev devoted particular attention in his report to the 27th Party Congress.[89]

The Gorbachev leadership

The advent of a new general secretary had normally meant a significant change in the direction of Soviet public policy, although any change took some time to establish itself as the new leader gradually marginalised his opponents and coopted his supporters on to the Politburo and Secretariat. At the outset of his administration Gorbachev's objectives, and indeed his personal background, were still fairly obscure even at leading levels of the party. Gorbachev, unlike his two main rivals Grigorii Romanov and Viktor Grishin, had not addressed a party congress; he had still no published collection of writings to his name; and he had made only a couple of official visits abroad, to Canada in 1983 and to the United Kingdom in late 1984, on both occasions as the head of a delegation of Soviet parliamentarians. Andrei Gromyko, proposing Gorbachev's candidacy to the Central Committee, explained what had convinced him personally that Gorbachev would be a suitable general secretary: Gorbachev, he indicated, had chaired meetings of the Politburo in Chernenko's absence and had done so 'brilliantly, without any exaggeration'.[90] Gorbachev himself told the Politburo that agreed to nominate him there was 'no need to change their policies',[91] and in his acceptance speech he paid tribute to the late general secretary and promised to continue the policy of his two predecessors, which he defined as 'acceleration of socioeconomic development and the perfection of all aspects of social life'.[92] At the same time there were some elements in the new general secretary's biography which suggested that this new administration would be more than a continuation of the ones that had immediately preceded it.

One of those elements was Gorbachev's own background, particularly his education and age group, which placed him among the reform-minded '1960ers' who had been inspired by the 20th Party Congress in 1956 and by the process of destalinisation that followed it, rather than the Brezhnev generation, whose formative experience had been their military service during the Second World War and who had in turn been led to believe that the Soviet system rested on popular support and that it was capable of supreme achievement.[93] Gorbachev himself, born on 2 March 1931 to a peasant family in the north Caucasus, was too young to have taken a direct part in the hostilities, although he had vivid memories of the German occupation of his native village and of the destruction that had taken place in other parts of the country.[94] His father was wounded in the conflict and he was brought up mainly by his maternal grandparents, who were poor peasants of Ukrainian origin.[95] He worked first as a mechanic at a machine-tractor station and then in 1950, with the help of his local party organisation, enrolled in the Law Faculty at Moscow State University. Gorbachev was a Komsomol activist while at university, and joined the CPSU itself in 1952. He graduated in 1955, the first Soviet leader since Lenin to receive a legal training and the first to complete his education at the country's premier university, although it was an institution in which the Stalinist *Short Course* still held pride of place and in which the 'slightest deviation from the official line . . . was fraught with consequences'.[96]

The Czech communist and later dissident Zdenek Mlynar, who was Gorbachev's friend and classmate at this time, recalled him as an open-minded student who had particularly liked Hegel's dictum that the truth was 'always concrete' and who was prepared, even before the death of Stalin, to take issue with the purges (Lenin, he pointed out, had at least allowed his Menshevik opponents to emigrate).[97] Gorbachev himself remembered objecting when one of his instructors insisted on reading out Stalin's newly published *Economic Problems of Socialism in the USSR* page by page (there was an immediate investigation); one of his fellow students, indeed, recalled him as 'all but a "dissident" at this time'.[98] But he graduated without incident – there had even been a possibility that he might take up a career in the KGB – and returned to Stavropol', where he worked in the Komsomol and party apparatus and later completed a correspondence course at the local agricultural institute. In 1966 he became first secretary of the city party committee, in 1970 he was appointed to head the territorial party organisation, and the following year he joined the Central Committee as a full member. In 1978 Gorbachev replaced his mentor Fedor Kulakov in the Central Committee Secretariat, taking responsibility for agriculture. In 1979, in addition, he became a candidate and then in 1980 a full member of the ruling Politburo; this made him, in his late forties, one of the very few 'super secretaries' who were represented on both of the party's leading bodies and who formed the most obvious pool of candidates for the succession.[99]

Gorbachev met his wife Raisa, a philosophy graduate, while they were both at Moscow University (they met during a class in ballroom dancing[100]). Born in the town of Rubtsovsk in Siberia in 1932, Raisa Maksimovna was the eldest daughter of a Ukrainian railway engineer. Like Gorbachev's, her family had suffered during the Stalin years: Gorbachev's grandfather had been released after torture had failed to extract a confession; Raisa's own father had been arrested, and her grandfather had been shot for 'counter-revolutionary agitation' (it was not until 1988 that the family received a formal certificate of rehabilitation).[101] The Gorbachevs married in 1953 and then moved to Stavropol' two years later, after their graduation; Raisa was able to pursue research into the nature of social relations in the nearby countryside and was awarded a candidate of science degree (roughly equivalent to a Western doctorate) in 1967. In the 1970s she lectured for some years at Moscow University.[102] Previous party leaders' wives had played a very discreet role in Soviet public life: it was not even known that Andropov's wife was still alive until she appeared at his funeral in 1984. Mrs Gorbachev, however, swiftly assumed a prominent position in domestic and international affairs, acting as a Soviet 'First Lady' when the general secretary travelled abroad on official occasions. Her views, equally, had a strong influence upon him: they discussed 'everything' at home in the evenings, Gorbachev told an NBC interviewer in late 1987 in remarks that were censored for Soviet domestic consumption; others, including his bodyguard, thought he was even 'subordinate to her'.[103]

It was not customary for a Soviet leader to discuss his personal affairs with the mass media, but Gorbachev did venture some information on this subject when he was interviewed by the Italian communist paper *L'Unità* in May 1987. His main weakness, Gorbachev believed, was that he had too many interests. He had enrolled in the law faculty at university, but had originally intended to study physics. He liked mathematics, but also history and literature. In later years he had turned more and more to the study of economics, while remaining interested in philosophy.[104] This was not, to put it mildly, the intellectual background of his immediate predecessor. Interest in the general secretary's personal life was hardly satisfied by such revelations and there were further queries in the spring of 1989. Did Mikhail Sergeevich, for instance, like fishing? And why did *glasnost'* not apply to the person who had invented it?[105] Gorbachev obliged with some further information in an interview in a Central Committee journal later the same year. He earned 1,200 rubles a month, he explained, the same as other members of the Politburo. He had a considerable additional income from royalties and other sources (his book *Perestroika* alone had appeared in more than 100 countries), but he had donated any earnings of this kind to the party budget and charitable causes. Literature, theatre, music, and cinema remained his hobbies, although he had less and less time to devote to them.[106] The general secretary, it also emerged, had been baptised; though not himself a believer, he supported the constitutional provision by which citizens were free to practise their faith if they wished to do so, and his mother was known to be an active worshipper.[107]

As well as his personal characteristics, there were also clues in Gorbachev's speeches before his assumption of the general secretaryship as to the direction of policy he was likely to pursue. Perhaps the clearest indication of this kind was a speech Gorbachev delivered to an all-union conference on ideology in December 1984. The speech contained positive references to self-management, which Lenin had 'never counterposed to Soviet state power', and drew attention to the various interests of different social groups and to the need for a greater measure of social justice (which had become a coded form of attack upon the Brezhnev legacy). There was enormous scope, Gorbachev went on, for the further development of the Soviet political system, and of socialist democracy. This was partly a matter of developing all aspects of the work of the elected soviets, and of involving workers more fully in the affairs of their own workplace. It was also a matter of securing a greater degree of *glasnost'* or openness in party and state life. As well as tributes to Chernenko, there were clear and positive allusions to Andropov in his remarks about the 'two previous years' and the need to avoid 'ready-made solutions'.[108] Gorbachev's electoral address of 20 February 1985, made at a time when Chernenko's serious illness was widely known, repeated many of these themes, combining almost populist references to Soviet power as a form of rule 'of the toilers and for the toilers' with more abrasive remarks about the need for self-sufficiency in enterprise management and better discipline on the shopfloor.[109]

The direction of reform became still clearer at the April 1985 Central Committee plenum, the first that Gorbachev addressed as party leader and the one from which it became conventional to date the start of *perestroika*. There had been significant achievements in all spheres of Soviet life, Gorbachev told the plenum. The USSR had a powerful, developed economy, a highly skilled workforce, and an advanced scientific base. Everyone had the right to work, to social security, to cultural resources of all kinds, and to participation in the administration of state affairs. But further changes were needed in order to achieve a 'qualitatively new state of society', including modernisation of the economy and the extension of popular self-government. The key issue was the acceleration of economic growth. This was quite feasible if the 'human factor' was called more fully into play, and if the reserves that existed throughout the economy were properly utilised. This in turn required a greater degree of decentralisation of economic management, including cost accounting at enterprise level and a closer connection between the work people did and the rewards that they received.[110] The months and years that followed saw the gradual assembly of a leadership team to direct these changes and the further extension of what was already a challenging reform agenda.

The formation of a new leadership was the easier of these two tasks and the one that advanced more rapidly. The April 1985 Central Committee plenum itself made a start with the appointment of Yegor Ligachev and Nikolai Ryzhkov, both Andropov appointees, to full membership of the Politburo without passing through the customary candidate or nonvoting stage. There had been no promotions of this kind for at least twenty years and it was an early demonstration of Gorbachev's control over the vital power of appointment.[111] There were further changes in July 1985: Grigorii Romanov, Gorbachev's principal rival for the leadership, retired from both Politburo and Secretariat 'on grounds of ill-health' (he was just over sixty and a rumoured weakness for women and alcohol hardly suggested infirmity), and two new Central Committee secretaries were elected, one of them Boris Yeltsin, who had been party first secretary in Sverdlovsk.[112] At the Supreme Soviet session that took place the following day Foreign Minister Andrei Gromyko, rather than Gorbachev himself, was elected to the vacant chairmanship of the Presidium, and the Georgian party leader Edward Shevardnadze became foreign minister in his place (he had no diplomatic experience but was committed, like Gorbachev, to a change in Soviet relations with the outside world);[113] and then in September Ryzhkov replaced the veteran Brezhnevite, Nikolai Tikhonov, as prime minister.[114] A still more extensive restructuring took place at the 27th Party Congress in March 1986, including the appointment of five new Central Committee secretaries: one of them was Alexander Yakovlev, a close Gorbachev associate who had previously served as ambassador to Canada and as director of one of the institutes of the Academy of Sciences; another was Alexandra Biryukova, a former secretary of the All-Union Council of Trade Unions and the first woman member of the leadership since the early 1960s. Remarkably, nearly half the members of this newly elected Politburo and Secretariat were people who had not served in either body before Gorbachev's election to the general secretaryship the previous year.[115]

There were further changes in the leadership in the months that followed, all of which tended to strengthen Gorbachev's position still further. The Central Committee plenum that took place in January 1987 brought Alexander Yakovlev into the Politburo as a candidate member; he and Alexander Luk'yanov, a leading jurist and head of the general department in the Central Committee apparatus, both became Central Committee secretaries (Luk'yanov, it later emerged, had been a member of the Komsomol committee at the same time as Gorbachev when both of them were at Moscow University in the early 1950s[116]). Two Brezhnev appointees, Dinmukhamed Kunaev and Mikhail Zimyanin, left the Politburo and Secretariat respectively at the same time; Kunaev, whose resignation was ostensibly 'in connection with his retirement on a pension', was expelled from the Central Committee itself the following June for 'serious shortcomings' in his tenure of the Kazakh first secretaryship.[117] At the same meeting Yakovlev moved up from candidate to full Politburo membership, and Dmitrii Yazov, the new defence minister, became a candidate member, replacing Marshal Sokolov who had been discredited by the ability of a young West German, Matthias Rust, to land a small plane in Red Square (which was soon being called 'Moscow's fourth international airport').[118] Changes in the party leadership were only a part of a much wider-ranging replacement of leading officials at all levels. All the fourteen republican first secretaries had been replaced by 1989, some more than once, and there was an equally far-reaching turnover in the Central Committee, an overwhelming 84 per cent of whom when elected in 1990 had never previously held party office of any kind.[119] Two-thirds of the leading officials of lower-level party organisations had been replaced by late 1988,[120] and 88 per cent of the deputies elected in March 1989 to the Congress of People's Deputies were entirely new to representative duties;[121] in the economy, Gorbachev himself reported, more than two-thirds of the country's industrial managers and farm directors had been replaced by early 1989.[122]

Of all the policies that were promoted by the Gorbachev leadership, *glasnost'* was perhaps the most distinctive and the one that had been pressed furthest by the end of communist rule.[123] *Glasnost'*, usually translated as openness or transparency, was not the same as freedom of the press or the right to information; nor was it original to Gorbachev (it figured, for instance, in the constitution that had been adopted in 1977 under Leonid Brezhnev). It did, however, reflect the new general secretary's belief that without a greater awareness of the real state of affairs and of the considerations that had led to particular decisions there would be no willingness on the part of the Soviet people to commit themselves to his programme of *perestroika* ('the better the people are informed', he told the Central Committee that elected him, 'the more consciously they act, the more actively they support the party, its plans and programmatic objectives').[124] Existing policies were in any case ineffectual and often counterproductive. The newspaper *Sovetskaya Rossiya* reported the case of Vladimir Polyakov of Kaluga, a well-read man who followed the press closely and never missed the evening television news. He knew a lot about what was happening in various African countries, Polyakov complained, but had 'only a very rough idea what was happening in his home town'.[125] In late 1985, another reader complained, there had been a major earthquake in Tajikistan, but all they were told was that 'lives had been lost'. At about the same time there had been an earthquake in Mexico and a volcanic eruption in Colombia, both covered in full with on-the-spot reports and details of the casualties. Was Tajikistan really further from Moscow than Latin America?[126]

Influenced by considerations such as these, the Gorbachev leadership made steady and sometimes dramatic progress in broadening the scope of public debate and exposing the Soviet past as well as the Soviet present to critical scrutiny. The Brezhnev era was one of the earliest targets. It had been a time, Gorbachev told the 27th Party Congress in 1986, when a 'curious psychology – how to change things without really changing anything' – had been dominant.[127] There had been real achievements in the early years of his rule, with the development of new branches of industry, an improvement in living standards, and an increase in the Soviet Union's international influence. But the promise of these achievements had been dissipated by a failure to carry the reforms through to their logical conclusion, or to make the changes that had become necessary in social policy and in the leadership itself; the result had been a period of 'stagnation', with the economy slipping into crisis and party and government leaders lagging increasingly behind the needs of the time.[128] The Stalin question was a still more fundamental one, for all Soviet reformers. Gorbachev, to begin with, was reluctant even to concede there was a question. Stalinism, he told the French press in 1986, was a 'notion made up by enemies of communism' which was 'widely used to discredit the Soviet Union and socialism as a whole'; Stalin himself, he insisted elsewhere, had made an 'indisputable contribution to the struggle for socialism [and] to the defence of its achievements'.[129] By early 1987, however, Gorbachev was insisting that there must be 'no forgotten names, no blank spots' in Soviet literature and history,[130] and by November of that year, when he came to give his address on the seventieth anniversary of the revolution, he was ready to condemn the 'wanton repressive measures' of the 1930s, 'real crimes' in which 'many thousands of people inside and outside the party' had suffered.[131]

Plate 1.3 'Never again!' (an anti-Stalinist poster, 1990)

In the course of his speech Gorbachev announced that a Politburo commission had been set up to investigate the repression of the Stalinist years, and this led to the rehabilitation of many prominent figures from the party's past (and thousands of others) from 1988 onwards. The most important figure to be restored to public respectability in this way was the former *Pravda* editor Nikolai Bukharin, whose sentence was posthumously quashed in February 1988 (his expulsions from the party and from the Academy of Sciences were also rescinded).[132] Trotsky had not been sentenced by a Soviet court and there was therefore no judgement to be reconsidered; but his personal qualities began to receive some recognition in the Soviet press, and from 1989 onwards his writings began to appear in mass-circulation as well as scholarly journals.[133] An extended discussion took place about the numbers that Stalin had condemned to death: for some it was about a million by the end of the 1930s, but for others (including the historian Roy Medvedev) it was at least 12 million, with a further 38 million repressed in other ways.[134] Some of the mass graves of the Stalin period began to be uncovered at the same time, the most extensive of which were in the Kuropaty forest near Minsk. The victims, as many as 40,000, had been shot between 1937 and 1941;[135] this, and the other graves that were still being discovered in the early 1990s, was an indictment of Stalinism more powerful than anything the historians could hope to muster.[136]

Glasnost' led to further changes in the quality of Soviet public life, from literature and the arts to statistics and a wide-ranging discussion about the future of socialism itself. There was new information about infant mortality and life expectancy, the figures for which had been suppressed since the early 1970s, and there was information on abortions and suicides, which had not been reported since the 1920s.[137] Subjects that had been unmentionable in the Brezhnev years, such as violent crime, drugs, and prostitution, began to receive extensive and even sensational treatment. Many events of the past, such as the devastating earthquake in Ashkhabad in 1948 and the nuclear accident in the Urals in 1957, were belatedly acknowledged. Figures for defence spending and foreign debt were revealed to the newly elected Congress of People's Deputies when it met in 1989; figures for capital punishment followed in 1991. Virtually all the banned writers had been published by the same date, including Pasternak's *Doctor Zhivago*, Zamyatin's futuristic *We*, and Vasilii Grossman's *Life and Fate* (all in 1988); Alexander Solzhenitsyn's *Gulag Archipelago* and Nabokov's *Lolita* both appeared in 1989 (so did Orwell's *1984*), and by 1990 some extracts from Hitler's *Mein Kampf* were being published in the main military-historical journal. Libraries opened up their closed stacks; museums brought out their Chagalls and Kandinskys; and archives introduced a thirty-year rule. The new press law, adopted in June 1990, went even further by abolishing censorship entirely.[138] Opinion polls suggested that *glasnost'*, for all its limitations, was the change in Soviet life that was most apparent to ordinary people, and the one they were most likely to think had done more good than harm.[139]

The 'democratisation' of Soviet political life was an associated change, and one that was intended to unlock the human energies that, for Gorbachev, had been choked off by the bureaucratic centralism of the Stalin and Brezhnev years. The Soviet Union, he told the 19th Party Conference in the summer of 1988, had pioneered the idea of workers' control, and the right to work, and equality for women and national minorities. The political system established by the October revolution, however, had undergone 'serious deformations', leading to the development of a 'command-administrative system' that had made possible the 'omnipotence of Stalin and his entourage' and then a 'wave of repressive measures and lawlessness'. The role of party and state officialdom had increased out of all proportion, and a 'bloated administrative apparatus' had begun to impose its own priorities in political and economic matters. Nearly a third of the adult population were regularly elected to the soviets, or to the commissions that advised them, but few had any real influence over the decisions that were taken by their executives. Social life as a whole had become 'straitjacketed' by controls of various kinds, and ordinary working people had become 'alienated' from the system that was supposed to represent their interests. It was this 'ossified system of government, with its command-and-pressure mechanism', that had become the main obstacle to *perestroika*.[140]

The Conference agreed to undertake a 'radical reform' of the political system, and this led to a series of constitutional and other changes from 1988 onwards that – for the reformers – had as their ultimate objective the development of a model of socialism that would recover the democratic gains that had been won in the early postrevolutionary years while still retaining a framework of public ownership and comprehensive welfare. An entirely new election law, approved in December 1988, broke new ground by providing for – though not specifically requiring – a choice of candidate, and giving ordinary citizens the right to make nominations (see chapter 2).[141] A new state structure was established, incorporating a smaller working parliament for the first time in modern Soviet history and – from 1990 – a powerful executive presidency (see chapter 3). A reform of the political system would not be enough, however, unless it was accompanied by a strengthening of the rule of law; this led to a series of related changes, including a constitutional supervision committee that had the right to consider the legality of government decisions, and reforms in court procedures that strengthened the independence of judges. Ultimately, it was hoped, these and other reforms would help to establish a 'law-based state', first mentioned in 1988 and the subject of a resolution at the Party Conference in the summer of that year.[142] The CPSU itself was meanwhile 'democratised', although the changes took rather longer to come into effect.

Leading officials, it was agreed, should be elected by competitive ballot for a maximum of two consecutive terms; members of the Central Committee should be involved much more directly in the formulation of policy; and there should be much more information about all aspects of the party's activities, from its income and expenditure (members had complained they knew more about the financial affairs of the British royal family) to the composition of its mass membership (including such details as the presence of 125 Eskimos, 7 Englishmen, 3 Americans, 2 'negroes', and 1 Bolivian).[143]

There was a still larger objective, discussed by academics and commentators as well as the political leadership: the elaboration of a 'humane and democratic socialism' that would build on Soviet achievements but combine them with the experience of other nations and schools of thought into a body of social thought that could serve as the basis of a global civilisation in the new century. Khrushchev had promised that the USSR would construct a communist society 'in the main' by 1980 in the Party Programme that had been adopted under his leadership in 1961. His successors dropped that commitment and began to describe the USSR, from the early 1970s, as a 'developed socialist society', whose evolution into a fully communist society was a matter for the distant future. Gorbachev, for his part, avoided the term 'developed socialism'[144] and opted instead for 'developing socialism', in effect a postponement into the still more distant future of the attainment of a fully communist society.[145] In 1990, in a Programmatic Declaration that was approved at the 28th Party Congress, the objective became 'humane, democratic socialism' (did this mean, some asked, that there could be a socialism that was inhumane and undemocratic?);[146] later still, in a revised version of the Party Programme that was approved by the Central Committee in the summer of 1991, the slogan had changed to 'Socialism, Democracy, Progress', with communism mentioned only as the 'epitaph on a tombstone'.[147] The new Programme committed the party to 'all-human values', democracy, 'freedom in all its forms', social justice, and a 'new world civilisation'; it was also, in Gorbachev's words, an acknowledgement that the communist ideal was unrealisable in the foreseeable future.[148]

It remained unclear, these generalities apart, how a 'humane and democratic' socialist society of this rather different kind was to be constructed. Gorbachev resisted calls to set out the way ahead in any detail: did they really want a new *Short Course*, he asked the Party Congress in 1990, referring to the discredited Marxist primer that had been produced under Stalin's auspices in 1938? And what was the point of programmes like railway timetables, with objectives that had to be achieved by certain dates; wasn't an authentic socialism the achievement of working people themselves, not something they were directed towards by others?[149] Gorbachev's objectives emerged as a set of fairly abstract propositions; they were set out, for instance, in the 'seven postulates of *perestroika*', which were formulated in his address to the Central Committee meeting that took place in January 1987. These included a 'resolute overcoming of the processes of stagnation, destruction of the retarding mechanism, and the creation of dependable and efficient machinery for expediting the social and economic progress of Soviet society', as well as a greater reliance on the 'creative endeavour of the masses', including greater socialist self-management. There would be a greater emphasis upon intensive factors of growth, including what Gorbachev described as 'socialist entrepreneurship'; there would also be a 'constant concern for the spiritual wealth and culture of every person and of society as a whole', and the elimination of 'any deviation from socialist morality'. The ultimate aim, as Gorbachev explained, was to achieve a 'fundamental renewal of all aspects of public life' and the 'fullest disclosure of the humanistic character of our social order in all its decisive aspects'.[150] However persuasive this might have been as a statement of the leadership's philosophy, it offered little guidance to party officials in their practical activity, nor did it carry conviction for a wider public at a time of economic difficulty, more assertive nationalism, and an increasingly open acknowledgement of mistakes in policy for which a party that had monopolised political power for seventy years could scarcely avoid responsibility.

It was one of Gorbachev's central assumptions that it had been 'subjective' factors and in particular the quality of leadership, rather than more deep-seated causes, that had led to the degeneration of Soviet socialism over the whole postrevolutionary period. What was the reason for their difficulties, he asked the Central Committee in April 1985? Natural and external factors were certainly important; but the main reason was that the necessary changes had not taken place in the management of a changing society.[151] For years, Gorbachev explained to the 27th Party Congress in 1986, party and government leaders had failed to challenge the bureaucratic 'command-administrative system' that had developed in the Stalinist years; it was a failure that was 'above all of a subjective character', and one that would be remedied only when leaders brought their methods of government into line with changing circumstances.[152] Speaking in July 1990, Gorbachev acknowledged that the replacement of leading officials was 'not a panacea'; but people mattered more than institutions, and the right appointments were of 'decisive' significance.[153] The 'root cause' of their difficulties, he told the Central Committee the following October, was the 'inertia of old thinking'.[154] And in a speech in November 1990 he declared that the 'most important revolution' was the 'revolution in minds, in our heads, in us ourselves'.[155] There could be little doubt, as the Gorbachev leadership drew to a close, that the Soviet leadership had been renewed more extensively than at any time in postwar history; but it was much less obvious that an attack on 'conservative thinking' was decisive to the success of *perestroika* and that deeper, more systemic choices could be avoided.

The August coup and the end of party rule

The attempted coup of August 1991, which led directly to the end of communist rule, was itself a demonstration of the limits of a leadership style that placed its main emphasis upon personal rather than institutional factors. Many of the conspirators had been Gorbachev's own appointees, even friends, and he was affected more profoundly by this than by any other aspect of the short-lived emergency (the whole family had been particularly close to Gorbachev's head of staff, Valerii Boldin, and had 'told him everything, even the most personal things').[156] The coup, in fact, had not come without warning. Foreign Minister Shevardnadze, tendering his resignation in December 1990, had told the Soviet parliament that a 'dictatorship' was approaching, although no one yet knew what form it would take.[157] Speaking in early August 1991, he again thought it possible there would be an attempt to resolve the country's difficulties by resorting to a 'strong-hand' policy'.[158] An 'Appeal to the people', published in the newspaper *Sovetskaya Rossiya* in July, called for national and patriotic unity and was signed by two of the organisers of the coup as well as other prominent hard-liners.[159] Alexander Yakovlev, in a television interview on 12 August, warned that 'conservative and reactionary forces' had been mobilising and that they would be only too glad to 'turn back the clock'. Speaking a few days later, just before the conspiracy was launched, Yakovlev warned again that a 'Stalinist grouping' had become dominant in the party leadership and that it was preparing a 'party and state coup'.[160]

These warnings notwithstanding, the attempted coup of August 1991 was a shock as well as a surprise to the Soviet leader and to the outside world.[161] August, by a coincidence, was the month in which General Kornilov had attempted to overthrow the Provisional Government in 1917, and it was the month in which the Soviet president normally took his family holidays in the Crimea. In 1987, he spent the time writing his best-selling *Perestroika*. On 18 August 1991, he was working on the text of a speech when four emissaries arrived unexpectedly from Moscow. All his telephones had been disconnected, so this was clearly no ordinary visit. Gorbachev refused either to resign or to sign a decree instituting a state of emergency, and was thereupon placed under house arrest and isolated from the outside world.[162] In the early hours of 19 August a self-styled State Emergency Committee informed a startled world that Gorbachev was 'unwell', and that his responsibilities would be assumed in these circumstances by the vice-president, Gennadii Yanaev. The Emergency Committee, it later emerged, had eight members. Apart from Yanaev himself there was the KGB chairman, Vladimir Kryuchkov; the defence minister, Dmitrii Yazov; the interior minister, Boris Pugo; the prime minister, Valentin Pavlov; and three other members of less prominence, Oleg Baklanov, Vasilii Starodubtsev, and Alexander Tizyakov.[163] Yanaev and four other members of the Committee addressed a hastily convened press conference later the same day. The vice-president, they explained, had assumed power on the basis of Article 127 of the Soviet constitution, which allowed him to do so if the president was 'for whatever reason' unable to carry out his responsibilities; Gorbachev, they added, was 'very tired', but it was hoped that 'once he had recovered' he would return to his official duties.[164]

The Committee, in a series of decrees, meanwhile suspended the activities of all parties (other than those that had supported the emergency), banned the publication of all but a small number of newspapers (including *Pravda*), ordered the surrender of firearms, and prohibited meetings, strikes, and demonstrations. The Committee's message was not simply a coercive one; it also promised to cut prices and increase wages, and to place food supplies under strict control with priority being given to schools, hospitals, pensioners, and the disabled.[165] In a 'message to the Soviet people', broadcast on the morning of 19 August, the Committee offered a more extended justification of its action. The Soviet people, it explained, were in 'mortal danger'. *Perestroika* had reached an 'impasse'. The country had become 'ungovernable', and 'extremist forces' were seeking to break up the Soviet state and seize power for themselves. Meanwhile the economy was in crisis, with the breakdown of central planning, a 'chaotic, ungoverned slide towards a market', and famine a real possibility; and crime and immorality were rampant. The Committee, it promised, would reverse these trends, strengthen public order, arrest the fall in living standards, and restore the Soviet Union's international standing; it appealed, in turn, for the support of 'all true patriots and people of goodwill', but made no reference of any kind to socialism.[166]

The coup, it soon became clear, had been poorly planned – two of its principal members, Yanaev and Pavlov, were drunk for most of its duration[167] – and it was opposed from the outset by Boris Yeltsin, who had been elected Russian president two months earlier, and who made a dramatic call for resistance on 19 August standing on one of the tanks stationed outside the Russian parliament building. Yeltsin denounced the Committee's action as a 'right-wing, reactionary, unconstitutional coup' and declared all its decisions illegal. Gorbachev, he insisted, must be restored immediately to his position, and he called for an indefinite strike until the Soviet parliament had met and constitutional propriety had been restored.[168] Huge demonstrations in front of the Russian parliament the following day were addressed by Shevardnadze, Yakovlev, Andrei Sakharov's widow Yelena Bonner, and other democrats. The critical moment was the evening of 20 August when about 70,000 Muscovites defied the curfew and assembled in front of the 'White House' to defend it against an expected attack by pro-coup forces. That night, three men were killed – one shot and two crushed by tanks – but the attack on the Russian parliament itself did not materialise.[169] It later emerged that substantial sections of the armed forces had declared against the coup, and that the elite KGB 'Alpha' anti-terrorist group had rejected the order they had been given to storm the building.[170]

On Wednesday 21 August the coup began to collapse. The Russian parliament met in emergency session and gave Yeltsin their unqualified support; media restrictions were lifted, and the Ministry of Defence ordered troops to return to their barracks. The USSR Supreme Soviet Presidium declared the action of the Emergency Committee illegal, and the procurator general's office announced that criminal proceedings for high treason had been instigated against its members. One of the coup leaders, Boris Pugo, committed suicide; several others went to the Crimea to seek Gorbachev's forgiveness (the Russian parliament sent its own representatives to bring the Soviet president back safely); and others still, such as Foreign Minister Alexander Bessmertnykh, tried to explain why they had – in his case – suffered a sudden 'cold' while the emergency was in force (he was dismissed two days later). The most ambiguous figure of all was the chairman of the Supreme Soviet, Anatolii Luk'yanov, who had refused to denounce the coup at the time and was accused of being its 'chief ideologist' (by the end of the month he was one of the fourteen people involved in the coup who had been arrested and charged with high treason).[171]

Gorbachev was flown back to Moscow in the early hours of 22 August, where he later addressed a crowded press conference. He thanked Yeltsin as well as the Russian parliament for securing his release, and then described the difficult circumstances under which he

Plate 1.4   Felix Dzerzhinsky (originally in Lubyanka Square opposite the KGB headquarters, but moved in August 1991 and now in the Tret'yakov Gallery sculpture park, Moscow)

had been held. He had refused to accept the conditions his captors had tried to dictate to him or the food they had provided, but had been able to rig up a makeshift radio on which he had been able to listen to Western radio broadcasts; he had even recorded four copies of a video message to the Soviet people explaining the real nature of the emergency. There was some surprise that the Soviet leader continued to defend the Communist Party, whose rule in the attempted coup had been obscure.[172] Later, however, when the complicity of the party leadership became clear, Gorbachev resigned the general secretaryship and called upon the Central Committee to take the 'difficult but honourable decision to dissolve itself'.[173] Yeltsin had signed a decree suspending the activity of the Communist Party throughout the Russian Federation on 23 August, at a meeting of the Russian parliament that Gorbachev attended.[174] Another decree on 25 August transferred all the assets of the party into the hands of elected bodies of government, and froze its bank accounts;[175] and then in November 1991 the party was suppressed entirely.[176]

The Soviet Union itself was a still greater casualty of the coup. Although they had aimed to block the signature of a new union treaty that would have approved a loose confederation, the conspirators – in the event – accelerated the collapse of the state they had sought to preserve (see chapter 7). Lithuania had already declared its independence, in the spring of 1990; the other Baltic republics followed immediately; and by the end of the following year all of the republics – apart from Russia – had adopted declarations of a similar kind. The Ukrainian decision, backed by the support of over 90 per cent of its population in a referendum on 1 December, appears to have convinced Yeltsin that there was no future in a reconstituted USSR of which the second largest republic would not be a member, and on 8 December he met the Ukrainian president and the Belorussian parliamentary chairman at a country house near Minsk and concluded an agreement establishing a Commonwealth of Independent States. The new Commonwealth was not a state, it had no common parliament, and in particular it had no presidency; but with its establishment, according to the agreement, the USSR as a subject of international law and a geopolitical reality had 'ceased its existence'.[177] On 12 December the Russian Supreme Soviet approved the agreement, and withdrew from the treaty of union that had been concluded in 1922 (in cases of this kind the constitution made clear that the full Congress of People's Deputies should have considered the matter, and almost certainly a referendum);[178] a further agreement on 21 December in Alma-Ata brought all the remaining republics apart from Georgia and the Baltic ones into the new association.[179] With the disappearance of the USSR the position of its president had obviously become untenable and Gorbachev resigned his last remaining public office on 25 December; as *Pravda* pointed out, the exchange rate had slid from 0.6 to more than 90 to the dollar during his incumbency and the gold reserves were almost exhausted, but there were twelve registered political parties instead of one and the sale of Big Macs had increased from zero to 15 million.[180]

2   Parties, voters, and government

Voting was still quite new in early postcommunist Russia.[1] Voting, that was, in the sense of choosing. Under the Soviet system there were frequent votes but no opportunity to choose, not just between candidates or parties but (in practice) whether to vote at all. In a variation on Brecht's suggestion that the government 'elect a new people', it was the leadership that determined the composition of each new parliament and the constituencies in which they would themselves be nominated. Voters had only to drop the ballot paper, unmarked and possibly unread, into the box: if they left the single name it was regarded as a vote in favour; if they wished to vote against they had to go to the screened-off booth at the edge of the polling station, where 'everyone could guess their intentions'.[2] The results were so predictable that newspapers could prepare their front pages with pictures of the successful candidates before the election had taken place, and the Politburo could itself approve the report of the Central Electoral Commission two days before the polls had opened.[3] In 1987, in the first partial break with this practice, a small number of constituencies in local elections were allowed to nominate more candidates than seats available;[4] and then in 1988, as 'democratisation' developed further, a new electoral law was adopted that allowed any number of candidates to be nominated, with ordinary citizens as well as approved organisations making the nominations, and with the result determined by a vote that had to be cast in a polling booth and not openly affirmed as in the past.[5] The outcome, in the election to a new Congress of People's Deputies that took place in March 1989, was described as 'political shock therapy' by the party's leading conservative, Yegor Ligachev; there were, in fact, more party members among the successful candidates than ever before, but thirty-eight party secretaries including a member of the ruling Politburo were rejected by a newly enfranchised electorate, and Boris Yeltsin won nearly 90 per cent of the vote in Moscow in a result that was the clearest possible rebuff to the party leadership's attempt to marginalise his challenge to their authority.[6]

A Russian parliament was elected on the same partly competitive basis, in March 1990; and it was this parliament, a Congress of People's Deputies with a smaller working Supreme Soviet, that took Russia into the postcommunist era. Tensions were always likely to develop between a parliament and a president who both enjoyed a mandate from the electorate; they were still more likely between a parliament that was overwhelmingly communist at the time of its election and a president who had resigned from the CPSU, banned it after the August coup, and dissolved the state it had created. Those tensions, in the end, were resolved by another coup when President Yeltsin, emboldened by the results of a referendum in April 1993 in which the policies of his government had been given majority support, dissolved the parliament the following September and then ordered the army to shell the parliament building in early October when a popular demonstration broke through the blockade and encouraged the parliamentary leaders to seek control of the state itself. According to official sources, 145 lost their lives and more than 800 were wounded in the bloodiest street fighting since the October revolution – a confrontation that, for Yeltsin, had been an 'armed rebellion', and for First Deputy Prime Minister Gaidar nothing less than a 'short civil war'.[7] The suppression of parliament was an acknowledged violation of the constitution, which explicitly prohibited any attempt by the president to dissolve the Duma or suspend its operation; it was a constitution, moreover, that Yeltsin had pledged himself to uphold when he was sworn in as Russia's first elected president in July 1991. Many of Yeltsin's closest supporters had doubted the wisdom of his action and counselled against it,[8] and the minister of defence had insisted on written instructions before ordering his troops to take action.[9] Yeltsin himself, however, had decided some time previously that the country could 'no longer have such a parliament'[10] – there had been a plan to disperse the deputies with CS gas if they had voted in favour of impeachment the previous March[11] – and he did not regard himself as bound by a constitution that had been amended many times since he had sworn to uphold it.[12]

The suppression of the parliament allowed Yeltsin to introduce and then secure approval for an entirely new and postcommunist constitution within which the powers of the presidency were still further enhanced. The new constitution, ratified in December 1993, abolished the Congress of People's Deputies and established a two-chamber Federal Assembly in its place (see figure 2.1). The upper house, the Council of the Federation, was a 'Senate' that represented Russia's eighty-nine republics and regions, and which drew two of its members from each of them. The lower house, the State Duma, was a 'House of

Representatives', half of whose 450 members were drawn from individual constituencies with the result determined by simple majority, the
other half from a nationwide competition among parties and electoral
alliances with the seats distributed proportionally among all that secured
at least 5 per cent of the vote. The election would be regarded as valid, in
both cases, if the level of turnout was at least 25 per cent. The president,
strictly speaking, had no authority to call a referendum and what took
place was a 'national vote' in which 54.8 per cent were reported to have
taken part (at least 50 per cent was required for the vote to be valid and
there were persistent reports that the turnout had been artificially
inflated); of those who voted on 12 December, 58.4 per cent approved
the presidential text.[13] The new constitution, whatever the circumstances of its adoption, set a framework for postcommunist politics; it
was unclear, at the same time, how a directly elected parliament would
interact with a directly elected president, and whether Russians could be
persuaded to express their political preferences through the forms of
multiparty politics – or indeed if they would bother to vote at all.

Parties and party politics

Under the Soviet system only a single party had enjoyed a legal existence
('two parties?', local humorists had asked; 'isn't one bad enough?').
Although the Communist Party of the Soviet Union (CPSU) had been
mentioned in passing in earlier versions, the constitution that was
adopted under the guidance of Leonid Brezhnev in 1977 had converted
the Party's effective dominance into a formal political monopoly. The
CPSU, according to an entirely new Article 6, was the 'leading and
guiding force of Soviet society and the nucleus of its political system, of
all state organisations and public organisations', and it imparted a
'planned, systematic, and theoretically substantiated character to their
struggle for the victory of communism'. In 1990, however, the party
agreed to relinquish its monopoly, and Article 6 was amended to read
'The Communist Party of the Soviet Union [and] other political parties,
as well as trade union, youth, and other public organisations and mass
movements, participate in shaping the policies of the Soviet state and in
running state and public affairs through their representatives elected to
the soviets of people's deputies and in other ways.' Article 7 was also
revised to make clear that 'all political parties, public organisations, and
mass movements' had to operate within the law, and Article 51 added
the right of all citizens to 'unite in political parties and public organisations and to participate in mass movements contributing to their greater
political activity and to the satisfaction of their diverse interests'.[14] The

party, Gorbachev told a meeting of the Central Committee in February, was not so much abandoning its political monopoly as acknowledging that the USSR had already become a multiparty society, although the parties and movements that had come into existence in the late 1980s had not yet acquired a legal basis; it would certainly make every effort to retain the leadership of a changing society, but it could do so only 'within the framework of the democratic process', without any kind of 'political or legal privileges'.[15]

A legal framework for multiparty politics was established the following October when a new law on public associations was adopted, covering political parties as well as trade unions, women's and veterans' associations, and sport clubs. At least ten citizens were required to establish an association under the law, and they were required to hold a founding congress at which their statutes were adopted and executive bodies elected. The statutes of an association had then to be registered with the USSR Ministry of Justice or its counterparts at other levels of government, which could refuse registration if (for instance) the objectives of the association appeared to conflict with the constitution. Political parties, in particular, were supposed to have the basic goal of participation in elected institutions and in government; they were expected to have a programme, which had to be published for general information, and they had the right to nominate candidates for election, to campaign on their behalf, and to form organised groups in the bodies to which their candidates were elected.[16] The registration of new and existing parties, including the CPSU, began on this basis in 1991; twenty-five parties had been registered by the summer of 1992, though many claimed no more than a few hundred members and there were no more than 30,000 active members of all political parties put together.[17] The new constitution nonetheless made clear that postcommunist Russia was firmly committed to 'political diversity and a multiparty system', subject only to the requirement that parties and associations refrain from a forcible challenge to the state and from incitement to social, ethnic, or religious strife; the same principles were affirmed in a new law on public organisations, approved by the Duma in April 1995, pending the adoption of a special law on parties themselves.[18]

The first test of this emerging but still weakly formed party system was the election of December 1993, and in particular the election to the lower house, the State Duma, which was based in part upon a national competition among party lists and in part upon a series of contests in single-member constituencies (see figure 2.1). The suspension and bombardment of the parliament had created an inhospitable environment for the conduct of these first postcommunist elections. Yeltsin's main rivals, parliamentary speaker Ruslan Khasbulatov and his vice-president Alexander Rutskoi, had come out of the parliament building with their hands in the air and were in prison facing serious charges. There was a brief period of censorship; fifteen newspapers were banned on the grounds that they had contributed to the 'mass disorders in Moscow', and three others were suspended. *Pravda* and *Sovetskaya Rossiya*, two of the papers that had been suspended, were also instructed to change their names and replace their editors (in the end both retained their distinctive titles, but did not appear for an extended period); the parliament's own paper, *Rossiiskaya gazeta*, was taken over entirely by the Russian government. A state of emergency in Moscow, incorporating a ban on demonstrations and a curfew, lasted until 18 October. The Constitutional Court, which had ruled that there were grounds for Yeltsin's impeachment, was suspended and its chairman forced to resign; the prosecutor general was dismissed and replaced by a Yeltsin loyalist. Sixteen parties or organisations were suspended on the grounds that they had been involved in the 'events' of 3–4 October; the Communist Party of the Russian Federation (CPRF), whose leader had urged both sides to 'refrain from provocations', was eventually legalised, but most of the others, including the National Salvation Front and the hard-left Russian Communist Workers' Party, remained subject to a ban that deprived them of any opportunity to take part in the contest. In the end, thirty-five parties or alliances began a campaign to collect the 100,000 signatures that they required to secure the right to put forward candidates; twenty-one claimed to have collected the number that was needed; and, of these, thirteen were included on the ballot paper after their documentation had been verified.[19]

Western governments had supported Yeltsin's moves against parliament on the grounds that he had promised to submit himself personally for re-election in the summer of 1994 (an undertaking that was later withdrawn), and in the expectation that a new election would allow Russians to rid themselves of a 'communist parliament' that had represented an obstacle to reform. The result was a considerable shock, not just in Russia but also to the wider international community. Most successful of all were the independents, who won 141 of the 225 single-member constituencies; this gave them nearly a third of all the seats in the new parliament. The most successful of the parties was Russia's Choice, led by former acting prime minister Yegor Gaidar and fully committed to the policies of the Yeltsin administration, with a total of seventy seats. But there was a sensational result in the party-list contest, which was won by the right-wing nationalist Liberal Democratic Party led by Vladimir Zhirinovsky with nearly a quarter of the vote, with the

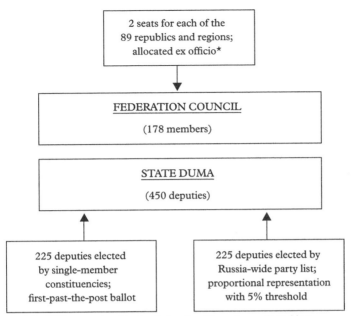

* In 1993, exceptionally, the Federation Council was elected in a
first-past-the-post ballot.

Fig. 2.1   The Russian Federal Assembly

Communists in third place; and there was some disappointment that the
level of turnout was just 54.8 per cent, continuing a steady decline from
the heady days of the first competitive elections in the last years of Soviet
rule (see table 2.1). The result was a 'fiasco' for Russian pollsters, who
had predicted a win for Russia's Choice with Liberal Democrats in the
'zone of defeat';[20] it was still more serious for the regime itself. Television coverage was suddenly suspended in the early morning because of
'technical difficulties', and US Vice-President Al Gore, who had been
present to welcome the birth of Russia's new democracy, had to leave in
some embarrassment. Gaidar's own reaction was that the reformers had
suffered a 'bitter defeat'; the Moscow evening paper put it even more
dramatically, warning that Russians had 'woken up in a new state' after
the 'Communo-Fascists' success'.[21] The new Duma, however, was an
extraordinary one, elected for a limited period of two years; its successor
would define the shape of parliamentary politics for a normal four-year
term and perhaps for rather longer.

According to the Central Electoral Commission, 273 parties or other
organisations had the right to nominate candidates to the Duma that

Table 2.1. *Elections to the State Duma, December 1993*

Party/bloc	Party lists			Single-member constituencies		Total seats	
	% votes	number of seats	% seats	number of seats	% seats	number	%
Russia's Choice	15.51	40	17.8	30	13.3	70	15.6
Liberal Democratic Party of Russia	22.92	59	26.2	5	2.2	64	14.2
Communist Party of the Russian Federation	12.40	32	14.2	16	7.1	48	10.7
Agrarian Party	7.99	21	9.3	12	5.3	33	7.3
Women of Russia	8.13	21	9.3	2	0.9	23	5.1
Yabloko	7.86	20	8.9	3	1.3	23	5.1
Party of Russian Unity and Concord	6.76	18	8.0	1	0.4	19	4.2
Democratic Party of Russia	5.52	14	6.2	1	0.4	15	3.3
[5 per cent threshold]							
Democratic Reform Movement	4.08	–		4	1.8	4	0.9
Dignity and Charity	0.70	–		2	0.9	2	0.4
Civic Union	1.93	–		1	0.4	1	0.2
Russia's Future-New Names	1.25	–		1	0.4	1	0.2
Cedar	0.76	–		–		–	
Against all	4.36	–		–		–	
Spoiled ballots	3.10	–		–		–	
Independents	–	–		141	62.7	141	31.3
Postponed	–			6		6	
Total		225		225		450	

Sources: Based on *Rossiiskaya gazeta*, 28 December 1993, p. 1, and *Byulleten' Tsentral'noi izbiratel'noi komissii Rossiiskoi Federatsii*, no. 12, 1994, p. 67.

was elected in December 1995, and there were fears that Russia might set a 'world record for the number of electoral associations per head of population'.[22] Nominations in the 225 single-member constituencies, under the law, required the support of at least 1 per cent of the local electorate; 2,627 candidates were successfully nominated on this basis, 1,055 of whom had been put forward by electors rather than the political parties.[23] Parties or 'electoral associations' that wished to put forward candidates in the national competition for the other half of the Duma had this time to collect the signatures of at least 200,000 electors, not more than 7 per cent of whom could be drawn from any one republic or region; forty-three parties and movements eventually satisfied these requirements, with a total of 5,746 candidates on their lists[24] (the

Table 2.2. *The Russian political spectrum in the 1990s*

Reformist	Centrist	National-patriotic	Communist-agrarian left
Russia's Democratic Choice (Gaidar)	Our Home Is Russia (Chernomyrdin) Women of Russia (Lakhova)	Liberal Democratic Party (Zhirinovsky)	Communist Party of the Russian Federation (Zyuganov)
Yabloko (Yavlinsky) Forward, Russia! (B. Fedorov) Workers' Self-Management Party (S. Fedorov) Pamfilova–Gurov–Lysenko bloc (Pamfilova)	Trade Unions and Industrialists (Shmakov, Shcherbakov, Vol'sky) Ivan Rybkin bloc (Rybkin) Cedar (Panfilov)	Congress of Russian Communities (Lebed, Skokov) Derzhava (Rutskoi) Govorukhin bloc (Govorukhin)	Power to the People! (Ryzhkov, Baburin) Communists–Working Russia–For the Soviet Union (Anpilov)

Source: Adapted from A. G. Beloborodov et al., *Vybory deputatov Gosudarstvennoi Dumy. 1995. Elektoral'naya statistika* (Moscow: Ves' mir, 1996), p. 242; limited to parties or movements that secured at least 1 per cent of the national party-list vote in the December 1995 election, and to their more prominent leaders.

Central Electoral Commission claimed later that it had validated 933,000 nomination papers containing a total of 12 million signatures[25]. The election law made it illegal to offer financial inducements to potential supporters, and it was also illegal to contribute to the nomination of more than a single list of candidates. Press reports, however, made clear that many of the parties ignored these requirements in obtaining their signatures: a week before nominations closed prospective signatories in the Belgorod region were being offered two kilograms of flour, and in Krasnodar a bottle of beer; the average price of a signature had reached 2,000 rubles (about 50 cents at the prevailing rate of exchange), and it increased still further as the deadline for nominations came closer.[26] Indeed there were 'centres for political consulting' that were prepared to organise the entire campaign for their clients, from the collection of signatures to public speeches and, 'for the laziest', an electoral programme.[27] Very provisionally, the parties and alliances that were included on the ballot and that were active in Russian political life in the 1990s could be divided into four broad groups (see table 2.2).[28]

There were (i) several *'democratic' or reformist groupings*, of which the most substantial was 'Russia's Democratic Choice – United Democrats', led by Yegor Gaidar and committed to the fullest possible transition to a private ownership economy. The bloc was based around Gaidar's own Russia's Democratic Choice Party, founded in June 1994, which had emerged from Russia's Choice, the broadly based coalition that had been formed to 'express the interests of all who in the referendum of 25 April [1993] had supported the reformist course of President Yeltsin'.[29] It had been the largest of the parliamentary fractions after the 1993 elections, but lost ground as some of its deputies gravitated towards the Chernomyrdin government while others took up a more sharply critical position; so did Gaidar after the outbreak of the Chechen war, although this led to an open rift with President Yeltsin when Gaidar announced in February 1995 that the party would not support him for a second term.[30] Russia's Democratic Choice adopted 'Peace, Prosperity, and Justice' as its pre-election slogan; its immediate priorities included tax reform, the private ownership of land, and a transition to a professional rather than a conscript army; it also favoured a more limited role for the state, a cut in the government bureaucracy, support for small business, and a reduction in military expenditure.[31] The party list in the election was headed by Gaidar, an economist with a Moscow University doctorate who had worked for *Pravda* but who had become increasingly persuaded of the merits of a free-market approach to economic management. Gaidar's grandfather had been a popular children's writer, but

Gaidar himself had a bookish and well-nourished appearance that was less appealing to a mass electorate, particularly at a time of economic difficulty. The party itself was represented in seventy-eight of Russia's regions, with 5,000–10,000 members throughout the country; the largest party organisation was in Moscow, with a thousand, but branches more typically had between 100 and 150 members on their books.[32]

'Yabloko' (Apple), led by economist Grigorii Yavlinsky, shared a commitment to economic reform but on a more gradual basis, and it was sharply critical of the policies that Yeltsin and Gaidar had been promoting since the start of 1992. It had officially been founded in January 1995, although its three founding members (whose surnames gave the party its distinctive title) had already combined to contest the 1993 election and had then formed a fraction in the new Duma. Yabloko's programme, adopted in September 1995, declared it a 'democratic movement committed to the creation of a rule-of-law state with a market, socially oriented economy, and a strong army'.[33] Their aim, Yavlinsky told *Izvestiya*, was to demonstrate that there was a 'democratic alternative to the current regime'; they were critical of the bombing of the White House in October 1993 and the increasingly corrupt nature of the ruling elite, and anxious to strengthen the place of parliament within the existing Russian constitution.[34] Yabloko supported the free market, but not at the expense of those who were unable to defend their own interests; their aim was 'reforms for all, not just for a narrow section whose aim is rapid enrichment', and they deplored the widening division between rich and poor, increasing crime, and the 'weakening and partial destruction of the state'. Nor did they believe that science, education, health, and culture could simply be handed over to the private sector. Their electoral programme placed considerable emphasis in addition upon public morality, the environment, and evolutionary rather than more rapid change (they refused in this connection to engage in a 'denial of the past', or in anti-communism for its own sake).[35] But if Gaidar had become leader of Russia's Democratic Choice because he more than any other could articulate its political philosophy, Yabloko was much more clearly an organisational extension of its party leader, and in practice 'its leader G. Yavlinsky *was* its political line'.[36]

Among the other pro-reform movements, 'Forward, Russia!' was headed by former finance minister Boris Fedorov; founded in February 1995, it was particularly conspicuous for its firm defence of Russian unity, including the Chechen republic (what would the US government have done, Fedorov asked, if Texas had tried to leave the Union?). At the same time Forward, Russia! took a sharply hostile position towards the Yeltsin government and called for faster, more extensive privatisation and measures to curb the state bureaucracy.[37] The Party of Beer-Lovers was also regarded as 'democratic' in orientation; its aim was to turn Russia into a 'country with a secure, well-fed, and peaceful life, based on honest labour and comfortable beer drinking' (its ranks were however threatened by a pro-vodka secession[38]). Other reformist groupings included the Social Democrats, headed by former Moscow mayor Gavriil Popov, who called for a model of reform that would combine democratic change with measures to support the living standards of ordinary people, and the Party of Workers' Self-Management, headed by the famous eye surgeon Svyatoslav Fedorov. As Fedorov put it in one of his campaign publications, it was 'shameful that the people whose eyesight I have restored see a country that has collapsed', and for some analysts these last two parties occupied a distinctive, 'democratic leftist' position of their own in that they allowed for public as well as private ownership and rejected the 'comprador-mafia capitalism' that was being promoted by reformers within the government.[39] Another left-centrist party emerged at the end of 1998 under the auspices of Moscow mayor Yuri Luzhkov, and with the backing of a wide range of trade union, employer, and national-patriotic organisations; entitled 'Fatherland' (Otechestvo), it was sharply critical of the economic policies of the Yeltsin–Chernomyrdin government and respectful of the achievements of Soviet rule, but put its main emphasis upon a 'strong, but not authoritarian state power capable of combating crime, collecting taxes, and preventing separatism', and a more assertive foreign policy.[40] As Luzhkov explained, Russia needed a state system of the social-democratic type that would 'combine a market economy and social policies';[41] the new movement was intended to mobilise the support that evidently existed for such objectives, and at the same time to provide Luzhkov himself with a position from which he could challenge for the presidency.

The (ii) *'pro-government centre'* was based around 'Our Home Is Russia' (Nash dom – Rossiya), founded in the spring of 1995 as a political movement that could sustain the Chernomyrdin government in the Duma elections and then provide the basis for a presidential campaign by Boris Yeltsin in the summer of 1996. In practice, Our Home was the 'party of power': a coalition of the postcommunist political and economic *nomenklatura*, with differing views but a common interest in maintaining their privileged position. The prime minister himself attracted some attention in this connection because of the wealth he had accumulated through the privatisation of the gas industry, and some dubbed the group 'Nash dom – Gazprom' after the name of the immense concern of which he had been chairman. Our Home sought the support of 'all who value our common home – Russia, who want progress without revolutionary upheavals, who are tired of disorder, and who are devoted to the Fatherland';[42] its election programme, adopted in August 1995, emphasised three priorities: the 'spiritual renewal of Russia', including the rights and freedoms of the individual; the 'integrity of the country', including public order; and the 'development of a market economy together with a greater degree of social protection'.[43] Our Home's most obvious advantage was the support it received from big business, together with its access to the machinery of government and the mass media; it was able to spend liberally on campaign publicity, and to attract celebrities (like the German supermodel Claudia Schiffer) to its public events, although it was not clear that this would compensate for the middle-aged image of the prime minister – who had never before run for public office – and his ministerial colleagues. As a 'party of power' Our Home could claim to exercise considerable influence on government, but this was true only as long as Chernomyrdin was prime minister; when he was dismissed in 1998 it became no more than a 'party of influence on power', with the rather nebulous objective of 'helping people to find their place in our complicated life'.[44]

'Women of Russia' had an even more ambiguous position; based on the Soviet-era Committee of Soviet Women and relatively successful with 8 per cent of the party-list vote in the 1993 elections, it had come to reflect the centrist views of the president and of its leader Yekaterina Lakhova, a doctor who came from the same part of Russia as Boris Yeltsin and who had organised a commission on women, the family, and demography within his administration. It was, in this sense, the female half of the 'party of power'; yet it had also supported a move by the Communists and Agrarians to halt the process of privatisation which led it to be called the 'women's department of the CPRF'. Women of Russia, *Izvestiya* explained, was 'one of the most pragmatic' of the Duma parties, in that it 'more often than others voted for diametrically opposite proposals';[45] and when it came to voting on the 'most bitterly contested questions of principle, it usually abstained or voted in a way that suited the government'.[46] For its opponents, Women of Russia offered a form of 'politics without politics'; for Lakhova herself it was simply a party that 'always supported consensus', and Duma speaker Ivan Rybkin emphasised the 'stabilising' role it had been able to play in the Russian parliament.[47] Women of Russia had lost their unique claim to represent the female constituency with the inclusion of women in prominent positions in other blocs or indeed as the leaders of blocs, like former social security minister Ella Pamfilova who headed the Pamfilova–Gurov–Lysenko bloc, and businesswoman Irina Khakamada of the pro-market grouping Common Cause; at the same time they had the good fortune to obtain first place on the ballot paper, a source of advantage in all electoral systems. The Women of Russia programme emphasised social issues, including state support for health, education, housing, and child care, a '*de facto* equalisation of the position of women and men' including equal participation at all levels of decision-making, a 'socially oriented market economy' with state and co-operative as well as private ownership, and the resolution of armed conflicts 'only through political negotiation'.[48] As their very first press release had pointed out, 'Without women there's no democracy!'[49]

A further group of parties occupied a (iii) *national-patriotic* position, including a new and apparently promising grouping, the Congress of Russian Communities. Its leaders were certainly representative of key constituencies: former chairman of the Security Council Yuri Skokov, who had close ties with the military-industrial complex; economist Sergei Glaz'ev, who had been minister of foreign trade up to October 1993 when he resigned in protest over Yeltsin's suspension of parliament; and the formidable figure of Alexander Lebed, the gravel-voiced general who had led the 14th army in Transdnestria region until a ceasefire was concluded and who was then dismissed when his outspoken views began to embarrass the Ministry of Defence. Opinion polls suggested Lebed was the most popular politician in the country;[50] newspaper commentaries credited him with the 'brain of Albert Einstein and the physique of Arnold Schwarzenegger'.[51] Lebed's autobiography, *Za derzhavu obidno . . .* (It's Shameful for a Great Power), was published in the late summer of 1995; it recalled his arduous military training, his service in Afghanistan and Moldova, and his commitment to the Orthodox Church, the army, and the Russian people – but not necessarily democracy.[52] The Congress had been founded in March 1993 to represent Russians living outside the Federation, gradually evolving into a moderate national-patriotic grouping. Its programme was egalitarian, but also eclectic; its central elements were the gradual reconstitution of the USSR by peaceful means, defence of Russians abroad, a crackdown on crime, support for traditional Russian institutions such as the church and family, the restoration of Russia's great-power status, and the formation of a 'highly effective and socially oriented market economy' in which there would be a 'sensible defence of domestic producers' as well as 'support for the high technology core of the Russian military-industrial complex'.[53] The Congress was very critical of the government's economic programme and blamed Yeltsin for the collapse of the USSR, the 'October events' of 1993, and the excesses of privatisation; but it had its own difficulties, partly because of the inconsistencies in its

Plate 2.1   Three ballot boxes in search of a voter (*Izvestiya*, August 1995)

programme, but also because of the unresolved ambitions of its leaders (Skokov, for instance, told journalists that Lebed 'lacked education' and was unready for the post of defence minister, let alone the premiership; Lebed formed his own grouping in early 1997 and won the governorship of the vast Krasnoyarsk region a year later to become a challenger for the presidency itself).[54]

The other national-patriotic parties were 'Derzhava' (Great Power), headed by former vice-president Alexander Rutskoi, and Vladimir Zhirinovsky's Liberal Democrats. The Liberal Democrats had been the sensational winner of the 1993 party-list election, but their parliamentary fraction had been unstable and Zhirinovsky himself had shown some willingness to co-operate with the Chernomyrdin government, in particular through his support of successive budgets. The party's earlier appeal had also been undermined by the emergence of other radical nationalist groupings, including the Congress of Russian Communities. The Liberal Democrats, founded in 1989 with what appeared to be the tacit support of the KGB and Communist Party, were nationalist and anti-Western in their foreign policy, strongly in favour of the restoration of federal control in Chechnya, and pro-market but also protectionist in their domestic economic strategy.[55] They were equally opposed to the dissolution of the USSR, and called for it to be restored within its earlier boundaries or 'ideally' the boundaries the Russian Empire had enjoyed after the Crimean War, including Finland, the Baltic states, and Alaska;[56] they also favoured the restoration of at least indicative planning.[57] The Liberal Democrats were well financed, had a national network of activists, and enjoyed a high level of support within the armed forces;[58] but they owed most of all to their leader, a charismatic campaigner who successfully identified the problems of ordinary Russians and suggested simple ways of dealing with them, like shooting the leaders of organised crime or providing 'a man for every woman and a cheap bottle of vodka for every man' (in 1998 he called for state-sponsored sex and an end to the American 'masturbatory hegemony').[59] The Liberal Democrats, indeed, were 'less a political party than an organisation serving the ambitions of a single person, its leader Vladimir Zhirinovsky', and it was no more than a recognition of this when in 1994 the Liberal Democrats added 'the party of Zhirinovsky' to their official title and elected Zhirinovsky chairman for ten years with the right to form the party leadership in any way he chose.[60]

A more conventional range of parties occupied the (iv) *communist-agrarian left*, of which by far the most important was the CPRF, founded in 1990 within the framework of the CPSU and led by Gennadii Zyuganov. It was a distinctive party in many ways: it was the only one with a mass membership, and it had the best network of local activists throughout the country; indeed for some it was the only one of these organisations that could properly be called a political party.[61] In 1991, the party explained in its election platform, there had been a 'state coup' led by the 'old *nomenklatura*'. The Communists called for a 'national-patriotic majority' in the new Duma so that they could restore a system based on the elected soviets with guaranteed socioeconomic rights for working people, the renationalisation of 'strategic' sectors of the economy, and priority for domestic producers of all kinds.[62] The party had been suspended and then banned after the attempted coup of 1991, but the Constitutional Court ruled in November 1992 that, although its leading bodies had usurped the functions of government, its rank-and-file members had the right to form the political organisation of their choice; they did so in February 1993, adopting a commitment to 'socialist ideas and people's power' as well as to the 'formation of a planned market economy' based on an 'optimal combination of different forms of property'.[63] The party's new programme, adopted in January 1995, called for a 'return to the path of socialist development' but without going back to the 'society that existed before the start of so-called *perestroika*'. Its main aims were the restoration of elected soviets, guaranteed employment, free education and health care, the formation of a 'government of national confidence' that would restore state regulation of the economy, the reconstitution of a single union state, and more generally the conduct of an 'independent foreign policy' that reflected the 'national-state interests and strengthened the international authority of the Russian state'; it was also committed in the longer term to communism as the 'historic future of humanity'.[64] The party's list of candidates in the 1995 elections was headed by Zyuganov, who represented the dominant 'popular-patriotic' section of the leadership; it could claim 570,000 members and a presence in all of Russia's republics and regions, making it by far the most significant of all the postcommunist groupings.[65]

The Communists had a close ally in the Agrarian Party, founded in 1993 and representing state and collective farms rather than commercial agriculture. It was a party, its leaders explained, that had emerged 'not in the offices of rural functionaries, but in the thick of the peasant movement of the late 1980s and early 1990s', and in the 'vacuum' that had developed with the collapse of the CPSU. The party's aims and methods 'largely coincided' with those of the Communist Party, but the Agrarians had their own programme and insisted they were more than the 'younger sister' of the Communists. The land, they believed, should 'belong exclusively to those who worked and lived on it', and they were against any 'hasty moves' towards a free market, arguing that in the circumstances of early postcommunist Russia this would lead to a 'random redistribution' that would simply 'open the road to speculation and the extraction of unearned income'.[66] The party chairman was Mikhail Lapshin, director of the 'Behests of Lenin' farm in the Moscow region. Addressing the party's fourth congress in September 1995, he deplored the introduction of 'foreign models' in the management of the Russian economy, and called for the buying and selling of land to be banned by law; he also supported the 'natural wish of the CIS countries to restore a union state'.[67] The Agrarians' election slogan was 'Fatherland, People's Power, Justice, Welfare'; their pre-election programme called for a 'new political and economic course', which in practice meant a greater degree of state support for agriculture and the prohibition of private ownership of natural resources.[68] There were two other left groupings, 'Power to the People!' led by former prime minister Nikolai Ryzhkov and Duma deputy Sergei Baburin, which sought to defend the living standards of working people but without returning to a 'supercentralised planning and distribution system';[69] and the harderline 'Communists–Working Russia–For the Soviet Union', a coalition of the Russian Communist Workers' Party and the Russian Party of Communists which was committed to the restoration of soviet power and of the USSR and socialism more generally, and which was led by one of the most effective of the street orators, Viktor Anpilov.[70]

Patterns of electoral behaviour

With forty-three parties or alliances competing for places in the party-list section of the Duma, it was clear from the outset that few of them would be able to surmount the 5 per cent threshold. In the event, only four did so: the Communist Party of the Russian Federation, with more than a fifth of the total vote; Zhirinovsky's Liberal Democrats and Our Home Is Russia, each of which secured just over a tenth; and Yabloko, with just under 7 per cent (see table 2.3). The Liberal Democratic vote fell by more than half, but this was an improvement on poll forecasts; there was more surprise that the Congress of Russian Communities had failed to reach the threshold, a failure that was attributed to its amorphous programme and to its uncertainty about a possible coalition with other parties, in particular the Communists.[71] Most of the parties that had won seats in 1993 were also unsuccessful, including the Agrarian Party, Women of Russia, Russia's Democratic Choice, and the Party of Russian Unity and Concord; the Democratic Party, which had won party-list seats in the earlier election, put up no candidates at all. The hard-line grouping Communists–Working Russia–For the Soviet Union, by contrast, came close to the threshold, reflecting a general leftward shift in the electorate; and it was one of the parties, together with the Agrarians, Women of Russia, Russia's Democratic Choice, and the Party of Russian Unity and Concord, that won some representation in the single-member constituencies. But with only four parties able to secure seats in the new Duma, nearly half the party-list vote was wasted, and the successful parties obtained a share of the party-list seats that was twice their share of the vote. There was no precedent anywhere in the world for this degree of disproportionality, and there were understandable complaints that the 'rights of millions of voters had been violated'.[72]

Elections in the single-member constituencies did something to rectify these imbalances and many of the parties that obtained no seats in their own right were able to win some representation, often through a strong campaign by a party leader with local links. The Communists, again, were the most successful, but the Agrarians also did well, and parties in general increased their control as the share of the seats that were won by independent candidates fell by half (they still won more seats than any of the parties). Alexander Lebed won a seat in Tula, although the Congress of Russian Communities had fallen below the party-list threshold; his brother won a seat as an independent in neighbouring Khakassiya. Yekaterina Lakhova, one of the leaders of Women of Russia, won a seat in the Ul'yanovsk region; the leader of the Party of Russian Unity and Concord, Sergei Shakhrai, won his party's only seat in the Rostov region. Yabloko campaigned more effectively than before in the single-member constituencies, and won nearly half as many seats as in the party-list competition (it won more than any of the other parties in reform-minded St Petersburg). The Liberal Democrats, by contrast, won just a single constituency seat, in spite of their network of activists. It was notable that the most successful party in the single-member constituencies (apart from the Communists) was the Agrarian Party, which had failed to secure representation in its own right; the Liberal Democrats, conversely, had finished second in the party-list contest but once again did very poorly in the single-member districts even though they had nominated the largest number of party-sponsored candidates. Party labels, admittedly, were often misleading, as many candidates preferred to fight as independents in the belief that their chances would be improved: outgoing foreign minister Andrei Kozyrev, for instance, fought his Murmansk constituency as the nominee of his constituents and not as the sponsored candidate of a political party.

There had, in fact, been relatively little movement in the overall distribution of party preferences. As before, there were several large

Table 2.3. *Elections to the State Duma, December 1995*

	Party lists			Single-member constituencies		Total seats	
	% vote	number of seats	% seats	number of seats	% seats	number	%
Communist Party	22.3	99	44.0	58	25.8	157	34.9
Liberal Democrats	11.2	50	22.2	1	0.4	51	11.3
Our Home Is Russia	10.1	45	20.0	10	4.4	55	12.2
Yabloko	6.9	31	13.8	14	6.2	45	10.0
[5% threshold]							
Agrarian Party	3.8	–	–	20	8.9	20	4.4
Power to the People!	1.6	–	–	9	4.0	9	2.0
Russia's Democratic Choice	3.9	–	–	9	4.0	9	2.9
Congress of Russian Communities	4.3	–	–	5	2.2	5	1.1
Women of Russia	4.6	–	–	3	1.3	3	0.7
Forward, Russia!	1.9	–	–	3	1.3	3	0.7
Ivan Rybkin bloc	1.1	–	–	3	1.3	3	0.7
Pamfilova–Gurov–Lysenko bloc	1.6	–	–	2	0.9	2	0.4
Communists–Working Russia–For the Soviet Union	4.5	–	–	1	0.4	1	0.2
Party of Workers' Self-Management	4.0	–	–	1	0.4	1	0.2
Trade Unions and Industrialists	1.6	–	–	1	0.4	1	0.2
Govorukhin bloc	1.0	–	–	1	0.4	1	0.2
Fatherland	0.7	–	–	1	0.4	1	0.2
Common Cause	0.7	–	–	1	0.4	1	0.2
Transformation of the Fatherland	0.7	–	–	1	0.4	1	0.2
Party of Russian Unity and Concord	0.4	–	–	1	0.4	1	0.2
Party of Economic Freedom	0.1	–	–	1	0.4	1	0.2
89 Regions of Russia	0.1	–	–	1	0.4	1	0.2
Bloc of Independents	0.1	–	–	1	0.4	1	0.2
Other parties	8.9	–	–	0	–	0	–
Independents	–	–	–	77	34.2	77	17.1
Against all lists	2.8	–	–	–	–	–	–
Invalid vote	1.2	–	–	–	–	–	–

Registered electorate: 107,496,558. Total vote: 69,204,819. Valid vote: 67,884,200.
Turnout (total vote as percentage of electorate): 64.4 percent.

Source: Vestnik Tsentral'noi izbiratel'noi komissii Rossiiskoi Federatsii, no. 1, 1996, pp. 49–51 (party-list vote) and 18–47 (deputies elected by single-member constituencies).

blocs: the organised left, with about a third of the party-list vote; and then three blocs with about a fifth of the vote each, representing the national-patriotic, pro-government, and reformist parties and movements (figure 2.2). The Communists had certainly advanced their position, winning a larger share of the vote in the country as a whole and the largest share of the vote in sixty-two of the eighty-nine regions and republics. But their successes were most often at the expense of the Liberal Democrats, not of the pro-government or pro-reform parties, while their 1993 allies, the Agrarians, lost more than half their share of the party-list vote and failed to secure representation in their own right. The leading reform party in 1993, now known as Russia's Democratic Choice, lost even more heavily, but Our Home Is Russia, which had not been in existence at the time of the 1993 election, took more than a tenth, and taken together, the main pro-government vote had not fallen substantially. The biggest loser was the Liberal Democratic Party, with a drop in its share of the poll in all but one of the regions and an overall loss of 4.6 million votes; it was particularly unsuccessful in the larger cities, and in regions with a substantial non-Russian population. Our Home Is Russia, by contrast, did well in the cities (particularly in Moscow) and in the non-Russian republics, and Yabloko won more votes than in 1993, although its share of the party-list vote fell slightly; it won two of the regions, St Petersburg and Kamchatka, and had the most concentrated of the party electorates, with more than a fifth of its voters resident in St Petersburg and Moscow. At the other extreme, as many as sixteen of the forty-three parties and movements that contested the party-list election secured fewer than 200,000 votes, which was fewer than the number of signatures they had been obliged to collect in support of their original nomination.[73]

How had voters made their choices? Some of the characteristics of the party electorates are shown in table 2.4, which is based on a nationally representative survey conducted just after the vote.[74] As had been true at the time of the 1993 Duma election,[75] Communist voters were older than those of other parties; Women of Russia, by contrast, had the youngest of the party voters, but those who had not voted at all were even younger. Women of Russia, predictably, had the highest proportion of female voters, the Liberal Democratic Party the lowest. The reform parties, Russia's Democratic Choice and Yabloko, had the most highly educated electorates; the Communists and Liberal Democrats, conversely, had the highest proportion with only a basic education and the lowest with a university or college degree. The reform parties were also the most likely to draw their support from the biggest cities, although Our Home Is Russia, with its appeal to officialdom, had a similar

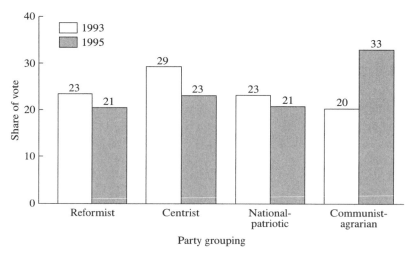

Source: Adapted from A. G. Beloborodov et al., *Vybory deputatov Gosudarstvennoi Dumy. 1995. Elektoral'naya statistika* (Moscow: Ves' mir, 1996), pp. 241, 243.

Fig. 2.2   The distribution of the party-list vote, 1993–5

profile. Similarly, there were marked differences between the parties in terms of the beliefs of their supporters. Those who had voted for reform parties were the most committed to the market economy; Communist voters, followed by Liberal Democrats, were the most hostile. Communists and Liberal Democrats were also the most likely to resist the claims of any of the Russian regions to leave the federation, although voters and nonvoters alike were also opposed. There were further contrasts in attitudes to parties and party systems: Communist voters, followed by Liberal Democrats, were the most likely to favour the restoration of a single-party system – for the Communists, though not the Liberal Democrats, this was the view of the largest number of their supporters. Few supported the multiparty system that had come into existence by the mid-1990s; the reform parties, Russia's Democratic Choice and Yabloko, were the most supportive of a multiparty system of a more coherent kind, and this was the most strongly supported position across the electorate as a whole. Congress of Russian Communities voters were more pro-market and pro-multiparty than the average, but (in spite of their party programme) also more likely to support the right of regions to leave the federation; sociologically, they were close to a cross-section of the electorate.

How important were attitudes in determining party choice, as distinct from social characteristics such as gender, age, income, and education?

Table 2.4. *The correlates of voting, 1996 (percentages)*

	All	In December 1995 voted for:							
		Communist Party of the Russian Federation $n=404$	Congress of Russian Communities $n=53$	Liberal Democratic Party $n=126$	Our Home Is Russia $n=153$	Russia's Democratic Choice $n=49$	Women of Russia $n=75$	Yabloko $n=132$	Non-voters $n=347$
Male	40.5	42.1	41.5	61.1	42.5	30.6	13.3	37.9	37.8
Female	59.5	57.9	58.5	38.9	57.5	69.4	86.7	62.1	62.2
Age: 18–30	20.6	8.7	16.98	18.3	18.95	8.2	25.3	21.96	34.9
31–60	56.1	54.7	66.0	69.0	54.2	65.3	60.0	57.6	50.1
61+	23.3	36.6	16.98	12.7	26.8	26.5	14.7	20.5	14.98
Education:									
Basic secondary	45.3	56.2	43.4	49.2	38.6	24.5	38.6	28.8	48.99
Specialised secondary	28.7	23.5	37.7	28.6	34.6	26.5	37.3	27.3	27.95
Higher	20.3	15.3	16.98	12.7	23.5	49.0	18.7	41.7	14.4
Residence:									
village	23.3	26.98	20.8	27.8	18.3	20.4	42.7	15.9	21.0
town of 1k–100k population	25.1	28.96	30.2	23.0	22.2	12.2	16.0	20.5	25.9
town of 100k–1m population	31.5	32.2	30.2	41.3	33.3	28.6	30.7	30.3	29.7
city of 1m+	20.1	11.9	18.9	7.9	26.1	38.8	10.7	33.3	23.3
Market economy:									
for	53.9	33.4	64.2	45.2	66.0	87.7	65.3	75.8	55.3
against	28.1	48.0	20.8	37.3	15.0	6.1	16.0	11.4	25.4
Regions should be allowed to separate:									
yes	31.2	27.5	39.6	34.1	28.8	42.9	36.0	34.1	35.4
no	48.5	56.7	47.2	54.8	47.7	38.8	42.7	44.7	45.8
Favours:									
one party	29.9	48.5	15.1	34.9	15.7	2.0	28.0	12.1	32.3
multiparty system	5.9	1.2	11.3	5.6	11.1	6.1	9.3	10.6	5.5
multiparty with fewer parties	49.4	41.6	64.2	47.6	61.4	83.7	48.0	69.7	37.5
no parties	7.0	2.2	3.8	4.8	7.2	6.1	9.3	5.3	10.95

Source: Derived from a national representative survey conducted for the author and associates by Russian Public Opinion and Market Research (ROMIR) in January–February 1996, n = 1581.

In a Western country, using the classic model developed by Lipset and Rokkan,[76] it would be customary to start with the formation of regional, occupational, and religious identities over time, and then move on to shorter-term determinants including assessments of economic performance and future expectations. Russians, however, have had to acquire their political preferences in a society in which ownership and occupation are still fluid and in which there has been little opportunity for party choices to become rooted in social cleavages and transmitted across the generations by a process of political learning.[77] A multiple regression analysis suggests that, at least in the 1995 election, party vote was much more likely to be predicted by attitudes than by the social characteristics that shape most Western electorates.[78] The Communist vote, for instance, was heavily influenced by age, but even more heavily influenced by hostility to the market economy and to the government. The Liberal Democratic vote was better predicted by gender than by attitudes, but the next most important determinants were hostility to the market, hostility to the government, and (most of all) their willingness to support military action if there was an ethnic conflict in a neighbouring country in which the rights of Russians were being threatened; age, education, and income made relatively little difference. Our Home supporters were older, but even more likely to favour the market, and almost as likely to be distinguished from other voters by their support for a multiparty system. Yabloko voters were better educated and more affluent than the electorate as a whole, but still more readily predicted by their commitment to multiparty politics and (most of all) by their support for a market economy.

Survey evidence made clear other characteristics of party choice.[79] The Communist vote, for instance, was the most consistent: more than two-thirds of those who had voted Communist in 1995 reported that they had also done so in 1993. Liberal Democratic voters were the next most likely to have supported their party in both elections (47 per cent), followed by Yabloko with 43 per cent; by contrast, only a third (34 per cent) of those who voted for Women of Russia had voted for them in 1993, and of those who voted for Russia's Democratic Choice only 19 per cent had voted for Russia's Choice in the earlier election.[80] The Communist vote was the 'hardest' in several other respects: its supporters, for instance, were more likely to have decided at an early stage on their choice of party, and they were more likely than any other group of party supporters to agree that the party reflected the 'interests of people like me' (see table 2.5). Yabloko and the Congress of Russian Communities did best when voters were asked if they trusted the party leaders (Communist voters, by contrast, were the least likely to say they had

Table 2.5. *The motivations of party voters, 1995 (percentages)*

	It reflects the interests of people like me	I trust its leader(s)	It is strong enough to change things	Out of habit or I know this party, but have barely heard of the others	The majority of my peers supported it	It isn't so good, but the others are worse	To protest about what is going on in the country	These are people not involved in financial scandal or corruption	This is a new fresh political force	I like its name
All	30	28	21	7	8	12	5	5	5	2
Communist Party of the Russian Federation	43	12	28	15	12	7	7	2	0	0
Congress of Russian Communities	15	48	19	6	8	13	8	19	13	2
Liberal Democrats	21	39	30	5	9	18	6	3	2	0
Our Home Is Russia	18	28	31	5	9	18	1	0	2	2
Russia's Democratic Choice	29	38	16	10	9	14	0	2	3	0
Women of Russia	39	18	8	3	4	15	5	9	8	4
Yabloko	31	40	19	4	6	9	2	9	12	2

Note: The question asked was 'Why did you vote for this party or bloc?' More than one answer was allowed; other answers and don't knows are not reported.

Source: Derived from a national representative survey conducted for the author and associates by the All-Russian Centre for the Study of Public Opinion (VTsIOM) in late December 1995, n = 1568.

voted for their party because of their confidence in its leaders). Our Home Is Russia voters, on the other hand, were the most likely – and with some justification – to believe their party was 'strong enough to change things' (Women of Russia voters were the least likely to think their party could make a difference of this kind, although they did like its name); and voters for the Congress of Russian Communities were the most likely to have been impressed that its candidates had not 'been involved in financial scandal or corruption'. Communist voters were also the most likely to report that they 'fully and unconditionally' identified with the party's programme and slogans: 43 per cent did so without reservation, compared with just 17 per cent of those who had voted for Our Home Is Russia.

As well as differentiation by social characteristics, there was a sharp differentiation in the support that was offered to the various parties across the republics and regions. There was nothing accidental about this differentiation: it had been apparent in 1993 as well as 1995, and it was reflected in the way that neighbouring regions shared a common political orientation rather than a random distribution of preferences. The Communists, for instance, did particularly well in the north Caucasus (they won more than half of the vote in North Ossetia), and in the regions in middle Russia that had become known as the 'red belt'; but they also did well along the boundaries of the Russian Federation with the newly independent former republics, where the collapse of established trading relations had been especially marked and where flows of inward migration were particularly large. Communists did better in rural areas, and in those with processing industries, less well in regions that were rich in natural resources and heavily involved in the export of their output; nonetheless, they were the only party that exceeded the 5 per cent threshold in all republics and regions. Yabloko did particularly well in the Far East, especially in Kamchatka, where it won more than a fifth of the vote, and in the north-west; it also did well in regions that had embraced market reforms more enthusiastically than others, including Nizhnii Novgorod, Rostov, and Tomsk as well as Moscow and St Petersburg, but it performed poorly in rural areas and in those with a large non-Russian population. The Liberal Democrats did best in regions that were economically depressed, and badly (as has been noted) in regions with an ethnically mixed population; Our Home Is Russia, predictably, was the most popular party in Moscow with its large proportion of government officials, and it also did well in St Petersburg and the Moscow region. The regions, obviously, varied in their social composition, and it was necessary to allow for these characteristics before specifically local effects could be identified; and there were many individual results that clearly owed most of all to the techniques of political management, such as the 34 per cent that was won by Our Home Is Russia in Ingushetia, or the 48 per cent it was reported to have obtained in neighbouring Chechnya even though the republic was still at war with the federal authorities.[81]

Russia by the late 1990s was certainly a multiparty state; and yet it was difficult to say that parties were central to the political process. There were certainly bodies that called themselves parties and nominated candidates for public office; at the same time they were often no more than vehicles for ambitious politicians, with negligible memberships and poorly defined programmes. Forward, Russia!, for instance, had no individual membership at all, nor did the Party of Economic Freedom, headed by wealthy businessman Konstantin Borovoi, nor did Our Home Is Russia[82] – one of the questions considered by its congress in 1997, indeed, was whether it should 'become a political party'.[83] There were parties that had a mass membership and a functioning organisation, like the Communists and (according to its own estimates) the Liberal Democrats; at the same time there were parties that had a membership of no more than a hundred or so, like the incongruously named People's Party,[84] and there were organisations of a quite different character that also had the right to put forward candidates, like the Automobilists' Club of Russia.[85] All the parties, moreover, exaggerated their memberships. Zhirinovsky had included all who attended its inaugural congress as members of the Liberal Democratic Party; the Party of Workers' Self-Management claimed 350,000 members, but had evidence of only 2,685 at the moment of its official registration.[86] Equally, there was double counting, even at leading levels. The governor of Samara, Konstantin Titov, was a member of Russia's Democratic Choice but at the same time a deputy chairman of Our Home Is Russia; the chairman of the upper house, Yegor Stroev, was simultaneously a member of the Central Committee of the Communist Party, the National Council of the Congress of Russian Communities, and the Central Council of Our Home Is Russia.[87] And there were fringe, mostly short-lived parties like the Idiots' Party of Russia with its persuasive slogan, 'Give the People Bread and Sausages.'[88]

Given their loose organisation, it was not surprising that many of the new parties divided into smaller and sometimes hostile groupings. Democratic Russia, which was the earliest coalition of reformers, quickly fell apart; and then Russia's Choice, which was the most substantial of its successors, suffered a split of its own when Gaidar left to form Russia's Democratic Choice (in his memoirs he complained bitterly of the inability of the reform-minded intelligentsia to form a coherent political organisation).[89] Later still his own party lost about a third of its members to Our Home Is Russia, which was the 'party of power' after the 1995 election, and found it very difficult to agree a common position during the 1996 presidential contest: Gaidar himself favoured Chernomyrdin, but when the prime minister refused to stand the party formally associated itself with Yeltsin, although some of its leading members joined the Yavlinsky campaign.[90] Splits, however, were at least as characteristic of the left as of the reformist right. The CPSU had itself fragmented into as many as eight distinct tendencies during its last years of rule, including a 'silent majority',[91] and most of these became independent parties in the postcommunist years. The Republican Party, for instance, evolved from the 'Democratic Platform' that had been formed within the CPSU, while the 'Marxist Platform' developed into a Union of Communists, a short-lived Party of Labour, and a strongly orthodox Russian Party of Communists.[92] Other parties remained coherent but at the cost of a harsh internal discipline, like the All-Union Communist Party (Bolsheviks), headed by chemistry lecturer Nina Andreeva, which saw itself as a continuation of the party over which Stalin had presided and which accordingly rejected the 1993 constitution and took no part in the postcommunist electoral process.[93]

Many of the new parties avoided the word altogether if they could possibly do so, a legacy of the time when 'the party' meant a CPSU that had monopolised power and (for most Russians) abused its position. As a teacher from Vitebsk wrote to *Izvestiya*, 'wouldn't it be better without parties altogether?' What was a party anyway but 'always and everywhere a struggle for posts and positions', fed by a lust for power that was 'more powerful than any narcotic?'[94] Or as a 45-year-old woman, formerly a member of the CPSU, told *Argumenty i fakty*, 'I don't believe in any of the parties any more . . . All the ones we have at the moment are only interested in getting into power, and no one is concerned about ordinary people. Not even the communists.'[95] It was equally clear that ordinary Russians were reluctant to associate themselves with the parties that had begun to compete for their support. According to the survey evidence, just 22 per cent of Russians identified to some degree with a political party, compared with 87 per cent of the electorate in the United States and more than 92 per cent in the United Kingdom.[96] Parties, indeed, were the most distrusted of all the political institutions, and they were even more distrusted in Russia than in the postcommunist countries of Eastern Europe.[97] There were much lower levels of membership or participation in the activities of political parties than in Eastern Europe, and 'extraordinary levels of electoral volatility, even by postcommunist standards': the shifts that took place in voting support between elections in postcommunist Russia were six times as large as in

Plate 2.2   The voters decide . . . (*Izvestiya*, November 1995)

Western Europe in the 1980s, and twice as large as in Eastern Europe.[98] The Russian electorate, in these and other ways, was 'very fluid', cleavage formation was 'indefinite', and there was 'little sense of patterned interaction or "systemness"'.[99]

The weakness of parties in postcommunist Russia was partly a consequence of the fluidity of social structures, and partly a consequence of the length of time that Russians had been denied an opportunity to form their own organisations and choose among them at the ballot box. It was also a consequence of the political system itself. For a start, Russia had a strongly presidential system, with a head of state who claimed to govern in the interests of the nation as a whole and who enjoyed a mandate of his own; this undermined the position of political parties, whose purpose was typically to mobilise a section of the electorate in order to achieve a parliamentary majority.[100] But even if they did so, a majority in the Russian Duma had no direct implications for the composition of the government or the direction of public policy. The prime minister owed his position to the confidence of the president, not the support of the electorate, and indeed Chernomyrdin's immediate reaction to the defeat of Our Home Is Russia in the 1995 election was to declare that there would be no changes at all in the policies he was pursuing[101] (conversely, the dismissal of the entire cabinet that took place in March and August 1998 and then again in May 1999 had nothing to do with a change of party balance in the

Duma, still less a national election). The situation, journalists suggested, was quite similar to the one that had existed before the revolution: a monarch, with enormous power concentrated in his hands, who could issue laws, nominate those who were to carry them into effect, administer justice, and even – in Yeltsin's case – control the mass media.[102] Why, in these circumstances, should parties seek to gather the support they needed to win a majority of seats? And why should ordinary Russians believe their choice of party gave them any influence over the conduct of public affairs?

The choice of party at the ballot box was in any case rather loosely related to the distribution of party support within the Duma. This was partly because of the disproportionality that operated in a system that allowed a large number of parties to compete for seats, while at the same time insisting on a 5 per cent threshold. But it was also because of the way in which seats were redistributed after the election had taken place. In a Western democracy, deputies sit with other members of their party after an election; and if their party is in a majority, at least in a parliamentary system, they form the new government. The position in Russia was rather different. Only the Liberal Democratic fraction in the new Duma coincided with the number of seats the party had won in the 1995 election. Yabloko gained an independent, Our Home Is Russia gained ten independents and a deputy who had been nominated by Forward, Russia!, and the Communists added six independents and another deputy who had originally been elected on a different party list. Most 'independents', in fact, joined one or other of the party groupings in the new Duma; the 'independent' group, conversely, was mostly composed of deputies who had originally been elected on a party ticket.[103] Parties, in these circumstances, were less a means of attempting to 'win power' or even to influence a new government; they were more important as a device through which prospective presidential candidates could obtain media exposure (including free air time), and in this way strengthen their position in the contest that really mattered.[104]

Elections and government

Just as its elections lacked any element of choice until the late Gorbachev years, so too the Soviet system had lacked any element of parliamentarianism. Soviets were meant to be very different: there was no separation of powers, for a start, as working people were assumed to have a common interest that was based upon their ownership of the means of production, and it was that common interest that was reflected in a single slate of candidates in local and national elections.

Why, it was asked, should working people need courts that were a separate branch of government, any more than they needed different parties to reflect social interests that were in basic agreement? The USSR Supreme Soviet, for these reasons, met very rarely, for no more than a week of the year, and its votes were always unanimous, although there was a complex procedure for resolving disputes between the two chambers. It was hardly surprising that speakers were in agreement as the texts of their contributions had normally been prepared beforehand by party officials, leaving them with barely enough time to read through 'their' speech before delivering it;[105] parliamentary journalists, for their part, could file their story before the session they were reporting had taken place.[106] Much of the work of the Supreme Soviet was in fact conducted through a committee system, and the budget in particular was given quite detailed consideration; but all the deputies were part-timers, deliberately so as they were supposed to combine parliamentary duties with their daily work and not become a separate, 'parasitic' class. There was a high rate of turnover, which gave the largest possible number of working people the opportunity to run their 'own' state, and deputies at all levels were chosen so that they reflected the society they represented: about a third were women, more than half were workers or collective farmers, and many were under thirty; fewer than half of the deputies, in fact, were Russians, which was less than their share of the total population.[107]

All of this was changing in the late Soviet period. A part-time parliament, certainly, was unlikely to offer a direct challenge to the dominance of the CPSU; but it was also a parliament that had little opportunity to hold government to account, or to criticise any of its members who were guilty of incompetence or corruption. Ministers, as a consequence, held their position for long periods of time: Yefim Slavsky headed the Ministry of Medium Machine-Building almost without a break from 1957 to 1986 (when he was in his late eighties); Andrei Gromyko, foreign minister from the same year up to 1985, was old enough to have taken part in the foundation of the United Nations. Equally, the lack of effective public scrutiny meant that policies were poorly considered, and there were more likely to be serious and costly mistakes. It was not until 1986 that an ambitious plan to divert the Siberian rivers southwards, with enormous implications for the global environment, was formally abandoned;[108] the same ministry, *Izvestiya* reported, had made plans to irrigate the Sahara desert.[109] All of this, as Gorbachev pointed out in his speech to the 19th Party Conference in 1988, had encouraged the formation of a massive governmental apparatus that had begun to 'dictate its will' in political and economic matters, and to a corpus of officials who had become indifferent to the responsibilities with which they had been entrusted and in some cases involved in the abuse of their office for private gain.[110] Responding to this lead, an entirely new representative system was established at the end of that year as part of a deliberate move towards 'Soviet parliamentarianism': there would be a large, 2,250-member Congress of People's Deputies and a smaller working body, the Supreme Soviet, which would be in session for six to eight months of the year; ministers, too, would be elected by direct competitive ballot and hold their positions for a maximum of two five-year terms. This was the parliament that was elected in March 1989, with responsibility for the whole of the USSR; there was also a Russian Congress of Deputies, elected in March 1990, and it was this parliament that took Russia into the postcommunist era.

The constitution that was approved in December 1993 established another new representative system, as we have seen (figure 2.1): an upper house, the Council of the Federation, which was composed of deputies from each of Russia's regions and republics, and a lower house, the State Duma, which was elected by a combination of single-member constituencies and a national party list. The Federation Council had 178 members, two from each of the republics and regions, and it was accordingly the chamber that considered all questions of federal significance. It was the Federation Council, for instance, that approved boundary changes and the introduction of martial law or a state of emergency; it appointed judges to the Supreme Court on the nomination of the president, and authorised the use of Russian armed forces beyond the boundaries of the state; it also considered legislation emanating from the Duma on the budget, taxes and currency matters, international treaties, and war and peace (Art. 102). The Federation Council was a chamber of full-time politicians: two-thirds worked in central or (more often) local government, most were in their forties and fifties, and an overwhelming 95 per cent were men.[111] Equally, it was a chamber that met irregularly, for just one week in three, with a further period before its regular sessions in which its committees could hold their meetings.[112] At least in the view of its own chairman, it was a chamber that was less politicised than the Duma, where half the deputies had been returned by party lists, and its members were 'closer to life', as they had direct responsibility for their own regions.[113] For its critics it was an anomaly that it met infrequently, despite the constitutional requirement that the Federal Assembly be a 'permanently working body', and that it was not directly elected, but drew its membership from the administrations and legislatures of the republics and regions on an *ex officio* basis (this was difficult to reconcile with

Article 10 of the constitution, which insisted on a separation of powers).[114]

The lower house, the State Duma, had a range of more conventional parliamentary prerogatives. It was the Duma, first of all, that approved nominations to the prime ministership on the nomination of the president (Art. 103); if it failed to do so three times in succession the president was obliged to appoint his own candidate, dissolve the Duma, and call fresh elections (Art. 111). The Duma, equally, could express its lack of confidence in the government as a whole; if it did so twice within three months the president was bound to announce the resignation of the government or the dissolution of the Duma itself (Art. 117). The Duma had other powers of appointment: it confirmed and dismissed the chairman of the State Bank, the chairman of the Accounting Chamber, and the Commissioner on Human Rights or ombudsman, and it had the exclusive right to declare an amnesty (Art. 103) – as it did, controversially, when it pardoned all who had been implicated in the attempted coup of 1991 and the confrontation of September–October 1993. The Duma, in addition, adopted federal legislation; its decisions had to be confirmed by the Federation Council, but the Duma could override a veto if it voted in favour a second time by more than a two-thirds majority (Art. 105). The president, equally, could refuse to sign a law that had passed the Duma and the Federation Council, but his decision could be overridden by a two-thirds majority in both chambers (Art. 107); in 1997, for instance, he was obliged to approve a land code he had sought to veto, and to accept a parliamentary ban on the return of objects of value that had been seized in the later stages of the Second World War.[115] Most proposals, in practice, were accepted by the upper house and president after they had been approved by the Duma, and about three-quarters of all draft legislation eventually became law after a further hearing had allowed the Duma to use its right to override their opposition.[116]

The Duma was overwhelmingly a male assembly: only forty-five women deputies were elected in December 1995, a proportion even lower than in the previous Duma in which Women of Russia had secured some representation in the party-list contest and women had won fifty-nine seats altogether. Women were particularly badly represented on party lists, accounting for just 6 per cent of all the deputies that were elected on this basis as compared with 13 per cent of the deputies that had been elected by single-member constituencies.[117] It was, however, a relatively youthful assembly, with most deputies in their thirties (20 per cent) or forties (44 per cent); 4 per cent were in their twenties; and only 5 per cent were over sixty. Most had a background in central or local government (56 per cent of the total), and nearly half (46 per cent) had previous experience in an elected body; indeed, 156 had been elected to the previous Duma, and another eleven to the Federation Council. As these backgrounds suggested, the deputies of 1995 were overwhelmingly from nonmanual occupations (95 per cent); just 2 per cent were workers by social origin and another 2 per cent were pensioners, and two deputies were unemployed at the time of their election. But this was a very different assembly from the Soviet-period parliaments that had been directly representative of the population in terms of age, gender, occupation, and nationality. Equally, in terms of their place of residence, the deputies elected in 1995 represented eighty of the eighty-nine Russian regions, which was more than in 1993, but Muscovites accounted for more than a quarter of the total (29 per cent) and another 5 per cent were from St Petersburg.[118]

The Duma soon became an active legislator: the first Duma alone, between 1993 and 1995, adopted more than 400 laws, many of which were designed to consolidate the postcommunist state system.[119] There were new laws on the Constitutional Court and on the referendum, on elections to the presidency and to the Duma itself, on the government, and on electoral rights. And there were new law codes – a Civil Code in two parts, a Family Code and a Water Code, an Air Code and a Forestry Code, and a new Criminal Code. Much of the work of the Duma was conducted through its twenty-eight committees, whose chairmen were often figures of some significance in their own right. General Lev Rokhlin, a hero of the Chechen war who had later moved towards the opposition, chaired the defence committee until his murder in 1998; film director Stanislav Govorukhin chaired the committee on culture, and former ambassador Vladimir Lukin the committee on international affairs. The work of the Duma more generally was organised through fractions and groups of deputies: fractions were based on the parties that had contested the election and secured representation in their own right, groups could be formed by other deputies provided they were at least thirty-five in number. The largest of the fractions after the 1995 election was that of the Communist Party, with 149 of the 450 seats; Our Home Is Russia had 66, the Liberal Democrats 51, and Yabloko 46. There were three deputies' groups, 'Russian Regions', 'People's Power', and the Agrarians, and twenty-five independent deputies who stood outside the organised framework of representation altogether.[120] Few, however, managed to preserve their unity when it came to voting: on the final reading of the budget in 1998, for instance, all the Yabloko deputies voted against but seventeen Communist deputies voted in favour (ninety-five voted against), six Our Home deputies voted against and

Plate 2.3   The State Duma in session (Novosti)

only three in favour (fifty-seven abstained), and all the Liberal Democrats abstained as well.[121] Equally, coalitions across the fractions were
unreliable, although there was a large degree of common purpose
between the Communists and two of the deputies' groups, People's
Power and the Agrarians, and a corresponding degree of hostility
between Yabloko and the Liberal Democrats.[122]

The conduct of the Duma and its members did not always encourage
respect for their position. One nationalist deputy, for instance, a deputy
chairman of the committee on women, families, and youth, lived openly
with three women and proposed a bill to legalise polygamy – because, he
explained, there weren't enough sober and gainfully employed men to
go around. 'The majority of Russian men are too poor to support one
family, let alone several', he told reporters; 'I have the money and energy
to keep all my women fully satisfied, materially and physically.'[123] A
sitting on 9 September 1995, which had been meant to discuss the
NATO bombings in Bosnia, was particularly remarkable. The deputy
who set things in motion was Nikolai Lysenko, leader of the far-right
National Republican Party. Desperate to attract press attention, he
chose this moment to attack a long-time foe, Orthodox priest Gleb
Yakunin of the Democratic Party. As Yakunin was returning to his seat,
Lysenko seized his cross; another deputy from the Stability group

rushed forward to separate them but became involved in the melee. Two women deputies tried to restore order – 'women have always interfered in fights', one of them told journalists – but at this point Vladimir Zhirinovsky joined in. He elbowed one of the women out of the way (she suffered concussion) and then turned on the other, seizing her in an armlock and removing her spectacles. A bloodied Yakunin later announced that he would be taking legal action against Lysenko for the theft of his cross, for banditry, and for offending the sensibilities of believers; the press gave rather more attention to Zhirinovsky's assault on a women deputy, describing it as 'the Duma's solution to women's issues'.[124] There was another incident in the spring of 1998, again involving Zhirinovsky, when the Liberal Democratic leader pushed the speaker from his seat, threatened to beat up the Rules and Procedures Commission chairman, and finally spat in the faces of several fellow deputies.[125]

Deputies had other faults as well. As a cleaning lady told the Moscow evening newspaper, they stole whatever they could from the parliament building: soap, towels, cups, telephones, mirrors, light bulbs, and toilet paper; none, however, had been called before its committee on ethics. There were no financial scandals, Russian journalists explained, 'because nobody even tries to hide their conflicts of interest'. There were rules that were intended to prevent legislators from engaging in commercial business, but many did so, using their wife's name. And there was 'almost no way to trace illicit money. There is no oversight and no paper trail. You can't prove anything.'[126] Criminals were often eager to become deputies, because of the parliamentary immunity it afforded them. Indeed entire fractions, according to press reports, were willing to trade their support for financial rewards; this was 'all but the most reliable source of income for individual and party budgets', and one reason the federal budget took so long to negotiate.[127] Duma support staff were even more likely to be engaged in criminal activity, and on average one of them was shot dead every month; some had bought their position because of the opportunities for enrichment that it afforded, and deputies were for their part willing to employ assistants with a criminal background because they could 'get things done'.[128] Not surprisingly in these circumstances, the Duma had an indifferent public reputation. In a national survey in 1997, 51 per cent were entirely negative in their assessment, 25 per cent were mixed, and only 10 per cent took a positive view; at the same time only a quarter thought Russia could do without the Duma altogether.[129] In another survey that was published in 1998, the Duma was given an 'approval rating' of just 28 per cent, with little variation across the age groups, the genders, and the occupations.[130] There was no alternative to an elected institution if Russians were to express their views and advance them through a legislative process; but they were almost as far from representative and accountable government by the late 1990s as they had been at the end of the Soviet period, when the first steps had been taken away from a single-party monopoly towards a form of rule that rested upon the freely expressed choice of the electorate.

3   Presidential government

The end of the Soviet period saw the establishment of an executive presidency in Russia as well as in the USSR itself, although the dominance of a single leader was of much older origin. Indeed, by the time Brezhnev took over the chairmanship of the Supreme Soviet Presidium in 1977 and thus became the Soviet head of state, it was already conventional in foreign capitals to refer to him as 'President Brezhnev' or at least as the 'first person' in Soviet political life. The move to a formally constituted presidency came in 1990, as a part of the reform of political institutions that was being undertaken throughout the Gorbachev era. Gorbachev himself became the first (and as it turned out, last) head of state of the USSR in March 1990, when he was elected to the newly established presidency by the Congress of People's Deputies; Russia gained its first president a year later, in June 1991, when Boris Yeltsin defeated five other candidates in a popular election. Several of the republics and regions had adopted presidential systems even earlier, as part of a general movement towards a pattern of executive rule that prevailed very widely in the world community, and Russia soon 'led the world' in the number of such positions it had established at various levels of government.[1] The presidency, it was agreed, should normally be an elective office, and a position of executive authority: neither Gorbachev nor Boris Yeltsin, as former prime minister Nikolai Ryzhkov remarked, liked the idea of 'reigning like the Queen of England'.[2] After December 1993, indeed, it was the presidency that defined the character of the entire political system, as Yeltsin used his ascendancy after the dissolution of parliament to secure the adoption of a constitution that extended his already impressive powers. 'I don't deny that the powers of the president in the draft constitution are considerable', he told *Izvestiya*, 'but what do you expect in a country that is used to tsars and strong leaders?'[3]

A strongly personalist leadership, as Yeltsin implied, was indeed a longstanding Russian tradition, extended into the Soviet period by the dominance of the general secretary within a Communist Party whose formal dominance of the system as a whole had itself been confirmed by Article 6 of the 1977 constitution. At the time he secured this position for himself, Gorbachev recalled, 'not one world leader had more power than the general secretary of the CPSU',[4] and the party itself appeared to be in a position of permanent government, beyond the reach of ballot box, media, or courts of law. And yet, even in the Soviet period, there were countervailing forces. Leadership, after Stalin, was increasingly collective. The general secretaryship had been separated from the position of prime minister after 1964 to avoid an excessive concentration of power in the hands of a single person. The state system itself was strengthened, through the reform of local government and an expanded committee system within the Supreme Soviet, and ministries began to acquire more autonomy in their day-to-day activities.[5] Indeed effective authority was already migrating from party to state in the late communist years as Gorbachev was elected first to the chairmanship of the Supreme Soviet Presidium in 1988, then to a newly established chairmanship of the Supreme Soviet in 1989, and then to the presidency itself in 1990.

Developments in Russia were part of a wider trend towards executive presidencies, not only in the former Soviet republics but throughout the postcommunist world. Turkmenistan had been the first to institute a presidency of this kind, in 1990; Georgia followed in May, Russia in June, and most of the other republics by the end of 1991; and by 1994, when Belarus (the former Belorussia) adopted a new constitution, all the members of the Commonwealth of Independent States had moved to a presidential form of government based upon direct election. A few, indeed, had moved even further, towards what was virtually the restoration of 'emirs',[6] with presidents – often their former communist first secretaries – who had been able to secure almost unanimous support for their election and then for an extension of their mandate for periods up to 2002 (the most egregious case was Turkmenistan, where a full-scale personality cult had developed in which the president, Saparmurad Niyazov, had been invested with the title of Turkmenbashi or 'leader of the Turkmen people').[7] Most of Eastern Europe had moved towards an executive presidency by the same time, with Albania, the Czech Republic, Hungary, and Slovakia, where a more ceremonial president was elected by parliament, the main exceptions.[8] The late 1980s, however, had also seen the development of a body of Western scholarship that 'took institutions seriously', and there were many indications, in this literature, that an executive presidency was unlikely to contribute towards the formation of a party system or political stability more generally.[9] Did the Russian experience, by the late 1990s, bear out these gloomy forecasts? Had a working balance been found between an elected president, the government that he appointed, and a parliament that was also directly elected? And how did the institution of presidential government relate to a society that was familiar with a strong leadership, but also with its tendency to abuse the powers it had been given?

The emergence of presidential government

The creation of the new presidency had been among the radical proposals announced by Gorbachev at the Central Committee plenum in February 1990 at which the constitutionally guaranteed 'leading role' of the Communist Party had been relinquished.[10] The idea of a Soviet presidency, in fact, was a good deal older than this. It had been under discussion at the time of the adoption of the 1936 constitution; Stalin, however, told the Congress of Soviets that there was 'no place for an individual president elected by all the people, like the Supreme Soviet, and able to oppose the Supreme Soviet', and the proposal made no further progress.[11] A presidency was considered again in 1964 when Khrushchev suggested it to the commission that was preparing a new constitution, and of which he was the chairman; a chapter was drafted accordingly, but the discussion lapsed when Khrushchev was forced out of office later in the year, and the constitutional commission itself ceased to meet. The commission renewed its work in the mid-1970s, when what was now the Brezhnev constitution was under discussion, but it took the view that the Presidium of the Supreme Soviet should continue to serve as a collective presidency, and any anomaly was resolved when Brezhnev himself took over the chairmanship of the Presidium and brought together the real as well as formal functions of a chief executive.[12] In 1985, after Gorbachev had become party leader, the idea was put forward once more by two of his senior advisers, Georgii Shakhnazarov and Vadim Medvedev. Gorbachev, however, was still committed to a system of elected soviets, and in a system of this kind there was 'no place for a presidency'.[13]

The idea of presidential government was discussed again before and during the 19th Party Conference in the summer of 1988. Some, Gorbachev told delegates, had argued for a return to the practice of Lenin's day, when the party leader was also the head of government. Others wanted to separate party and government entirely, and others still favoured the introduction of a Soviet presidency. But a presidency, Gorbachev argued, would 'concentrate too much power in the hands of a single person', and in the end it was decided to introduce a different position, a chairman of the Supreme Soviet or, in effect, a parliamentary speaker.[14] The following year he was still arguing that it would be 'very stupid' to introduce a sort of 'saviour of the fatherland' when what was needed was a form of rule that allowed the people themselves to become the 'main actor in the political arena'.[15] The new chairmanship of the Supreme Soviet, however, proved an unhappy compromise, and the discussion continued; Andrei Sakharov, released from exile in Gorky, suggested the direct election of the chairman of the Supreme Soviet in his election address in the spring of 1989, and in the draft constitution that he proposed later in the year he included a 'president of the Union of Soviet Republics of Europe and Asia' who would be elected by the population every five years and would 'hold supreme power in the country, not sharing it with the leading bodies of any party'.[16] It was already clear to Gorbachev's associates that they would have to recapture the initiative on political reform, and in late 1989 they resumed their discussion of a presidency as part of a larger series of changes in the structure of government.[17] Gorbachev, it appears, was finally convinced of the need to move to a presidential system during a discussion with his closest advisers that took place after the Second Congress of People's Deputies in December 1989. The discussion was based upon a memorandum prepared by Medvedev and Shakhnazarov, which was very close to the proposals that were put into effect early the following year.[18]

As Medvedev and Shakhnazarov explained, the new state system was working badly. The chairman of the Supreme Soviet was fully engaged in the management of parliamentary proceedings and had no means of enforcing his own decisions. The Soviet government was busy defending its position in the committees of the new parliament; and parliament was itself holding up the implementation of important state policies. Medvedev and Shakhnazarov proposed a rather different system, based upon a directly elected president who would head a Cabinet of Ministers that would itself be approved by the Supreme Soviet. The CPSU would nominate its own general secretary, elected at a party congress, to this position; he would preside over meetings of the Politburo in his presidential capacity, and the general secretaryship as such would be abolished. It was agreed that, in the first instance, the president would be elected by the Congress of People's Deputies, and not by the population at large. 'There was no time', Shakhnazarov recalled; Gorbachev would certainly have had more authority if he had submitted himself to a popular election, but the result would have been 'unpredictable' given the rapidly increasing popularity of Boris Yeltsin, and in any case a direct election would have raised procedural difficulties – the president would have needed the support of a majority of the republics, not just of voters, and this made it possible that a decision might be deadlocked indefinitely.[19]

The first steps were taken to sound out the opinions of deputies at an informal meeting in February 1990. Opinion, it emerged, was evenly balanced. Fedor Burlatsky, an independent-minded scholar and journalist who was already associated with the cause of political reform, began by setting out the case for a presidential system.[20] Others, in reply, argued that an elective presidency would strengthen the party leadership even further by adding to the already considerable powers of the general secretary. Why was a change of this kind being introduced so hastily? Wasn't there a danger that the president, as a CPSU member, would simply carry out the instructions of the Central Committee? And that the Presidential Council through which he ruled would become a 'new Politburo'? But for others again, the attraction of an elected presidency was precisely that it would allow Gorbachev to develop a political base that was independent of his more orthodox colleagues in the party leadership. Deputies were also interested in the possible extension of a presidential system to the republics. What, it was asked, would be the relationship among the fifteen presidents that might emerge as a result? Shakhnazarov urged Gorbachev to ensure that there was just a single president in such circumstances; Gorbachev, in a fateful decision, preferred to allow the institution to develop more widely, with 'thirty–forty presidents' at lower levels of government;[21] in the event they became a challenge to his authority and to the existence of the state itself, particularly when they had been legitimated through popular election and on the basis of a demand for the supremacy of local decisions over those of the central authorities.

Following the discussion, it was agreed to place the question of a presidency on the agenda of the Supreme Soviet; and after the Supreme Soviet had approved the introduction of a presidency by a very large majority, the issue was placed before a specially convened session of the Congress of People's Deputies. Anatolii Luk'yanov, who presented the proposals, argued that a presidency would allow the political leadership to take action promptly in the event of public disorders or other emergencies, nor was there any reason to fear that the presidency would lead to a new form of authoritarian rule: there was an 'entire system of safeguards' against this, including limits on age and length of tenure, and the ability of Congress – if a sufficiently large majority decided accordingly – to recall the president and overrule his decisions.[22] Understandably, perhaps, some deputies were still concerned that an elected presidency of the kind that had been proposed would lead to the 'concentration of enormous power in the hands of a single person',

Plate 3.1　The Gorbachevs during their official visit to India, 1986 (Novosti)

which was a 'danger for the process of democratisation of our society'. They might be willing to trust Gorbachev himself; but if conditions worsened, was there not a danger that many would look for a tsarist 'little father' who might bring about a 'return to dictatorship'? Others thought the proposals, at best, were premature; first of all, they argued, there should be a new treaty of union among the Soviet republics and a new and democratic constitution, and then the president should be elected by direct and popular vote. Many of the republican leaders, equally, were concerned about the possible exercise of presidential power to suspend the operation of their own parliaments, and there was a majority, though not a sufficiently large one, in favour of a formal separation between the presidency and the party leadership.[23] Most of those who spoke, however, accepted the proposals as a means of ending what was described as a 'vacuum of power', and in the end the establishment of the presidency was approved by 1,817 votes to 133, with 61 abstentions.[24] Gorbachev was the only candidate when elections to the new post took place on 14 March, and he was sworn in the following day with the support of 71 per cent of the deputies who had voted.[25]

Any citizen aged between thirty-five and sixty-five could be elected to the presidency of the USSR for a maximum of two five-year terms. The president would normally be elected by universal, equal, and direct suffrage, although it was agreed that Gorbachev – exceptionally – would be elected by the Congress itself: the 'father of the house', literary scholar Dmitrii Likhachev, carried the day with an impassioned warning that if they did not elect a president without further delay – and he was old enough to remember the revolution of 1917 – there was a real danger of civil war.[26] The president, under the terms of the legislation, was to report annually to the Congress of People's Deputies and would brief the Supreme Soviet on the 'most important questions of the USSR's domestic and foreign policy'. He would propose candidates for the premiership and other leading state positions, he could veto legislation, and he could dissolve the government and suspend its directives. He could also declare a state of emergency, and introduce direct presidential rule. The president headed a new Council of the Federation, consisting of the presidents of the fifteen union republics; he also headed a Presidential Council, which was responsible for the 'main directions of the USSR's foreign and domestic policy'.[27] In September 1990 these already impressive powers were extended by parliamentary vote, giving Gorbachev the right to institute emergency measures to 'stabilise the country's sociopolitical life' for a period of eighteen months;[28] and further changes were made by the Fourth Congress of People's Deputies in December 1990, completing the move to a fully presidential administration.[29]

Formally, at least, these were greater powers than any Stalin had commanded, and they deepened the concern of deputies and of Gorbachev's opponents outside parliament that they could open the way to a further period of dictatorial rule. For reformist deputies, once again, the new presidency represented an 'usurpation of power', leaving too many responsibilities in the hands of a single person. Gorbachev, claimed one deputy, was 'demanding more and more powers for himself', and 'creating the legal foundations for a dictatorship'. Did the president lack formal powers, or was it rather that he had no 'firm position' on matters of the day?[30] Boris Yeltsin went even further, charging that the president was being given 'unlimited powers', more than Stalin or Brezhnev had ever commanded, which would 'constitutionalise an absolutist and authoritarian regime that could ultimately be used to provide a legal pretext for any high-handed act'.[31] Gorbachev himself drew attention to a cartoon in which he had been shown with a tsar's crown in his hands, trying it on for size.[32] There were, in fact, considerable limitations upon the powers of the new president, extensive though they undoubtedly were. For a start, he could be impeached by a two-thirds vote of the Congress of People's Deputies; indeed, attempts were made to do so at the Fourth Congress, although the vote in favour was a long way short of the number that would have been required to place the question on the agenda.[33] Ministerial nominations, equally, required the approval of the Supreme Soviet, which could force the resignation of the Cabinet as a whole if it voted accordingly; and the president had to report annually to the Congress of People's Deputies upon the exercise of his responsibilities. In any case, as Gorbachev told a gathering of miners in April 1991, he had voluntarily surrendered the extraordinary powers that he possessed as general secretary of the CPSU. Would he have done so if he had been seeking unlimited personal authority?[34]

The Russian presidency

In March 1991, as the wider population took part in a referendum on the future of the USSR as a 'renewed federation', voters in Russia were also being asked if they would support the institution of a directly elected presidency. They declared overwhelmingly in favour; and at the election that subsequently took place, in June 1991, Yeltsin was a clear winner on the first ballot (table 3.1). The decision to create the office of president within what was still one of the Soviet republics had not originally been controversial.[35] At the first Russian Congress of People's Deputies, in May and June 1990, the proposal had the support of deputies from all of the parliamentary factions; Yeltsin himself was elected chairman of the Supreme Soviet after several inconclusive ballots, and on 12 June the Congress adopted a 'declaration of sovereignty' in terms of which the Russian constitution was to prevail upon its territory, and Russian laws would have precedence over those of the USSR.[36] But once Yeltsin had resigned from the CPSU and become, in effect, the leader of the extraparliamentary opposition, the issue of the presidency became more partisan and the question of who might fill the position became a bitterly contested one. At the second Russian Congress of People's Deputies, in December 1990, all that was agreed was that the Supreme Soviet and its constitutional committee should consider appropriate amendments to the Russian constitution and submit them to the full Congress.[37] As a constitutional amendment would require a two-thirds majority in the Congress, Yeltsin's hard-line opponents seemed well placed to resist any change that would be to their disadvantage. The decision to call a referendum on the future of the USSR, however, altered the situation once again. In January 1991 the Presidium of the Russian Supreme Soviet proposed an additional ques-

Table 3.1. *The Russian presidential election, 12 June 1991*

Candidate	Votes	Percentage of vote
Boris Yeltsin	45,552,041	57.3
Nikolai Ryzhkov	13,395,335	16.9
Vladimir Zhirinovsky	6,211,007	7.8
Aman-Gel'dy Tuleev	5,417,464	6.8
Al'bert Makashov	2,969,511	3.7
Vadim Bakatin	2,719,757	3.4
Against all	1,525,410	1.9
Invalid votes	1,716,757	2.2
Turnout	79,507,282	74.7

Source: Pravda, 20 June 1991, p. 1 (the registered electorate was 106,484,518).

tion on the establishment of a directly elected presidency; its proposal was approved by the Supreme Soviet the following month; and then in March Russia's voters were asked to express their views. A resounding 70 per cent approved the change.[38]

The Congress of People's Deputies had originally been elected in March 1990, with a substantial representation of Communists. Led by its influential speaker, Ruslan Khasbulatov, it took an increasingly hostile attitude towards the market-oriented reforms that were being promoted by the president and his government. The outcome of the referendum and the open expression of public support for changes of this kind, however, influenced the Congress in a different direction and on 5 April it was resolved that a presidential election would be held on 12 June 1991. The Supreme Soviet, meanwhile, was asked to prepare a law on the presidency as well as any amendments that might be necessary to the Russian constitution.[39] A new Law on the Presidency was duly approved by the Supreme Soviet on 24 April,[40] and a month later the full Congress of People's Deputies agreed a series of amendments to the Russian constitution that incorporated these changes, adding an entirely new chapter. According to these provisions, candidates for the Russian presidency must be citizens aged between thirty-five and sixty-five. They could not hold any other public or private office, they could not engage in commercial activity, and they could hold the presidency itself for no more than two consecutive five-year terms. The president was described as the 'highest official of the Russian Federation and the head of executive power'; he enjoyed the right of legislative initiative and could veto the legislation that went through the Supreme Soviet, he reported to the full Congress of Deputies at least once a year, and he appointed the premier 'with the consent of the

Supreme Soviet'. There was also a vice-president, elected at the same time on the president's nomination; Yeltsin's choice was Alexander Rutskoi, a fighter pilot who had been a hero of the war in Afghanistan and who then went on to head a moderate Communist grouping in the Russian Supreme Soviet. The Supreme Soviet, for its part, could over-rule a presidential veto by a simple majority in both houses, and the Congress of Deputies could impeach the president or vice-president if they violated the constitution or laws, or if the president violated his inaugural oath.[41]

Yeltsin owed much of his authority to the fact that he had been directly elected, unlike Gorbachev who had been chosen – in the first instance – by Soviet parliamentarians; and he had also won respect when he faced down the attempted coup of August 1991, at some risk to his own life. At the same time he had to govern through a Congress of People's Deputies that had also been chosen by a popular vote, and which was able to claim the same right to represent the will of the electorate. The Congress had initially been supportive, electing Yeltsin its chairman and then, in the aftermath of the coup, granting him additional powers.[42] Yeltsin, however, used his position to launch a programme of radical reform under the guidance of Yegor Gaidar, who had become a deputy premier with responsibility for economic policy in November 1991, and parliamentary resistance strengthened as the consequences of those reforms became clearer. In April 1992, at the first Congress after the abandonment of most forms of price control, an attempt to debate a motion of no confidence in the government was narrowly defeated and a resolution was adopted that called for 'major changes' in the reform programme, including a substantial increase in public spending.[43] Gaidar, who had been appointed acting prime minister in June, was forced to stand down at the Seventh Congress in December 1992 at the same time as the economic performance of the government was pronounced 'unsatisfactory';[44] and at the Eighth Congress, in March 1993, the president was stripped of his emergency powers and ordered to act in accordance with the constitution, in terms of which the Congress was itself the 'supreme body of state power'.[45] Yeltsin's supporters had already talked of extraordinary measures in response to what they regarded as parliamentary sabotage of their programme of reforms, and on 20 March, in a television address, the president called publicly for a 'special form of administration' under which the Congress would continue to meet but would be unable to challenge his decisions.[46] The Congress, hurriedly convened for an emergency session, voted to impeach him but not by the necessary two-thirds majority; the outcome was an agreement that a referendum, originally approved the previous December, would be held on 25 April 1993 to decide 'who rules Russia'.[47]

The referendum, in the event, did little to resolve a continuing impasse. Voters were asked if they 'had confidence' in Yeltsin as Russian president, and if they approved the policies that president and government had been pursuing; they were also asked if they favoured early presidential or parliamentary elections. Of those who voted, 58.7 per cent supported the president and 53.1 per cent approved his policies; 49.5 per cent favoured early presidential elections and a more substantial 67.2 per cent early parliamentary elections, but in both cases this fell short of the majority of the electorate – and not just of voters – that was necessary for constitutional changes. These were better results than the polls had forecast, although there were substantial regional variations: eighteen of the eighty-nine republics and regions declared a lack of confidence in the president (another eight gave him less than majority support), and in thirty there was a majority against his social and economic policies; there was no voting at all in the Chechen republic, and in Tatarstan the turnout was so low the whole exercise was invalid.[48] For Yeltsin and his supporters, nonetheless, this was a verdict that justified pressing ahead with a constitution that provided for a presidential republic with a much more limited legislature, and by the end of the year they had attained their objective. Yeltsin had already made clear, in an uncompromising address in December 1992, that the Congress was creating 'intolerable working conditions for the government and the president', attempting to turn the 'Supreme Soviet, its leadership, and its chairman into the absolute rulers of Russia', and aiming in the last resort at the 'restoration of the totalitarian Soviet-communist system'. It had, he warned deputies, 'become impossible to go on working with such a Congress', and he had called for a referendum to resolve the tension between 'two irreconcilable positions'.[49]

For parliamentarians and their speaker the issue was a rather different one: whether government should be accountable to elected representatives, and whether a broadly representative parliament should be allowed to act as a counterbalance to what would otherwise be an overwhelmingly powerful executive. For Khasbulatov, in Russia the state had for centuries been identified with the power of an autocratic ruler. Marxism-Leninism had not only continued this tradition but taken it to 'absurd lengths'; indeed, the party general secretary had 'practically become a tsar'. It was vital, in these circumstances, to establish a secure division of powers, which was the basis of democratic states in other countries. Not only did it guarantee the effective operation of the state machine, it also had a 'deeper humanistic meaning' in that it helped to defend individual liberties based on the rule of law. A parliament, in this context, was the 'institutionalisation of democracy'; it represented the society as a whole and helped to reconcile its various interests, it acted as a 'counterbalance' to the executive in matters such as public spending and the composition of government, it encouraged the formation of political parties, and it helped to stabilise the entire system.[50] Opening the Russian parliament in March 1992, Khasbulatov accused the government of an 'attack on democracy' and complained that individual ministers had a dismissive attitude towards the representative institutions through which it was expressed.[51] He insisted that government should be accountable to the Congress and Supreme Soviet rather than to the 'collective Rasputin' that surrounded the president.[52] And he argued more generally that a presidential republic was not appropriate to the particular circumstances of postcommunist Russia, with its need to maximise consensus and public understanding.[53]

These differences, in the end, were resolved by force, when parliament was dissolved by presidential decree on 21 September 1993 and then seized by the Russian army on 4 October following an attempt by parliamentary supporters to occupy the Kremlin and establish their own authority (see chapter 2). Yeltsin had produced his own draft of a new constitution in April 1993, in the immediate aftermath of the referendum, and a constitutional conference that met in June and July with a number of deputies in attendance produced another version that was in Yeltsin's view 'neither presidential nor parliamentary'.[54] Yeltsin had however predicted a 'decisive battle' between the supporters and opponents of his programme of reforms, and in the different circumstances that obtained after the suppression of what he described as a parliamentary insurrection it was a rather more centralist draft that was published in November 1993 and approved at a referendum the following month.[55] Most of the changes in the draft were minor, but several were significant, particularly those that concerned the relationship between the central government and the republics and regions. The constitution as it stood incorporated the Federation Treaty, concluded in the spring of 1992, which defined relations between the state as a whole and its constituent republics and regions; the November draft left it out, undermining the position of what were now to be known as 'subjects of the Federation'. The republics and regions, in a related change, were no longer to be 'sovereign', with their own citizenship. And the position of the government in relation to the president was further weakened: under a new article it would be required to resign on the election of a new president, the president would have the right to preside over its meetings, and he could dismiss it without reference to parliament.[56] The outcome was what an *Izvestiya* journalist described as a 'superpresidential republic'; others thought it 'monarchical'.[57]

The newly defined presidency was certainly a formidable one. The newspapers dubbed him a 'president-tsar' (Gorbachev, indeed, claimed that the Russian president was *more* powerful than the tsar had been before the revolution);[58] opponents argued that his powers were 'dictatorial' and compared them with those of Napoleon III in nineteenth-century France.[59] The president was head of state and guarantor of the constitution itself, to which he swore an oath. It was the president who represented the Russian Federation at home and abroad and who defined the 'basic directions of the domestic and foreign policy of the state' (Art. 80), particularly in the 'annual address on the situation in the country' that he gave to both houses of parliament (Art. 84). The president was directly elected for four years by universal, direct, and equal ballot, and could not be elected for more than two consecutive terms (Art. 81; unlike his American counterpart, he could be re-elected on a future occasion). A Russian president had to be at least thirty-five years old, and had to have lived in the Russian Federation for at least ten years (Art. 81); this ruled out the émigré candidatures that had been seen in Eastern Europe in the postcommunist period, some of whom had been very successful (an émigré, indeed, won the Lithuanian presidency in early 1998). The president, moreover, had extensive powers of appointment. He appointed the prime minister 'with the agreement of the State Duma', and could preside at meetings of the government. He nominated candidates to head the State Bank, he appointed and dismissed deputy premiers and ministers, and he nominated candidates to the Constitutional Court, the Supreme Court, and the Procuracy. He formed and headed the Security Council, and appointed and dismissed his representatives in the Russian regions as well as the high command of the armed forces and diplomatic representatives (Art. 83). In addition, he could initiate legislation and dissolve the Duma in specified circumstances (Art. 84); and he could issue his own decrees, which had the force of law throughout the Federation (Art. 90). The president, finally, headed the armed forces, and could declare a state of war as well as a state of emergency (Arts. 87 and 88).

There were in fact few limits on the powers of a Russian president. He could still be impeached, but less easily than before: the Duma had first of all to vote in favour of proceedings by a two-thirds majority on the initiative of at least a third of the deputies after a special commission of deputies had decided he had been guilty of treason or a crime of similar gravity; the Supreme Court had to rule that there were grounds for such an accusation, and the Constitutional Court had to confirm that the proper procedures had been followed; and the Federation Council had then to vote in favour by a two-thirds majority, not later than three months after the original charges had been presented (Art. 93). It was unlikely, given this elaborate procedure, that Yeltsin or any future president would be forced out of office on this basis, although the Duma might sometimes find a sufficiently large majority to initiate proceedings. There was no upper age limit, as there had been in the April draft, presumably because Yeltsin would just have passed his sixty-fifth birthday when his first term came to an end. There was no provision, as there had been in the constitution that was valid at the time of Yeltsin's September decree, that the president could not dissolve the Congress of Deputies or Supreme Soviet, or suspend their operation. It was for the president to approve the 'military doctrine of the Russian Federation', which was a constitutional novelty (Art. 83); and it was for the president, not the parliament, to call a referendum once the necessary procedures had been completed.[60] Nor was there any provision for a vice-president, who could deputise for the president and, as Rutskoi had done, offer a political alternative as well as a mechanism that could be invoked if the president were to die or become unable to exercise the functions of his office. Symbolically, the April draft had placed its chapter on the president after the chapter on the Congress and Supreme Soviet; in the version that was approved in December 1993 the chapter on the presidency came first.[61]

The president, indeed, had additional powers that were not fully specified by the constitution. The constitution, for instance, mentioned that the president formed the 'Administration of the President of the Russian Federation' (Art. 83), but gave no other indication of its role in government. It was, in fact, almost a government in itself, with a staff of nearly 2,000 that was in many ways reminiscent of the central bureaucracy of the CPSU, housed in the same buildings, and headed by presidential counsellors whose influence could eclipse that of the corresponding ministers.[62] In 1999, after its sixth reorganisation, the presidential administration included (i) a main supervisory board, (ii) a department of internal policy, (iii) a department of regional policy, (iv) an economic department, (v) a personnel department, (vi) a separate personnel department for the presidential administration itself, (vii) a department for the Cossacks, (viii) a department for state decorations, (ix) a main legal department, (x) a pardons department, (xi) a department on citizenship, (xii) a department for the work of presidential representatives in the regions, (xiii) a public relations department, (xiv) a foreign policy department, (xv) a presidential chancellery, (xvi) an information department, (xvii) a department for appeals, (xviii) the presidential archives, (xix) an organisation department, which looked after a variety of consultative bodies, (xx) a protocol department, (xxi) a business management department, (xxii) a department ensuring the operation of the consultative agencies under the president, and (xxiii) a press service, as well as (xxiv) a group of presidential advisers.[63] The head of the presidential administration was a figure of considerable influence in his own right; up to the end of 1998 it had been Valentin Yumashev, a journalist who had identified with Yeltsin at the outset of his career, masterminded his campaigns, and ghosted his memoirs. Yumashev had limited experience of government but considerable skill in corridor manoeuvres; crucially, he enjoyed the president's entire confidence, and was a part of his 'family circle' together with his immediate predecessor, Anatolii Chubais (all three had children or relatives attending the same school in England). He also played tennis, although he had taken it up 'long before the whole Kremlin elite began to play it'.[64]

The prime minister had a distinct but subordinate position within this structure of executive authority. He was appointed by the president 'with the consent of the State Duma' (Art. 111); the entire government submitted its resignation to a new president (Art. 116), and the president had in turn to submit his prime ministerial nomination within two weeks of taking office (Art. 111). But unlike parliamentary systems, there was no question of the prime minister submitting his resignation to a newly elected Duma and securing the support of deputies in order to continue. On the contrary, as Chernomyrdin made clear after Our Home Is Russia had secured just over 10 per cent of the party-list vote in the December 1995 parliamentary election, he would not be considering resignation and there would be no changes in the policies the government had been pursuing.[65] Equally, the dramatic dismissals of the entire cabinet in March and August 1998, and then again in May 1999, were quite unconnected with the balance of power within the Duma, still less the outcome of a new election. The Duma, for its part, did have some influence over the choice of prime minister, but it was a power of last resort. The Duma had a week to vote on any nomination; if it rejected three nominations in a row the president was required and not merely empowered to dissolve the Duma and call a new election (Art. 111). The Duma had another power of last resort, which was its right to call a vote of no confidence in the government as a whole. If it did so twice within three months the president had either to announce the resignation of the government, or dissolve the Duma; the government could also decide to offer its own resignation, which the president could accept or reject (Art. 117). Both of these powers, however, were unlikely to be used in normal circumstances, as they would precipitate a constitutional crisis and almost certainly the dissolution of the Duma itself.

It was the prime minister, in turn, who took responsibility for the ordinary business of government. He made proposals to the president on the structure of the government as a whole, and on the appointment of deputy premiers and ministers (Art. 112). More generally, he was supposed to identify the 'basic guidelines' of government activity, and to 'organise its work' (Art. 113). It was the government that submitted an annual budget to the Duma, and reported on its fulfilment; ministers, under the Law on the Government of 1997, could also be required to respond to the questions that were addressed to them by members of the Duma or Federation Council (Art. 38). The government, similarly, took responsibility for finance, credit, and currency matters, and it conducted a 'uniform state policy' in culture, science, education, health, social security, and the environment. The government was also responsible for state property, for public order and the rule of law, and for foreign policy (Art. 114), and it could issue resolutions and directives in order to carry its decisions into effect (Art. 115). Under an amendment to the 1997 law it had the additional responsibility of 'co-ordinating' the defence and foreign ministries, although the president remained commander-in-chief and headed the Security Council, which had ultimate authority in all matters of this kind.[66] As reconstituted in May 1999 the Russian government included twenty-four federal ministries, among them defence, justice, foreign affairs, finance, economics, health, culture, and education. There were also eleven state committees, including youth, the environment, telecommunications, and housing;; two federal commissions; fifteen federal services including tax collection, foreign intelligence, security, broadcasting, and currency; ten agencies; two inspectorates; and three other bodies that were associated with the presidential office. [67]

Viktor Chernomyrdin had been appointed prime minister in December 1992 when the Congress of Deputies refused to accept Yeltsin's nomination of Yegor Gaidar, and he was confirmed in his position after the 1996 presidential election. Yeltsin, however, was apparently jealous of the prominent role that Chernomyrdin had been playing in domestic and international affairs – newspaper commentaries suggested he had made the president 'almost redundant'[68] – and in March 1998 he unexpectedly dismissed the entire government and appointed Sergei Kirienko acting prime minister, explaining at the same time that there would be 'no change in policy'.[69] Kirienko, a boyish 35-year-old who had served as energy minister since the previous November, was virtually unknown to the wider public ('Sergei who?', asked *Moscow*

News[70]); but he was formally nominated as prime minister four days later, Yeltsin introducing him as a 'technocrat' who was 'able to conduct a dialogue with all who [we]re ready to hear a variety of opinions'.[71] Kirienko, it emerged, was a graduate of the Gorky Institute of Water Transport Engineering and a former Komsomol official from Nizhnii Novgorod, who had then moved into factory management and banking. As he told journalists, he had a Russian mother, a Jewish father, and a Ukrainian surname, and there was general agreement that he had a 'disarming and easygoing manner'.[72] Kirienko, nonetheless, was rejected in a first vote on 10 April and by a larger majority on 17 April; he was finally approved a week later, many deputies aware that if they rejected his nomination a third time not simply would the Duma itself be dissolved but the president would be able to impose his own choice at least until the new Duma had been convened.[73]

Political life was thrown into disarray once more in August 1998 when the president made another unexpected change of prime minister and government. Yeltsin, who was on holiday at this time, had told journalists just a few days earlier that he was 'quite satisfied' with his youthful premier, and Kirienko himself had been giving interviews to mark his 'first hundred days' in office.[74] But on 23 August, in a country already destabilised by a sudden collapse in the ruble (see chapter 4), the Russian president dismissed the entire government once again and nominated Viktor Chernomyrdin to the premiership, just five months after he had dispensed with his services.[75] In a 'difficult' economic situation, Yeltsin explained in a television address, they needed a 'heavyweight' with the kind of 'experience and authority' that the former prime minister could provide; and they also needed someone who could ensure the 'continuity of power', which suggested that Chernomyrdin would be his favoured candidate at the next presidential elections.[76] Chernomyrdin, however, had still to secure the endorsement of the Duma, which showed no willingness to accept a candidate whose policies had so manifestly failed; he was rejected on 31 August by a large majority, and then on 7 September by an equally decisive margin.[77] Yeltsin told interviewers he would 'insist' on Chernomyrdin in the third and decisive vote, dissolving the Duma if necessary;[78] but he had no wish to face an even more hostile parliament, which opinion polls suggested was the most likely outcome, and in detailed negotiations with the party leaders a different and more widely supported candidate emerged, Foreign Minister Yevgenii Primakov. He was nominated on 10 September and endorsed by the Duma the following day by 317 votes to 63 with the support of the Communists and of Yabloko, who had first proposed his name earlier in the year.[79]

Primakov, Yavlinsky explained, was not their ideal candidate, but he was a 'flexible politician without personal ambitions, whose main goal would be to maintain stability',[80] and he had made clear he would not be using the premiership to position himself for the presidency.[81] Yeltsin himself, in another television address, emphasised that Primakov was a 'consensus candidate', and one who for the first time would be able to count upon the support of the Federal Assembly as well as of the president.[82] This was nonetheless the first time Yeltsin had been obliged to yield ground to his opponents, and it marked a significant shift towards what was at least *de facto* a more balanced relationship between president, government, and parliament. Indeed there were moves against the president himself: the Duma had voted in favour of his resignation in the immediate aftermath of the collapse of the ruble in late August, and it began to gather evidence that could be used to press impeachment charges.[83] Yeltsin himself told interviewers he would not be resigning, and that he would be remaining until the end of his second term;[84] but his spokesmen also made clear that he would be withdrawing to a more distant role, no longer allowing himself to be 'distracted by day-to-day issues', although he was still reluctant to consider any formal transfer of his considerable powers or – still more so – any modification of the constitution that would diminish them.[85] What this could mean became clear in May 1999 when the president dismissed his government once again and appointed interior minister Sergei Stepashin as acting premier. Primakov, Yeltsin complained, had shown 'insufficient dynamism', but it appeared more likely that the president had again become jealous of the popularity of a subordinate and of one who was allowing the affairs of the presidential family to be investigated by the procurator general (Stephashin was replaced three months later by security chief Vladimir Putin, an even more committed Yeltsin loyalist, in another unexpected move that, for *Izyestiya*, was the 'president's way of showing the Duma who's boss').[86]

Yeltsin and the Russian presidency

The man who now exercised the far-reaching powers of the Russian president had been born in the village of Butko in the Sverdlovsk region of western Siberia in 1931, the son of peasant parents. According to his autobiography, Yeltsin was lucky to be alive at all: the priest nearly drowned him when he was being baptised, remarking calmly, 'Well, if he can survive such an ordeal it means he's a good tough lad.' Both his father and his uncle were persecuted in 1934 when they fell foul of the campaign against kulaks, who were rich or simply more efficient farmers. They were accused of conducting anti-Soviet agitation and, though they protested their innocence, given three months' hard labour; Yeltsin himself, though only three, remembered the 'horror and fear' years later.[87] Yeltsin's childhood was a time of the famine that followed agricultural collectivisation: there were always shortages of food, and the family might not have survived the war but for the milk and sometimes the warmth of their nanny-goat. Yeltsin lost two fingers in an accident; he broke his nose and contracted typhoid fever; his father, a harsh disciplinarian, beat him regularly. Later, he lost almost all hearing in his right ear – not an unmitigated loss for a Russian politician, as his bodyguard pointed out in his memoirs.[88] But he did well at school and graduated as an engineer at the Urals Polytechnical Institute, where he perfected his volleyball technique and met his future wife (they had fallen in love during their second year of study, she told journalists).[89]

After completing his studies, Yeltsin worked as a construction engineer managing a large state enterprise that specialised in prefabricated housing. In 1961 he joined the CPSU, becoming a full-time party functionary in 1968 and in 1976 first secretary of the Sverdlovsk regional party organisation. He joined the Central Committee at the next party congress in 1981, and as a full member. One of Yeltsin's decisions as party first secretary was to order the destruction of the Ipat'ev house in which the tsar's family had been shot in 1918, and which had become a place of pilgrimage. The decision, he explained later, had been taken secretly by the Politburo and there was no alternative but to carry it out, although he knew that 'sooner or later' they would all be ashamed of what they had done (much later, in 1998, he was able to make atonement in a dignified speech when the remains of the royal family, as verified by scientific analysis, were buried in the Cathedral of St Peter and St Paul in St Petersburg).[90] Yeltsin's managerial qualities – he had, on his own admission, become 'steeped in command-administrative methods' by this time; for others he was even 'totalitarian'[91] – caught the attention of the central leadership, and early in 1985 he was invited to Moscow to take up a position in the party apparatus as head of its construction depart-ment. In December 1985, after Gorbachev had taken office, he was transferred to the position of first secretary of the Moscow party organisation in succession to a disgraced Brezhnevite, Viktor Grishin.[92]

Yeltsin's outspoken comments soon attracted attention. His speech at the 27th Party Congress in early 1986 began with references to the 'Bolshevik spirit' and 'Leninist optimism' that prevailed at their delib-erations, but went on to ask why over so many years the party had failed to eliminate social injustice and the abuse of official position.[93] Then in October 1987 – according to those who were present, almost by accident[94] – he was called to speak to the Central Committee plenum

Plate 3.2 'Muscovites have made their choice' (Boris Yeltsin and Yuri Luzhkov, a 1996 election poster)

that was considering Gorbachev's draft report on the seventieth anniversary of the revolution. Yeltsin wanted, he wrote later, to 'screw up [his] courage and say what [he] had to say'; his speech was no more than a few headings on a sheet of paper. It was nonetheless the decisive moment in his political career. There had been no changes in the way the party secretariat operated, Yeltsin told the delegates, or in the conduct of its head Yegor Ligachev. More and more instructions were being issued, but they were receiving less and less attention. Meanwhile in the Politburo there had been a 'noticeable increase' in what he 'could only call adulation of the general secretary'. In seventy years, he declared in another version of the speech, they had failed to feed and clothe the people they claimed to represent, while providing for themselves abundantly. And there were criticisms of the general secretary's wife, who was being paid for what was thought to be voluntary work and acquiring her own 'cult of personality'.[95]

Yeltsin knew what would happen next: he would be 'slaughtered, in an organised, methodical manner, and . . . with pleasure and enjoyment'.[96] The plenum itself described his speech as 'politically mistaken' and called for his dismissal as Moscow party secretary; Gorbachev, 'almost hysterical', denounced him at the Politburo and complained that everything in the Soviet capital was 'going badly'.[97] The Moscow party organisation, when it met in November, dragged a 'barely conscious' Yeltsin out of a hospital bed to listen to a series of charges of incompetence and even 'Bonapartism' in what was the political equivalent of a Stalinist show trial, and then voted to remove him from his post.[98] Yeltsin himself, after an 'almost fatal' dose of painkillers, spoke briefly and like a 'hypnotised lunatic'; the plenum itself affected his health and left him in a 'very low mood, confined to bed, and if anyone visited him he shook the hand that was extended to him with two cold fingers'.[99] He was dropped from the Party Politburo in February 1988 and urged to retire, but in the end moved to a junior ministerial position at the State Construction Committee. A 'political outcast, surrounded by a vacuum',[100] Yeltsin seemed to have reached the end of his political career; even his membership of the CPSU was in doubt as the Central Committee, in a decision without postwar precedent, voted to investigate his increasingly outspoken views to determine if they were compatible with party policies.[101]

But the more Yeltsin was attacked by the party leadership, the more he came to be seen as a champion of ordinary citizens against an overpowerful, often corrupt establishment; and the introduction of competitive elections at the same time as his disgrace allowed him to turn this popular following to his advantage. In March 1989, standing for the Moscow national-territorial constituency, he had won over 89 per cent of the vote against a party-approved competitor;[102] his winning margin, over 5 million votes, was so large it entered the Guinness Book of Records, and it contrasted sharply with Gorbachev's decision to take one of the hundred seats that had been reserved for the CPSU and for which a hundred candidates had been nominated, avoiding a direct appeal to the electorate and still more so a direct confrontation with his leading opponent. A year later, in elections to the Russian parliament, Yeltsin won another popular mandate when he took over 80 per cent of the vote in his native Sverdlovsk in elections to the Russian Congress of Deputies;[103] and he began to use his position, once he had been elected parliamentary chairman at the end of May 1990, to advance the claims of the republics and especially of Russia against the central state and its ruling party.

Yeltsin's appeal was based on his open opposition to the party-state bureaucracy, but he also advanced more specific proposals. Speaking to the Central Committee in February 1990 he called for the private ownership of land, independence for the republics, financial autonomy for factories and farms, freedom of political association, and freedom of conscience.[104] Asked in the summer of 1990 if he was still a socialist, Yeltsin turned the question round: what was meant by socialism? It could mean the 'developed socialism' that the USSR itself had experienced under Brezhnev, or Pol Pot socialism. In Hitler's Germany there had been national socialism; and there were many different kinds of capitalism too. What was the point of arguing about definitions?[105] His models, he told interviewers, were Peter the Great and Yaroslav the Wise, grand duke of Kievan Rus' in the early eleventh century;[106] but in general, he confessed, he was happy to rely on his intuition.[107] A study of his speeches by three academics found that the Russian president was 'predictable in only one respect – his unpredictability'; and ordinary Russians felt he was just as 'unpredictable' when they heard his public performances.[108]

Yeltsin admitted in the memoirs he published in 1994 that he relied on his self-image as a 'wilful, determined, strong politician'. But he also confessed that he was easily influenced by the opinions of people he respected; and sometimes his ideas were changed completely by 'a word said in passing or a line in a newspaper article'. There was, it seems, a decisive moment in this intellectual trajectory, in late 1989 when Yeltsin visited a Moscow bathhouse. He found himself surrounded by a crowd of about forty naked men, all insisting he should maintain his challenge to the leadership. It was, he recalled, 'quite a sight'. And it was at this moment in the *banya*, with everything reduced (so to speak) to its essentials, that he had 'changed [his] world view, realised that [he] was a communist by Soviet tradition, by inertia, by education, but not by conviction'.[109] Yeltsin was also influenced by a visit to the United States in September 1989, his first to a capitalist country. Amazed by the array of foodstuffs that was readily available in a Houston supermarket, he commented that this disproved the 'fairy tales' that were being peddled in the USSR itself about the superiority of socialism. In the view of Lev Sukhanov, one of his closest aides, it was at this time Yeltsin decided to leave the ranks of the CPSU;[110] it could in fact have seen the end of his career entirely as he chose to take his staff swimming late at night in shark-infested waters, paying no attention to the warning notices or to the 'little wave' that appeared beside him.[111]

In a newly established and weakly institutionalised system of the Russian kind, formal position mattered rather less than the shifting patterns of influence that revolved around the president himself. A great deal of importance attached, for instance, to relations with the president's younger daughter, who had become responsible for his 'image' in 1997 and who wielded a great deal of influence over other matters including appointments and larger questions of strategy.[112] A common regional background was also important (a 'Sverdlovsk mafia' provided many of the president's closest advisers, particularly during his first term), and so were services to his expensive re-election campaign in 1996, or even his choice of tennis partner – including the national coach, with whom he played four or five times a week.[113] The head of presidential security up to 1996, for instance, Alexander Korzhakov, held a position of no constitutional significance. But he saw the president daily, played tennis with him regularly (making sure to lose more often than he won), and began to offer views on current politics that appeared to carry considerable weight at the very centre of the administration.[114] When Korzhakov sought to bring his influence to bear upon the role that foreign companies should play in energy policy, *Izvestiya* was moved to ask in a front-page headline: 'Who rules Russia: Yeltsin, Chernomyrdin, or General Korzhakov?'[115] And there was intensive speculation when Korzhakov, in an interview with a British newspaper, suggested publicly that the 1996 presidential elections should be postponed or called off altogether, even though these views were immediately disowned by the president.[116] Korzhakov himself found that Yeltsin was influenced more than anything else by the 'interests of his family clan, not of the state', and in particular by his daughter Tanya and her 'chosen circle', which included Anatolii Chubais and the financier Boris Berezovsky (Chubais, after the 1996 elections, had even remarked 'let's make her vice-president!').[117] Berezovsky was in turn the main shareholder in the international carrier Aeroflot, whose director was the husband of Yeltsin's elder daughter, and he took personal responsibility for the second volume of Yeltsin's autobiography, which was published without particular success in 1994.[118]

The result was what Yavlinsky described as a 'Byzantine court', with members who were constantly engaged in 'palace intrigues';[119] it was a system of 'checks and balances', as others put it, but one in which, in the president's absence, 'the "checks" immediately declare[d] war on the "balances"'.[120] There was constant competition among the president's associates 'for which of the "closest" persons [wa]s the closest of all', just as Politburo members had jostled for the central positions above the Lenin Mausoleum for the parade on the anniversary of the revolution.[121] And there was a pervasive atmosphere of suspicion, in which telephones were tapped and presidential aides exchanged their views in the form of notes that were later destroyed.[122] It was also a male environment, in which there could be physical threats, off-colour anecdotes that were 'reminiscent of the mores of the time of Ivan the Terrible', drinking bouts, and buffoonery.[123] Annoyed by his press secretary during a visit to Krasnoyarsk in which they were taking a boat trip on the Yenisei, for instance, Yeltsin brusquely demanded that Kostikov be 'thrown overboard'; Korzhakov, admiring the Siberian countryside from the lower deck, thought at first it was an 'enormous bird' as Kostikov sailed past him, flailing the air with his arms and legs.[124] Kostikov himself 'mainly invited members of the sexual minorities' to join his staff; one of its members who regularly staged homosexual orgies was found under the window of his flat one morning with most of his bones broken, after he had been ritually beaten for his 'complete sexual satisfaction' and then thrown from the third floor (this did not improve Kostikov's own position).[125] The president himself had more traditional tastes and simply 'love[d] a good time', according to the testimony of his former bodyguard. He was fond of drinking songs, and was a skilful instrumentalist with a good sense of rhythm; even on official trips he would demand 'bring spoons!' His 'favourite trick', Korzhakov recalled, 'was to play knick-knack-paddy-whack with his spoons' on the head of his chief of staff. At first he would beat on his own leg,

and then he would beat loudly on the head of his subordinate. The latter did not dare to take offence, and just smiled affectedly. The audience burst out laughing. On one occasion, Yeltsin took aside the president of one of the former Soviet states, Askar Akayev of Kyrgyzstan, and played the spoons on his head. He could torture one to death with this musical instrument.[126]

Several other members of the president's staff offered their evaluation in memoirs and interviews. Yekaterina Lakhova, for instance, a qualified doctor who came from the same part of Russia and who worked latterly within his administration, found the president a contradictory character: 'by nature very stern, strong-willed, even dictatorial', a man who 'did not tolerate verbosity and vagueness', who always wanted the tasks before him to be set out 'clearly and precisely', and who set out tasks in this way before his subordinates. But he was also 'kind and responsive', even 'overly trustful', which meant that his relations with others were often based on his personal impressions rather than a balanced assessment of their performance.[127] Press secretary Kostikov also found him a person of moods, who rose to the occasion when it was necessary but fell into depression at other times, who liked to be the centre of attention and feel that 'all the applause belonged to him', and who was 'very jealous' of the success of others but also 'trustful'. He had found it difficult to adapt to democratic politics, Kostikov believed, and was happier dealing with practical matters than with abstractions. He had no interest in culture and his musical tastes did not extend further than folksong, but at the same time he could reproduce an entire passage from Shostakovich's 'Leningrad Symphony'. He found it difficult to establish a relationship with other Russian politicians and increasingly referred to himself in the third person, but liked to speak of 'my friend Bill' or 'my friend Helmut'; and he had no particular philosophy, in Kostikov's view, other than the 'ideology of power itself'.[128]

Former prime minister Yegor Gaidar was another who had roots in the Sverdlovsk region, and he knew from his own sources that Yeltsin had been well regarded locally and that there had been disappointment when he was transferred to Moscow. His speeches at the October 1987 plenum and at the Party Conference in 1988, thought Gaidar, had shown his 'strength and political potential, his ability to seize on problems that really concerned people', but also 'complete uncertainty about where this political potential would be directed', especially in economic matters. Equally, when he won the Moscow seat in the Congress of People's Deputies in 1989 it was clear that this was a 'real political leader', but there were few clues about the ways he would use the popular support he had been able to mobilise. Yeltsin, for Gaidar as for others, was a 'complicated, contradictory character'. His strongest quality was the 'ability intuitively to feel the popular mood and take account of it before taking the most important decisions', and in questions of principle he trusted his instincts more than his advisers. He was able to listen, but could also be manipulated. And, like Kostikov, he noted that the president was capable of 'very long periods of passivity and depression'.[129] Closest of all was Yeltsin's former bodyguard Alexander Korzhakov, whose revealing memoir appeared in 1997. Yeltsin, he disclosed, had several times tried to kill himself, the first occasion in 1990 when he jumped off a bridge into the Moscow river in what had been thought at the time to be a drunken escapade, and on another occasion when Korzhakov had to break into a sauna to rescue him.[130] Others still consulted the stars: Yeltsin, they noted, was an Aquarian, like three other heads of state in the CIS: this meant they were 'strong-willed, ambitious people, able to achieve what they wanted whatever the cost'.[131]

The 1996 election and the problems of presidential power

The struggle for influence within the presidency took place against a steady fall in the public standing of the president himself. Yeltsin had clearly overtaken Gorbachev in public support before he became Russian president: in 1989 it was the Soviet president who was 'man of the year', and by a wide margin, but by 1990 Yeltsin (with 32 per cent) came first, ahead of Gorbachev with 19 per cent.[132] Indeed Yeltsin, in one survey at this time, came first among all Russian leaders of the twentieth century, ahead of Lenin, Gorbachev, and (by a wide margin) Nicholas II.[133] Yeltsin, in more qualitative terms, was seen as 'open and straightforward' (34 per cent), 'ambitious' (26 per cent), but also 'resolute' (24 per cent). Gorbachev, by contrast, was 'hypocritical' (28 per cent), 'weak and lacking in self-confidence' (20 per cent), and 'indifferent to human suffering' (19 per cent), although he was also 'flexible and capable of adapting to change' (18 per cent).[134] According to the All-Union Centre for the Study of Public Opinion, it was in the summer of 1990 that Yeltsin's popular support overtook that of the Soviet president. The peak of his popularity, with an approval rating of 80 per cent, was in July 1990 soon after he had been elected chairman of the Russian parliament; his support rose again, to 74 per cent, after the attempted coup in August 1991.[135]

Once in office, however, Yeltsin's support declined rapidly. It had fallen to about 45 per cent at the time of the collapse of the USSR at the end of 1991, and fell still further after the spring of 1992 as Gaidar's economic policies began to bite. The president's popularity recovered a little at the time of the April 1993 referendum, and again during the conflict with the Russian parliament in September and October 1993, but then resumed its earlier decline, and by the end of 1994 his support was down to 34 per cent. Just 3 per cent of Russians, by this time, were ready to say they 'completely shared' his views and policies; 10 per cent supported him 'in the absence of other worthy political leaders'; but 25 per cent had become 'disappointed' in the Russian president and 26 per cent were his declared opponents.[136] It was at this point, in December 1994, that Yeltsin sent Russian forces into Chechnya to restore federal authority and perhaps to recover his personal standing in what was expected to be a 'short, victorious war'.[137] If this was the intention, it came badly unstuck. Chechen resistance proved unexpectedly stubborn; the Russian campaign was incompetently conducted, particularly at the outset, and losses were heavy, up to 30,000 within the first year. Yeltsin's support, in the event, plunged still further, a majority holding him personally responsible for the war and just 5.8 per cent prepared to support him in the event of an early presidential election.[138]

What kind of president did Russians really want? The survey evidence suggested that Russians would be prepared to accept a woman president, particularly if they were younger; and they were quite prepared to accept a former member of the Communist Party, although there were many who wanted a candidate with a 'fresh view of things'. Far more important, for most Russians, was that the president should be a 'highly educated specialist' (75 per cent), that he should be 'decisive' and 'self-confident' (59 per cent), and that he should be a Russian (59 per cent). But little importance was attached to whether the president was a religious believer or not, or a particular age, and there was majority agreement that the president could be a figure with the 'usual human failings', although a substantial minority insisted on a figure 'completely beyond reproach in personal and family life'.[139] The surveys that were conducted by the president's own staff found there were certainly some ways in which he appealed to ordinary Russians, and this was particularly in the way that he reflected what ordinary Russians thought was their 'national character': he was direct, honest, and firm, an impression that was reinforced by the president's massive Siberian figure and blunt features.[140] On the other hand, a substantial number (31 per cent) held the Russian president responsible for the 'crisis in the economy'; others pointed to the 'mistakes of recent years' (27 per cent), Yeltsin's 'responsibility for the war in Chechnya' (24 per cent), and his 'lack of a programme for getting the country out of its crisis' (20 per cent). In addition, the president was seen as 'uninterested in the social problems of ordinary people' (19 per cent) and 'remote' (12 per cent). Indeed, a majority (52 per cent) thought he should resign.[141]

Yeltsin, in the event, announced on 15 February 1996 that he would be seeking a second term – he had lost his voice and made the announcement with 'some difficulty'[142] – and then mounted a remarkable campaign which carried him to victory in the two rounds that took place in June and July. It was a victory, in the end a decisive one, that owed a good deal to the prerogatives of the presidency itself. Yeltsin made full use of his influence over the state media, and particularly television. He invited the head of Russia's newly established independent television service, which had been critical of his policies in Chechnya, to join his campaign staff. He committed public funds with increasing abandon: to small businesses and the Academy of Science, to pensioners and those who had lost their savings. An end was declared to the conscription in the armed forces, and the troops themselves were allowed to avoid compulsory duty in Chechnya and other hot spots.[143] Perhaps as much as $500 million was spent on his campaign, and certainly much more than the $3 million allowed by the electoral law.[144] But most important of all, Yeltsin campaigned with increasing confidence, travelling the country with an energy that belied his sixty-five years, and presenting himself as the only serious alternative to a return to the Soviet system. After one of his trips at least four of the accompanying journalists suffered pneumonia, and so did two of Yeltsin's own staff.[145] The changes in his behaviour were so extraordinary that ordinary Russians began to believe he had been connected to a battery; another view, put about by a financier involved in his campaign, was that 'At key points in his life, Yeltsin wakes up.'[146]

The outcome in the first presidential ballot, on 16 June 1996, was a narrow plurality (see table 3.2). But within a few days Yeltsin had received the third-placed candidate, former general Alexander Lebed, and offered him a place in his administration as secretary of the Security Council with particular responsibility for public order. Gennadii Zyuganov, the Communist candidate, found himself unable to extend his coalition of supporters between the two rounds, despite a series of attempts to form a broadly based 'government of national confidence'; and Yeltsin, in the second round, won a clear victory with most of Lebed's voters behind him as well as the overwhelming majority of the voters that had backed liberal reformers like Grigorii Yavlinsky (see table 3.3).[147] It was a striking success; yet it also made clear that Yeltsin's committed supporters were only a quarter of the electorate, a smaller share than nonvoters, and a much smaller number than had been prepared to support him in June 1991 and again in the April 1993 referendum. The distribution of support for pro-Yeltsin reformers and for Communists and their allies, in fact, had scarcely changed between the December 1995 Duma election and the first round of the presidential contest in June 1996: the broadly Communist electorate was 32.2 per cent in 1995, and 32 per cent exactly in the first round of the presidential elections; nationalists secured 20.7 per cent in 1995 and 20.2 per cent in the first round in 1996; and centrists and reformists

Table 3.2. *The first round of the Russian presidential election, 16 June 1996*

	Vote	
Candidates	Percentage	Number
Boris Yeltsin	35.3	26,665,495
Gennadii Zyuganov	32.0	24,211,686
Alexander Lebed	14.5	10,974,736
Grigorii Yavlinsky	7.3	5,550,752
Vladimir Zhirinovsky	5.7	4,311,479
Svyatoslav Fedorov	0.9	699,158
Mikhail Gorbachev	0.5	386,069
Martin Shakkum	0.4	277,068
Yuri Vlasov	0.2	151,282
Vladimir Bryntsalov	0.2	123,065
Aman-Gel'dy Tuleev[a]	0.0	308
Against all candidates	1.5	1,163,921
Invalid ballots	1.4	1,072,120
Turnout	69.7	75,587,139

[a] Withdrew from race at last minute in favour of Zyuganov.

Source: Derived from Tsentral'naya izbiratel'naya komissiya Rossiiskoi Federatsii, *Vybory Prezidenta Rossiiskoi Federatsii. Elektoral'naya statistika* (Moscow: Ves' mir, 1996), p. 128 (the registered electorate was 108,495,023).

Table 3.3. *The second round of the Russian presidential election, 3 July 1996*

	Vote	
Candidates	Percentage	Number
Boris Yeltsin	53.8	40,203,948
Gennadii Zyuganov	40.3	30,102,288
Against both candidates	4.8	3,604,462
Invalid ballots	1.0	780,592
Turnout	68.8	74,691,290

Source: As table 3.2, pp. 128 and 130 (the registered electorate was 108,589,050).

took 42.2 per cent of the vote in 1995 and just slightly more, 44.6 per cent, in the first round of the presidential contest.[148] Yeltsin, as before, polled most strongly in Moscow, St Petersburg, his native Sverdlovsk region and most of the north and the Far East, winning forty-six of the eighty-nine regions in the first round and fifty-seven in the second and decisive vote; the Communists retained most of their 'red belt' around Moscow and along the western and southern borders, taking forty-three of the regions in the first round and just thirty-two in the second.[149]

Although he had been successfully and, in the end, decisively re-elected, the experience of the early years of Russian presidentialism suggested a number of weaknesses in what had been intended as a system of firm and effective authority. One of these was the extent to which the discharge of executive functions depended upon the person of the president, and upon his physical health as well as his policy priorities. The 1993 constitution added to these concerns by abolishing the position of vice-president (in the postcommunist world only Bulgaria, Kazakhstan, and Kyrgyzstan retained a position of this kind).[150] Under the constitution, for instance, the president relinquished office ahead of time in the event of his resignation, impeachment, or 'stable inability to perform the duties of his office for reasons of health'. In these circumstances the powers of the president passed on a temporary basis to the prime minister, and new elections had to be called within three months (Art. 92). But who, asked commentators, was to decide if the president was 'totally unable to exercise his powers? The patient himself, by signing a decree? Or the prime minister? Or a special conference of doctors? Including whom? Or, perhaps, a presidential assistant – but which one?'[151] Yeltsin was generally hostile towards the medical profession, and he resisted the idea of a health bulletin of the kind that was regularly issued in France and the United States, and which was demanded from time to time by the parliamentary opposition.[152] The issue came up with particular force during his heart surgery at the end of 1996. Did surgery, or a lengthy hospitalisation, count as a 'stable inability to perform the duties of his office'? Did the transfer of his powers to the prime minister require a formal decree, or was it sufficient for the president to issue the appropriate instructions? Or should it require the approval of a state body? And if so, which one?[153]

Yeltsin himself complained that 'as soon as [he went] on holiday, speculation [began] about [his] health'.[154] But there were many such absences, and it was not surprising that every visit to the hospital was accompanied by 'arguments and rumours that undermine[d] his authority'.[155] In 1993 Yeltsin was confined to hospital with a nervous disorder. In December 1994 he underwent an operation on his nose. In April 1995 a spring holiday was extended by a further week because of the president's high blood pressure, and in July he was rushed to hospital complaining of acute chest pains. In October 1995 there was a recurrence of the same cardiac difficulties; he was in hospital for more than a month and did not return to his Kremlin desk until the end of December. There were further rumours when Yeltsin disappeared from public view between the two rounds of the presidential election in 1996, and a wooden television appeal on the eve of the decisive vote was not reassuring. The president had become a 'painted mummy', complained one of Zyuganov's supporters; 'they're suggesting we vote for a living corpse'.[156] Yeltsin underwent a multiple bypass operation in early November 1996 with Western specialists in attendance, but resumed his powers the following day and was soon 'back at work';[157] then he was ill again in January 1997 with double pneumonia, and a planned visit to the Netherlands had to be postponed. 'The president is ill. The prime minister is on vacation. The country is adrift', announced *Izvestiya*.[158] Allowing for public holidays, the paper calculated, the president had exercised his official functions for just ten days since the election.[159] The Liberal Democrats, unsportingly, called for him to be declared a 'missing person'.[160]

Concerns about the presidential role were not allayed by repeated reports of alcoholism. The president himself admitted, in an interview in 1993, that he 'sometimes' allowed himself a glass of cognac on a Sunday evening with his family, or some beer after visiting the bath-house.[161] His parliamentary critics were more forthcoming. 'It's time to stop the public drunkenness of our president', a Communist deputy demanded after an unsteady performance during the president's first visit to the United States. 'When he's shown on television, he can't stand up without support.'[162] There was criticism in early 1993 when the president, defending himself against impeachment, spoke uncertainly before the Russian parliament and had to be assisted from the hall (deputies agreed he had 'created a strange impression').[163] And there were further excesses when Yeltsin arrived in Berlin to take part in the withdrawal of Russian troops from Germany. The president was already 'tired' the morning after his arrival, but nonetheless suggested he 'relax a bit' before the official ceremony. He took some medicine and had a facial massage, which helped to improve his appearance, but the German chancellor had to support him at the ceremony, and at the official lunch, where there was an abundance of red wine, Yeltsin became particularly animated. The two leaders went afterwards to lay a wreath in a specially equipped bus, in which Yeltsin ordered coffee but then poured it all over his shirt (his support staff, fortunately, always carried a complete change of clothing).[164] There followed a 'stirring rendition of Kalinka' by the Berlin police band under the impromptu conductorship of the president,[165] and later in the evening a well-watered reception in the Russian embassy.[166] A number of advisers who had expressed their concern at his performance were simply left behind on the president's next foreign trip, which concluded with his controversial nonappearance at Shannon airport to take part in discussions with the Irish prime minister. Yeltsin, his staff explained, had simply overslept; his political opponents took a less charitable view and accused him subsequently of being in a 'permanent state of visiting Ireland'.[167]

Whatever the circumstances, the president was certainly capable of behaving erratically. Arriving in Sweden on a state visit in December 1997, he plunged into the crowd to bring forward a twenty-year-old beauty and introduced her to First Deputy Prime Minister Nemtsov, who was accompanying him.[168] Then he 'astonished the assembled crowd' at a reception in the Royal Palace by publicly demanding that Nemtsov settle his differences there and then with the chairman of the gas concern Gazprom, who was also a member of the party.[169] Yeltsin's formal speech made no less of an impression: it mistakenly identified Germany and Japan as nuclear powers (he appeared to believe he was himself in Finland) and then offered to dismantle a third of the Russian nuclear arsenal in Europe in a 'surprise for diplomats and generals', apparently to enliven an otherwise rather formal oration.[170] His press secretary explained that the president was 'tired after a busy day'; for the Western press the speech 'renewed speculation about his health and drinking habits'; for the Moscow Komsomol paper the president had 'created the impression of a computer that has gone haywire'.[171] There was a 'severe respiratory infection' in March 1998, which meant a CIS summit had to be postponed,[172] and then at the end of the month there was an uncertain appearance at a 'big three' meeting with President Chirac and Chancellor Kohl, when the president had to be 'rescued by his press secretary as he fumblingly handed a parting gift to his guests'.[173] A trip to Central Asia in October 1998 was cut short when he had to be supported on his arrival at Tashkent airport.[174]

The Russian presidency raised still more serious questions of a constitutional kind, and by the late 1990s there was strong pressure for a reconsideration of the superpresidential document that had been approved in 1993 (some, indeed, were urging its entire replacement). Yeltsin himself insisted that Russians were used to having one person and 'some sort of vertical power structure, a strong hand, which can not only talk, but act'. Parliamentary government, on the other hand, 'cannot solve anything because no one is responsible'; a strong parliament would be subordinated to parties, and 'there would be no kind of democracy'.[175] Yeltsin, in some interviews, was rather more sympathetic to the idea of restoring the monarchy, which could guarantee the stability of the state as it appeared to have done during the Spanish transition, although there was little public support for such a view and even less clarity about the descendant of the Romanovs that had the strongest claim to the succession.[176] But he was hostile to proposals for

constitutional change; in his opinion the potential of the current constitution had 'not yet been exhausted' and any attempt to change it
could 'only destabilise the situation in the country'. As 'long as I am the
president', Yeltsin declared, 'I will not have the constitution
changed.'[177]

Several of the parties, however, took a quite different view. Yabloko,
for instance, had campaigned against the 1993 constitution, and did not
themselves 'exclude the possibility in the future of the transition of
Russia to a form of rule under which the president would retain only the
functions of a head of state and all executive power would be held by a
government based on a majority in the Federal Assembly'; in all the
post-Soviet states, they argued, the president had become a 'constant
source of political instability and a threat to the security of citizens'.[178]
The Communists, equally, pressed for a series of changes, including the
reinstitution of a vice-presidency (the calculation appeared to be that
their own candidate, Gennadii Zyuganov, would not be able to win a
straight fight for the presidency itself but would be an obvious choice for
the second most important position in the state – and for the most
important, at least on a temporary basis, if Yeltsin were forced to leave
office).[179] Communist spokesmen generally suggested that the presidency would be retained 'temporarily', at least for two or three years,
until a new constitution had been prepared; but 'in the long run' they
saw Russia as a parliamentary republic, without a presidency at all.[180]
Montesquieu's principle of the separation of powers, they argued, had
been 'completely discredited' in the former Soviet republics; all it had
given them was 'confrontation between the president and the Supreme
Soviet, and then the president and the State Duma', with the president
himself an 'unaccountable monarch'.[181]

There were calls for reform from other quarters, including the
chairman of the Federation Council Yegor Stroev, who was the elected
governor of Orel region and also its former party first secretary. The
constitution, Stroev argued, was 'not an icon';[182] indeed there was 'no
constitution in the world' that had not evolved over time.[183] More
specifically, he argued that the country should 'increasingly be governed
by laws passed by the Federal Assembly and signed by the president'. In
the first instance the constitutional powers of the Duma and Federation
Council in economic and social policy should be increased.[184] And the
parliament as a whole should play a greater part in the formation of
government: the Duma in the confirmation of deputy premiers, the
Federation Council – as the 'chamber of war and peace' – in approving
appointments to the defence and other 'force ministries'.[185] Equally,
there was a case for new mechanisms of consultation such as a State

Council that would include the president and representatives of the two chambers and of the largest cities.[186] Other members of the Federation Council agreed that government should be accountable to the upper house, not just (in limited respects) to the Duma;[187] and there were suggestions from the leader of the Our Home Is Russia faction in the Duma, Alexander Shokhin, that the chairman of the Federation Council might become a 'number two in the state', or in effect a vice-president.[188] The restoration of a vice-presidency found support elsewhere, including former prime minister Chernomyrdin;[189] and there were suggestions for a change in the way in which the president himself was chosen, perhaps by an electoral college of parliamentarians and regional representatives rather than by a 'populist' and expensive direct election.[190]

There were other suggestions from constitutionalists. A Moscow University professor, Suren Avak'yan, called for a series of amendments that would ensure a better balance between the branches of government – 'a balance that simply does not exist today'. It should be less easy for the president, for instance, to dissolve the Duma; and members of the government should be required, not just requested, to report on their implementation of its decisions. There were particular problems with Article 80, under which the president 'determined' the basic principles of domestic and foreign policy. Properly speaking the president, as head of state, should not be allowed to do more than implement those principles, which should be for the president and parliament to determine together.[191] In a larger study Avak'yan argued for a series of further changes. The constitution, for instance, divided up the legislative, executive, and judicial functions, and allocated the executive function to the government. Where did the presidency fit into a separation of powers of this kind? Equally, the Duma had too little influence upon the formation and conduct of government; in order to redress the balance he suggested that appointments to deputy premierships and to the more important ministries should require its approval, not just appointments to the prime ministership. Rather than undertake the complicated task of detailed amendment, Avak'yan favoured the adoption of an entirely new constitution in these circumstances, using the mechanism of a national referendum.[192]

Where, others asked, was the principle of accountability in the Russian constitution? It was the government, for instance, that conducted the affairs of the nation; but it was responsible for its actions and its composition, in practice, 'only to the president', with parliament taken into account only when the annual budget was being negotiated. The president himself was responsible to the electorate as a whole, not to a representative institution, which meant that he was accountable, at best, in a 'moral-political' sense. Even the annual address, unlike the State of the Union address in the United States, was less a rendering of account than a statement of government objectives for the future. For Piskotin, the president should be required to present a report on his tenure of office over the previous year, and it should be discussed rather than simply presented to the two chambers. Deputies, equally, should have the right to interrogate ministers and to vote their lack of confidence in individual ministers as well as in the government as a whole; it should be less easy for the president to dissolve parliament in the event of a disagreement; and it should be easier for the Duma itself to institute the process of impeachment. All of this would require amendment of the 1993 constitution; but constitutions, he pointed out, were most likely to require amendment in their early years, and even the American constitution, held out as an example of stability, had been amended ten times in its first four years.[193]

Viktor Sheinis, a senior Yabloko deputy and one of the authors of the election law, shared the general view that the constitution had a 'series of serious defects'. The main one, as for other critics, was the misallocation of power between the branches of government and the concentration of 'enormous power' in the hands of the president, placing him in effect 'above parliament, and above the government'. Theoretically a balance had been observed: parliament could impeach the president, and the president could dismiss the Duma. But it was virtually impossible, in practice, to secure a vote in favour of impeachment, while the threat of the dissolution of the Duma was a much more powerful weapon in the hands of the president than the vote of no confidence in the government that was within the competence of the Duma. For Sheinis, the constitution was less 'superpresidential' than 'insufficiently parliamentary'. The president, for a start, should not be the 'guarantor of the constitution', a formulation that could allow him to take almost any action he thought necessary such as launching a war in Chechnya on his own authority without the approval of parliament. Nor should the president alone define the 'basic directions of domestic and foreign policy'. Parliament, moreover, should have stronger supervisory powers, including the right to conduct investigations into the performance of members of the government; and any deployment of armed forces by the president at home or abroad should require its approval. Like others, Sheinis thought the Duma should be required to approve more of the key appointments, and it should have to endorse a presidential decision to dismiss the prime minister or the government as a whole, not just to appoint them.[194]

Others still were less persuaded that legal changes, of these or any other kind, were likely to be crucial; there was a more fundamental problem, they thought, which was Russia's low level of legal and political culture. Once Russia had become a cultured society, they argued, even the defects of the existing constitution – which were significant – would not impede the democratic process, any more than they did in France, where presidential powers were also excessive and the constitution a long way short of perfection. If every president or parliament tried to introduce a new constitution that would operate to its advantage, there would be 'neither a legal state, nor democracy, nor anything good for the society as a whole or for its individual members'.[195] It was equally clear that amendment would not be easy. The Russian constitution was 'probably the most complicated in the world in its procedure for amendment and supplementation'; not only did two-thirds of the republics and regions need to agree upon a change, there was also a problem in that chapters 1, 2, and 9 (which covered its basic principles) could not be altered by parliament but only by a full-scale constitutional convention. There was no law to regulate the composition and powers of a constitutional convention, however, nor was there even a 'clear idea' about the role it should perform.[196]

A larger conclusion was that Russia was experiencing a 'crisis of government'. There was a bureaucracy that was bigger than ever before, staffed by the same people as before; a parliament that had no real influence on government, and a government that was itself dependent on a president who acted as a 'stern headmaster' but who was often unable to put his own decisions into practical effect; and a 'deepening cleavage between government and society'.[197] Soviet government had at least been effective government, based on a monopoly of political power in the hands of the Communist Party and, within the party, a concentration of decision-making authority in the hands of the leadership. The partly reformed system that existed after 1988 was an uneasy combination of party direction 'from above' and electoral control 'from below', a tension that was eventually resolved in favour of the voters. The postcommunist system, however, introduced a new source of tension with the separate election of an executive president and a working parliament. The tension between the two led to a governmental impasse throughout 1992 and 1993; the constitution that was introduced in December 1993 appeared at first to have resolved this tension in favour of the president, but it became increasingly clear that this had led to new forms of tension rather than a long-term solution. A workable system, it seemed clear, would require a move to semi-presidentialism: towards a system more like the French, in which the president enjoyed a popular mandate but the government required a parliamentary majority.[198] The Russian tradition was strong in its attention to centralised direction; its future was likely to depend upon the extent to which it could incorporate other, more Western traditions of accountability and popular consent.

4   Reforming the economy

Lenin, in one of his later writings, had insisted that socialism would prevail 'in the long run' because of the greater productivity that was inherent in a system whose only purpose was the satisfaction of human need.[1] In the end it was capitalism that prevailed, and it appeared to have done so, more than anything else, because of its ability to secure a greater return from the resources that it commanded and, as a result, to satisfy a higher level of human requirements. Capitalism, it was accepted, led to social divisions and a reserve army of unemployed; and although it was also capable of generating higher levels of prosperity, for some time the Soviet authorities could claim their system was superior in that it provided in a comprehensive way for the needs of all its citizens, whatever their income, family status, gender, or age group. This was what Gorbachev called the 'security' (*zashchishchennost'*) of the Soviet citizen:[2] it included the right to work, adequate and modestly priced housing, and a free medical service. Whatever their inadequacies, it was these 'social guarantees' that gave ordinary citizens their confidence in the future;[3] and in these terms, he told television interviewers in December 1987, the USSR was not a poorer but a much more advanced society than its American counterpart.[4]

For many, during the Brezhnev years, it began to appear as if the USSR and its counterparts in Eastern Europe had found an enduring formula of government on this basis, sustained by what could be described as a 'social contract' between the communist authorities and the societies over which they ruled. There was no suggestion that governments of this kind were freely elected, although they were usually willing to concede some forms of consultation; but equally, they maintained an acceptable standard of living for the mass of ordinary citizens, including heavily subsidised prices for basic foodstuffs, rents for housing that had remained unchanged for decades, free education and health care, and guaranteed employment. Gorbachev had already identified these 'social conquests of the Land of Soviets' as an 'important factor in [its] political stability',[5] and addressing his first Central Committee meeting in 1985 he described them as the 'basic source of political stability, social optimism, and confidence in the future'.[6] Some Western scholars, indeed, spoke more broadly of a 'corporatist polity' that allowed a variety of organised interests to take a direct part in policy formation on the basis of this wide-ranging consensus.[7]

Once economic growth started to slow down in the 1970s, however, it became increasingly difficult for the regime to satisfy its part of the 'bargain'. If output stagnated but incomes went up, there would obviously be shortages. And the more consumption increased at prices that were maintained by government, the heavier the burden of budgetary subsidy. Higher prices, however, prejudiced the assumption that they would remain unchanged, at least for fundamentals. Less rapid growth also meant it was no longer possible to satisfy all important interests at the same time – consumers as well as generals, health as well as education, poor regions as well as rich ones, the elderly as well as schoolgoers. And as pressures increased for price rises, lower subsidies, and even unemployment, the more difficult it became to sustain the claim that Soviet-type systems offered a degree of economic security to their populations that made up for lower living standards and their lack of a full range of political freedoms. As Chingiz Aitmatov, a writer who was also a Communist member of the Congress of People's Deputies, pointed out in 1989, workers in countries like Sweden and the Netherlands earned four or five times as much as their Soviet counterparts; even if they were out of work their social security and welfare rights were vastly superior.[8] Indeed, others suggested, it was perhaps societies such as these that had come closest to a viable 'socialism' in the late twentieth century.[9] Did they really want to work for the capitalists, Gorbachev had asked a mass meeting at the Izhorsk factory in Leningrad when he visited in July 1989? 'Yes, if they pay well', answered a small but vocal section of his audience.[10]

This, in the end, was a metaphor for the collapse of the regime itself, unable to sustain living standards with which its people could be satisfied, and yet unwilling to offer them the alternative of a form of government through which they could hold the party and state leadership to account for any shortcomings in their performance. But it left many questions unanswered. Had the existing system, based on public ownership and planning, been incapable of reform, or was its collapse at least compounded by errors of judgement?[11] How was it that the Chinese, with fewer natural advantages, had managed to sustain a high level of growth without rejecting communist rule?[12] How important were exogenous factors, such as the Chernobyl nuclear explosion in 1986 or the Armenian earthquake in 1988? Equally, if the existing system was incapable of reform, how was it to be replaced – quickly or gradually, in all sectors at once or in a few to begin with? And what was the alternative – a wholly privatised economy, or one in which (as in many other noncommunist countries) the state played a substantial role in regulation, and even in ownership? Just as the USSR had pioneered a system based on central direction, so too it led the way in a complex process of economic change for which there were no obvious precedents outside a number of the other 'countries in transition'; among them, in turn, it was by far the largest, and the only one that had for more than two generations been committed to what it defined as socialism.

The crisis of Soviet planning

At the time, the historical record of Soviet economic management seemed to be one of impressive achievement. Russia in 1913 was a backward country by the standards of the time, 'the poorest of the civilised nations' in the words of a contemporary but still authoritative account.[13] There was an active manufacturing sector, and levels of production in some areas – such as oil and textiles – were high by world standards. But the Russian share of world industrial output was also very small: just 5 per cent, compared with 14 per cent for the United Kingdom, 16 per cent for Germany, and 36 per cent for the USA.[14] The overwhelming mass of the population – 77 per cent in the 1897 census – were classified as peasants, and only a small minority – 21 per cent in the Empire as a whole, and just 5 per cent in Central Asia – could read and write (this compared with a figure of nearly 90 per cent in the United States and almost universal literacy in the United Kingdom).[15] Russia's relative backwardness was reflected with particular clarity in the development of modern communications. By 1900 Russia had an extensive railway network, with the Trans-Siberian nearing completion; but there was twice the length of track in the United Kingdom and ten times as much in the United States, and there were ten times as many passengers in the United States and more than forty times as many in the United Kingdom, relative in each case to population. More than fourteen times as many letters were sent in those two countries as in Russia, and more than a hundred times as many telegrams;[16] most strikingly of all, there was a single telephone subscriber for every thousand Russians as compared with thirteen in Britain, fifteen in Germany, and seventy-six in the USA.[17]

Just two generations later, the contrast could hardly have been greater. The USSR was one of the world's economic superpowers, with a level of gross domestic product that was second only to that of the

United States. In many areas – including oil, gas, cast iron, steel, and tractors – Soviet levels of production were the highest in the world. The USSR had pioneered the exploration of outer space, and led the world in the number of its scientific staff. The Soviet natural gas distribution system was one of the largest in the world, and Soviet oil wells were the deepest. The USSR maintained one of the world's largest merchant marines, and deployed one of its most formidable concentrations of military might. According to official sources, Soviet national income had increased 149 times between 1917 and 1987, and industrial production 330 times. National income, 58 per cent of that of the USA in 1960, had increased to 67 per cent by 1980, and industrial production had increased from 55 to more than 80 per cent of the US total. Soviet industrial production, about 3 per cent of the global total in 1917, had increased to 20 per cent by 1987; indeed, the USSR by this date produced more than the whole world had done in 1950. Other indicators of development, less dependent on methods of calculation, showed a broadly similar picture: in numbers of students, hospital beds, newspaper circulations, calorie consumption, or scientific research the USSR was clearly one of the world's leading nations.[18]

These achievements, moreover, had taken place in historical circumstances that could hardly have been more difficult. As Gorbachev reminded interviewers from *Time* magazine in 1985, there were many problems that had simply been inherited as a 'grim legacy' from the old regime: 'a backward economy, strong vestiges of feudalism, millions of illiterate people'. To this had to be added the effects of two world wars, which had ravaged a large part of the USSR and destroyed much that had been created by the Soviet people. There had also been 'irreparable losses' of population: more than 20 million Soviet citizens had perished during the Second World War (the numbers, in fact, were much higher),[19] and millions more had been wounded (Gorbachev, too young actually to have fought in the war, saw the damage it had wrought during his railway trips from southern Russia to Moscow in the late 1940s).[20] It had been asserted by the West at the time, Gorbachev went on, that fifty to a hundred years would be needed to make good what had been destroyed by the Nazi invaders. By doing so in a much shorter period the Soviet people had achieved what had been thought to be impossible. The fact remained that, since the revolution, something like two decades had been devoted to wars and reconstruction, leaving barely fifty years in which they had turned the USSR into a 'world economic power'[21] (although the calculations remained controversial, most economists agreed that the Soviet economy had grown much more rapidly than at any time in prerevolutionary Russia, and at a more rapid rate than anything the capitalist world had achieved up to that point).[22]

Yet if the economic achievements of the USSR over the longer term were clear, particularly when war and other factors were taken into account, it was equally apparent by the late 1970s that there were deep-seated difficulties that had still to be resolved. The most striking indicator of these difficulties was the rate of economic growth, which fell consistently from the 1950s to the 1980s with only a slight reversal in the late 1960s. Levels of economic growth, by the late 1970s and early 1980s, were the lowest ever recorded in Soviet peacetime history. In 1979 national income rose just 2.2 per cent, and labour productivity a bare 1.4 per cent; agricultural output actually fell, by 3.2 per cent or more than this if a modest increase in population was taken into account.[23] The 11th Five Year Plan, covering the first half of the 1980s, was in turn substantially underfulfilled: the 26th Party Congress, in 1981, had approved directives that provided for an 18–20 per cent increase in national income by 1985, but the actual increase was 16.5 per cent, and the figures for grain production were so bad they had to be suppressed entirely.[24] The target for industrial output, in fact, had not been met in any of the five year plans that had been adopted after 1970, whereas only once before that date – in the very first five year plan – had there been a shortfall. And each extra unit of output had been bought at the cost of an increasing consumption of energy and raw materials, at a time when the leading Western countries were finding new ways of using their resources more efficiently.[25]

Even these figures, moreover, tended to exaggerate the real level of Soviet achievement. In particular, they concealed a steady increase in overreporting, amounting to 3 per cent of total production by the 1980s or up to a third in sectors such as cotton or road transportation.[26] And they concealed a high level of waste (as much as 40 per cent of the potato crop, for instance, was lost before it reached the consumer).[27] Nor did they allow adequately for concealed inflation, as cheaper goods were withdrawn and replaced by more expensive and not necessarily superior alternatives.[28] According to a controversial reassessment of official figures that was published by economists Vasilii Selyunin and Grigorii Khanin in early 1987, taking such factors into account Soviet national income had increased six or seven times between 1928 and 1985 – a creditable performance, but far short of the ninetyfold increase claimed by official statistics.[29] Much of Soviet industrial output, in any case, was hardly a contribution to real wealth. More tractors and combine harvesters were produced than workers were available who could operate them, and the quality of farm machinery was such that

Table 4.1. *Soviet and Russian economic performance, 1951–85 (average annual changes, official data, percentages)*

USSR	1951–5	1956–60	1961–5	1966–70	1971–5	1975–80	1981–5
Produced national income	11.4	9.2	6.5	7.8	5.7	4.3	3.6
Gross industrial output	13.2	10.4	8.6	8.5	7.4	4.4	3.7
Gross agricultural output	4.2	6.0	7.2	3.9	2.5	1.7	1.0
RSFSR							
Produced national income	n.d.	n.d.	7.2	9.4	6.6	4.6	3.0
Gross industrial output	15.8	11.6	9.0	9.8	8.4	4.4	3.3
Gross agricultural output	n.d.	6.4	1.8	5.0	−0.4	0.6	1.0

Source: Adapted from *Narodnoe khozyaistvo SSSR* and *Narodnoe khozyaistvo RSFSR*, various issues.

more than a million people were engaged in repair workshops, more than in the entire agricultural machinery industry.[30] More than twice as many pairs of footwear were produced as in the USA, but their quality was so poor that many more had to be imported; twice as much steel was produced, but there was a smaller output of finished products.[31] And even on official figures some alarming developments were beginning to occur. Soviet national income, 67 per cent of that of the USA in 1980, had slipped to 64 per cent by 1988, and labour productivity in agriculture had fallen from 'about 20 per cent' in the 1970s to 16 per cent in the late 1980s;[32] on other figures, released in 1990, Soviet consumption per head of population was just 25 per cent of the level of its major capitalist competitor.[33]

Several factors were usually blamed for the Soviet economic slow-down, both in the West and in the USSR itself. One reason, certainly, was that the increase in the size of the industrial labour force was levelling off. Throughout the 1950s and 1960s large numbers of people were leaving the land to work in industry, allowing output to increase through additional labour rather than higher productivity. By the early 1980s this outflow had diminished, leaving economic growth much more dependent upon the efficiency with which existing resources were used. The population, as in the West, had also been ageing: this meant an increase in the 'dependency ratio', or in the numbers of pensioners and others who had to be supported by the population of working age. Some 6.7 per cent of the Soviet population was aged sixty or over in 1939; by 1987 the proportion had more than doubled, to 13.5 per cent; and by the year 2000, according to Soviet demographers, the proportion of the elderly could be expected to increase still further, to about 17–18 per cent.[34] At the same time there was a steady falling off in the rate of growth of the population that was of working age,[35] and there was expected to be an absolute decline in Ukraine in the first half of the 1990s and in Russia itself during the first decade of the new century.[36] Indeed, in some areas in Russia, Ukraine, Belorussia, and the Baltic republics, there was already an absolute and not simply a relative decline in the population that was economically active.[37]

A further contribution to the economic slowdown came from the fact that raw materials which were conveniently located and of high quality had gradually been used up, making it increasingly necessary to extract resources from more remote locations and poorer sources of supply. By the 1970s fuel and raw materials were already running out in the European part of the USSR, where most of the population was concentrated, and efforts had to be made to develop new sources of supply: oil and gas production were increasingly located in western Siberia, and timber and precious metals came increasingly from the Far East; the world's largest nickel plant was developed at Noril'sk, above the Arctic Circle.[38] Resources of this kind, inevitably, were costlier, as they were more difficult to extract and more expensive to process and transport elsewhere. In the 1960s, it has been calculated, one ruble of production in the extractive industries required two rubles of investment; by the early 1980s the same level of output required not two but seven rubles. An example was the oilfield at Samotlar in western Siberia, which had provided two-thirds of the country's needs up to the 1980s but was steadily becoming exhausted. The most obvious alternative source of supply was Noyabr'skoe, 300 kilometres to the north; but it was far from roads and rivers, and the oil was deeper and more difficult to reach.[39] More attention had also to be paid to quality and design, if goods were to find buyers in an increasingly competitive marketplace, and to environmental conservation, which tended to raise unit costs still further.

Whatever the explanations that might be offered, it was clear that a steadily falling rate of economic growth could not be sustained much further without serious damage to the international standing of the USSR and to the 'social contract' between the regime and the population. Even the political stability of the USSR could not be taken for granted, several speakers warned the 27th CPSU Congress in 1986, if popular expectations of this kind continued to be disappointed: Ligachev, for one, emphasised that political stability was largely a function of the party's 'correct social policy', and Gorbachev, in his closing remarks, reminded the delegates of Lenin's warning at the Party Congress in 1922 that there were revolutionary parties that had 'perished' because they were 'afraid to talk about their weaknesses'.[40] As

Gorbachev had put it in a speech in December 1984, only a highly developed economy would allow the USSR to enter the twenty-first century as a great and flourishing power; the fate of socialism as a whole, not just of the USSR itself, depended upon their success.[41] Other writers argued, in still more apocalyptic terms, that unless the USSR achieved a transition to more efficient forms of economic management it would 'cease to be a great power' and would enter the new century as a 'backward, stagnating state and an example to the rest of the world how not to conduct its economic life'.[42]

The Gorbachev strategy

The broad framework of economic reform was set out in Gorbachev's address to the 27th Party Congress in 1986. The top priority, in his view, was to overcome the factors that had been holding back the country's socioeconomic development as quickly as possible and to resume the growth trajectory of earlier decades.[43] Not only was it necessary to accelerate the rate of economic growth: it must be a new kind of growth, based upon scientific progress and a more efficient use of resources. There had been 'impressive successes' over the previous quarter of a century, Gorbachev told the Congress; national income and living standards had risen rapidly, and there had been welcome advances in science, medicine, and culture. But difficulties had built up during the 1970s; growth rates had fallen, and plan targets had not been met. The main reason, Gorbachev suggested, was that they had failed to respond to the need for a shift from extensive growth, based on additional labour and raw materials, to intensive growth, based on higher levels of productivity.[44] In the light of these requirements, the new five year plan set out as its central objective a doubling of national income by the year 2000. This would require a thorough modernisation of the economy on the basis of the most advanced technologies, with particular priority for engineering and electronics. In agriculture the chief priority would be to satisfy the country's food requirements by giving collective and state farmers a greater degree of independence and more substantial incentives. The management of the economy as a whole would be decentralised, with Gosplan (the USSR State Planning Committee) concentrating its efforts on long-term objectives and with enterprises guided to a much greater extent by their performance in the marketplace. The financial system would be reorganised; prices would be more 'flexible'; and co-operatives of all kinds would be encouraged to extend the scale of their operations.[45]

More detailed guidelines for economic reform were approved by a

Central Committee meeting in June 1987, at which Gorbachev again delivered the key address. There had been outstanding successes in the years since the revolution, Gorbachev suggested, but the centralised form of economic management established at that time had outlived its usefulness. Attempts had been made to reform it from the 1950s onwards, but they had all proved ineffective. Now, in the 1980s, the Soviet economy was in not just a difficult but a 'pre-crisis' situation. The rate of economic growth had dropped to a level that 'virtually signified the onset of economic stagnation'. Resources were being wastefully used, technological levels lagged increasingly behind those of the rest of the developed world, and there were diminishing returns from capital investment. Budget deficits were being covered by the sale of raw materials on world markets and by duties from the sale of liquor, which had more than doubled over the previous fifteen years. Spending on wages had meanwhile exceeded plan targets, while increases in output had been less than predicted; this meant that there was more money in circulation than goods that were available for purchase. Shortages, inevitably, had become worse – of everything from cement and metal to consumer goods and manpower – and there was a growing shadow economy, particularly in services. Nothing less than a 'radical reform' in the whole system of economic management was needed to reverse these alarming trends.[46]

The centrepiece of the Gorbachev reform strategy was the Law on the State Enterprise, which was adopted the same month and brought into effect in January 1988.[47] The main aim of the law, as explained by Gorbachev, was to bring 'real economic independence' to the enterprise, freeing it from the dictates of ministries and higher-level economic bodies. This was not the end of central planning, as some Western press reports suggested, but it was certainly intended to represent a significant change in the nature of this kind of guidance, with the plan being drawn up by factories themselves upon the basis of 'control figures', which specified the desired level of production and other general objectives, and 'economic normatives', which covered the contributions that were due to the state budget for land, labour, and capital. Within this framework the enterprise would be expected to prepare its own plan, based upon 'state orders' placed by the central authorities and upon commercial orders placed by other enterprises. The income from these activities, in line with the principle of 'self-financing', was intended to cover all the costs that were incurred, including wages and investment in new technologies. Equally, the new law sought to bring the 'human factor' into play by democratising the workplace, allowing workers to elect their managers at all levels and 'as a rule' on a competitive basis.

The scope for rapid improvement – and the alleviation of the shortages of most immediate concern to ordinary citizens – was probably greater in agriculture than in industry, and this became the object of a wide-ranging package of reforms approved by a Central Committee plenum in March 1989. The reality, Gorbachev explained in his opening address, was that the USSR still lagged behind the Western countries in its agricultural productivity, and the gap was widening rather than narrowing. Part of the problem was historical, including the 'human tragedy' of collectivisation in the 1930s. But new equipment, roads, and buildings would not be enough by themselves to bring about the improvements they all wanted to see; what was needed was a much more far-reaching change in rural economic relations, giving farmers more opportunity to develop their own initiatives. There should be a diversity of forms of economic management, including collective and state farms, agricultural firms, and integrated complexes belonging to industrial enterprises. Family-run farms should be allowed to develop without the prejudice that they were 'lower' forms of economic activity. Above all, leaseholding, by which groups of farmers received land or livestock on a contract basis with the right to sell any surplus, should be encouraged, and farmers themselves should be persuaded to become collectives of leaseholders, paying their way on a profit-and-loss basis. All of this, in Gorbachev's view, represented a 'drastic revision of the CPSU's agrarian policy', to be carried forward by party and state authorities in the very different local conditions in which they operated.[48]

The strategy of reform was completed by a number of other measures, all of them designed to encourage a wide variety of forms of nonstate economic activity. Under legislation approved in late 1986, for instance, several forms of 'individual labour activity' were officially approved, including car repairs, tutoring, photography, handicrafts, and private car rental; more than 670,000 were employed on this basis by 1990.[49] A further, more significant change was the adoption in May 1988 of a Law on Co-operatives which was widely seen as the most radical economic measure to be introduced in the first years of the Gorbachev leadership.[50] No special permission was required to establish a co-operative, and formally speaking they were to have equality of status with the state sector; they could hire outside labour, raise capital through share issues, lease property, fix their own prices except when they were fulfilling state orders, and engage in foreign trade. By January 1991 there were 245,400 co-operatives of various kinds in operation, including a co-operative bank; most of them were small, with an average of just twenty-five employees, but they employed a total workforce of over 6 million and official sources suggested that they could account for 10–12 per cent of national income by the mid-1990s.[51] There were parallel reforms in foreign trade, designed to encourage more direct links at the level of individual factories and to deepen Soviet participation in the international division of labour, and plans were made for the ruble to become an internationally convertible currency.[52]

From plan to market

Gorbachev, his official spokesman explained, had won the Nobel Prize for Peace, not for Economics; and there would certainly have been no basis for such an award in the results that were announced over the later years of his general secretaryship. The 12th Five Year Plan, adopted in 1986, had specified an average growth rate of 4.2 per cent; the 'basic directives' adopted by the 27th Party Congress called for the rate of growth to rise still further, to 5 per cent a year by the end of the century, in order to double national income by the year 2000.[53] The average rate of growth recorded between 1986 and 1989 was in fact a more modest 3.7 per cent,[54] which was below the 'stagnation' years of the late 1970s; there was a fall in 1990, rather than an increase,[55] and then in 1991, as the state itself collapsed, a more dramatic decline as the economy moved into an open and deepening recession (see table 4.2). As the State Statistics Committee reported in February 1992, the last year of the USSR had been one of 'intensified decline in the economy and people's standard of living and an exacerbation of the social atmosphere'. Gross national product had slumped; soap, washing powder, and many other goods were being rationed; the output of oil and coal were down 10 per cent on the previous year, for reasons that included a wave of industrial action in the mines; and foreign trade turnover was down because of a fall in the export of fuel and raw materials, still the main sources of hard currency. Control over the money supply had meanwhile been lost completely (the value of currency that was in circulation had increased nearly five times over the previous year), and the consumer price index had risen by 196 per cent.[56]

Giving greater autonomy to industrial enterprises, it became clear, had allowed them more freedom to choose their output mix so that they were able to meet their obligations in the easiest possible way. One general response was to reduce or discontinue the production of cheaper and less profitable items, such as children's clothing. As enterprises became more independent, they also found it easier to raise their prices; and as up to 40 per cent of industrial output was produced by monopoly suppliers,[57] there was little consumers or other producers could do

Table 4.2. *Soviet and Russian economic performance, 1986–91*
(official data, percentage change on previous year)

USSR	1986	1987	1988	1989	1990	1991
Produced national income	2.3	1.6	4.4	2.4	−4.0	−15.0
Gross industrial output	4.4	3.8	3.9	1.7	−1.2	−7.8
Gross agricultural output	5.3	−0.6	1.7	1.3	−2.3	−7.0
RSFSR						
Produced national income	2.4	0.7	4.5	1.9	−4.0	−11.0
Gross industrial output	4.5	3.5	3.8	1.4	−0.1	−8.0
Gross agricultural output	6.7	−1.2	3.2	1.7	−3.6	−4.5

Source: Adapted from *Narodnoe khozyaistvo SSSR* and *Narodnoe khozyaistvo RSFSR*, various issues; *Ekonomika i zhizn'*, no. 5, 1991, p. 9, and no. 6, 1992, pp. 13–16.

about it. Enterprises, at the same time, had begun to enjoy a greater freedom in the payment of wages, whether or not there had been a corresponding change in productivity. As the Komi first secretary told the CPSU Central Committee in April 1989, wages were increasing ahead of productivity at such a rate that soon the whole of the economy would be devoted to printing banknotes;[58] rubles, others complained, were becoming a 'measure of weight' rather than a measure of value.[59] Government itself came under pressure to pay for social programmes that had become increasingly expensive at the same time as public spending was being forced up by the growing burden of consumer subsidies (which had cost 90 billion rubles in 1990 and were expected to cost half as much again in 1991).[60] The budgetary deficit, as a result, widened rapidly: by the end of 1991 it was approaching 30 per cent of gross domestic product[61] and the national debt, to which it contributed, was running at a level more than twice as high.[62]

Shortages, meanwhile, were becoming more acute as consumers did what they could to convert their rubles into something more useful than rapidly depreciating pieces of paper. In Tambov, by the late 1980s, there were 'huge queues' for matches, and salt had practically disappeared from retail sale.[63] In Saratov there were shortages of soap, washing powder, and toothpaste.[64] Elsewhere there were 'day and night' queues for sugar, queues 'like in the war' for bread, and a 'catastrophic' lack of medicines.[65] In Novosibirsk things were so desperate that local people began to spend the night in shops to be sure of obtaining their sausage in the morning, and there were assaults on sales staff by irate customers.[66] The shortage of soap and washing powder was a source of particular and understandable concern. 'What kind of a regime is it if we can't even get washed?', asked an indignant group of workers in Vladimir.[67] A housewife in the Moscow region threatened to send her dirty linen directly to the ministries: 'if they can't provide us with soap', she reasoned, 'let them do the washing themselves'.[68] Others approached the Central Committee directly, which had to explain that it was 'not a department store'.[69] Shortages, at the same time, encouraged a burgeoning black market; the authorities did what they could to counteract it by rationing meat and other basic commodities, but the coupons themselves became an item of underground commerce and in any case they could have no direct influence upon the level of output.[70]

Not all of these difficulties, admittedly, were the result of official policies. Their success was also prejudiced by external circumstances, including the Chernobyl nuclear explosion of April 1986 and the Armenian earthquake of December 1988. Despite early and alarmist reports, just thirty-one deaths, not all of them from radiation, occurred in the immediate aftermath of Chernobyl, but 600,000 had received a 'significant exposure' and there was a heavy and continuing loss of life, with up to 10,000 deaths over the following decade and an increased rate of serious illness among the children of survivors as well as among survivors themselves.[71] In addition, about 200,000 of the local population had to be resettled, 3.1 million hectares – an area the size of Belgium – were contaminated, and 250,000 hectares were so badly affected they had to be taken out of cultivation altogether.[72] The economic costs were estimated at about $200 billion, with continuing costs for Ukraine alone of $1 billion a year, and the accident – the worst that had occurred anywhere in the world – prejudiced a development strategy that had begun to place an increasing emphasis upon nuclear power as oil production fell off.[73] The Armenian earthquake in December 1988, meanwhile, left 45,000 dead and half a million homeless; it was the most powerful in the Caucasus for more than eighty years, and at its epicentre 'virtually nothing was left standing'.[74]

There were additional problems in foreign trade as the price of raw materials on world markets began to fall. About 12 per cent of Soviet gas was sold abroad, and about 20 per cent of the country's oil; in turn, fuel and electricity accounted for over 40 per cent of the value of all Soviet exports, allowing the USSR to import large quantities of Western manufactures and, by 1990, foodstuffs as well. Unfortunately for Soviet planners, the high world prices for oil that had sustained them through the Brezhnev years began to fall in the late 1980s. Oil lost about a third of its value on export markets between 1985 and 1990, and levels of output themselves began to decline; more natural gas was extracted but its value on export markets fell even more sharply, by nearly a half. The foreign trade balance, as a result, moved into deficit in 1989 and into a

Plate 4.1   A liquor queue in the mid-1980s

still deeper deficit in 1990; the biggest losses were in trade with West Germany, but there were relatively much heavier losses in Soviet trade with the USA, with imports four times the value of Soviet exports.[75] External debt rose as a result, from $5 billion in 1985 to $68.8 billion at the end of 1990, by which time there was a serious threat of 'international bankruptcy'.[76]

But as well as natural disasters and the terms of trade, there were mistakes in judgement such as the anti-alcoholism campaign that was launched at the start of the new administration, in May 1985. There was certainly no doubt that 'something had to be done'. Levels of alcohol consumption had more than doubled between 1960 and the mid-1980s, reaching a level of 15 or 16 litres a year for all adults or as much as a bottle a day in some industrial cities.[77] More women were drinking, and more young people; life expectancies were falling, and there were heavy costs for the whole society in terms of family breakdown, violent crime, and forgone production. Gorbachev himself was a moderate on such questions and the strongest pressure for a radical approach came from other members of the leadership, particularly second-ranking secretary Yegor Ligachev, whose nature inclined him to 'severe and administrative' measures,[78] as well as the chairman of the Committee of Party Control, Mikhail Solomentsev, who had himself 'enjoyed a rather good relationship with alcohol' in his earlier years.[79] Solomentsev, reflecting later on the campaign, pointed to the 'thousands of heart-rending letters', mostly from wives and mothers, that had persuaded the leadership to take action,[80] and Gorbachev was also convinced that 'the whole society' had called for the campaign.[81] Popular support, however, melted away as the campaign overreached its original objectives: there was an enormous increase in home brewing, a criminal underground became established, and the loss of tax revenues was one of the main causes of a deepening crisis in public finance.[82]

The collapse of the economy, in the event, was so quick and comprehensive that some members of the leadership were inclined to explain it in terms of conspiracy and not simply misjudgement.[83] Whether this was true or not, it was certainly relevant that reformers as well as conservatives had little first-hand experience of a market economy, still less of a successful transition to a 'socialist market economy' that would combine state ownership and guidance with private and even foreign initiative. Indeed there were few, particularly among the reformers, who had practical experience of economic management at the level of a ministry or a large plant: Ryzhkov, a moderate, had run one of the country's largest engineering factories, but Gorbachev had spent his life in Komsomol and party work, and his closest associates, like Yakovlev and Vadim Medvedev, had been academics. A more fundamental difficulty was the confused nature of *perestroika* itself. Was there, for instance, a basis on which public ownership could be reconciled with the disciplines of the market? Gaidar, at least, had 'more and more the impression of a dangerous disjunction between [Gorbachev's] good intentions and his actual economic policy'. He was always keen to find a consensus, but this led to a 'constant ambiguity'; and convinced that his task was to remove a number of isolated faults in Soviet socialism, he had no conception of the difficulties he would face and the resistance he would encounter. Confronted by powerful and incomprehensible processes, Gorbachev 'panicked and lost his bearings'; in the end it was clear he had no strategy at all.[84]

From socialism to capitalism

The practical and theoretical failure of the 'socialist market' meant that there was little resistance to a process of more broadly conceived reform with which the newly elected Russian president, Boris Yeltsin, was quick to associate himself. Many of the old orthodoxies, in fact, had collapsed even before his election and before the USSR itself had been dissolved. In 1990 a new law on property had established equality of status for all forms of ownership, including foreign ownership, and opened the way to private or 'non-socialist' ownership of the means of production.[85] In August there were government measures to 'create and develop small enterprises' and to 'demonopolise the economy'.[86] In July 1991 the Soviet parliament went even further, adopting a law on the 'denationalisation and privatisation of enterprises' on the basis of which up to half the assets of state-owned industry were to pass into private or co-operative hands by the end of the following year.[87] A law on entrepreneurship, adopted in April 1991, sanctioned the use of hired labour;[88] and employment exchanges reappeared in the summer, sixty years after the last of them had closed in what was seen at the time as a historic victory over one of the inherent flaws of the capitalist system.[89] Price reform had meanwhile been initiated by a reluctant Ryzhkov, in what he later recalled as the 'most traumatic, most difficult speech' of his life,[90] and by the middle of 1991 about 45 per cent of all output was being sold without restriction.[91]

The alternative offered by the Yeltsin government was what had become known in other countries as 'shock therapy'. It was foreshadowed in a wide-ranging speech by the Russian president in October 1991 in which he called for 'profound reforms' including the liberalisation of prices, cuts in public spending, privatisation, and military conversion. 'We must', Yeltsin insisted, 'provide economic freedom, lift all barriers to the freedom of enterprises and of entrepreneurship and give people the opportunity to work and to receive as much as they can earn, casting off all bureaucratic constraints.'[92] Yeltsin himself was given additional powers to rule by decree in economic matters, and in the month that followed there were presidential directives that abolished limits on earnings, liberalised foreign economic relations, and commercialised shops and services;[93] going still further, a decree on prices in December abolished controls on all but a 'limited range' of goods and services from 2 January 1992.[94] Prices were duly 'freed', not only in Russia but in most of the other post-Soviet republics; within a month they had risen by 350 per cent, within a year by 2,600 per cent.[95] Price reform, Yeltsin acknowledged in a national address, was a 'painful measure', but it was the path the 'whole civilised world' had been obliged to follow.[96]

A 'memorandum on economic policy' appeared in February 1992 which placed these changes within a broader context. Already, it noted, about 90 per cent of consumer goods were being sold without any form of administrative control; by the end of the following month all remaining price controls would be removed, apart from rents, municipal services, and public transportation. Energy prices would be allowed to move to world levels by the end of 1993. The most vulnerable sections of the population would be protected, so far as possible, in the form of cash benefits for those with the lowest income levels. A balanced budget would be achieved through a series of cuts in subsidies to enterprises and a reduction of up to 15 per cent in public sector employment. Exchange restrictions would be eliminated, and export licences would be abolished in all but a limited number of cases as a step towards Russia's full integration into the international economy.[97] A further, more elaborate 'Programme for the Deepening of Economic Reforms in Russia' was approved in July 1992; it dealt with the medium term, up to 1996, and set out the same kinds of goals – deregulation, a balanced budget, privatisation, an 'active social policy', structural change (including demilitarisation), and the creation of a 'competitive market environment'.[98]

The main outlines of Russia's privatisation programme had been approved by the Supreme Soviet on 3 July 1991 in a law on the privatisation of state and municipal enterprises that has been described as a 'watershed in the Russian privatisation process'.[99] Its aim, through a transfer of ownership from the state into private hands, was to establish an 'effective, socially oriented market economy', and a Committee for the Management of State Property, headed by a chairman of ministerial rank, was established to supervise its implementation.[100] A law on 'personal privatisation accounts' was approved the same day, establishing the principle that all citizens would be given a credit to the value of their notional share of public assets.[101] A more detailed programme was approved by the Presidium of the Supreme Soviet in December 1991;[102] under its provisions a whole range of economic activities were to be privatised in the course of the following year, including retail and wholesale trade, public catering, construction, the processing of agricultural produce, and road freight.[103] The programme was extended again in a parliamentary resolution of 11 June 1992, which made clear that the exercise would be conducted in the first instance through the issue of 'privatisation cheques' to all citizens.[104] A presidential decree of August 1992, accompanied by a more detailed set of regulations, set out a timetable according to which the first tranche of 'privatisation cheques', with a nominal value of 10,000 rubles each, would be distributed from 1 October onwards.[105]

Privatisation cheques – or vouchers, as they were called in spite of Yeltsin's objections[106] – would be issued to all permanent residents of the Russian Federation, including children, and to others, like diplomats and journalists, who were resident abroad for reasons connected with their work. The vouchers could be used to buy shares in their own enterprise, or to take part in an auction at which other firms and companies were being sold, or they could be placed in investment funds which could use them to buy company shares. Vouchers, equally, could be sold, given away, or bequeathed, but they could not be used for the purchase of commodities (which would have had enormous inflationary implications). All such transactions would have to be completed by the end of 1993 (a deadline that was later extended).[107] Privatisation vouchers, as the legislation had provided, began to be distributed on 1 October 1992. 'For the first time since 1917', commented *Izvestiya*, 'something is being given to us, not taken away.'[108] In Yekaterinburg, which was Yeltsin's home region, a newborn boy was christened 'Voucher'; a popular song, 'Wow, wow, voucher', reached no. 5 in the Russian hit parade.[109]

Under the legislation, privatisation could take three basic forms.[110] Under option 1, the workforce were given 25 per cent of the share issue in the form of nonvoting stock, and were allowed to buy a further 10 per cent for vouchers or cash at a 30 per cent discount (this, it emerged, was the option most likely to be chosen when the enterprise was capital-intensive, as was often the case in the energy sector, or where the relationship between workers and management was so tense that managers were reluctant to allow the issue of shares that would place voting rights in the hands of their employees). Option 2, which was by far the most popular, allowed 51 per cent of the voting equity to be sold to managers and workers at extremely low prices with the remaining 49 per cent sold at auction or held by the state for sale at a later date (this was essentially an employee–management buyout).[111] A more ambitious option 3 allowed larger numbers of workers – but not necessarily the entire workforce – to reorganise and develop their own enterprise, receiving up to 40 per cent of its share issue in exchange. The balance would be available for purchase by ordinary citizens, using their privatisation cheques, or by investment funds acting on their behalf; but it was not a popular option, in part because the regulations had been written in 'traditional Russian bureaucratese'.[112] 'We need millions of property owners, not just a handful of millionaires', as Yeltsin had explained in a nationwide television address. 'The voucher', he added, was a 'sort of ticket for each of us to a free economy. The more property owners and business people there are in Russia, for whom concrete action is more important than idle discussion, the sooner Russia will be prosperous and the sooner its future will be in safe hands.'[113]

The scheme, however, soon encountered difficulties. Despite an expensive advertising campaign, there was some uncertainty about who could receive the vouchers: they were clearly intended for all citizens, whatever their age, but it was not until January 1993 that the status of refugees and members of the merchant marine was clarified.[114] In other cases, vouchers were quite improperly exchanged for services: in Tyumen' they were used to cover the cost of dentistry, or sold for vodka or eau de cologne; in Yaroslavl' they were offered as advance payment for funerals.[115] Vouchers were also counterfeited and stolen; some fake certificates in Rostov on Don were intercepted simply because they had been so well produced that locals became suspicious.[116] There were larger questions as well. For instance, the value of the assets that were being distributed was itself somewhat notional: the last appraisal of fixed assets had taken place twenty years earlier, and there were no valuations of any kind that were based on Western accounting conventions.[117] In the end the face value of 10,000 rubles, about $10 at the rate of exchange that prevailed at the time, was chosen 'for reasons of simplicity';[118] it represented the book value of the country's productive resources, divided by the total population, and then rounded up from 8,476 rubles to a more manageable 10,000.[119]

These were new and unfamiliar procedures, and not surprisingly they led to a series of scandals as newly established funds began to compete for the vouchers of an inexperienced public.[120] In St Petersburg, three companies set up to receive investments simply disappeared – as did the

РОССИЙСКАЯ ФЕДЕРАЦИЯ

ГОСУДАРСТВЕННАЯ ЦЕННАЯ БУМАГА

Действителен
по 31 декабря
1993 года.

Подделка чеков
преследуется
по закону.

1992

ПРИВАТИЗАЦИОННЫЙ ЧЕК

10 000

16 1985359

РУБЛЕЙ

Plate 4.2   A 'privatisation cheque' or voucher

savings of about 400,000 of their depositors. The whole incident
became known as the 'affair of the century'.[121] The management of
NeftAlmazInvest, a fund that promised to invest in the oil and diamond
industries, got away with about 900,000 vouchers; another fund,
'Russkii dom selenga', collected the savings of 1.5 million luckless
investors and then relocated to the Bahamas.[122] The largest scandal of
all involved a pyramid investment company, MMMInvest, run by a
businessman and sometime Duma deputy, Sergei Mavrodi. MMM took
over the top floor of the Lenin Museum; its slogan, advertised all over
the Moscow underground, was 'We'll Make Your Voucher Golden.' The
company collapsed in 1994 and its director was seized in a spectacular
raid on his private apartment; but there were demands that the Russian
government redeem the claims of disappointed investors and Mavrodi
himself became something of a folk hero, winning a seat in the Duma in
a by-election which in turn secured his early release. Between 15 and 20
million had lost their investment, and some had suffered heart attacks or
been driven to suicide;[123] Mavrodi, meanwhile, had sent most of the
money abroad.[124] The 'party of the swindled', indeed, was already a
substantial electoral force, with an estimated 24 million voters among
the victims of one or other of these investment frauds.[125]

By the time voucher privatisation came to an end, in June 1994,
something like 100,000 enterprises had changed their form of ownership, and more than 40 million Russians had become property owners –
'a process unprecedented in its scale and speed', according to *Izves-*

tiya.[126] Indeed there were more private shareholders in Russia by this time than in Britain or the United States, and it seemed reasonable to claim that there had been a change of mentality and not simply of ownership, reasserting the rights of private property and 'sharply altering the "Soviet" mind-set'.[127] A second stage of privatisation began in 1994, involving the sale of large enterprises at auction;[128] a third stage, involving smaller individual projects, began in 1996. The pace of privatisation was slowing down, with 43,000 enterprises privatised in 1993 but just 22,000 in 1994, 10,200 in 1995, 5,000 in 1996, 3,400 in 1997, and 2,600 in 1998;[129] nonetheless by this time 87 per cent of all industrial enterprises were in private hands, although they accounted for no more than 25 per cent of total output and 35 per cent of all industrial employment (a much larger share of output, 61 per cent, came from enterprises that were jointly owned but in which there was no foreign participation).[130] Yeltsin congratulated the State Property Committee on its selfless labour, and claimed that 'the foundation of the new edifice of the reviving economy of great Russia' had been laid.[131] For some Western advisers the whole exercise had been an 'extraordinary achievement' and the 'most successful aspect of the Russian transformation'.[132]

Other views of the privatisation process were less complimentary. Indeed it was described not as privatisation at all, but as a '*nomenklatura* collectivisation of enterprises' that was simply another stage in the 'economic civil war' between the Yeltsin administration and the rest of the society.[133] Sergei Glaz'ev, who had been minister of foreign economic relations in the Chernomyrdin government, described it still more forthrightly as an exercise in which 'under the guise of "reforms" the most substantial property in world history [had] come into the hands of a criminal community'.[134] *Pravda* spoke similarly of an 'enormous swindle' in which '60 per cent of the national economy had fallen into the control of banks that were close to government . . . and groups of organised criminals', as a result of which 'industry was at a standstill, workers received no pay for months, and the number of unemployed had gone over 10 million', while a 'narrow stratum of "new Russians" feeding off the budget and raw material exports got richer and richer'.[135] Many identified privatisation with Western advice, or more precisely with the terms that had been imposed upon the Russian government as a condition of IMF support;[136] and there was particular indignation when a number of the ministers most closely identified with the programme were reported to have gained large sums as advances on a 'history of privatisation' that had not yet been written from one of the banks with an interest in the outcome.[137] Three senior officials were dismissed, and the former chairman of the State Property Committee was charged with abuse of his official position; Chubais offered to resign but was retained by an indulgent president.[138]

What did ordinary Russians make of it all? The popular response, it appeared, was 'massive disillusion'.[139] Russians, according to the survey evidence, were actually rather positive about the economic system they had enjoyed before the start of *perestroika*, but very critical of the economic system that had been introduced after the end of communist rule; and, unlike East Europeans, they thought the future would be worse than the past, although it would be a little better than the present.[140] The popular reaction was particularly sceptical of the programme of privatisation (in Russian, *privatizatsiya*) – some, indeed, preferred to call it *prikhvatizatsiya*, or 'seizure'. Not many thought it would 'make the economy more productive', 'give people a material stake in the economy', or 'put more goods in the shops' (between 35 and 40 per cent agreed with these propositions); it was much more likely, in the popular view, to 'make a few people rich' (86 per cent), 'increase prices' (84 per cent), and 'create unemployment' (82 per cent).[141] Another survey found that privatisation was widely seen as in the interests of 'a few' (42 per cent) and to some extent of enterprise management (23 per cent), but hardly of the 'whole society' (5 per cent);[142] in a USIA survey, similarly, there was overwhelming agreement (84 per cent) that privatisation had 'mainly benefited the mafia and members of the former CPSU *nomenklatura*'.[143]

Summing up the results of privatisation in 1995, the sociologist Tat'yana Zaslavskaya accepted that there had been a substantial change in property relations, although relatively few had received a dividend from their new investments. The change that had taken place, however, was not the establishment of a society of small proprietors, as the Yeltsin government had apparently intended, but an 'even greater concentration of wealth in the hands of a narrow group of people'.[144] The change of ownership had certainly had little effect on investment or enterprise behaviour. There was a fall, not an increase, in labour productivity.[145] Output was even more highly concentrated in a small number of factories than it had been before the move to private ownership.[146] Energy costs per unit of output had risen, not fallen.[147] And there were few signs of a revolution in managerial attitudes. Managers, on the contrary, were just as keen as their Soviet predecessors to retain state subsidies, cheap credits, and protection from foreign competition. And although there was an investment crisis of 'astounding proportions', managers as well as workers were opposed to the sale of shares in their enterprise even if a new owner was likely to bring them the resources they needed to expand and modernise.[148] The real change was the emergence of a 'broad stratum of private owners', and this appeared to reflect the overriding objective of securing a 'powerful social base for the market economy and a democratic society' just as Stolypin's 'wager on the strong' had sought to encourage a prosperous landowning peasantry that could sustain the prerevolutionary order (clearly, without much success).[149]

Privatisation of agriculture had been taken less far by the late 1990s, even though the private ownership of land had been incorporated into the Russian constitution in late 1990 and then formed part of the new constitution that was approved in December 1993. A presidential decree of March 1992 and a further decree of June had provided for the sale of private plots of land.[150] A more far-reaching decree of October 1993, hailed in the press as a 'historic step',[151] established that it was legal for those who owned it to buy, sell, lease, mortgage, or exchange land; every owner of a plot of land was to receive a certificate that would be entered in a state registry, compulsory deliveries were phased out, and the state itself guaranteed the 'inviolability and protection of the private ownership of land as well as the protection of the rights of landowners during land transactions'.[152] But there were problems about the physical separation of the land that individual farmers might claim: it had, among other things, to take account of the 'rational organisation of land areas and compact land use', which provided all kinds of opportunities for dispute and delay. Changes in ownership, for this and other reasons, advanced slowly: the number of commercial farms increased to about 280,000 in 1996 but then fell slightly, and there was a decline in the value of agricultural output from commercial farms in absolute and relative terms (by 1997 they accounted for only 2 per cent of the value of all agricultural output and were most important for their production of sunflower seeds).[153]

The privatisation of land encountered further difficulties because of the high proportion of collective and state farms that were unprofitable, which gave little incentive to take over their ownership (only 3 per cent of farms were running at a loss in 1990, but energy and other costs increased much more rapidly than whatever farmers were able to earn from the sale of their produce, and by 1997 as many as 82 per cent of farms were losing money).[154] There was strong opposition to the 'voucherisation of land relations' in any case, given the danger that it might lead to 'speculation' and the 'creation of a class of latifundistas'.[155] The Russian parliament, particularly its Communist and Agrarian deputies, pressed in these circumstances for lifetime leasing rather than outright ownership; fourteen of the Federation's eighty-nine subjects took no steps to legalise private land ownership within their own area, and one – the Karachai–Cherkess republic – went so far as to prohibit its sale, in spite of the provisions of the constitution.[156] A presidential decree in March 1996 sought to make more of a reality of the constitutional right to land, and to complete the issue of certificates of ownership.[157] But given high interest rates and competition from cheaper imports, it was more likely that farmers would simply 'pool their brand-new deeds, conclude contracts with the chairman, and work exactly as they had done before'.[158] Production, in the event, fell virtually everywhere there had been substantial changes in forms of rural ownership; land dropped out of cultivation, and family farms sank into a 'debt abyss'.[159] Across the economy as a whole, livestock numbers fell by a half between 1990 and 1999, the grain harvest fell by almost half (although there were considerable fluctuations from year to year), the output of meat and milk fell by more than half, and the output of flax and wool was down to less than a third of its level in the last full year of Soviet rule.[160]

Western assistance

The other vital element in the reform strategy was Western economic assistance, including direct investment. The USSR had already begun to move closer to the international economy, joining the European Bank for Reconstruction and Development in March 1991 and becoming a 'special associate member' of the International Monetary Fund later in the year;[161] a more favourable legislative environment was created at the same time for foreign investment.[162] Gorbachev, in a historic gesture, was invited to attend a summit of the Group of Seven industrial nations in the summer of 1991 at which the Western leaders agreed to 'assist the integration of the Soviet Union into the world economy'.[163] Russia became a member of the International Monetary Fund in April 1992, and joined the World Bank the following July.[164] The Group of Seven eventually became a Group of Eight, with Russia a full participant (see chapter 7); and a series of agreements was concluded with international financial institutions, starting with a ruble stabilisation fund in 1992 that was worth $24 billion.[165] A further $43 million was approved in 1993, although not all of it was new money;[166] and the repayment of Soviet foreign debt, an estimated $80 billion, was suspended for ten years.[167]

And yet the international economy, by itself, was unlikely to achieve the transformation that domestic reforms had not accomplished. Much of it, for a start, failed to materialise: only about $10 billion of the $24 billion agreed in 1992, for instance, and this was in the form of commercial credits.[168] Foreign debt mounted at the same time, from $97 billion in 1992 to $152 billion in 1998;[169] and the cost of borrowing rose in parallel, from about 30 per cent of GDP in 1994 to 60 per cent in 1997, much of it short-term and at high rates of interest (which meant that more than a third of government revenue had to be spent on servicing the debt).[170] Russian money was meanwhile being exported at a much faster rate. By 1996 it was estimated that about $700 billion had already been sent abroad, of which about half had been invested in property, and that a further $50 billion was leaving every year, much of it in the form of the illegal export of gold and other valuables on a scale that had not been seen since 1918; this was a loss of resources every year that was about ten times the value of inward investment.[171] Hard currency was one of Russia's 'staple exports', with up to 400 tonnes of dollars leaving every year in search of a more stable environment; indeed it emerged that the Central Bank had itself been moving its funds to the comparative safety of the Channel Islands.[172]

Much of the capital that flowed abroad went into property, some of it advertised in the Russian press. *Izvestiya* in April 1997 had advertisements for 'a marvellous hill-top VILLA with a sea view' in Marbella, retailing at $1.65 million, and in July it advertised a 'tax paradise' in the Bahamas, a castle near Munich, and a 'tsarist life in a villa palace in the Arabian style' in Palma de Mallorca. In August an 'incredibly beautiful villa on the sea front near Cannes' was on offer, with its own parkland and a swimming pool with waterfall.[173] There were specialised agencies catering for Russians who wished to invest elsewhere: several advertised in the publication *Property Abroad*, whose front-page offers in 1996 included a hotel near Prague and a house in a 'picturesque corner' of Spain, as well as a flat in Thailand with a 'view of the jungle'. For those who were worried by crime and instability and seeking a future for their children as well as themselves, a villa was on offer in Greek Orthodox Cyprus;[174] other agencies offered European Union passports for $15,000 ('100 per cent legality guaranteed'), or citizenship of one the Caribbean islands (the Dominican Republic found that nearly half its clients were from the former Soviet Union).[175] In Nice alone at least fifty villas valued at $850,000 or more were being sold to Russians every year in the late 1990s; [176] in the spa town of Carlsbad, in the Czech Republic, a 'rouble mafia' had bought up most of the hotels, and locals concluded it had become a '"zone of peace" for Russian godfathers seeking a break from life at home and a convenient place to launder their profits'.[177]

Foreigners, however, were slow to take the same interest in the postcommunist Russian economy as Russians were taking in the savings and investment opportunities that were available in other countries. Foreign direct investment worldwide was estimated at $325 billion in 1995; Russia's share was less than 1 per cent.[178] There was less foreign investment in Russia than, for instance, in Peru, and far less than in China ($2.8 billion as compared with $38 billion in 1995);[179] and there was much less than in the postcommunist countries of Eastern Europe – foreign investment in the Russian economy between 1989 and 1996 averaged $34 a head, which was more than the figure for Ukraine but much less than the East European average of $266 a head.[180] Foreign investment, in turn, accounted for only 4 per cent of all domestic investment in 1997, and it was concentrated in 'middleman' operations that yielded a relatively quick return such as banking and services, although there was also a significant presence in the oil industry.[181] Joint ventures with foreign participation accounted for no more than 1.6 per cent of all enterprises in the same year, and for only 5 per cent of the value of industrial output.[182]

Why were foreign investors reluctant to entrust their resources to a newly democratic Russia, but very willing to do so in the case of communist China? Some of them confided their reservations to the weekly paper *Argumenty i fakty*. A French electronics entrepreneur found the new Russian businessmen were simply too vulgar: they threw money around in the casino, while he read Tolstoy and Dostoevsky and developed his firm so that he could provide new forms of employment. A British computer manager who was a regular visitor thought 'serious big business' would never come to a country with such a level of crime, with 'bankers and businessmen being killed on your city streets every day'. And an Israeli banker was worried about political instability, and who would win at the next elections – if there were any.[183] A related concern was the level of corruption with which domestic and particularly foreign businessmen had to contend. Russia was the most corrupt country in Europe, according to the international rankings published by Transparency International, and the forty-ninth most corrupt of the fifty-two for which they published information.[184] Most Western businessmen found that 'key ministries would usually demand that large fees be paid to shadowy "consultants" before necessary approvals and licenses were issued', and that if they failed to oblige the contract would go elsewhere. 'How to make a million in the former Soviet Union?', asked one exasperated American investor. 'Bring two million and it will soon be down to one.'[185]

Table 4.3. *Russian economic performance, 1991–8 (official data, percentage change on previous year)*

	1991	1992	1993	1994	1995	1996	1997	1998
Gross domestic product	95	85.5	91.3	87.3	95.9	96.5	100.8	95.4
Index numbers [1990 = 100]	95	81	74	65	62	60	60	57
Industrial output	92	82	86	79	97	96	102	94.8
Agricultural output	96	91	96	88	92	95	101.3	87.7
Investment	85	60	88	76	90	82	95	93.3
Inflation rate (times)	2.6	26.1	9.4	3.2	2.3	1.2	1.1	1.8
Ruble/dollar exchange rate	1.7	193	927	2,204	4,559	5,121	5,785	20,650

Source: Adapted from *Rossiya v tsifrakh. Kratkii statisticheskii sbornik* (Moscow: Goskomstat Rossii, 1998), p. 11; *Biznes v Rossii*, 30 January 1999; *Izvestiya*, 18 February 1999, p. 2 (for 1998 GDP); *Economic Survey of Europe*, no. 2, 1998, appendix tables B7 and B14, for inflation and exchange rates; and *Segodnya*, 31 December 1998, p. 1, for the 1998 exchange rate.

Economic reform: a balance sheet

What, several years later, was the outcome of the reform programme? There had been a far-reaching change in ownership, but had there been any sign of the entrepreneurial energies that the old system was supposed to have held in check? What, for instance, about growth, for many years the most sensitive of the 'success indicators'? As table 4.3 makes clear, there had indeed been growth but it had been negative, as the economy experienced a series of contractions rather than (as the administration and its Western advisers had promised) a short-term loss to allow for an adjustment to market demand followed by a more vigorous and sustained advance. The fall in national income went back to the last years of Soviet rule, but several years of capitalist reform had certainly not reversed it. Indeed, in cumulative terms, the fall in national income that had taken place over the first four years of Yeltsin–Gaidar reform was unprecedented, greater than the Great Depression in the West in the early 1930s and greater than the country had suffered in the course of the First World War, the civil war, or even the Second World War.[186] In 1997, according to official figures, the contraction was at last arrested and even reversed (by just 0.4 per cent); other figures, which were based on physical indicators such as electricity consumption and goods traffic that were less open to manipulation and misreporting, suggested there had in fact been a further fall, of about 3–4 per cent,[187] and the collapse of the currency in the late summer of 1998 made it unlikely that significant real growth would be achieved until the early years of the new century.

Official statistics had never been entirely satisfactory (confidence was not improved when a group of senior officials at the statistical office were arrested in 1998 and charged with bribe-taking and systematic falsification),[188] and, although Russian statistics conformed more closely to international conventions in the 1990s, they still tended to understate activity in the private and 'black' or informal sectors (the official series was revised in late 1995 to take account of such factors and earlier estimates of decline were somewhat moderated).[189] The size of the informal economy was nonetheless the subject of widely differing estimates: officially it was about 25 per cent of gross domestic product, but some put it at 40, 60, even 80 per cent.[190] It could also be argued that a fall in national income was an inevitable and indeed desirable development in that it reflected an economy in structural change, one that was no longer producing military hardware and goods for which there was no consumer demand. But in the event, the decline in the output of modern consumer goods was even sharper than that of the heavy industries of the Soviet past: between 1990 and 1997 the output of coal, oil, steel, and gas fell by up to 45 per cent, but the output of personal computers was down by more than 60 per cent, of cameras and watches by more than 80 per cent, of colour televisions and tape recorders by more than 90 per cent, and of video recorders by no less than 99 per cent as compared with the last full year of Soviet rule. Investment, meanwhile, had fallen every year to just a quarter of its 1990 level.[191]

These rates of decline had obvious implications for Russia's level of development in relation to other nations. In 1990, at its peak, Russian gross domestic product had been about a third of that of the United States; six years later it was barely a fifth.[192] Its share of world trade, meanwhile, had fallen by almost half, from 2.5 to 1.3 per cent.[193] The Russian economy was still one the world's largest, ranked twelfth in 1997 by the World Bank, but by the late 1990s it had fallen behind Brazil, China, and South Korea as well as the major Western democracies. In relative rather than absolute terms, and expressed in purchasing power parity (which took account of local cost variations), it ranked much lower: it was a 'lower middle-income' country in World Bank terms, well below the global average in GDP per head of population and behind Latin American countries like Costa Rica, the Dominican Republic, and Ecuador, Asian countries like Thailand, and African countries like Gabon and Namibia.[194] Comparisons could be drawn with a number of other developing countries, and here again the results were unflattering. In the early 1990s, for instance, Russia had been overtaken in its per capita gross domestic product by Peru, Jordan, Iraq, and many others. If existing rates of growth continued, it was calculated, several more countries, including Morocco and Swaziland, would over-take Russia by the end of the century, and Vietnam and Mozambique were on course to do so by the end of the following decade.[195]

The Gorbachev leadership had insisted the USSR must play a full part in the international division of labour; and for the postcommunist reformers it was equally important that Russia be an open economy, trading with the rest of the world on the basis of a fully convertible currency, and drawing some of its growth dynamic from the pressure to compete successfully on price and quality with producers in other markets. The value of imports and exports both increased during the early postcommunist years, and there was a positive trade balance; Russia's main trade partner was Germany, accounting for 9.9 per cent of Russian exports and 16.4 per cent of imports, with the USA, China, Switzerland, Japan, and the United Kingdom the other main markets for Russian exports and the USA, Italy, Finland, and France the other main suppliers of Russian imports.[196] These figures, however, took no account of 'unorganised imports', conducted by individual traders; estimates suggested that this 'shuttle' trade, of goods carried from countries like Turkey or Poland, accounted for up to half of the value of all clothing and footwear that was sold on the domestic market.[197] Imports, at the same time, accounted for an increasing proportion of the Russian diet: for about a third in 1998, including half the cheese, tinned meat, and pasta.[198] And exports, in spite of the intentions of the reformers, were even more likely to consist of raw materials rather than manufactured goods. By 1997 mineral products, including oil, repre-sented nearly half the value of Russian exports (Russia, some suggested, was becoming the 'world's petrol pump').[199] Metals and precious stones accounted for another quarter, which was even more than in 1990; and the biggest imports were of machinery and foodstuffs.[200]

The reformers had more success with inflation, which rose to 2,609 per cent in 1992 but then dropped steadily to 940 per cent in 1993, 315 per cent in 1994, 231 per cent in 1995, 122 per cent in 1996, and 111 per cent in 1997.[201] Their achievement, however, owed much to unpaid wages or suppressed inflation. In 1998, according to the survey evi-dence, only 18 per cent of Russians were being paid regularly, 25 per cent were being paid irregularly, and 57 per cent were not being paid at all; the main reason they continued working was the fear of losing their job.[202] Workers in a Krasnoyarsk factory, where no one had been paid for a year, put up a gravestone in the form of a 500-ruble note to commemorate their last payday;[203] local utility workers held a 'wage funeral' to mark the period since they had themselves last been paid,

Plate 4.3 'The factory needs workers who don't need to be paid' (*Novoe vremya*, June 1996)

and threatened that if the deceased did not come back to life they would 'deluge their beloved city with sewage'.[204] One worker, after a year without pay, committed suicide by jumping from the roof of the factory in which he worked, leaving a message that the factory director should pay for his funeral.[205] Workers in Novosibirsk, in the late 1990s, were being paid 'almost two years late'; the record-holders were Eskimos in northerly Chukotka, who had not been paid their wages for five years.[206]

Another practice was to offer payment in kind rather than in cash. Workers at a Penza clock factory, for instance, were given rolls of toilet paper instead of their usual bonuses (one of them tried to pay her rent in the same unconventional currency but housing officials refused to accept it).[207] Workers elsewhere were being paid in tins of pineapple, or jars of pickled cucumbers; a collective farm offered payment in vodka.[208] Male workers were paid in gas pistols or, less appropriately, in brassieres; a doctor in the Archangel region suggested payment in gravestones; seamstresses in Siberia were offered coffins; teachers in the Altai were offered vodka after they had turned down toilet paper and funeral accessories.[209] There were particular problems with the payment of pensions, with delays of up to three months. 'You might just as well lie down alive in your grave', Valentina Korchenkova from the Tver' region told *Izvestiya*, as her savings dwindled away. 'If only presidential elections were more frequent, maybe we'd get paid more regularly, but this way I won't make it till the next ones.' Heart attacks and hysteria were 'routine' for the elderly these days, the paper reported, as they stood in line for their pension; and you couldn't feed people on promises.[210]

The state itself was in considerable difficulty because of a chronic failure to collect taxes. Of the 2.8 million enterprises and other bodies that were registered with the tax authorities in 1997, nearly half were behind with their payments and 35 per cent presented no accounts at all; only 16.5 per cent were up to date.[211] This meant that all the activities that were funded by the state were in the same situation. Frontier posts, for instance, were understaffed, leading to a substantial loss in customs revenue.[212] The legal system broke down in the Komi republic, as courts in the capital had no money for paper, pens, or envelopes; in Karelia the police were not being paid, and were responding only to emergencies.[213] The armed forces, although they continued to enjoy a large share of state spending, were in disarray, with unpaid salaries, serious shortages of housing, and numerous reports of suicides, and overall they represented 'a danger to themselves'.[214] Science, meanwhile, was 'on the brink of death', with the budget of the Academy of Sciences just 5–7 per cent of what it had been at the end of communist rule.[215] The director of a Chelyabinsk research institute, many of whose staff had been subsisting on bread obtained on credit, was so distressed by the situation in his institution that he committed suicide; substantial numbers, anxious to continue their work as well as to feed their families, emigrated to the West.[216]

Unemployment rose steadily throughout the postcommunist period, although it was often difficult to distinguish between the unemployed as they would have been defined in other countries, the rather smaller proportion that registered with labour exchanges, the much larger proportion that were nominally employed but in fact required to take a period of unpaid leave or work a reduced week, and the still larger numbers that were in employment but not being paid. So far as official figures were concerned, the unemployed rapidly increased, from 4.7 per cent in 1992 up to 14.2 per cent at the start of 1999; only a third of them were registered with the authorities and receiving a benefit, and an increasing proportion were the long-term unemployed, who had been looking for a job for a year or more.[217] There was, in fact, little incentive to register as unemployed because the benefits were so meagre, and enterprises had some incentive to keep surplus workers on their books to avoid the tax payments they would otherwise have to make. Taking these and other circumstances into account, the International Labour Organization estimated that the real level of unemployment in the late 1990s was closer to a third than a tenth of the total workforce.[218] Men were more likely to be unemployed than women, although women were a larger share of those who received unemployment benefit; equally, there were far higher levels of unemployment in some of the peripheral regions than in Moscow – more than half of the workforce in Ingushetia were out of work, and more than a fifth in Kalmykia, North Ossetia and Dagestan.[219]

The reformers' main achievement – perhaps their only one – had been a reduction in the rate of inflation; but even this became impossible to sustain in the late 1990s as the collapse of currencies in East Asia increased speculative pressure on the ruble and at the same time exposed the fundamental weakness of an economy that had been in almost continuous decline. There had already been several upsets on the money markets: on 'black Tuesday' in October 1994, on 'black Thursday' in October 1997, and then again in May 1998, when there was a sudden panic and exchange rates were increased sharply to ward off the threat of devaluation. A much graver crisis developed later in the year when the Russian government announced that the exchange rate against the dollar was going to be widened (this was in effect a devaluation of up to 50 per cent, with major inflationary implications) and that foreign debts would be converted into longer-term obligations (which was in effect a default). Yeltsin, seeking to reassure an anxious public, had insisted there would be 'no devaluation of the ruble' and that everything was 'carefully worked out',[220] but journalists found he had some 'strange things to say', including an apparent confusion between the 2,000th anniversary of the birth of Christ and the founding of the Russian state, and concluded he had 'little understanding of the kind of crisis the country was in'.[221] The official announcement, on 17 August, blamed 'world financial markets' and the 'latest drop in world oil prices' for an embarrassing volte-face,[222] and indeed for the collapse of the policies that had been followed since the end of communist rule. Prices rose sharply (food prices increased by 40 per cent in September alone);[223]

real incomes fell by about a third;[224] and many individual Russians, particularly its fledgling middle class, found their savings worthless and often inaccessible (even former president Gorbachev was ruined).[225]

An alternative set of policies took some time to emerge, but it was clear from the outset that they would place a greater degree of emphasis upon state regulation, the 'real economy', and the concerns of ordinary Russians even if they departed from the prescriptions of the IMF. They were shaped, in part, by the advice of some of the Russian economists who had been prominent in the Gorbachev years but who had been marginalised under Yeltsin and his Western advisers; they favoured the indexing of salaries, benefits, and savings, the establishment of a national food reserve, closer government control over foreign currency dealings, a 'controlled currency emission' that would allow salaries and pensions to be paid, and a greater emphasis upon reviving the domestic market as a means of stimulating growth and real incomes.[226] It had been the 'so-called reformers', insisted Prime Minister Primakov, who had been responsible for the financial collapse; they had pursued 'stabilisation for the sake of stabilisation', selling natural resources to buy manufactures and ignoring the 'social aspects of the economy'. Western economies had used the power of the state to pull themselves out of difficulties during the Great Depression, and in postwar Germany; it was only state regulation that could protect 'civilised capitalism' from 'wild capitalism', and only the state that could launch an effective attack upon corruption that was already 'widespread'.[227]

The programme that was approved by the Russian government in November 1998 reflected these priorities. The state itself would play an 'enhanced role', including direct government intervention to restructure larger enterprises, encourage small and medium businesses, and raise levels of technology. Privatisation would continue, but on a 'civilised basis' and where it was justified by economic and social considerations. There would be immediate measures to distribute food and medicines in short supply, and to reduce duties on their import and transportation. Wages, pensions, and other social benefits would be paid in full, and indexed; and the money supply would be sustained at a level that made it possible to do so. Measures would be taken to hold down the prices charged by local and national monopolies. The banking sector would be reorganised, and a new development bank established. Tax rates would gradually be brought down, but collection improved. In the longer term, there would be a shift from stabilisation towards 'socially oriented economic growth'.[228] One more specific measure had already been introduced, the restoration of a state vodka monopoly, which was intended to improve the flow of excise duties and at the same time to protect the domestic market from low-quality and sometimes dangerous imports.[229] It remained unclear how far it would be possible to print more money and at the same time avoid hyperinflation; or to attract new loans and foreign investment while suspending repayment; or to protect the domestic producer without resorting to protectionism; or to reduce taxation but at the same time sustain higher levels of public spending.

Russia and the market

By the late 1990s, the arguments were still continuing about whether the Russian reforms had 'failed', if they had succeeded, or indeed if they had even been tried at all. And if they had failed, who had 'lost Russia'? The view most closely associated with those who had persuaded the Russian government to adopt the policies in the first place was that they had, broadly speaking, been a success – or at least that any shortcomings were the result of individual misjudgements, not inherent in the strategy itself. An IMF 'stabilisation' package had worked for Latin America: why not in Russia? For the reformers, the fall in output had been greatly exaggerated, and so had the social costs; more generally, they argued that the process of reform had succeeded to the extent that Russia had 'become a market economy', and that an 'entire culture had been transformed'.[230] Another of the government's advisers, and the author of a study on the 'coming Russian boom', felt able to assure his readers in 1996 that there would be 'strong economic growth based on private enterprise', and that Russia's economy would 'grow faster over the next twenty years than that of most OECD countries and probably faster than most emerging markets (outside the Far East)'.[231] Writing elsewhere, he promised an 'upturn' as early as 1996.[232] There were similar assurances from members of the Yeltsin administration: Chubais, for instance, insisted in 1995 that the future sequence of events was 'absolutely ironclad: first financial recovery, and then the recovery of production'.[233] Yeltsin himself, in a television address at the end of 1991, had promised things would get better in 'six to eight months', and that if there was no improvement he would 'lie on the rails'.[234] Success would be apparent 'definitely this year', he promised in a television address early the following year.[235]

The reformers advanced a larger argument, which was that Russia was 'not essentially different from other countries'.[236] For the privatisers, Russians 'were "economic men" who rationally responded to incentives'; they were just as keen to take risks and work hard as anyone else, and they would find a market was as natural a vehicle for them to do so as it was in other countries.[237] As Petr Aven, minister of foreign economic relations in the Gaidar government, insisted, 'There are no special countries. All countries from the point of view of an economist are the same so far as the stabilisation of their economies is concerned.'[238] This was certainly the view of their Western consultants, who received several million dollars for their advice, and who were able to control millions more in aid budgets that went, in many cases, to nominally independent organisations they had helped to establish. 'Crony capitalism' was increasingly paralleled by a 'crony research and advice system stretching from Washington to Moscow';[239] more than 30,000 Western 'consultants' had visited Moscow since the change of regime, reported *Trud*, many of them interested in '"assistance" not to ordinary Russians but to themselves'.[240]

Even the reformers, however, had to accept that the outcome of their recommendations was far from a 'normal' capitalism, if indeed it was capitalism at all. Gaidar, for instance, concluded that Russia had established a 'corrupt bureaucratic capitalism',[241] and for him it was still an open question in the late 1990s if it would be a capitalism in which 'sharp social inequality leads to waves of sociopolitical instability or a civilised capitalism, controlled by the society'.[242] Elsewhere he called it a 'capitalism of officialdom'.[243] Boris Nemtsov, a first deputy prime minister from 1997 to 1998, spoke of a 'gangster capitalism', or of an 'oligarchic capitalism' that pumped income from the poor to the rich, or an 'administrative-oligarchic capitalism'.[244] Others still spoke of a 'crony capitalism', run by an 'interlocking clique of business elites who use[d] their political connections to shield themselves from domestic and international competition',[245] and there were some who thought the postcommunist system in Russia was something entirely new, a 'mixture of feudalism and capitalism', a 'strange and corrupt new system of its own invention', or even a 'mutant'.[246]

Many Russian economists were even more outspoken. For Petrakov and Perlamutrov, Russia was a 'zone of economic catastrophe'.[247] Others compared the economy in the early 1990s to Grozny at the end of the Chechen war, after 'monetarist "carpet bombing"'.[248] There was particular concern about the loss of national sovereignty that appeared to be taking place, which was turning Russia into a dependent territory for the supply of raw materials and a convenient storage place for dangerous waste.[249] This, it was argued, was 'colonisation', not development; it was being urged by Western 'experts' who had often been retained by the intelligence services of their own countries; it was leading to a progressive deindustrialisation;[250] and the result was a threat to the 'very existence' of Russia, the worst since the Mongol invasion.[251] Others went so far as to argue that 'what Hitler was unable

to achieve' was 'now being carried into practice'.[252] Alexander Solzhenitsyn, no economist but representative of a broad spectrum of nationalist opinion, argued similarly that what was taking place was nothing
less than the 'destruction' of the Russian economy, a conclusion reinforced by the impressions he had gained in a series of meetings with
ordinary people in twenty-six of the Russian regions.[253]

Even those who stopped short of these stark conclusions drew the
lesson, with economist Leonid Abalkin, that Russia must 'find its own
way without disregarding the experience of other countries'.[254] Russia's
own circumstances, Abalkin insisted, must not be forgotten: history and
culture, geography and attitudes.[255] For all the talk of globalisation, he
wrote elsewhere, it was no less valid to focus on the differences between
cultures and civilisations; indeed globalisation was associated with a
'deepening of the particularity of the cultures of different types of
civilisation'.[256] And equally, proper weight must be given to the 'historical experience, culture, and traditions of Russia'.[257] A greater willingness to take into account the specificity of the Russian experience –
its lack, for instance, of a developed legal system even before the
Bolsheviks had come to power – was associated with a more cautious
approach towards 'allegedly miraculous foreign prescriptions'.[258] There
was mounting scepticism about the 'young reformers', who (in Luzhkov's words) knew 'nothing about real-world economics and production' and spent their time playing 'monetarist games',[259] and increasing
resistance to the advice that was offered by 'young kids' from the IMF
who (in Primakov's very similar words) had 'seen almost nothing in
life'.[260]

Equally, there was an increasing recognition within as well as outside
the country that capitalism was compatible with a strong and even
interventionist state: indeed, that this might be a condition of its
successful operation.[261] The importance of a larger, even dominant role
for the state in the process of economic reform had been argued by a
number of economists including three Nobel prizewinners in a letter to
the Russian press in the summer of 1996. Shock therapy, they believed,
had been a failure. The state, they insisted, should play a 'central, co-
ordinating role', as it did in the mixed economies of the West. In its
absence, criminal elements had 'filled the vacuum', and they had helped
to bring about a transition 'not to a market, but to a criminalised
economy'. There should be more emphasis upon competition, rather
than privatisation (this, if anything, was the 'secret' of the market
economy). There should be a more sustained attempt to resume
economic growth, and to mitigate the social consequences of existing
policies. And more generally, there should be a gradual approach

towards the process of reform, not a continuation of the radical measures that had led to a 'deep crisis'.[262]

Some Western economists drew more general lessons from the Russian experience. It suggested, for a start, that more attention needed to be paid to history, culture, and society. The formerly communist countries, it had to be remembered, were a 'tabula non rasa'.[263] There was no need to suggest that Russians, or Poles, or Georgians were biologically different from anyone else in their economic behaviour. But the reforms that were being conducted in their countries had to take more account of context. Had there, for instance, been a private agriculture (as in Poland), or a community of small traders? Was there a functioning legal and financial system? And was there a state that was strong enough to break up monopolies, enforce its decisions, and collect the taxes that were needed to finance its policies?[264] The World Bank itself began to give more attention to these institutional factors as the century drew to a close: from clean water and sanitation to health, education, and international security. These were factors that depended on the quality of government; they suggested in turn that state and market were 'inextricably linked', and that the capacity for state action was 'central to providing a viable institutional framework for development'.[265] The USSR had shown the limitations of central planning; but its postcommunist experience was equally striking evidence of the limitations of a dogmatic commitment to market principles, and it was not only in Russia that the response was a shift back towards a more balanced relationship between private ownership and state regulation, and towards policies that took more account of domestic circumstances than of the advice of foreign moneylenders.

5   A divided society

The USSR was always a diverse society. It was European, but also Asian. It stretched over eleven time zones bordering twelve other states and three oceans, with much of its northern territory permanently frozen but its southern republics largely desert. It was a mostly Christian society, but it was also the world's fifth-largest Muslim state, and there were substantial Jewish and Buddhist communities. About half of its population was Russian, and three-quarters belonged to one of the Slavic nationalities; but there were more than a hundred recognised national groups, and on other, more inclusive counts as many as eight hundred.[1] Its language was predominantly Russian, and 82 per cent of the population spoke it fluently or as a native language, but about 130 other languages were spoken on Soviet territory using a variety of different alphabets.[2] Indeed the state itself was based upon diversity, as it was a 'voluntary union' of fifteen different republics within each of which a particular national group was supposedly predominant.[3]

But if the USSR was 'national in form', it was also 'socialist in content'. For a start, there was no private ownership of productive resources of a kind that would have led to a minority of owners and a majority of wage labourers. Private ownership was not illegal, and there was (for instance) a substantial private housing sector. But there could be no private factories or farms, and it was illegal to live off the labour of others – this was what the Soviet authorities defined as 'exploitation' – or indeed not to work at all (the Soviet constitution, following St Paul's Epistle to the Thessalonians, insisted that those who did not work 'should not eat').[4] It was illegal, equally, to own more than one house, or to own a house of more than a certain size, or to rent it out and live on the proceeds.[5] This was not a 'classless' society: official theory recognised the existence of workers and collective farmers, and of a 'friendly stratum' of white-collar employees. But there was in principle no antagonism between these various groups because they collectively owned the society's resources, and there was accordingly no basis (it was suggested) for the conflicts that were characteristic of capitalism and other class-divided societies.

Official theory was admittedly an imperfect guide to the realities of daily life under the Soviet system; and even official theory began to change as the society itself underwent a far-reaching transformation. For Yuri Andropov, as late as 1982, a socialist society was a society without social antagonisms, and there was accordingly no basis for an 'organised opposition' of a kind that Western exponents of 'pluralism' were making every effort to encourage.[6] Under Gorbachev, just a few years later, it became possible to speak of 'socialist pluralism', and then of a 'pluralism of opinion' or even a 'pluralism of interests' that logically entailed the articulation of political alternatives through which they could be expressed and reconciled.[7] Changes in official thinking reflected a society that was itself evolving and becoming more difficult to classify. In 1985, when Gorbachev succeeded to the party leadership, more than 85 per cent were employed in the state sector; by 1990, as the Ryzhkov government began to introduce a 'regulated' market, more than 80 per cent were still working in the state sector but nearly 5 million had taken up employment in trading co-operatives, commercial farming, or joint enterprises, and a further 2 million were unemployed.[8] By 1996, after still more extensive changes under the Yeltsin–Gaidar leadership, many more were unemployed and more than 7 million were working as wage labourers; 37 per cent were still working for the state or local government, but slightly more – 38 per cent – were in the private sector, and 23 per cent were working in enterprises with mixed forms of ownership.[9] Formally at least, a monolithic USSR had been succeeded by a postcommunist Russia with a diversity of ownership and occupation that matched the ideological diversity of its newly established political institutions.

Rich and poor in postcommunist Russia

One of the clearest results of the transition to an economy based largely on private ownership was a rapidly widening gap between incomes, and accordingly between living standards. In 1991, the USSR's last year, the least well-paid fifth of the population earned 12 per cent of all money incomes, and the best paid 31 per cent. By 1997 the poorest fifth earned half as much in relative terms as they had earned six years earlier, but the richest fifth earned half as much again – nearly half, in fact, of all earned income; and just 1.5 per cent had acquired 65 per cent of the national wealth.[10] Differences of this kind are conveniently expressed in terms of the 'decile ratio', which relates the earnings of the most prosperous 10 per cent of the population to those of the least prosperous 10 per cent. In 1990 it stood at 4.4, but by 1997 it had jumped to 13.2 per cent (see table 5.1); the richest 20 per cent of the population by this time earned a greater share of income than in any other European country for which the World Bank reported statistics, including all the former republics of the USSR, and more than in all but a few countries in Africa and Latin America.[11] Average incomes were about twice as high as the subsistence minimum in the late 1990s, but a fifth of the population – more than 30 million people – fell below it.[12] Of the poor, more than a third were in 'extreme poverty', with an average income that was less than half the subsistence minimum, and almost a fifth were in 'constant poverty'.[13]

Money incomes are only one of the ways in which living standards are generated, and this was particularly true of postcommunist Russia.[14] For a start, substantial numbers were not being paid all or even a part of their earnings, and official statistics distinguished accordingly between nominal incomes – the salaries and wages to which the working popula- tion were entitled – and the money incomes they actually received. Both of them, moreover, varied from year to year, falling sharply in 1992 as prices were allowed to find an equilibrium but recovering some ground the following year. By 1996, nonetheless, both had declined substan- tially in value, money incomes to 67 per cent of their 1990 value and nominal incomes to just 46 per cent; pensions also fell sharply, to 56 per cent of their value at the start of the decade.[15] Incomes could equally be expressed in terms of the commodities that they could buy. A Russian on average earnings, for instance, could buy more fruit in the late 1990s than at the start of the decade, but less meat, fewer eggs and potatoes, less than half the bread, and not much more than a quarter of the milk products.[16] Russians, as a result of these changes, were spending more of their income on food (nearly half by 1996),[17] while at the same time the quality of their diet was deteriorating. Bread and potato consump- tion remained stable or increased slightly between 1990 and 1996, but fruit and vegetables fell back, meat and milk consumption dropped by a third or more, and fish consumption was down by nearly half.[18] These, moreover, were average levels: the biggest earners, as in other countries, ate the same quantities of bread and potatoes but about twice as much fruit, vegetables, fish, and meat as the least prosperous 10 per cent of households.[19]

There were differentials not only between social groups, but also between regions, and within regions, in their patterns of income distribution. Across the entire country, in the late 1990s, money incomes were more than twice as high as the subsistence minimum.[20]

But in Dagestan, bordering the Caspian, average incomes were just below subsistence levels, while at the other extreme money incomes were highest in Moscow, both in absolute terms and in relation to the local cost of living.[21] Average incomes, clearly, lumped together the poor and the very rich, and their relative proportions varied from region to region. In Sakhalin, in the Far East, the richest 20 per cent of the local population earned just three times as much as the poorest 20 per cent; but in Moscow, they earned nearly twenty times as much.[22] This meant that there were large numbers of poor in Moscow, as well as most of the country's millionaires. In Moscow, similarly, 19 per cent of the population earned less than the subsistence minimum, but in Tyva, on the Mongolian border, an overwhelming 73 per cent had incomes below the local subsistence minimum and more than three-quarters of these lived in 'extreme poverty'.[23] There were related differences between occupations; rates of pay in agriculture dropped particularly sharply, from close to the national average in 1990 to less than half the average in 1996.[24]

Official statistics of this or any other kind could capture no more than a few of the changes that were taking place in patterns of social inequality. They could clearly take little account of illegal and undeclared earnings, or of the extent to which Russians were already living in an informal economy based upon the exchange of services and the bartering of commodities, or of the contribution to living standards that was made by suburban allotments.[25] But official figures seemed likely, if anything, to understate the differences that were opening up between rich and poor. The subsistence minimum, for a start, had been set at an unreasonably low level (much lower than prison rations in tsarist times, which had contained twice as much meat).[26] And income differentials were almost certainly much wider than official figures suggested, as the rich had found ways of concealing their income and could protect its value by investing in real estate, while the poor included vagrants, beggars, and alcoholics who often escaped the attention of official scrutineers entirely.[27] A number of Russians, similarly, had a second job; but only 11 per cent had an additional income of this kind on an occasional or more regular basis, their numbers were declining, and they were likely in any case to be those who were already earning the most in their principal employment.[28] As a result, while government statistics identified about a third of the population as living in poverty, calculations based on survey returns put the proportion as high as 80 per cent; and, of these, 20 per cent had an income so low that it covered no more than the physiological needs of family members with no provision for clothing, medical treatment, or holidays.[29]

Table 5.1. *Living standards in the 1990s*

	1990	1991	1992	1993	1994	1995	1996	1997
Incomes								
Real money incomes								
(% change)	–	116	53	116	112	84	100	103
Inequality (decile ratio)	4	5	8	11	15	14	13	13
Percentage below subsistence	–	–	34	32	22	25	22	21
Food consumption (kg/head)								
Bread	97	101	104	107	101	102	97	93
Meat	70	65	58	57	58	53	48	52
Milk products	378	348	294	305	305	249	235	219
Education								
Nursery enrolments								
(% of age group)	66	64	57	57	56	56	55	54
College enrolments (mn)	2.3	2.2	2.1	2.0	1.9	1.9	2.0	2.0
University enrolments (mn)	2.8	2.8	2.6	2.5	2.5	2.7	2.8	3.0
Culture								
Theatre visits (mn)	56	51	44	41	35	32	29	28
Books (mn copies)	1,553	1,630	1,313	950	594	475	421	436
Newspapers (mn daily copies)	166	160	144	86	86	122	114	125

Source: Adapted from *Rossiiskii statisticheskii yezhegodnik. Statisticheskii sbornik* (Moscow: Goskomstat Rossii, 1997), and from *Rossiya v tsifrakh. Kratkii statisticheskii sbornik* (Moscow: Goskomstat Rossii, 1998), various pages.

Up to 5 per cent of Russians, by the late 1990s, could be regarded as 'rich' (with their families, they accounted for between 4 and 7 million of the population). Another 15 per cent were 'comfortable', with a monthly income of at least a thousand dollars for each family member. The 'middle' accounted for a very varied 20 per cent, ranging from the staff of commercial firms, street traders, and junior government officials to more prosperous businessmen and criminals, some of whom could hope to sustain a standard of living that corresponded to that of the middle class in Western countries. Most of them were concentrated in Moscow, where they represented about a third of the population, and they were about 10 per cent of the population of most of the larger towns and cities. But the polarisation of incomes had gone so far that there were already 'two Russias', very different in their patterns of spending and housing conditions and not simply in their incomes. The 'relatively poor' accounted for another 20 per cent and the 'poor' for as many as 40 per cent, of whom about a quarter were destitute.[30]

Another, more sharply pointed classification was suggested by Tat'yana Zaslavskaya, perhaps the most eminent of Russian sociologists.

At the top, she suggested, was a 'renewed oligarchy' that accounted for just 1 per cent of the population, formed for the most part out of the most competent or fortunate members of the former *nomenklatura*, and with 'no less power and great deal more wealth' than their Soviet predecessors (the seven largest financial-industrial groups alone were estimated to control half the nation's assets). Below it, accounting for another 4–5 per cent of the population, was an 'augmented and strengthened ruling bureaucracy', twice as large as in the Soviet period and based on the 'total corruption of the state apparatus and the law enforcement agencies' together with the 'collapse of justice'. The third group (about 14–17 per cent of the total) were a 'middle class in the Western sense', but a relatively narrow, heterogeneous, and unstable one, without significant property, based for the most part in the towns, but 'because of their weakness not yet able to exercise a significant influence on social development'. The fourth and by far the largest group was what Zaslavskaya defined as the 'base', accounting for 60–65 per cent of the population. As a result of the economic reforms this was an even less prosperous group than it had been in the Soviet past; it had received no significant assets from the privatisation of state property, and at the same time it had lost the limited social security it had enjoyed in earlier times (it was affected, indeed, by growing unemployment and the nonpayment of wages and pensions). Below it came the 'honest poor', including the least qualified and those with the largest families (9–12 per cent of the total); and finally the 'underclass', a criminalised 7–9 per cent who had lost touch with most social institutions and lived by their own rules.[31]

The rich, as these accounts suggested, were a composite of several groups, including well-educated and usually hard-working businessmen who held high positions in commercial structures with links to the state, and less-educated entrepreneurs with closer links to organised crime and a greater propensity to lead a flashy, free-spending lifestyle. The businessmen were more inclined to advance their interests by lobbying within government, and tended to invest their earnings in real estate; the entrepreneurs, by contrast, lived in less luxurious surroundings but indulged a taste for expensive cars and relaxed in nightclubs and striptease bars. The business elite were usually married, with a wife who had given up working; almost all had one or two children, whom they brought up as lawyers or economists; and their favourite cars were Volvos, Lincolns, and Mercedeses, although they kept some Russian-made cars for their family members.[32] Very few had established their position independently, and there was little prospect of doing so without 'influential patrons'. In these circumstances, those who were most likely to get rich were those who were already rich, or who were in power, together with the members of criminal clans; it was least likely to be ordinary people, or the educated.[33] The survey evidence suggested similarly that it was 'connections with important people' (49 per cent) that made the greatest difference in matters of this kind, although it was also possible to accumulate wealth because 'the economic system in our country allows the rich to profit from the poor' (45 per cent) or because of 'dishonesty' (39 per cent); 'ability and talents' or 'hard work', by contrast, counted for very little (14 and 11 per cent respectively).[34]

Who were the seriously rich? For the public at large it was political figures like the leader of the Party of Economic Freedom Konstantin Borovoi, the former Moscow mayor Gavriil Popov, and his successor Yuri Luzhkov,[35] but for informed opinion the richest were almost invariably the country's leading bankers: figures such as Vladimir Potanin, a former official of the Ministry of Foreign Economic Relations who had founded an import–export bank at an advantageous moment and who later became, for a year, first deputy chairman in the Chernomyrdin government; or Vladimir Gusinsky, an oil and gas engineer who was also a qualified theatre director and who went on to head Most-Bank; or Mikhail Khodorkovsky, a Moscow engineer who had risen through the Komsomol and become the head of the banking and industrial group Menatep. Others owed their position to their control over the country's vast natural resources, including Rem Vyakhirev, an engineer who had risen from management of the gas industry in Tyumen' to a deputy ministerial position and the chairmanship of Gazprom; he had been closely associated with former prime minister Chernomyrdin, another gasman, for more than thirty years.[36]

Boris Berezovsky, perhaps the most influential of all, had been a mathematician with a doctorate in management who had gone on to become the head of an automobile dealership that became the centre of a group of companies, and a close friend of the Yeltsin family. He was also, for a year, deputy chairman of the Security Council and later, for another year, executive secretary of the Commonwealth of Independent States.[37] The influence of 'oligarchs' like Berezovsky was broadly based, and often included a segment of the media: Gazprom controlled the newspapers *Trud* and *Rabochaya gazeta*; Berezovsky held shares in Russian Public Television and the now ironically named *Nezavisimaya gazeta* (Independent Newspaper); Potanin's Oneksimbank owned *Komsomol'skaya pravda* and shared ownership of *Izvestiya* with Lukoil; Gusinsky and his bank owned a series of newspapers including the influential *Segodnya* as well as independent television and a radio station.[38] There was continuing controversy about the extent to which the oligarchs constituted the 'real government of Russia', as the *Financial Times* described them.[39] Surveys found that Berezovsky was perceived as the 'most influential person in Russian politics', but 63 per cent of those who were asked had difficulty in replying and 22 per cent thought there was no such person;[40] for the chairman of independent television, Igor Malashenko, 'all stories about the incredible power of the oligarchs' were 'pure nonsense', and often cultivated by the oligarchs themselves to exaggerate the political influence they could command.[41]

What did it mean to be rich in postcommunist Russia? First of all, surveys suggested, it meant having no worries about the future. It also meant having a business of one's own (the most profitable were currency dealing, property, electronics, and oil); and after that it meant having a car, a dacha, and a flat; earning enough to buy food in markets, to drink cognac, and spend time in restaurants; and being healthy.[42] The rich, surveys agreed, liked foreign cars (more Mercedes 500 and 600 saloons were sold in the Moscow region than in the whole of Western Europe in the mid-1990s);[43] and they liked property abroad, particularly in Spain but also in the USA, Cyprus, Portugal, Greece, and France (Berezovsky, for instance, was reported to have bought a Riviera chateau for $70 million in the summer of 1998; a British estate agent was 'dealing with so many Russians that he kept a bottle of Stolichnaya vodka permanently on ice in his Hampstead office').[44] The new rich had little time for holidays – on average just a week a year, nearly always in a foreign resort. More than half had a mistress, whom they visited two or three times a month, and they dined out in restaurants at least four times a week. As many as 40 per cent admitted they had been involved in criminal activity at an earlier stage in their career, and 25 per cent had current links with the criminal world.[45] Other studies found that the most important characteristic of a rich Russian was personal security, including a bodyguard (two-thirds of them 'lived and worked under the threat of terror'); a second characteristic was property, including a second home in the country, a well-appointed flat, and a car; and a third characteristic was links with the criminal world and with government. Clothes and personal appearance, by contrast, were relatively unimportant.[46]

How did the rich spend their money? By far the largest share of the income of the new rich was invested in their businesses, with just 15 per cent spent on their own needs (in some cases, where they felt their businesses had yet to establish themselves, they spent even less on their personal requirements). Beyond that, the easiest way of showing off new-found wealth was through the purchase of a prestigious motor car

Plate 5.1   'First say the magic word!' 'Dollar!' (*Izvestiya*, July 1997)

or a city-centre apartment,[47] although with rising levels of crime and popular hostility it became increasingly common to move to well-protected residences in the nearby countryside (by the late 1990s the cost of residences of this kind in the Moscow region was running at up to $700,000, and competitions were being organised to identify the most luxurious).[48] The new rich worked out at fitness centres where family membership cost more than four times the average annual income; their children attended special playgrounds where they could watch fashion parades for the pre-teens under the protection of armed guards ('Children need to be fashionable too');[49] and many went on to a foreign education, either at secondary or at university level (Yeltsin's grandson attended an expensive British public school and then went on to Oxford; Berezovsky's daughters were at Cambridge University).[50] Russians showed a similar interest in aristocratic titles, not their own but foreign and particularly British, chosen from a catalogue of the insignia of the impoverished gentry. 'Edward', a 41-year-old Moscow businessman, explained that he had 'always dreamed of a title', and that it 'didn't matter what it cost'; the main thing was that he could hand it on to his children and they would 'become British aristocrats'.[51]

But many of the new rich just liked to have a good time. There was a developing network of clubs to cater for their tastes, like the Golden Palace, which had a perspex floor with 'fish swimming below your feet' but also 'evil-looking Vietnamese clients and shotgun-toting security'; or Hippopota M ('pricey; must check guns at the door'); or Voyazh Club ('heavy leathers and bikers' but a 'critical crowd; singer killed on stage last year by angry audience').[52] Another favourite place was the Hungry Duck, particularly on its ladies' nights, which involved 'some fairly graphic interaction between Dylan, a Nigerian male stripper, wearing gold spangles and little else, and several female volunteers from the crowd, while the Soviet hymn blasted through the speakers' (not surprisingly, there were angry complaints in the Duma).[53] The consumption of Moscow's super-rich, foreign journalists reported, was 'conspicuous even by Western standards'. They were protected by bodyguards and the tinted windows of their Mercedes 600s; they bought villas in Europe, did their shopping in Paris and Milan, and thought nothing of spending $100 for lunch at one of the five-star Western hotels in the Russian capital. When they held a public event, like Most-Bank's fifth birthday party, a 'parade of Mercedeses, BMWs, and Cadillacs' wound their way round one of the city's most opulent hotels; security staff with walkie-talkies took up position outside the building; inside, 'men in Armani suits and women in diamonds, Versace cocktail dresses, and Chanel suits checked their furs and joined the receiving line', the 'champagne was flowing' and caviare was in 'buckets'. Later on, at somewhere like the Up and Down Club, they surrendered their pistols at the door and were frisked by armed guards before heading upstairs to watch young women in G-strings gyrate around a pole in the middle of the stage before taking it all off. 'We don't have any foreign customers', explained the bar manager, pouring another of the club's favourite drinks, a $100 Hennessy Paradis; 'they can't afford it.'[54]

The 'new Russians' were easy to identify on holiday, not least by their extravagant spending. During the winter they could be found at Alpine resorts, their suitcases full of foreign currency (one ski boutique had to close when a Russian lady, 'dollar bills fluttering from her bag', bought everything they had for sale).[55] During the summer they preferred the French Riviera, attracted by its 'snobbish reputation, high prices, and anonymity';[56] they were welcomed in their turn because they spent five times as much as British or German tourists – not including hotel bills, which most of them insisted on paying in cash. Newspapers, indeed, reported that new Russians had 'overtaken oil sheikhs as the biggest and fastest spenders'; staff at the most expensive hotels 'watched goggle-eyed as families plonked down heaps of cash to cover bills that ran into thousands'. The new Russians had at least one other common characteristic, and one Riviera hotel had to make changes in its catering arrangements when it was found that the small bottles of vodka in its minibars had 'usually been emptied by breakfast'; thereafter, it was supplied in litres.[57] Another had to change its bar regime, as its new Russian guests wanted to order vodka from ten o'clock in the morning. 'They choose all the dearest things on the menu', reported hotel staff in Cannes, 'like Arabs from the Persian Gulf twenty years ago', and 'usually ordered more than they could eat', including the most expensive wines, but rarely left any tips.[58] This was also the experience of local taxi-drivers: 'they never tip', one of them told journalists disgustedly, 'not like the British aristocracy'.[59]

Not only the rich were 'new Russians': so were the poor. The new poor were often those with large families, who were hit disproportionately hard by the rising cost of bringing up children.[60] And they included those who had lost their employment. Nina from St Petersburg, for instance, just nineteen years old, had no job and no money and was offering herself as a surrogate mother to foreign clients; so was Zhenya, with two children already, but with no job and no other means of support.[61] The poor included whole towns like Yuzha, 200 miles west of Moscow in the depressed Ivanovo region, where four out of every five were living below the poverty line and many of the unemployed, elderly, and sick were too poor to have regular meals. No one in the Lipatova family, for instance, had eaten for three days. 'The fridge still works', they told a Western journalist, 'but it's no use; it's empty.'[62] It was a town, *Izvestiya* reported, where school pupils fainted with hunger; where old people looked for food in rubbish tips but rarely found anything because nothing was thrown out; and where there were never any mouldy rolls or decomposing meat because it had all been eaten. Children visited graveyards to collect the sweets that were sometimes left there, and looked forward to Easter when offerings were particularly plentiful. There were few cars, leaving locals to make their way about town in the snow on bicycles; there was a children's library, but not a single restaurant in a town of more than 30,000 inhabitants. In the local hospital a doctor who had worked there since 1953 told *Izvestiya* that there had never before been so many lice-ridden patients, a result of malnutrition and the cost of admission to the public bathhouse. The spinning mill, which had been the main source of local employment, was working at just 20 per cent of capacity because the supply of cheap Uzbek cotton had dried up, although the coffin workshop had plenty to do with four deaths in the area for every live birth. A committee had been set up to help the starving, as in the famine of the early 1920s. 'It was better during the war', commented locals.[63]

Another letter came from Svetlana T., who lived in Yartsevo, a town of 60,000 not far from Smolensk. The town, she told the newspaper, was 'dead'. Almost all its factories had stopped working in 1993. To feed themselves and their families the men of the locality had to go to Moscow, about 200 miles away, and look for work. They had tried striking and stopped the Moscow to Minsk railway, but no one took any notice. It was cold; the gas company wanted payment before it would resume supply, and there was nothing to pay them with – the town's gas debts were already more than its annual fuel bill. Salaries were being paid in margarine or flour, even in bicycles. The local textile factory had gone bankrupt and been taken over by the municipality; it used to have 14,000 employees, but now it had 1,200.[64] In a mining town in Rostov region, according to another report, four of the five shafts had closed; there was an excavator factory, but it was usually closed as well, and so were the cotton and the knitwear factory. All this would have been bad enough if those who were still in work had been paid regularly, but as late as October they were still waiting for their wages for the previous year. 'My family has forgotten the taste of sausage', the wife of one of the miners who was still working told journalists.[65] In Ivanovo and Murmansk locals were supplementing their porridge with animal feed;[66] in Khakassiya, in western Siberia, more than 500 children did not go to school throughout the winter because they had no shoes.[67]

The new poor included many others who were continuing to work, but who had not been paid for – sometimes – a very long time. This, as we have seen in chapter 4, was one of the ways that inflationary pressures were contained, at least under Chernomyrdin and Kirienko; but it led to intolerable difficulties for many families. The armed forces shared many of these deprivations. Not all of its problems were new – the bullying of new recruits, for instance, was of long standing; but its housing problems became more acute as thousands of troops returned from Eastern Europe, and as pay levels fell steadily behind the rise in prices. There were deaths from malnutrition;[68] others were being fed with dogfood – so bad, apparently, that dogs themselves refused to eat it.[69] Substantial numbers, unable to endure the conditions in which they were living, committed suicide (more than five hundred in 1998 alone);[70] others still turned to 'commerce', including the illegal sale of arms and equipment.[71] The poor also included the homeless, about 4 million of them throughout the country,[72] and street urchins: there were 'at least half a million' of them in the late 1990s, and up to 100,000 in Moscow alone.[73] They could be found 'outside mainline stations, queuing at voluntary soup kitchens, or huddling in doorways or empty basements'; 600 died of exposure during the winter of 1997, and another 2,000 had to be treated for frostbite. 'To be homeless in Russia', reporters commented, 'amounts to a death sentence.'[74]

Pensioners, in the aggregate, were not disproportionately poor: the average pension, at any rate, was worth as much in relation to average earnings in 1997 as in 1990. But the real value of the pension had fallen in most of these years (in 1992 alone by almost half), and by the late 1990s it had reached a level that was just above the subsistence minimum; the number of pensioners, meanwhile, had increased every year to just over a quarter of the total population, and there were fewer people of working age to support them.[75] For many, clearly, life was simply unbearable. Mrs Romanova from the Kemerovo region sent President Yeltsin a letter in which she explained that she had not received a pension for three months, and was cold and hungry with no prospect of an improvement; so she collected a burial certificate from her housing manager, took a tablet, and lay down to sleep. 'By morning it will be all over.'[76] Many, however, were 'afraid of dying'. A funeral, with bottles of alcohol for gravediggers and the entertainment for the mourners, was likely to cost three times the minimum monthly wage. Not only this: local authorities, at least in Moscow, were refusing to make land available; graves were being reused with increasing frequency, with a threat of plague and cholera; and cemeteries had become breeding grounds for rats.[77] 'Refuseniks' were another problem – those who refused to take on the expense of burying members of their family. They filled out a form to this effect, and then it was 'just a matter of a truck and the crematorium'. There were usually several bodies in a single truck, to keep down the cost, although each body had a separate coffin, even if it was just temporary and rented. The number of burials of this kind was 'growing steadily' in the early 1990s; for instance, of husbands and wives who both filled out a form, 'and then they live out the rest of their days in unbearable torment because of what they have done and because the same fate will befall each of them'.[78]

Levels of poverty were at their highest in 1992, as prices were allowed to find a new equilibrium; a third of the population – more than 50 million people – had incomes below subsistence at this time, a proportion that had fallen to about a fifth by the later 1990s. But this was still more than 30 million people (other calculations, less dependent on official statistics, suggested much higher figures).[79] Poverty, moreover, had become self-reproducing: poorer parents were less able to provide an adequate upbringing for their children, including diet, health care,

Plate 5.2   Old and homeless (Novosti)

and education, and this made it much more likely that their children would also be poor. In addition, there was 'fluid' poverty, composed of the 'new poor' whose living standards were held down by low levels of pay in state-owned enterprises, and also by unemployment and delays in the payment of salaries and pensions. At the very bottom were 'social paupers', including beggars, the homeless, orphans, alcoholics, drug addicts, and prostitutes. Studies suggested that 'marginals' of this kind accounted for as much as 10 per cent of the whole population, and their chances of regaining a normal existence were extremely low.[80]

Living standards suffered a further fall after the collapse of the currency in August 1998. Prices went sharply upwards; wages remained the same, or even fell; and a few lost their entire income as their firms went into liquidation.[81] Real incomes, accordingly, dropped by about a third;[82] even in Moscow 'almost half' fell below the poverty line,[83] and in a number of regions people were 'simply starving', with a diet that included cats and dogs, crows, jackdaws, and pigeons.[84] In provincial Penza things were so desperate that a policeman held up and robbed a pedestrian so that he could get a decent meal.[85] The crisis had particularly alarming implications for Russia's emerging but still fragile middle class of professionals and traders. The seriously rich kept their money abroad, and had withdrawn much of the rest before their accounts were frozen. State employees were protected by their benefits in kind, such as access to subsidised meals in the Duma. But those who depended on wages and pensions were affected much more seriously, and the middle strata most of all: many had lost their savings, others had been thrown out of work, and almost all had been traumatised by the loss of so much that they had taken for granted.[86] In September 1997, 50 per cent of Russians had characterised their economic position as 'bad or very bad'; a year later 67 per cent did so, and the proportion who thought their position was 'intolerable' had risen from 36 to 61 per cent.[87] Even government statisticians recorded 44 million living in poverty by this time; the national living standards centre, using a different methodology, identified 79 million (which was more than half the entire population), and three times as many were living in poverty, on these calculations, as in the last years of Soviet rule.[88]

Crime and punishment

There had been relatively little crime in the Soviet system, for reasons that were connected with its lack of a full range of civil liberties. Hooliganism, robbery, violence, and corruption all existed, as *Izvestiya* explained, and on a significant scale. But crime was unable to gain enough momentum to compete with law enforcement. Money was influential, but not all-powerful. There were millionaires, but they were underground; gangs formed, but they had to take enormous risks to equip themselves with weapons.[89] In any case, there were relatively few rich people with objects of value in their homes; it was less easy than in the postcommunist years to leave the country or to send stolen goods abroad; and it was almost impossible to conceal the movement of large sums of money when the only banking system was operated by the state itself. Crime statistics were not reported until the late 1980s, when the party leadership decided to make them available;[90] the 1988 statistical yearbook contained a new section with a wealth of detailed information drawn from the files of the Ministry of Internal Affairs, but it also showed that overall rates of crime had been falling since the start of *perestroika* and that the most serious crimes, including murder or attempted murder, had been falling in parallel.[91] The 1961 Party Programme, still valid when Gorbachev came to power, claimed that with rising prosperity and a higher level of consciousness it would eventually be possible to 'eliminate crime' entirely and to replace sentencing with forms of moral guidance.[92]

The political and economic changes that took place at the start of the 1990s, in the event, 'swept away the dams of repression that had held back the potential for crime' and led to what *Izvestiya* described as a 'criminal revolution'.[93] Rates of recorded crime were already increasing in the late 1980s, and over the years of *perestroika* the number of cases more than doubled. There had been an almost continuous increase over a much longer period, with particularly sharp increases in 1983 (when Andropov was conducting an organised campaign and crimes were more likely to be reported), in 1989 and in 1992. By this time reported crime was running at three times the level of the late 1970s; the real level, as in other countries, was considerably higher, as only half of all victims bothered to inform the police.[94] There were further increases in the years that followed, and new forms of crime began to emerge on a significant scale including kidnapping, drug-running, contract killings, and the pirating of computer software. Other crimes were less novel, but their form had changed: the incidence of arson, for instance, was much the same, but there were far greater losses of life and property, and the cases that occurred were much more likely to stem from the struggle for dominance among criminal groupings.[95] About a fifth of the working population, by this time, were estimated to be engaged in various forms of criminal or 'pre-criminal' activity;[96] and levels of recorded crime were expected to rise still further as the economically marginal increased in number (almost half of those who were sentenced in the late 1990s had no regular employment),[97] and as even more Russians turned to drink (more than a third of all crimes were committed 'in a state of intoxication').[98]

There were changes among the criminals as well as in the crimes they committed. They were still overwhelmingly male (over 84 per cent in 1996), but their origins reflected a rather different society. In 1990 more than half of all offenders were workers, and just 17 per cent had 'no constant source of income'. By 1996, those who had 'no constant source of income' were the largest single category, responsible for 48 per cent of all those detained; and of these, about a tenth were unemployed.[99] About a third of all offenders had previous convictions, a proportion that had changed little over the years, and the proportion that were juveniles fell slightly, although their absolute numbers almost doubled.[100] But there was a very large increase in the number of offences that were committed by groups, and particularly by organised groups: from 3,500 in 1990 to 26,400 in 1996.[101] And the death penalty was clearly no disincentive: more sentences of this kind were carried out than anywhere else in the world apart from China and Ukraine,[102] and the 'ultimate measure of punishment' was retained in the new Criminal Code that came into effect in January 1997 in spite of strong pressure from the world community (in Chechnya, in accordance with Islamic law, there were public hangings).[103]

Table 5.2. *Recorded crime, 1990–7 (thousands)*

	1990	1991	1992	1993	1994	1995	1996	1997
Total cases	1,840	2,173	2,761	2,800	2,633	2,756	2,625	2,397
Murder or attempted murder	16	16	23	29	32	32	29	29
Grievous bodily harm	41	41	54	67	68	62	53	46
Robbery	83	102	165	184	149	141	121	112
Theft	913	1,243	1,651	1,580	1,315	1,368	1,208	1,054
Number of offenders	897	956	1,149	1,263	1,442	1,586	1,618	1,372
Number of sentences	538	584	661	792	725	1,036	1,111	1,013

Source: Rossiiskii statisticheskii yezhegodnik. Statisticheskii sbornik (Moscow: Goskomstat Rossii, 1997), pp. 269–71 (for 1990 and 1991); Rossiya v tsifrakh. Kratkii statisticheskii sbornik (Moscow: Goskomstat Rossii, 1998), pp. 119–20, 122.

There were significant regional differences in the forms and levels of reported crime. Moscow, for instance, favoured shootings as the ultimate means of resolving differences; St Petersburg preferred bombs.[104] The Far East, Urals, and north Caucasus were the parts of the country most heavily involved in the undeclared or illegal economy, according to the Interior Ministry, with more than half of all economic activity controlled by criminal groups; these included the resource-rich regions of Tyumen' and Tatarstan, and the major ports. In the Volga basin, which was more agrarian and more likely to have a Communist local administration, the corresponding figure was less than 20 per cent. Overall, black marketeers, criminals, and corrupt officials were estimated to control more than two-thirds of the natural resources and of the industrial potential of the whole country.[105] In terms of the number of reported crimes, several regions in the Far East had levels that were up to twice the national average, and these were also the areas with the highest levels of crime against the person as well as against property. The lowest levels – presumably because their peoples were too busy fighting a war of independence to be bothered to collect police statistics – were in the northern Caucasus, and in Moscow (but not St Petersburg).[106] Most violent of all was Tyva, with a rate of murder and of other crimes against the person that was nearly five times the national average;[107] perhaps not coincidentally it was also the region with the lowest life expectancy – for urban males, just forty-nine.[108]

The Far East, as these figures suggested, was an area of particular difficulty, and four of its towns headed the list of urban areas in which there was a particularly high level of organised crime (Vladivostok, Nakhodka, Ussuriisk, and Khabarovsk);[109] across the whole region there were further forms of specialisation in the kinds of crime in which its population typically engaged and in the ethnic groups with which they were most closely associated. A high level of crime was related to a number of circumstances, among them the region's relative openness to the outside world with border crossings into China, a free economic zone, and several busy trading and fishing ports. This encouraged a substantial 'market of intimate services' centred around restaurants, massage parlours, and casinos, extending in some cases to the export of prostitutes to nearby countries. There was also a substantial and illegal trade in weapons, many of them supplied by the armed forces that were based in the region (local police found 150 depth charges in the boot of a car whose driver had simply been presented with them after a particularly good-humoured drinking session on board one of the ships of the Pacific Fleet). There was a narcotics trade, in which the region had specialised since prerevolutionary times; Vladivostok connected the 'golden triangle' in South-East Asia with lucrative markets in Europe and the USA, and levels of addiction were themselves higher than in the parts of Asia from which the drugs originated. Other forms of organised crime were more characteristic of the country as a whole, such as the improper operations that had taken place in the privatisation of the fish processing industry and the illegal export of capital through fictitious joint enterprises which brought together the interests of former state directors, the new *nomenklatura*, and the largest criminal groupings.[110]

Russia, of course, was not alone in reporting an increase in crime, and in violent crime particularly. Equally, the incidence of crime appeared to have peaked in the mid-1990s, after which there was a slight fall in the number of reported cases and in the most violent crimes against the person. But the number of offenders, if not of individual cases, continued to rise, and it did so even though levels of reported crime were already very high by international standards. Levels of crime, for instance, were almost twice as high in relation to population as in any of the other post-Soviet states.[111] And levels were high as compared with the major Western nations. There were more murders in Moscow, for instance, than in New York;[112] indeed there were more murders in Russia in relation to its population than in any other country in the world, apart from South Africa: there were three times as many as in the United States, often considered a violent society, and more than thirty times as many as in the United Kingdom.[113] Russia was also distinctive in the extent to which organised crime – loosely described as 'the mafia' – had 'permeated every pore of entrepreneurship and trade' and was 'dominating both legitimate and illegitimate economic sectors simultaneously',[114] including half the banks and 80 per cent of joint ventures with foreign capital, and perhaps 40 per cent of the economy as a whole (there were even higher estimates).[115] A particularly alarmist report prepared for the US Congress in 1997 warned that criminals had already seized power and that the whole country was on the way to becoming an ungovernable and mafia-dominated nuclear super-power.[116] A Sicilian mayor, visiting the country the same year, was reminded of 'Italy after the Second World War'.[117]

Women were much less likely to engage in crime than their male counterparts, and they accounted for no more than 16 per cent of all offenders.[118] Women were particularly associated with certain forms of crime, such as the theft of personal or state property, abuse of office for private gain, consumer fraud, profiteering, and the illegal sale of alcohol; they also accounted for a significant proportion of other forms of criminal activity that were less easy to identify, such as bribery.[119] Women were less likely to find themselves in court, given that they could often plead the necessity of looking after young children and had the use of 'powerful emotional arguments such as tears, a confession, and a promise not to do it again'.[120] Women, nonetheless, made up an increasing share of all offenders in the late 1990s,[121] and they were involved in several new developments including an increasing number of cases in which they were used as 'bait' by gangs of criminals. There were also cases of 'outright emancipation' in which a woman herself assumed the leadership. A gang that had been responsible for seventeen murders in Moscow, for instance, had been under the command of a woman with a 'long criminal record' who directed twelve heavily armed associates; and women were also prominent in the drugs business, sometimes 'ladies with a higher and frequently medical education' who had formerly been law-abiding citizens.[122]

Contract murders were another new development. Until the 1990s, they were something that Russians 'used to know about only from films about the Italian mafia';[123] but 'these days', commented *Izvestiya*, 'reports that a banker's Mercedes has been blown up, that a general director has been shot down in the entranceway to his home, or that the entire family of a chief administrator has been slaughtered dot news-paper pages and fill the airwaves'. To begin with the criminals were settling scores among each other, and simply reducing their own numbers. But then the chairman of a Council of Entrepreneurs became the victim of a contract murder, and there was a series of attempts on the lives of enterprise executives as well attacks on those who were attempting to uphold the law. Weapons, at the same time, had become more widely available, many of them in the hands of private security forces.[124] Nor was it only the influential or prosperous that were being targeted: at least in Moscow there were increasing numbers of attacks on single people or the mentally ill, and on small shopkeepers and out-of-towners. The going rate was from $2,000 upwards, but for a really important figure more than $1 million was necessary.[125] A professional killing, by the late 1990s, could be as easily arranged as 'say, a restaurant dinner',[126] and hitmen were advertising their services in the local press, seeking 'any kind of one-off dangerous work' (they could also be hired to conduct 'conversations' with reluctant debtors).[127]

Crime was particularly pervasive in the sale of property. There were murders, for instance, of the owners of privatised housing; there were several Moscow 'firms' that specialised in the buying and selling of apartments on this basis.[128] Alcoholics could also be persuaded to sell their newly privatised flats, and if necessary to abandon their children.[129] Elderly people, particularly those who lived alone, were at particular risk from semi-legal firms that pressured them into signing over their property.[130] In 1993 more than 30,000 elderly Muscovites had been persuaded to sell their flats; enquiries later revealed that nearly 2,000 of them had come to a violent end.[131] A gang in Yaroslavl', less than 200 miles from Moscow, was found in 1998 to have established an entire system of this kind. They made friends with local people, many of them drifters or alcoholics, and offered them work outside the city. Once they had signed a contract they were lured to a property in the countryside and suffocated. The bodies were disposed of and the gang then took control of the flats by transferring ownership through a chain of middlemen, forging signatures from the victims' contracts. To avoid arousing the suspicions of relatives the gang sent telegrams home on behalf of the murdered owners and drew their pensions; they also killed one of their informers who had tipped them off about their fifteenth victim, a priest. The gang was finally caught as its members were covering the bodies of the last of their victims with concrete.[132] There were further conflicts over the control of graveyards, which had become a lucrative form of private business.[133]

More complicated arrangements had to be made when enterprises were being sold to their workforce. First of all retired workers would be visited under the pretence of distributing 'humanitarian aid', and for a symbolic sum of money or after a brief discussion would be 'persuaded' to part with their shares in the enterprise in which they had worked. The head of the personnel department would then be bribed or threatened to provide a list of the current workforce, who would be visited systematically in the same way. The plant's managers would typically be offered 'advantageous terms of surrender', or if necessary threatened. The public auction of shares was turned into a 'stage play with extras in place and roles assigned in advance'; then the sale itself took place, with a representative of the interested criminals in a prominent position in the hall and with an entourage of thugs. As much as 70 per cent of the real estate put up for auction in St Petersburg, in the early stages of privatisation, ended up in the hands of purchasers who had been identified in advance, and who were often mafia kingpins laundering the money they had obtained through other activities.[134] More generally, an estimated 35 per cent of all capital and 80 per cent of all voting shares had passed by the late 1990s into criminal hands,[135] and they also had access to a 'parallel monetary system' consisting of dollars and a variety of surrogates that allowed them to escape state control entirely.[136]

Crime had also become more inventive. There were 'ambulancemen', for instance, who called at the front door to tell unsuspecting parents that their children had been involved in an accident. This was often enough to allow them to gain entrance to the family home, and then to take whatever they wanted; there were 'dozens' of such cases in the late 1990s.[137] There were body-snatchers, who called distraught relatives and offered to relieve them of a corpse for the relatively modest charge of a million rubles (about $70 at the time) and more promptly than the state's free collection service, which might take three days to arrive. The body-snatchers were mostly off-duty or former health department workers who bought up old ambulances and who found their opportunities when they were tipped off, for a percentage, by the police or by a doctor or nurse involved in registering the death. The typical fee, for health service workers, was the equivalent of an average monthly salary.[138] The repair of motor vehicles, particularly if they were Western and expensive, was another means of potential enrichment; in a spectacular case in the summer of 1998 the staff of a back-street and apparently innocuous Moscow garage were arrested after police exhumed the bodies of ten victims from their workshop floor.[139] Crops were seized from the fields, forcing farmers to organise armed patrols;[140] there were even cases of the theft of therapeutic mud from lakeside health resorts.[141]

Most serious crime was carried out by organised gangs, of which there were an estimated 3,000 in the late 1990s with a total 'staff' of about 60,000 – the equivalent of three divisions during the Second World War, or in other words a 'real army'.[142] They had divided up the country into their respective spheres of influence, and often had a wider network of international contacts. Many were based on a particular nationality, often from the Caucasus, and these were distinguished by their particularly high level of commitment. In Moscow they were most often Azerbaijani or Chechen, each group with its own specialisation: drugs and gambling in the case of the Azerbaijanis, oil and banking in the case

Plate 5.3 'Look, I've bought myself a pistol with a silencer' (*Izvestiya*, July 1996)

of the Chechens; Armenians, by contrast, specialised in car theft and swindling, Dagestanis in rape, Georgians in robbery and hostage-taking, the Ingusheti in gold mining, weapons, and precious metals.[143] Around the country there was a further specialisation into 'zones of influence': there were three main criminal gangs in St Petersburg, for instance, who among them controlled the entire city; in Krasnodar territory a Kemerovo group dominated the city of Novorossiisk, Abkhazians were in charge of Krasnodar itself, and an Omsk group commanded the coastline.[144] Gangs of this kind, moreover, were 'virtually uncatchable', as they had good connections within the police and local government; figures with a criminal record, indeed, were elected mayors in a number of Russian towns and cities including the third largest, Nizhnii Novgorod, as part of what *Izvestiya* called a 'criminalisation of power'.[145]

Corruption, particularly within government itself, was a more general issue.[146] In the view of Transparency International, a Berlin-based body that gathered the opinions of businessmen on such matters, Russia had one of the highest levels of state corruption in the world, ranking forty-seventh out of the fifty-four countries that were assessed in 1997.[147]

Another organisation, Control Risks Group, put Russia at the top of its world corruption league, with Nigeria a close second.[148] Up to half of the income of criminal associations, it was estimated, was used to bribe officials at various levels. Indeed there were indications, by the mid-1990s, that the criminal and governmental worlds were becoming so closely associated that they had become a single entity.[149] It was an impression reinforced by the number of state officials that were found guilty of serious offences, including the chief prosecutor himself, Alexei Il'yushenko, who was arrested and imprisoned in 1996 on charges of abuse of office and bribe-taking, and the former minister of justice.[150] Ordinary people were less frequently involved in cases of this kind, but according to the survey evidence about 14 per cent had been swindled, 13 per cent had been obliged to pay bribes, and 5 per cent had been involved in protection racketeering.[151]

Russian crime, by the late 1990s, was often conducted on an extravagant scale (after eleven people had been shot in a single incident in Saratov newspapers remarked that even Al Capone had eliminated no more than seven at a time).[152] And the whole of public life was affected. Several Duma deputies, for instance, were murdered.[153] General Lev Rokhlin, chairman of the Duma armed forces committee and chairman of the oppositional Movement for the Support of the Army, the Defence Industry and Military Science, was shot dead in the summer of 1998 in what was apparently a domestic disagreement.[154] An attempt was made to blow up the leader of the Party of Economic Freedom, Konstantin Borovoi, but he 'survived by a miracle'.[155] The prominent liberal politician, Galina Starovoitova, was less fortunate: she was shot dead in November 1998 with her aide in what appeared to be a political murder.[156] There was a still higher level of fatalities among deputies' assistants, who had increased rapidly in number. Positions of this kind conveyed a number of advantages, including easy access to buildings, and some politicians were prepared to offer them for sale, for between $4,000 and $5,000 each; deputies, for their part, found that assistants with a criminal background were well informed and often in a position to 'get things done' when more conventional methods were unavailing. For these and other reasons, there were as many as 15,000 assistants by the late 1990s: one deputy alone had 132;[157] others, it emerged, had simply obtained false documents.[158] By the late 1990s they were being killed at the rate of one a month.[159]

There were equally heavy losses among government officials and ministers. A deputy minister of justice, for instance, was found 'lying in a pool of blood' after being attacked with a kitchen knife, with his breakfast on the table and his tea still warm.[160] Another minister was killed in a drunken brawl.[161] In other cases, also in the summer of 1996, the head of administration in a Moscow region was shot, the general director of the federal food agency was killed in his office, and a deputy head of administration in the Moscow region was shot dead at her own front door.[162] In the summer of 1997 the deputy governor of St Petersburg, a reformer who had been responsible for the city's privatisation programme, was shot dead in his car in the city centre; the director of the city's seaport and his deputy had been killed the previous month.[163] Several regional governors were attacked, although none was fatally injured,[164] and judges were killed in their courtrooms.[165] Mayors were also at risk: the mayor of Nefteyugansk, a major oil-producing city in central Russia, was shot dead in the summer of 1998 in a contract murder after he had led rallies of local oil workers who were demanding their back pay; his aide was badly wounded.[166]

There were still more numerous casualties in the economy, a reflection of the extent to which business and crime had become interconnected. Bankers were particularly vulnerable. The chairman of the Russian Agricultural Bank, for instance, was shot dead in the entrance to his home when he was returning from work,[167] the chairman of a business bank was shot dead in 1995,[168] and there was an attack on the chairman of the central bank in 1996;[169] altogether, more than a hundred bankers had lost their lives over the previous three years.[170] There were similar losses at the level of enterprise management: the commercial director of a publishing firm was shot by snipers in 1997 as he left his home, in spite of the protection of a bodyguard; the same firm's deputy director had been shot dead in his car the previous year in intrigues that were apparently connected with the lucrative contract to print schoolbooks – publishers' incomes were otherwise too small to interest serious criminals in matters of this kind.[171] Three executives at the motor company Avtovaz were killed in a single month, and its management had to appeal to the government for assistance.[172] The head of Russia's largest diamond-processing company was shot in the summer of 1998 in a suspected contract murder that took place near his country home, and the director of the Rossiya hotel, on Red Square and Europe's largest, was shot as he made his way to the office (his predecessor had also been murdered).[173]

The sporting world was another area that attracted criminal activity, not least because of the substantial sums that were transacted. The manager of Moscow Spartak soccer club was murdered at her dacha in a Moscow suburb, in what was clearly a contract killing; the club manager, an 'unwanted witness', was killed in the same attack, and the director's brother was seriously wounded. It was organised crime's 'first open demarche in the realm of soccer'.[174] The president of the Russian Hockey Federation, Valentin Sych, was shot dead and his wife was wounded in the spring of 1997.[175] Many sports clubs became 'offices' for mafia groups, where they held regular meetings; a 'love of sports [had become] a sign of membership in the mafia, as it were'.[176] Organised crime reached beyond clubs themselves into sports schools and charitable foundations for the support of athletes. The first such foundation, named after legendary goalkeeper Lev Yashin, was set up by Otari Kvantrishvili, himself a former athlete who was 'known for his philanthropy' but who was also 'one of the leaders of organised crime in Moscow', and who was gunned down in the spring of 1994. The funeral was attended by particularly large numbers of 'foreign cars and people in cashmere coats and jackets'.[177]

A number of particularly brutal murders were associated with the Afghan veterans' association and its chairman, Mikhail Likhodei, who had been blown up together with his bodyguard in the entrance to his home.[178] In an unprecedented development, a bomb was set off at a mourning service in Kotlyakov cemetery in Moscow on the second anniversary of his killing – 10 November 1996, which as it happened was 'Police Day'. The bomb went off when the new chairman of the association was making the funeral oration; he and twelve others, including Likhodei's widow, were killed instantly, and about eighty were wounded.[179] The association, it emerged, had been given two sanatoria by a government anxious to honour its wartime heroes, and it had enjoyed a number of additional and very lucrative privileges such as the right to import all kinds of commodities duty-free and to export petroleum, timber, and metal. The veterans, however, needed money rather than commercial opportunities, and so they had reached an accommodation with the criminal underworld.[180] The outcome was a rapid growth in the volume of imported alcohol, cigarettes, and food, free of taxes and customs; soon the association was turning over about $100 million a year and making large profits, few of which were used for the benefit of the veterans.[181] The murder of one of the leading members of the All-Russian Society for the Deaf had a similar explanation.[182]

Journalists reported these and similar developments at some risk to their own lives. More than twenty journalists were killed in 1994 alone,[183] among them Dmitrii Kholodov, an investigative journalist for *Moskovskii komsomolets* who had uncovered evidence of the illegal sale of arms by troops returning from Germany and who was killed by a booby-trapped suitcase that he had been told contained incriminating evidence.[184] Another spectacular murder took place in 1995 when the popular television producer Vladimir List'ev, who had just been appointed executive director of Russian Public Television and who had begun to clean up the sale of advertising, was shot dead in what was evidently a contract killing; Yeltsin described it as a tragedy for 'all of Russia'.[185] Some journalists – including Westerners – lost their lives covering the war in Chechnya;[186] others died when their investigative reporting began to inconvenience important interests in the business and political world in their locality. The deputy editor of a local newspaper in St Petersburg died in the summer of 1998 after he had been beaten up by thugs outside his home; his briefcase was seized, together with the material on the political activities of local banks that he had collected for the next issue.[187] The editor of an independent paper in Kalmykia who had been a consistent source of embarrassment to the republic's authoritarian president was killed earlier in the year.[188] Altogether, 135 journalists had died during the five years up to 1997.[189]

Most gruesome of all were the cases of serial murder and even cannibalism that were reported in provincial Russia in the 1990s. The most spectacular was the 'Russian Ripper', Andrei Chikatilo, who was pronounced sane and sentenced to death in a court in Rostov in 1992.[190] A graduate of Rostov University and a former party member, Chikatilo had been suspected of child abuse while a schoolteacher but was allowed to leave quietly so as to preserve the reputation of the institutions in which he had worked. He was brought to trial in 1991 and accused of fifty-three murders over a twelve-year period, and of mutilating and occasionally eating parts of his victims (the balance of his mind had apparently been disturbed when his younger brother had been cannibalised during the Ukrainian famine of the 1930s, and he had difficulty sustaining normal sexual relations).[191] Few were aware that another serial killer had been on trial at the same time in an adjoining courtroom; or that there had been ten serial killings in the region in the previous three years, a Russian and (apparently) a world record.[192] There was another serial killer in Taganrog, with an obsession for girls in black stockings;[193] yet another, arrested in 1997, had kept five women in an underground dungeon where he tortured and sexually abused them before forcing some of them to take part in the ritual murder of the others.[194]

Human flesh, indeed, was 'back on the menu' more generally. In Saratov, a watchman was arrested in 1994 after he had broken into a hospital morgue, stolen human remains that had been removed during surgery, and sold them as meat in the local market.[195] Others carried out the surgery themselves. In 1997, an elderly woman was arrested after the half-eaten body of her husband was found in her flat. Two unpaid soldiers in the Far East were reported to have eaten one of their colleagues. And a 'quiet street sweeper with a keen interest in cookery and pets' was picked up in St Petersburg after an inspection of his flat and particularly of his kitchen revealed various parts of three of his friends; he urged arresting officers to take the buckets of human bones for stock 'so they wouldn't go to waste'.[196] In the city of Novokuznetsk in Siberia the same year, a killer responsible for as many as eighty deaths was believed to have eaten 'at least some' of his victims, parts of whose dismembered bodies were found in his flat.[197] In the same city a mother and her son and daughter had combined to murder thirty women and then turn them into meat pies which they sold as snacks at street corners, making cannibals out of their unsuspecting customers.[198] In a city in the Urals the following year, a man was arrested as he left a shop where he had gone to get mayonnaise and meat cubes to use in preparing dinner from the dismembered body of a dinner guest that he had suspected of trying to molest his girlfriend.[199]

The next generation of Russian businessmen, some hoped, would inherit the wealth that had been created for them by what were often criminal means and would be able to limit themselves to 'mere tax evasion, as is the case in civilised countries'.[200] There was no evidence, however, that the incidence of crime was levelling off, as the newly rich consolidated their acquisitions. On the contrary, there was a further rise in the late 1990s in all notified crime, and serious crime was up by more than the average;[201] there appeared to be some connection with the economic difficulties that had included the collapse of the currency, and with the uncertainties in the banking world that led more Russians to keep their valuables at home. Domestic difficulties had meanwhile encouraged the Russian mafia to enterd a 'higher, international stage of its development',[202] with at least a thousand organised groups relocating some of their activities to the West including the laundering of funds, mass hijacking of luxury cars, prostitution, drug trafficking, illegal immigration, and 'even the murky world of international football transfer fees'.[203]

There were few means of dealing with the problem, moreover, given the understaffing and underpayment of the police and of the court system. Russians, explained *Izvestiya*, 'fear[ed] not just criminals but the police too'.[204] No fewer than 11,000 law enforcement officers were arrested in 1997 alone; some had been responsible for a crime wave of their own, as in the case of a group of officers who were charged with a 'four-year reign of terror in which they murdered, robbed, tortured, and extorted money from businessmen in a manner no different from [that of] the gangsters whom they were employed to suppress', all of this under the guidance of a senior official in the Interior Ministry.[205] The prison system was itself a danger with about a million in detention, a figure that was about a half of the entire prison population of Europe,[206] and with many of them suffering from tuberculosis and other illnesses that represented a threat to the whole population. A United Nations official compared Russia's pre-trial detention centres, where many of the prisoners were held, to Dante's Inferno.[207] And a 'nuclear mafia' was developing, taking advantage of poorly guarded weapons sites and of scientists who had to maintain their families by whatever means were available to them.[208] At least for some, there was a danger that Russia could become a 'mafia state' or a 'corporatist, criminal oligarchy' on Latin American lines;[209] at a minimum, it greatly complicated any attempt to establish a genuine market economy, or a political system that was based upon the accountability of government to elected representatives rather than a small number of powerful interests. Equally, it threatened to leave a 'whole generation' for whom it would appear more normal to 'hire a killer to punish a partner who [had] wronged them than to go to court or arbitration'.[210]

Gender, politics, and society

Women, the Soviet constitution stated, had 'equal rights'. They had equal rights to training and remuneration; they were expected to take an equal part in social and political life; and 'special conditions' would allow them to combine these duties with the responsibilities of motherhood, including paid maternity leave and a gradual reduction in working hours for women with young children. Nearly all women, in fact, had a job, and women represented just over half the workforce. They predominated in traditionally female occupations like book-keeping and librarianship, but they also accounted for 60 per cent of engineers and nearly two-thirds of all doctors (as compared with 12 per cent in the USA), and even in the chemical and petrochemical industries they were as numerous as their male counterparts.[211] Women could retire at fifty-five (men only at sixty, even though women lived longer). Women, moreover, were excluded from particularly arduous forms of employment such as night shifts and mining; they had the right to be transferred to lighter work during the later stages of pregnancy; and they were guaranteed nearly four months of maternity leave at full pay – or a year's unpaid leave, if they preferred – without losing their position or seniority. Women made up half of all the deputies to the elected soviets, and they accounted for about a third of the seats in the national parliament; and there were signs, as Gorbachev told the 27th Party

Congress in 1986, that they were being 'more actively promoted to leadership positions' at all levels of the state and party.[212]

Despite these achievements, it was widely recognised that a real and not simply a formal measure of equality had yet to be established. Women, for a start, were concentrated in less well-paid positions, so that their average earnings were only two-thirds of male earnings.[213] Within each occupation, women were concentrated in less senior positions – they were 75 per cent of all schoolteachers in 1990, for instance, but just 39 per cent of secondary school directors; and they were just 6 per cent of factory directors.[214] The same was true of political life. Women had secured the right to vote in 1917, well ahead of other countries, and they had more seats in the USSR Supreme Soviet (as the authorities proudly claimed) than in 'any capitalist parliament'; but only one or two ministers were women, or about 1 per cent of the total (in the government that was formed in 1984, indeed, there was not a single woman).[215] Women, similarly, accounted for about a third of all the members of the CPSU, but they were just 8 per cent of its Central Committee and almost non-existent within its leadership (only 3 women out of a total of 157 had ever been elected to the party's ruling Politburo, and only 6 out of 103 had ever been members of its Secretariat).[216] The outcome, the Central Committee's commission on women and the family concluded, was the 'effective removal of women from decision-making', and a more general neglect of the 'energies and potential' that they could bring to public life.[217]

Some of the shortcomings in official policies had already been identified in the late Soviet period. Zoya Pukhova, chair of the Soviet women's committee, pointed out that the USSR lagged behind many developing not to speak of developed countries in its attention to women's rights, and called for 'more profundity' in the speeches of Gorbachev and other leaders on these matters.[218] She told the 19th Party Conference in the summer of 1988 that nearly 3.5 million women worked in conditions that contravened the labour law, and 4 million were employed, supposedly on a voluntary basis, on night shifts (this was twice the number of men who were employed at such times). Wage rates were formally equal, but women's pay was actually less than that of men because they were concentrated in less well-paid occupations and at lower levels of seniority. The economic reforms had added to their difficulties, as under conditions of self-financing enterprises were less willing to take on women with small children or to grant them the shorter working day and longer holidays to which they were entitled. And so far as careers were concerned, 48 per cent of men but only 7 per cent of women with a college or higher education were in managerial positions.[219]

Some sociological research on women's 'double burden' was presented by a deputy culture minister in early 1989. Women, it was found, spent an average of forty hours a week on domestic duties, while men spent just six. An average woman brought home 2.5 tonnes of shopping a year, and walked about 12 kilometres about the house every day in carrying out her domestic duties. This left, on average, just seventeen minutes a day for the upbringing of her children.[220] A woman's working week, others calculated, averaged over seventy-six hours, a man's just fifty-nine.[221] And women, as Pukhova had noted, were much more likely to suffer from the changes that were taking place as the central planning system gave way to a more uncertain and commercial environment. Women, for instance, were the first to be sacked when there were economic difficulties. Many of them worked in the textile industry, which began to contract when supplies of cotton from Central Asia dried up; many more were single parents, for whom a salary was normally their only source of income. Kindergartens, meanwhile, were being sold off, and children's clothes had become much more expensive. Women were working longer hours to maintain their earnings, or just to keep their jobs. Fewer were taking training courses, and fewer still were going on to management positions.[222]

Inequalities of this kind were not new; but what was novel was a developing discussion on women's social roles which reflected Western feminist influence, and was also a response to Gorbachev's somewhat old-fashioned views on such matters. Addressing the 27th Party Congress in 1986 he called in wholly conventional terms for a shorter working week and longer periods of maternity leave in order to allow women to combine motherhood with employment.[223] In his book *Perestroika*, published the following year, Gorbachev was equally concerned to encourage the active involvement of women in working life and in politics; at the same time he insisted that more attention should be paid to women's 'specific rights and needs arising from their role as mother and home-maker, and their indispensable educational function as regards children'. While they were out working, he went on, women no longer had enough time to devote to their 'everyday duties at home – housework, the upbringing of children, and the creation of a good family atmosphere'. Many social problems had arisen from the weakening of family responsibilities; there was also the danger of women working in strenuous occupations that were a danger to their health. All of this, in Gorbachev's view, had led quite properly to a discussion of 'what we should do to make it possible for women to return to their purely womanly mission'.[224]

These were not necessarily the views of Soviet women themselves,

Plate 5.4   The last inhabitants of a village in the Yaroslavl' region (Novosti)

more than 80 per cent of whom wanted to work even if there was no economic necessity for them to do so,[225] and perhaps the most distinctive element in the debate on the 'woman question' in the Gorbachev period was the cautious articulation of a specifically feminist perspective. An Irkutsk professor, for instance, asked why women party officials were always given secondary and unimportant posts. Why, in their society of supposedly equal opportunities, had they no Indira Gandhi or Margaret Thatcher? And why were there no new women's organisations or movements, as in other countries?[226] Despite 'male *perestroika* eloquence', another writer pointed out, it was women who had to deal with long queues, runaway price increases, poorly stocked chemists' shops, and illegal night work. Again, wasn't it time for a 'really serious women's movement, with its own programme, its own ideas, its left and right, even its hecklers'?[227] A still more far-reaching discussion on the whole question of gender roles began with an article by three feminist academics in the party theoretical journal *Kommunist*. Earlier Soviet writings on the subject, they suggested, had been biologically determinist. Zakharova and her colleagues argued by contrast that the division of labour was cultural in character, and that this allowed for a freer and more egalitarian choice of occupational and domestic roles. Equally, the emancipation of women made no sense without the emancipation of men, involving them, for instance, to a greater extent in the care of their children, and endowing them with 'paternity rights' as in the Scandinavian countries.[228]

The fall in female representation in the local and national elections of 1989 and 1990 led to a still more energetic discussion of women's social roles. The number of women, it emerged, had fallen from 32.8 per cent in the outgoing Supreme Soviet to 15.7 per cent in the Congress of People's Deputies that was elected on a largely competitive basis in 1989, and then to just 5 per cent in the Russian parliament that was elected in 1990.[229] This, complained a feminist academic, was 'manocracy', not democracy, and the party was itself setting a poor example, with the few women in senior positions no more than an 'alibi for men'.[230] The letters that flowed up to the Central Committee reflected similar concerns. Why, for instance, were there no women in Gorbachev's Presidential Council, established in 1990? Why could they not adopt the practice of foreign countries, in which many women were ministers and some headed the government itself?[231] Why were there only five women speakers at the 19th Party Conference in the summer of 1988 when there were 1,258 women delegates? Why had only one of those speakers given women's issues a 'political dimension'? Why were Soviet contraceptives 'roughly on a par with personal computers: rock bottom'? Why, in decision-making areas, could women 'raise their hands to vote, but not their voices'?[232]

Party leaders were slow to respond to the pressure for change, but in March 1991 the Secretariat adopted a resolution – the first of its kind since 1929 – that required women to be represented in its elected bodies in proportion to their share of the total membership. More positively, the Secretariat called for courses to be organised for prospective businesswomen and political leaders, and for the works of 'ideologists of the women's movement' to be published.[233] Women themselves had several other suggestions to make. One was to return to the quota-based representation that had prevailed in earlier years, by which women were guaranteed a certain proportion of seats in all elected bodies;[234] another was to establish a specifically women's political party,[235] or at least to ensure that a woman was nominated as a candidate in the next presidential elections, taking their cue from the election of a woman president in Ireland and a woman prime minister in Norway.[236] To help prepare women candidates for these contests of the future, 'politological courses' were organised by the women's commission of the CPSU Central Committee and the party's Academy of Social Sciences; they involved instruction in current affairs and public speaking, and a range of meetings with officials, 'American sociologists', and others.[237]

There was, in fact, no return to quota-based representation in the postcommunist period, and the special provision for women and their concerns that had appeared in the Soviet constitution was replaced by a more general statement that men and women had 'equal rights and freedoms and equal opportunities for their realisation' (Art. 19.3), and that motherhood, childhood, and the family were 'protected by the state' (Art. 38.1). In these circumstances, female political representation continued to decline. Women accounted for just 13 per cent of seats in the new State Duma that was elected in December 1993, and a single seat among the 178 that were filled in the Federation Council; in December 1995 female political representation fell still further, to 10 per cent, in part because Women of Russia had failed to win seats in the party-list section of the Duma, although three of the candidates it had sponsored were successful in single-member constituencies (see chapter 2). There was just a single woman in the presidium of the new Russian government that was formed in October 1998.[238] And there was a 'dramatic drop' in the proportion of women in local government: in Moscow region, for instance, they made up 47.7 per cent of the deputies that had been elected in 1987, but by 1992, in what was now a genuinely competitive exercise, their proportion had fallen to 9.5 per cent.[239] This, clearly, was a long way from the practice in the Scandinavian countries, where women were represented equally with men in all bodies of state power (and where men, including single fathers, had equal rights in domestic and family matters).[240]

The fall in female political representation took place against a background of social and economic change that affected women even more directly than their male counterparts. It was women, for a start, who suffered most directly from the 'feminisation of poverty'. Families with children were in the most difficult position of all, especially those that were headed by a single mother (there were about 6 million such families). Among single-parent families with children under the age of six, more than half had incomes below the poverty line, as did nearly half the single-parent families with children under sixteen.[241] Women were less likely to be unemployed than men, and the proportion of women among all those unemployed was falling, not increasing.[242] Women, however, were a majority of the rural unemployed, they were a still larger proportion (63 per cent) of those who were registered with the federal employment service and receiving benefit, and it took them slightly longer to find a new job.[243] Women were still concentrated in certain occupations, such as education and the health service; more than a fifth of all women were working in industry, although this was much less than in the Soviet period; and women had been losing their position in trade, finance, and insurance as they became better paid and, in practice, male professions.[244] Women's earnings, for such reasons, fell even further behind, from about two-thirds to just 45–50 per cent of those of their male counterparts.[245]

With economic difficulty came a wider deterioration in family life. Kindergartens closed down, or charged the kinds of fees that put them beyond the reach of ordinary parents; as a result, there was a fall of about a quarter in the number of such institutions in the early post-communist years, and of about a half in the number of children that attended them.[246] There was a similar fall of about a third in the number of children that spent their summer in holiday camps, particularly residential ones.[247] There were fewer hospital beds for sick children, or for their pregnant mothers; but there were more children in orphanages (the number that had been left without parents more than doubled between 1990 and 1996).[248] Social benefits were still being paid, but they were estimated to cover no more than 8 per cent of the cost of bringing up a school-age child.[249] More children became homeless, as their parents found it impossible to maintain them or indeed to sustain a family home; and there was a 'new category of homeless', children whose parents were alcoholics who had been persuaded to sell their apartments and then 'disappear who knows where', leaving the children to their fate.[250] The figures were contested, but there was general agreement that the problem was worse than it had been during the postrevolutionary or postwar years.[251] Between 1 and 2 million neither attended school nor had any form of employment.[252] And there was more violence against children than before; every year up to 2 million were subjected to regular beatings, 10 per cent of them were beaten to death, and 2,000 were driven to take their own lives.[253]

Fewer Russians were getting married, in the early postcommunist years (the level fell by about a third between 1990 and 1996), and more were getting divorced (the highest levels ever recorded were in 1995, although they moderated the following year).[254] There were fewer births than at any time since the war, and more abortions; already twice as numerous as births, they were expected to increase still further as economic difficulties pushed up the price of contraception.[255] A higher proportion of births than ever before were to unmarried parents (more than a quarter of the total in 1997).[256] Marriages themselves, moreover, were far from tranquil. Every year about 14,000 Russian women died as a result of domestic violence, about four times as many as in the United States, and more than 50,000 were maimed or otherwise injured.[257] The first crisis shelter in Moscow opened in 1993; it had about 2,000 visitors a year, including all kinds of women – 'housewives, women who hold Candidate of Science degrees, and businesswomen'. The police could intervene, under the criminal law; but all too often 'the wife changes her mind: how can she put the father of her children in jail?'[258]

Sexual harassment was also increasing, as employers took advantage of their position. Lena, for instance, was delighted to get a job at a water plant in Murmansk until the division head started showing up at night to see if she was 'following instructions', and then to demand 'sexual services'. He was drunk, he stank, and on every shift the same thing happened. In the end she had to go to the police. Women employees elsewhere were 'often forced to provide sexual services to a firm's clients and its bosses or were forced to have sex when they [came] to interview for a job'. In the 'kiosk business', where there were no laws and rarely any documents, sales staff were 'reduced to the status of concubines of medieval feudal lords'. Businesswomen had the same problems when it came to finalising a contract; 'sexual services' were sometimes demanded, in addition to payment, for the 'most ordinary commodities'. There had always been problems of this kind; but with jobs hard to find and insecure, it had become much worse. According to what survey evidence was available, one out of every four women had been a victim of a sexual assault – and not simply verbal innuendo – at the workplace during the first five postcommunist years.[259]

Another result of women's postcommunist 'emancipation' was a rising incidence of prostitution. Originally, in the Soviet period, it had been considered a phenomenon that was confined – at least in principle – to capitalism; but in the Gorbachev years its existence was openly acknowledged, and not just as an 'integral part of Moscow's tourist "service"'.[260] In one of the earliest studies, *Sovetskaya Rossiya* interviewed a police chief in the district that accommodated three of Moscow's largest railway stations who had made a special study of the 3,500 or so prostitutes that had come to the attention of his department. They were of various ages and origins, but the typical case was a 'dynasty' of mother, grandmother, and daughter, all working the same patch, and all displaying the same physical attributes, 'the vacant look, the puffy and unwashed faces, and tousled hair'.[261] Legislation was introduced in 1987 to deal with the problem (it had not, up to this point, been illegal), but the fines involved were so small that it was scarcely a disincentive. Some, even in the Ministry of Internal Affairs, were prepared to argue in favour of the legalisation of prostitution under these circumstances.[262]

The problem took on new dimensions in the postcommunist period, and became increasingly closely associated with organised crime. It was estimated to be the third-largest sphere of criminal activity in terms of the amount of money involved, after gambling and the drugs business.[263] In Moscow, the city's smartest shopping street, Tverskaya, was also the busiest;[264] but, as the popular press reported, 'for $200 you can have oral sex in the very centre of our motherland – on Red Square'.[265] It was the responsibility of the police, in the first instance, to deal with matters of this kind; but so far from regulating it, the police (it emerged) had become increasingly involved. They provided the girls with a cover by registering them as 'undercover agents', and helped madams to keep track of their girls by reporting the whereabouts of any who ran away. The policeman, in these circumstances, could claim that his 'regular contact with the madam' was for 'information-gathering purposes', while the madam, if arrested, could claim that she was not breaking the law but, 'on the contrary, working to enforce it'. A favourite stratagem was for a policeman to stop the car once a client had got in and made his payment; it would then be discovered that the girl had no internal passport or proof of registration, and she would be put into a patrol car and driven back to her point of origin.[266]

As in other societies, there was male as well as female prostitution. Many of them advertised their services in local papers: 'Sympathetic young man, sixteen, will place his well-built body in the lustful hands of a woman up to forty. Your every fantasy will become a reality'; or 'Blue-eyed blond, twenty, wants to be the sex toy of an older woman (or two)'; or 'man, twenty-two, seeks a well-off virgin who would like to become a woman and is in a position to pay for her education'. The main requirements, it appeared, were that the man should be well-dressed, clean-shaven, sweet-smelling, in good physical form, and of course his 'organ must always be in working condition'. Yelena, for instance, was a businesswoman who had divorced a first husband, and lost a second; but a woman had to be 'physiologically satisfied'. So she engaged Vladimir, ten years younger, and treated him as a 'stern mistress'. Irina had parted from her husband, who 'drank like a swine', but she was bringing up a teenager and could afford to engage a lover only once a week. Vera had lost both her legs, but her parents – at what cost she had no idea – had engaged Valerii, a 'high-class professional'. Now she always looked forward to Thursday – 'Valerii day'. Although a relative novelty in Russia, male prostitution of this kind was apparently 'growing more quickly than in other countries'.[267]

There was also underage prostitution. Sveta, for instance, was just nine years old, and had been abandoned by her mother. A car used to come for her every week and she would spend two or three days at a Moscow address, where several young girls would '"serve" five or six men'. By the mid-1990s this was a 'real social phenomenon, not something out of the ordinary', involving perhaps 20,000 cases every year.[268]

The Komsomol newspaper talked to another girl, just past her sixth year of schooling, who was involved in work of this kind, but only with Germans, British, and Americans ('I can't stand the smell of Arabs, Negroes, or Poles: I'd rather lie under a train than under those guys'). She sometimes obliged Russians, but just 'once in a while'. Many of these unfortunates were picked up at train stations; some were abducted; and some were bought from their parents, who were often alcoholics.[269] There had traditionally been a lot of demand at Black Sea coastal resorts as well as in the cities, but business declined sharply because of the war in Chechnya and the girls had to go elsewhere, some to Moscow, some to St Petersburg, and some to Odessa ('there are no punters at all because of that damned war', Lucy, a 'long-legged blonde from Kislovodsk', told *Argumenty i fakty*).[270] Prostitution was, however, a 'part of everyday life for most homeless children', and their number was increasing rapidly.[271]

Prostitution was also a thriving export trade. Using marriage agencies as a cover, girls with 'good physical attributes' were being offered highly paid work abroad, including the opportunity to find a foreign husband or become a photographer's model. At first they went to Yugoslavia, but there was a risk of 'ending up as a slave for some military unit'; more preferred Budapest, in spite of 'fierce competition from the Romanians', because of the large number of Germans from the former GDR who came there on sex tours. The first 'ladies of the night' had gone to Israel, where language was not a problem, and to Greece, because of its relatively easy passport regime; they also went to China, where they started as waitresses and were then required to 'entertain the guests'. Russian girls were 'very popular among the hot-blooded Turks', who were also popular with 'our Natashas';[272] 'new Russians', they complained, were 'almost all impotent' because of the 'nervous nature of their business'.[273] The 'richest and most attractive country' was Germany, where Russians were 'creating some serious competition for girls from Eastern Europe', although 'top-quality' girls also went to Sweden, where they worked in expensive hotels and restaurants.[274] Russians were travelling to Asia as well, in the late 1990s, encouraged by lax immigration regimes and corrupt officials; and they were popular with locals, who found they were unusually accommodating: 'in fact', a Colombo businessman told Western journalists, 'they'll do anything'.[275]

Inevitably, there was cost to pay in public health as well as moral terms. Levels of syphilis, in particular, increased spectacularly. There were five cases in 1990 for every hundred thousand Russians, which was a lower level than in earlier years; by 1996 there were 265. Levels of gonorrhoea also increased, though much more modestly.[276] The first

AIDS death had occurred in 1987; there had been 173 deaths by 1997; and it was estimated that there would be as many as 800,000 HIV carriers by the turn of the century.[277] The whole question was debated in the Duma in the spring of 1997, in the form of a bill that sought to restrict the sale of sex products to a number of specially licensed shops. There were over 4,000 illegal brothels in Moscow alone, deputies were told, sales of sexual products were running at $5 million a month, and about a thousand pornographic journals were in national circulation. At the same time the nation's 'golden genetic pool' was being exported to the sex markets of the West. Vladimir Zhirinovsky, always inventive, suggested a different approach: after all things were 'much calmer' on a nudist beach than on an ordinary one. Often, he pointed out, 'when certain parts are covered, you start to think what might be hidden there'. Wasn't it all a matter of sex education? Or take Russia's Muslim regions; women were covered from head to foot, and 'there's no sex'. As for the charge that there had been 'no sex under the Communists', on the contrary, pointed out Al'bert Makashov, 'I have three children and five grandchildren already, and we get along fine without your pornography.'[278] Clearly, there would be no early solution to a set of problems that existed in all industrial societies, and which in Russia had become entangled with a number of much more specific difficulties associated with organised crime, falling living standards, and a loss of moral bearings.

6   Changing times, changing values

Just as the Soviet Union – or so its citizens told Western television interviewers – 'had no sex', it also had no 'public opinion'. Social consciousness, in the official view, was a reflection of forms of property; in a socialist society, based on public ownership, it was characterised by the 'dominance of Marxist-Leninist ideology in all spheres of the spiritual life of citizens'.[1] In a society of this kind, it was argued, there was 'sociopolitical and ideological unity', and the views of workers, collective farmers, and members of the intelligentsia were 'identical on the basic questions of social development'.[2] It was a unity, moreover, that extended across the nationalities as well as the social groups, genders, and generations. Nationalism, the official view maintained, was a 'bourgeois ideology' that developed under capitalism, and whose purpose was to set worker against worker.[3] Under Soviet conditions it had been superseded by 'socialist patriotism', a set of beliefs that included 'boundless love for the socialist homeland, a commitment to the revolutionary transformation of society [and] the cause of communism', and by a 'proletarian internationalism' that brought together the peoples of the USSR and of other countries, particularly those under communist rule.[4] All were entitled to express their views; but there were no differences of opinion, and certainly no fundamental differences of interest, that could not be reconciled through the leadership of a broadly based Communist Party.[5]

There could clearly be little scope, in these circumstances, for Soviet social scientists to explore any of the issues that might have exposed the limitations of this basic unity. A centre for the study of public opinion had been established as early as 1960 by a Moscow University philosophy graduate, Boris Grushin, under the auspices of the youth newspaper *Komsomol'skaya pravda*. Taking advantage of the paper's enormous circulation, Grushin and his colleagues used its pages to distribute a series of questionnaires and then to publish their analyses of the very numerous responses they received. The questions ranged from the causes of war to living standards and the qualities that were typical of Soviet youth: patriotism and collectivism were represented, but so too were alcoholism and delinquency, and there were no questions at all on which there was a single opinion.[6] In 1967, however, the newspaper was obliged to close its public opinion department, and although Grushin was able to establish another centre within the Academy of Sciences it survived for just a couple of years.[7] Official policies were hardening by this time, in the aftermath of the suppression of the Prague Spring, and the study of public opinion was 'effectively banned';[8] the sociology institute attached to the Academy of Sciences came under heavy pressure, and a hard-line director was imposed in order to restore orthodoxy.[9] Yuri Levada, a Moscow University professor who had published a two-volume set of *Lectures on Sociology*, was attacked in the party's theoretical journal and forced to resign his academic position; Grushin himself found it impossible to publish the results of the surveys he had conducted in the Taganrog area in the late 1960s and had four manuscripts turned down by Soviet publishing houses between 1967 and 1981. When he took his study of *Soviet Society in Public Opinion Polls* to one of them, the response was 'Are you crazy or what?'[10]

In spite of these restrictions, there were still some indications in officially sanctioned publications that party and people were not quite as 'closely united' as the slogans claimed. Grushin's study of the Taganrog area, for instance, was finally published in 1980, although it had to have a coauthor from the Central Committee apparatus. Entitled *Mass Information in a Soviet Industrial Town*, it was able to identify a number of shortcomings in the regime's self-image including a considerable disparity between the mostly negative letters that local newspapers received and the mostly positive articles they published.[11] A legal scholar, Rafael' Safarov, was able to undertake a parallel investigation of the relationship between citizens and local government, based on surveys in Moscow and the nearby city of Kalinin. Safarov found that the existing forms through which public opinion could influence public decisions were 'not always effective'; members of the public were much less likely than officials to suggest that local administrators took public opinion into account, and 32 per cent reported that the decisions taken locally were often at odds with the views of local people.[12] Workers, similarly, were in theory the 'masters of production'; but as empirical inquiries established, they were often reluctant to play a part in management, or even in the discussion of enterprise affairs.[13] For attentive readers, it was clear that there could often be tensions between official orthodoxies and the world in which they actually lived; indeed it was for this reason that wits demanded an 'ear and eye' hospital, as they 'heard one thing, but saw something completely different'.

Not even the Soviet system, in fact, could operate in an informational vacuum. Local organisations of the Communist Party had been conducting their own inquiries, in some cases since the mid-1960s,[14] and there were repeated calls for a centre or institute that could conduct investigations of this kind on a more comprehensive basis.[15] In 1986, in his first address to a party congress, Gorbachev pointed out that no laws had yet been drafted to provide for the nationwide discussions that were mentioned in the constitution, and he went on to urge that better use be made of all the means that were available for 'eliciting public opinion and quickly and sensitively responding to the people's needs and attitudes'.[16] *Perestroika*, Gorbachev made clear, could succeed only if ordinary people were persuaded to identify with it; equally, public policy would be soundly based only if it took account of the realities of daily life, and not just of abstract principles. The party leadership, indeed, began to call directly for the 'use of sociological research in the practice of decision-making', and for a public that was 'better informed about the main questions of social development'.[17] Public opinion had certainly become legitimate by the late 1980s – official sources suggested that its role was already 'hard to overestimate'[18] – and an infrastructure had been established for its study that was expanded further in the postcommunist period. What, so far as these methods could establish them, were the concerns of ordinary Russians over nearly a decade in which their country had undergone a fundamental change in its forms of ownership and political management?

Public opinion and its study

The Communist Party had committed itself to a national public opinion centre as early as 1983, when a plenary meeting of the Central Committee agreed that a 'feedback mechanism' was needed of a kind that would allow the party to take account of changes in the public mood. It was time, officials insisted, to move from individual studies to a more broadly based examination of public opinion, 'and perhaps to the organisation of a centre for the study of public opinion'. The resolution that was adopted went still further, providing for the establishment of an 'all-union centre for the study of public opinion' that would be located within the Institute of Sociology of the Academy of Sciences.[19] Gorbachev, at an early stage, had identified the need for a more informal, interactive relationship with the society over which he ruled. How, he asked a group of writers in June 1986, could they monitor their own activities? The answer was 'most of all through *glasnost'*', but also through a 'responsible opposition' of the kind that existed in parliamen-

Plate 6.1 'Your attitude to opinion polls?' (*Izvestiya*, January 1994)

tary democracies.[20] Speaking to the 19th Party Conference in 1988, Gorbachev pointed to the need, under conditions of single-party rule, for a 'constantly operating mechanism for the comparing of opinions, of criticism and self-criticism in the party and in society', or in other words a 'permanent and constructive political dialogue' that would involve the 'study and taking account of public opinion', and he reminded delegates of the damage that had been done in environmental and other matters when proposals had gone ahead without the 'broadest possible consultation'. No one, as the Conference made clear in its resolutions, could have a 'monopoly on truth'.[21]

A national public opinion centre had already been established at the end of the previous year, under the direction of the outspoken sociologist Tat'yana Zaslavskaya.[22] The Centre, in the first instance, was concerned with the study of public attitudes on 'social and economic issues', and it was sponsored by the All-Union Council of Trade Unions as well as the State Committee on Labour and Social Questions. The purpose of its work, Zaslavskaya explained in an interview in March

1988, was to 'provide the most accurate possible guidance for the organisations that are responsible for making decisions'. There would be an emphasis upon speedy responses, and upon the fullest possible distribution of the Centre's findings; and there would be about ten-to-twelve national surveys every year, concentrating initially on prices, wages, and pensions. Decisions taken at the highest level, she pointed out, might often be well founded. But were they transmitted in their original form to those who would have to carry them out? And what did the broader public think of them?[23] The Centre's first survey, on the election of managers by the workforce, was published shortly afterwards,[24] and its bulletin, *Obshchestvennoe mnenie v tsifrakh* (Public Opinion in Figures), began to appear in 1989. The Centre – better known by its Russian initials VTsIOM – soon built up a Moscow staff of about a hundred, with thirty-five regional offices elsewhere in Russia or in the former Soviet republics, and by the late 1990s it was interviewing nearly a quarter of a million of its fellow citizens every year in more than 170 nationally representative surveys as well as about 100 exercises of a more commercial character.[25]

Vox Populi was established two years after VTsIOM, in 1989, under the direction of Boris Grushin. In 1993 alone the service conducted 106 surveys, asking over 15,000 respondents a total of about 800 questions.[26] Vox Populi came to specialise in work with the political elite, or 'leaders of public opinion'; based on interviews, it reported their changing assessment of government performance and of questions such as the position of Russians in the 'near abroad' and the relative standing of Yeltsin's political opponents. A regular feature was the 'political Olympus', a league table of the 100 most influential politicians based upon the judgements of fifty journalists, commentators, and analysts, and normally published in the newspaper *Nezavisimaya gazeta* as well as in the service's monthly bulletin. Apart from VTsIOM, Vox Populi, and several other Russian bodies such as the Public Opinion Foundation and ROMIR (Russian Public Opinion and Market Research), surveys were regularly conducted by the Centre for the Study of Public Policy at the University of Strathclyde, whose New Russia Barometer first appeared in 1992,[27] by Eurobarometer, which was sponsored by the European Commission,[28] and by the United States Information Agency, in each case working through a local agency.[29]

Surveys were the best way of establishing the distribution of opinion across a heterogeneous and changing society; but, in part because the society was changing so rapidly and because there was still some reluctance to express views on public issues (or even, with the increase in crime, to open the front door),[30] they were often ambiguous and – in their election forecasts – a poor guide to future behaviour ('Why', asked *Segodnya*, 'does Russia never vote the way it is supposed to?'[31]). Telephone surveys were particularly problematic because not much more than a third of the population had access to a receiver, and the last available census, conducted in 1989, was increasingly irrelevant as hundreds of thousands became refugees or changed their address for other reasons. As elsewhere, surveys could in principle provide a representative impression of the public mood, but they were best interpreted within a context that took proper account of the ways in which ordinary citizens were inclined to conceive of their own problems, on the basis of their own experience. And this, in turn, could be gathered from letters to the newspapers, from the wider world of cultural expression and from behaviour itself as well as from methodologies that were more familiar in a Western context. Russia, the poet Tyutchev had insisted, could not be 'understood', it could only be 'believed in'; and some of the questions that were being considered in the late 1990s, including what it meant to be a Russian in the first place, were resistant to almost any form of conventional inquiry.[32]

What, so far as surveys were concerned, were the main concerns of ordinary Russians as the century drew to a close? For the most part, they had little to do with constitutional design, or Russia's place in a very different world, or even the crisis in culture and public morality: most people were more concerned about how they were to earn a living in a rapidly changing economic environment (see table 6.1). In the late 1990s, it was prices and delays in the payment of wages that came first in the list of public concerns (only a third of those who were asked in 1999 had received the previous month's salary in full and on time).[33] The next most important public concerns were unemployment, the economic crisis, increasing crime, and the widening gap between rich and poor.[34] The conflict in Chechnya had become a less acute concern after a settlement was brokered in 1996, and the problem of 'shortages' almost disappeared as the shops began to fill up with goods for those who could afford them. There were few worries, equally, about the 'threat of fascism and extremism'. Unemployment, however, was a cause of mounting apprehension in the late 1990s; only 16 per cent thought it was unlikely they would lose their job in a 1997 inquiry, nearly three times as many thought it quite likely they would do so, and more than a quarter reported that there had been mass sackings at their workplace over the previous three months.[35]

What about the market, to which Russians had been committed by their government even before the end of communist rule? To begin with, the popular view was broadly supportive; but as the consequences of a

Table 6.1. *Public concerns, 1991–8 (percentages)*

	1991	1992	1993	1994	1995	1996	1997	1998	1999
Prices	69	62	84	84	77	63	47	40	87
Shortages	56	50	28	10	12	8	7	5	13
Increasing crime	28	37	64	68	58	60	54	50	43
Weakness of state power	20	21	33	34	35	29	40	37	34
Environment	19	15	29	26	31	27	26	24	13
Unemployment	18	22	30	49	48	63	54	65	60
Moral crisis	16	22	25	26	27	28	26	26	20
Nationalities	14	22	20	12	25	20	15	13	9
Economic crisis	–	–	45	51	47	54	47	57	58
Leadership divisions	–	–	30	16	12	10	15	12	9
Corruption	–	–	19	22	23	26	38	32	25
Social inequality	–	–	–	–	33	37	45	41	36
Unpaid wages	–	–	–	–	–	–	–	67	56

Source: National representative surveys conducted by the All-Russian Centre for the Study of Public Opinion as reported in *Moskovskie novosti*, no. 38, 1991, p. 5; *Nezavisimaya gazeta*, 7 March 1992, p. 2; *Ekonomicheskie i sotsial'nye peremeny*, no. 2, 1994, pp. 52–3, no. 5, 1995, pp. 57–8, no. 6, 1996, p. 61, no. 5, 1997, pp. 47–8, no. 5, 1998, p. 57, and no. 2, 1999, p. 56. Not all questions were asked in all years, and not all responses are included (in 1996 one of the main public concerns was the Chechen war, at 51 per cent, and in 1997 the 'threat of a military dictatorship', at 63 per cent).

market became apparent, including unemployment and higher prices, ordinary Russians became increasingly disillusioned (see figure 6.1). By the late 1990s, in the surveys that were conducted by VTsIOM, Russians were more favourable to a system 'based on state planning' (37 per cent) than to one 'based on market relations' (28 per cent), with a substantial 35 per cent who found it difficult to make up their minds.[36] Eurobarometer, in a separate exercise, found similarly that 24 per cent of Russians thought a 'market economy, largely free from state control' was 'right for [their] future' but that more than twice as many (59 per cent) took the opposite view, with support for the market at a lower level than in any of the other postcommunist countries that formed a part of the survey.[37] There was overwhelming agreement, in particular, that the state should provide a job for all who wished to work, and that it should guarantee a basic standard of living for all its citizens.[38] At the same time, a majority thought a free-market economy was 'necessary for Russia's economic development',[39] and there were as many who thought the reforms 'should be continued' as who believed they 'should be ended' (29 and 28 per cent respectively)

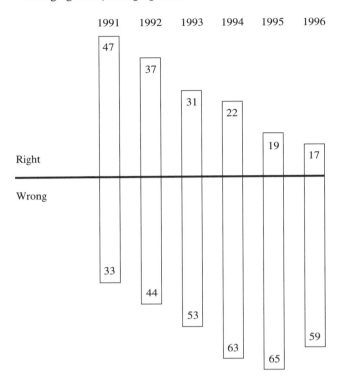

The question was: 'Do you personally feel that the creation of a market economy, one that is largely free from state control, is right or wrong for Russia's future?'
Source: Adapted from the *Central and Eastern Eurobarometer*, 1992–7.

Fig. 6.1 Attitudes to the market, 1991–6

– still larger numbers (44 per cent) had no view one way or the other.[40] Russians, it seemed, wanted a 'socialism that worked': one that had all the advantages of the market economy (including a greater availability of consumer goods and incentives for harder work) as well as what they saw as the positive qualities of a command economy (including a comprehensive welfare system, limited inequality, and guaranteed employment).[41]

Russians, in fact, were not entirely dissatisfied with the economic position of their own family, which they presumably knew best: for the largest number (41 per cent) it was 'average', and for 4 per cent even 'good' or 'very good'. But for 39 per cent it was 'bad' and for 15 per cent 'very bad',[42] and increasing numbers – 46 per cent in 1998 – told interviewers it was already 'impossible to put up with such a miserable existence'.[43] Russians were still gloomier about the economic position of the country as a whole: just 1 per cent, in 1998, thought it was 'good', and 14 per cent thought it 'average'; by contrast, 49 per cent thought it was 'bad' and another 30 per cent thought it 'very bad' – this, moreover, before the collapse of the currency and the sharp increase in prices that took place later the same year.[44] Confidence in the economy had been steadily declining, and few thought there would be an early economic improvement.[45] Only 8 per cent thought the 'hardest times' were already behind them; 23 per cent thought they were living through them; but twice as many (47 per cent) thought the hardest times were still ahead.[46] And how long would it take the government to 'solve the economic problems in the country'? For the largest single group (35 per cent), it would take from six to ten years; but for the next largest group (24 per cent) it would 'never happen' (24 per cent).[47]

What kind of a system did they actually have, Russians were asked in 1998? An enthusiastic 16 per cent thought they were experiencing the 'development of democracy', but 14 per cent thought it was the 'preservation of the old order under a new name' and much larger numbers (48 per cent) thought it was simply 'anarchy'.[48] The great majority of Russians defined the political situation as 'tense' (53 per cent) or even 'explosive' (34 per cent).[49] And few thought the government was in effective command: 17 per cent took this view, but more than three times as many (56 per cent) thought national affairs had already 'escaped from their control'.[50] In these circumstances, there was strong support for the idea that Russia needed 'order' (77 per cent) more than it needed 'democracy' (9 per cent).[51] In broader terms, 32 per cent of Russians had thought their country was 'going in the right direction' in 1991, as communist rule came to an end, but only 19 per cent did so five years later; conversely, 41 per cent thought their country was going in the 'wrong direction' in 1991, but 67 per cent did so five years later.[52] Eurobarometer, in a similar exercise, found that 18 per cent thought their country was 'going in the right direction' in the late 1990s but that 63 per cent took the opposite view, and that (once again) Russians were more dissatisfied than their counterparts in any of the other postcommunist countries.[53]

At least in retrospect, the principles of socialism were also attractive. Who, for instance, were the 'most outstanding political leaders in Russia's history since 1917'? The first choice was Lenin (21 per cent), followed by Stalin (15 per cent) and then Andrei Sakharov (11 per cent).[54] For whom did ordinary Russians feel the greatest sympathy, in 1997? Lenin again came first, followed by secret policeman Felix Dzerzhinsky (both, admittedly, with much less support than they had enjoyed at the start of the decade), and then by Nicholas II and Stalin.[55] Russians, it emerged, were as likely to think that the Stalin years were the 'best for their country' as they were to cite the postcommunist period, and although the prerevolutionary period was more widely favoured, the most popular choice of all and by a very wide margin was the late Soviet years when Brezhnev had been in power (59 per cent).[56] What, in fact, would today's Russians have done in October 1917? About a third (31 per cent) told interviewers they would have supported the Bolsheviks; 42 per cent would have taken no direct part; and only 6 per cent said they would have fought against the new regime (overall, 49 per cent took a broadly positive view of the revolution and 35 per cent were generally negative).[57] More than half of those who were asked, similarly, thought it would have been 'much better if the situation had remained the way it was before 1985',[58] and about a third, asked to 'base themselves on their own experience', were 'completely in favour of that form of socialism that existed in our country before 1985', with fewer (30 per cent) opposed and many others 'neither for nor against' (25 per cent).[59] These, however, were abstract choices, and more typical of older generations and rural residents; only a minority, although a very large one, thought it would actually be better in the circumstances of the late 1990s to 'restore the communist system', and only a quarter wanted the Communist Party to 'become the most influential political force in Russia again'.[60]

Russians were still more emphatic in regretting the passing of the USSR. Although the level fluctuated, about two-thirds of those who were asked in a succession of surveys were generally inclined to think it a 'great misfortune' that their old state no longer existed.[61] And it was clear why they regretted its passing: in particular, it was the most obvious cause of their economic difficulties.[62] The weekly paper *Argumenty i fakty* went out into the streets to ask ordinary Russians to put their responses into their own words. The first person they talked to, a young man temporarily out of work, was 'for the USSR, however stupid that might sound'. Yelena, a businesswoman, was against – it could 'only mean the return of psychiatric prisons, lies, and censorship'. But Ruslan from Tajikistan wanted 'everything to be like it was before'. Sergei from Moscow thought the three 'Slavic brothers' were 'simply fated to live together'. A visitor from Grozny was 'for the Soviet Union, naturally'. And Boris, a down-and-out, had a simple explanation:

'When there was a USSR, I had a flat. Now there is no USSR – and I've no flat either.'[63] The largest proportion of those who were asked in 1996 to identify their 'homeland', in fact, told interviewers it was the USSR (28 per cent), just ahead of the proportion who thought it was Russia (27 per cent), and nearly as many thought it was the region in which they lived.[64]

The worst feature of communist rule, respondents agreed, was certainly bureaucracy. The old regime had also 'oppressed rights' and it had been corrupt to some degree, although there were also some who thought it had no faults. The best features of communist rule were more obvious: there was guaranteed employment (indeed for most of the Soviet period it was illegal not to work); there were no ethnic conflicts (not least because any nationalist activity was suppressed); and there was a stable economy, with prices for basic foodstuffs, housing, and public transport that (until the last years of Soviet rule) had not changed for decades.[65] What, asked VTsIOM, were the main characteristics of the Soviet system that ordinary Russians had experienced between the 1970s and 1990s, and of the postcommunist system that had succeeded it (table 6.2)? The Soviet system had certainly been 'bureaucratic' and 'short-sighted'; but much larger numbers thought it 'accessible' or at least 'familiar', in spite of its lack of more conventional democratic attributes. The postcommunist system, by contrast, was just as 'short-sighted' as its Soviet predecessor, but the most general opinion was that it was 'corrupt and criminal', 'remote from the people', or even 'illegal', in spite of its foundation in a freely adopted constitution.[66] As for the postcommunist government, the most common view was that it was composed of 'people who were only concerned about their privileges and income', or for whom 'the main thing was power itself' (57 and 49 per cent respectively).[67]

The Russian government, admittedly, was not the only one that found it difficult to retain the support of those who had elected it, or to sustain a commitment to the political process itself. Russians, however, were much more dissatisfied than their East European counterparts. As the New Democracies Barometer discovered, East Europeans were also unhappy with their current economic situation, rating it below the communist past, but they saw the future as an improvement on both the present and the communist past. Russians, by contrast, saw the future as an improvement on the present but rated the future as well as the present below the economic system they had known in the communist years.[68] East Europeans, equally, were more satisfied with the system of government under which they were living than with the system of government they had known in the communist past, and they expected

Table 6.2. *The 'most characteristic' features of communist and postcommunist rule (percentages)*

Soviet rule, 1970s–80s		Postcommunist rule, 1990s	
Close to the people	36	Criminal, corrupt	63
Legal	32	Remote, alien	41
'Our own', familiar	32	Irresolute	32
Bureaucratic	30	Weak, powerless	30
Strong, firm	27	Short-sighted	28
Short-sighted	23	Bureaucratic	22
Authoritative, respected	21	Parasitic	18
Secretive, closed	17	Illegal	12
Just	16	Unprofessional	12
Honest, open	14	Incompetent	11

Source: Derived from *Ekonomicheskie i sotsial'nye peremeny*, no. 3, 1998, p. 57 (national representative survey, February–March 1998, n = 1500).

to be still more satisfied in the future. Russians, by contrast, were once again more discontented and more pessimistic: for them the postcommunist political system was less satisfactory than the one they had left behind, and although they expected some improvement in the future they still took the view that the political system that was likely to have developed in five years' time would be worse than the one they had experienced in the Soviet past.[69] Overall, a majority in Central and Eastern Europe had negative views about the communist system and positive views about the present and future; in the former Soviet republics the opposite was the case.[70]

In these circumstances, in whom could ordinary Russians place their confidence? In practice, in the late 1990s, they asked their family or friends about the difficulties they encountered (59 per cent), or else they relied upon their own resources (33 per cent).[71] There was little confidence, certainly, in politicians: more than half of those who were asked were unable to name a single figure in public life that they could trust (53 per cent), and only 4 per cent chose President Yeltsin.[72] There were low levels of confidence, indeed, in almost all public institutions: just 11 per cent had confidence in the president, fewer had confidence in the government and the Federal Assembly, and fewest of all – less than 5 per cent – had confidence in the political parties. There was rather more support, but still less than a majority, for the churches, the mass media, the armed forces, and the agencies of state security.[73] Nor was it clear that there were ideas or principles in which ordinary Russians could put their faith for the future. If there was any idea of this kind, it was 'law and order' (39 per cent) or 'stability' (36 per cent), and there was some support for 'social security' (24 per cent), 'great-power status' (23 per cent), or a 'worthy life' (23 per cent). But more ambitious philosophies had little following: just 6 per cent thought Russians could be rallied around the idea of 'freedom', 4 per cent thought Orthodoxy could play such a role, and only 1 per cent thought Russians could once again be persuaded to put their faith in 'communism'.[74]

The flow of political communication

Petitioning the authorities was a tradition that went back to medieval times, when a bucket was lowered from a window in the Old Kremlin Palace in which petitioners could place their grievances.[75] It developed in the Soviet period into one of the principal forms of communication between regime and society. The Council of People's Commissars, in the early postrevolutionary years, received about 10,000 letters a year, many of which were taken into account in the elaboration of government decrees; citizens could also address themselves to the reception offices of the Communist Party Central Committee.[76] Lenin's own postbag was itself a substantial one, including many missives that directly challenged official policies.[77] They were, he told a colleague, 'real human documents' without which 'not a single one of his speeches' would have been complete.[78] The postbag of the major newspapers was even larger: the peasant paper *Krest'yanskaya gazeta*, for instance, received more than 5 million over the ten years from 1923 to 1933 as its readers sought advice, appealed for assistance, or reflected on a socialism that was 'like the building of the Great Wall of China, which had swallowed up a lot of energy but to no obvious effect'.[79]

During the 1920s and 1930s, as the emphasis of party and state policy shifted from discovering what popular preferences might be to mobilising the masses towards the achievement of objectives that had already been centrally determined, 'work with letters' began to receive rather less attention. The soviets lost most of whatever democratic content they had originally possessed; newspapers devoted more space to record-breaking economic achievements than to the legitimate complaints of citizens; and the style of party leadership became increasingly remote and hierarchical.[80] The Stalin constitution, published in draft for national discussion, involved nearly 34 million members of the public, who among them suggested over 150,000 changes.[81] The new family legislation of 1936, however, was a better indicator of the use that was made of communications from ordinary citizens at this time. A sharply retrogressive measure, it was intended to strengthen marriage, and (among other things) outlawed abortion. A few letters appeared pointing out that 'lack of living space' was often the real problem; but the published correspondence as a whole, together with the editorial coverage, was overwhelmingly favourable. It later emerged that the great majority of letters had in fact opposed the new law but that only a few had been published, while every single communication in favour had been selected. 'The Boss says we must have more children' was the simple explanation.[82]

Letters and other forms of communication from ordinary citizens began to receive more attention during the Khrushchev period, as dictatorship mellowed into consultative authoritarianism. A Central Committee resolution of 1967 made clear that letters were 'one of the main forms of strengthening and broadening the links between party and people';[83] the first comprehensive legislation was adopted the following year,[84] and then in 1977 the new Soviet constitution established the right of citizens to submit proposals and criticisms to public bodies, and to lodge complaints against the actions of officials.[85] The discussion of the constitution that took place over four months in the summer of 1977 showed both the strengths and limitations of the exercises of this kind that were staged during the late Soviet years. More than four-fifths of the adult population were reported to have taken some part in the discussion, and letters arrived in an 'unending flow' at party headquarters; they had, Brezhnev reported, overwhelmingly said 'yes, this is the Basic Law we had been waiting for'.[86] Only much later did it emerge that the letters that were received at this time, while generally supportive, had also raised all kinds of awkward issues. Why, for instance, was there no choice of candidate at elections? Why had the CPSU been given a political monopoly in Article 6 of the constitution? And why had Brezhnev been given two Hero of the Soviet Union awards thirteen years after hostilities had formally concluded?[87]

Gorbachev had given particular attention to letters from the public during his party career and he made frequent reference to them after he had been elected general secretary, sometimes quoting directly. In April 1985, for instance, he mentioned that party members had been asking why officials held the same posts for years on end,[88] and in Kiev in early 1989 he quoted from some of the complaints that had reached him about the food supply.[89] Gorbachev was asked, during a visit to Leningrad in October 1987, if letters from ordinary people actually reached him. Yes, they did, he replied; he tried to read as many of them as possible, and took many home with him for further study.[90] A substantial part of Gorbachev's postbag came from abroad, particularly from Germany, Sweden, and the USA.[91] Paul McCartney wrote to suggest the issue of a special album of rock-and-roll tunes; Americans

Plate 6.2   In the *Pravda* correspondence department in the 1980s (Novosti)

suggested building a bridge from Alaska to Siberia ('we could then visit friends of ours on both sides'), asked for his help in completing college assignments, and offered to take the Gorbachev family to Disneyland.[92] Many others raised the same theme as a letter from which Gorbachev quoted at a press conference during his visit to the USA in 1987: if the family of man did not learn to live together, a seventeen-year-old girl had written to him, they would surely die together.[93] Gorbachev responded directly to an appeal from a retired US admiral when he announced his moratorium on nuclear testing in 1985,[94] and he used his correspondence once more when he was seeking to end the Soviet military presence in Afghanistan, circulating his Politburo colleagues with a 'flood of letters' from soldiers asking why they had been sent, and from mothers pleading to have their sons brought home.[95]

Gorbachev's postbag remained a substantial one, even in the last year of his presidential rule: more than 220,000 letters from various parts of the Soviet Union, and a further 70,000 from abroad (of which more than 40 per cent came from the USA). A special group, including lawyers and economists, had been established within the presidential administration to deal with this massive inflow. The 'most significant' of the letters, about 1,500 every year, were handed to the president personally, the remainder were used to prepare a weekly overview, 'The Post of the USSR President'. It began with a statistical summary and an indication of the main concerns that had been raised in that week's communications. In the first week of October 1991, for instance, there had been 'numerous telegrams' about the possible transfer of the Kurile islands to Japan, and from veterans who were 'angered by the renaming of Leningrad'; for the year as a whole by far the largest volume of correspondence had been concerned with relations among the nationalities. As well as summaries, the weekly digest also contained extracts from the letters themselves: from the mother whose son had died in Afghanistan who would 'strangle [the president] with her own hands', or from the St Petersburg pensioner whose ration cards had been stolen ('there was nothing like this even during the blockade').[96] Gorbachev himself told interviewers that he began and ended each day by reading from correspondence of this kind,[97] and as late as August 1991 he still read 'a proportion' of everything he received.[98]

There was a still more substantial flow of communications into party headquarters, where they were seen as a 'sensitive barometer of public opinion'.[99] More than half a million arrived every year during the 1970s, rising to more than a million in 1988 at the time of the 19th Party Conference.[100] In order to deal with this heavy correspondence the Central Committee established a Letters Department in 1978, which was later merged with the General Department.[101] Many of the letters he received, its head, B. P. Yakovlev, explained, required no particular reply: such as the letter from a captain in the Vladivostok fleet who reported to Brezhnev that his ship had 'worthily fulfilled the Ninth Five Year Plan', or from a Mr Il'in in Archangel who wrote to thank the party leader for his 'necessary, simply indispensable books' and for his 'measureless contribution to the cause of world peace'.[102] But as perestroika ran into difficulties, the letters became increasingly disillusioned and outspoken:[103] more of them were from the poor, increasing numbers were openly anticommunist,[104] and it was discontent of various kinds that predominated in the letters that were circulated to the delegates that attended the CPSU's 28th Congress in 1990.

Life, a party member and invalid complained, had 'become unbearable'. There was nothing in the shops, the shelves were empty, and they lived on vegetables from their allotment, macaroni, and milk.[105] The most basic goods, reported a veteran from Khabarovsk, had started to disappear: sugar, tea, matches, soap, washing powder, and toothpaste.[106] In the Sverdlovsk region it was 'impossible to buy painkillers'.[107] They had been 'waiting for five years for an improvement in their life', wrote Mr Zhuravlev from Tambov, but there was 'still no real change', just shelves in the shops that were getting 'emptier and emptier'.[108] The general view, in these circumstances, was 'categorically against a transition to the market by raising retail prices'.[109] The market, wrote equipment workers from the Moscow region, was 'just another robbery of the working class'.[110] A mother from Krasnoyarsk warned that her family was 'practically starving' with prices at their existing level.[111] Five years of perestroika, wrote Mr Anosov from the Kemerovo region, had been 'five years of belt tightening' for ordinary people.[112] The 'shelves were bare' in the shops, there were no socks (you couldn't, after all, 'put statistics on your feet'), and the health service was in a 'catastrophic state'.[113] Mrs Kolomnikova, a metalworker from Zlatoust, took her concerns directly to the party paper. She came back from work exhausted, she told Pravda, but there was nothing in the shops; sometimes things were so bad she just went into the bathroom to cry, turning on the shower so that her husband and children would be unable to hear her. When would the slogans about social justice finally become a reality?[114]

Similar themes were reflected in the newspapers, many of which were receiving up to half a million letters a year in the late 1980s: Argumenty i fakty received 480,000 in 1989, the trade union paper Trud 475,000, Pravda 473,000, Izvestiya 350,000.[115] A substantial staff had to be engaged to deal with these massive postbags: about ninety in Trud, and about seventy in *Izvestiya*.[116] Relatively few letters could be published in full, but *Trud* was one of the papers that could devote an entire issue every month, apart from foreign news, to the communications from its readers;[117] and *Izvestiya*, in 1987, began to publish special articles based on readers' letters – readers were even described, in a published collection, as the paper's 'main correspondent'.[118] Letters could sometimes take initiatives, even if they had presumably been authorised in advance (it was in a weekly paper, for instance, that the first public call was made for the restoration of Solzhenitsyn's Soviet citizenship; and it was a letter from a Saratov worker that asked 'How long are we going to put up with drunkenness?', just weeks before the Gorbachev leadership launched its ill-fated campaign[119]). Letters were also passed on to party headquarters: like the war veteran from the Tambov region, who complained to *Pravda* that people in the countryside harvested the grain but couldn't find any bread in their own shops; or the widow from Kishinev, who wondered how she could live on a pension of 55 rubles a month; or Mr Ledentsov from the Kirov region, who wondered how they had been constructing socialism for seventy years but there was nothing in the shops.[120] Newspapers made a telephone line available for those who wished to report their concerns directly; and the larger ones maintained reception offices that dealt with thousands of individual approaches.[121]

Letters maintained their significance into the postcommunist period; they were, Boris Yeltsin explained, one of the 'seven channels' by which he kept in touch with the opinions of ordinary people.[122] Every day up to 1,500 letters reached the Russian president, dealing with a 'broad spectrum' of problems. A department of letters and the reception of citizens with a hundred staff was set up in the presidential administration to deal with these communications, and it reported to him regularly; it prepared an analytic overview every week, as well as briefings on particular subjects. About 80 per cent of all the letters made inquiries of some kind – for instance, about the social benefits to which war veterans were entitled; 11 per cent were complaints; 4 per cent were proposals for some improvement in public life; and there were also 'quite a few' letters, usually anonymous, written in 'uncensored terms'. In all, about 350,000 letters arrived every year, raising matters from the state of the Tolstoy Museum at Yasnaya Polyana to a student dormitory in Voronezh; the information they provided, the head of the letters department explained, was 'much broader and more varied' than could possibly be obtained by stopping a thousand people in the street and asking them to say something into a microphone.[123] The president, in addition, gave interviews for the newspapers that were based on his responses to their readers' letters;[124] he occasionally replied directly;[125] and about 25,000 citizens were received every year by a member of the presidential staff.[126]

Letters, clearly, had a different function in a political system in which alternatives could be formulated in an independent press and put forward for approval by opposition parties at elections. Most of the papers, however, continued their 'work with letters' in the postcommunist period, and they remained a central feature of Russia's and for some time the world's best-selling paper, the weekly *Argumenty i fakty* (Arguments and Facts), where the editorial day began with the 'enormous bags of mail' that had come in from their readers.[127] There were, it emerged, four main kinds of correspondent. The 'irreconcilables', usually of advanced years, wanted to disagree with what the paper had to say; the 'analysts', usually over fifty, had their own ideas for the improvement of the society in which they lived; and there were the 'fighters for justice', usually over thirty, who were concerned with matters like the poor quality of the food that was provided in kindergartens. Others still had a personal concern: El'vira from Tyumen' wanted the paper to send her an electric milking machine, Viktor from Orsk wondered where he could find an egg incubator, Oksana and Valera from Kostroma wanted to get married but were short of the rubles they needed for the reception and hoped other readers could help. And there were individual but well-intentioned citizens like Mr Polevik of Moscow, who had observed a 'large collection of condoms of various sizes' floating down the river and wondered 'which institution (?!) abuses sex and throws these objects into the river' (it was letters of this kind, the paper explained, that it received with the greatest satisfaction).[128]

The letters that appeared in *Argumenty i fakty* in the 1990s raised all kinds of public issues – sometimes, indeed, the entire newspaper was devoted to them. How much, for instance, did the presidents of the CIS states earn? (Yeltsin, it emerged, was not the best paid.)[129] What about Yeltsin himself: was it true that his father had served in Kolchak's anti-Bolshevik army during the civil war? (No, but he and his brother had suffered political persecution in the late 1930s.)[130] Many letters in the summer of 1996 warned of the dangers of a Communist victory at the forthcoming presidential elections: would the Berezka shops come back, where Soviet goods were sold for foreign currency? Would soap operas on television be banned? And would sausage keep four years, until the following elections?[131] Other questions reflected the economic changes that were taking place over the same period. What, for instance, was an *off-shornaya zona*?[132] And what was a 'golden share'?[133] What were 'notebook computers', and where could you buy them?[134] Could an elderly woman bequeath her apartment to her cat? (She could, so far as the law was concerned.)[135] How could you open a licensed brothel?[136] Where could former prisoners invest their vouchers?[137] Where had members of the leadership invested their own vouchers? (Chubais, it emerged, was still making up his mind.)[138] And could you sell your body in advance of your death, asked I. Ivanov of Moscow region, who was trying to survive on a 'small pension'?[139]

Letter-writers raised personal questions more often than politics and public policy. It was to the press, for instance, that Russians turned to find out if they could take a dog on the underground, if they could buy a place in a graveyard with their privatisation voucher, if the Russian government had an astrological service, and if the presidents of the CIS states had been born under a particular sign of the zodiac.[140] And some had still more intimate concerns. Which men, for instance, were the most sexually potent, asked a women for whom it was 'very important'? (The Finns, it emerged, had the highest sperm counts per cubic centimetre.)[141] Another wrote to *Argumenty i fakty* to ask what to do with her thirteen-year-old brother who masturbated regularly but was 'too ashamed to go to the doctor'. Yuri of Saransk was in despair because he appeared to have transmitted the same unfortunate practice to his children: the 'only way out', it appeared, was 'alcoholism'.[142] The paper advised others who had asked how much it cost to engage the services of a prostitute: no more than five rubles or a glass of port wine, it reported, on Komsomol Square, where three of Moscow's main railway stations were located, but up to $300 in an Intourist hotel, and rather more for special services like a lesbian show or a bisexual act (foreigners apparently thought these charges were rather high).[143] Letter-writers were mostly pensioners and the elderly, but they also included the very young, like nine-year-old Anastasia of Irkutsk, who asked *Argumenty i fakty* to make sure that Father Christmas visited their apartment on New Year's Eve, rather than Ded Moroz, as Ded Moroz (the Russian equivalent) was 'suffering from a shortage of presents'.[144]

Russians raised a still wider range of personal concerns in their letters in the 1990s. How, for instance, could women lose weight? Polina from Penza had given up: 'diets are no use; in the evening all the same I fill myself up'.[145] Others were more successful: a thirteen-year-old girl from Chelyabinsk claimed to have lost 20 kilograms in a month by sticking to juice and porridge, and a correspondent from St Petersburg recommended apples – one for breakfast, two for lunch, and three for dinner. A more exotic proposal came from a reader in Uzbekistan, who told the magazine *Rabotnitsa* that women in her republic drank their own urine: 'It keeps us thin and makes our complexion smooth.'[146] There was

Lena, aged sixteen, who wondered what she could do about her hair, which was falling out in great quantities.[147] Others were interested in various forms of cosmetic surgery. Was it dangerous, for instance, to have silicone breast implants? (Not at all, the operation could be done in Russia itself and to 'great effect'.)[148] Was it safe to take a flight in such circumstances, or would they burst? (The paper was reassuring.)[149] And how did women with large busts manage with such a 'heavy load'?[150] A male correspondent, N. Z. of Moscow, had a rather different problem: he was a necrophile. Dead dogs no longer satisfied him, and he was going to look for employment in a morgue; but were his activities illegal? (Apparently not.)[151]

There were particular difficulties in reconciling a wider range of personal freedoms with the views of older generations, and indeed with a shortage of living space. What could you do, for instance, if your grown-up children wanted to use your apartment for their sexual encounters? When you were reaching the 'most interesting moment' and there was the sound of a key in the door?)[152] A husband and wife wanted to know what 'swinging' was. And N. Z. of Novosibirsk had 'no idea what to talk about in bed with [her] lover – not the cost of living presumably?'[153] Another inquiry was prompted by Sergei Mikhalkov's prize-winning film *Burnt by the Sun*, in which 'it was not he who was on top of his wife, but she on him!' In twenty years, wrote Mr Akulov from Krasnoyarsk, he and his wife had never thought of trying 'Mikhalkov sex'; could the paper please tell them about 'Gaidar sex' and 'Zhirinovsky sex' as well?[154] But another correspondent had no sex life at all because her husband washed very rarely and the smell in the house was unbearable.[155] Husbands themselves wrote in to ask what they should do because they had a problem sustaining an erection and as a result were unable to satisfy their wives.[156] Some wanted advice about less conventional relationships. L. P. of Lipetsk, for instance, wanted to know 'Can a woman love another woman?'[157] Thirteen-year-old Olga wrote in similar terms to share the 'problem, even misfortune' that she was obsessed with a female singer.[158] There were girls who were in love with their brothers ('unfortunately, he loves me too').[159] L. M. of Nizhnii Novgorod wanted to know if two cousins, 'secretly in love', could get married, as aristocrats used to do (it all depended how closely they were related).[160] Others still wanted to know if inflatable dolls were 'sold anywhere for sex in our shops' (they were, but not as often as vibrators; so it might be men, not women, who became redundant).[161]

But most often readers were just curious. Had Graeme Greene, for instance, been a spy? (He had.)[162] Did cosmonauts, after a long time in space, have dreams in which they were flying?[163] And a married pair of cosmonauts had been sent into space by the United States: a reader wanted to ask the 'delicate question' whether they had made love in these weightless conditions, 'at least for scientific purposes?'[164] Other readers asked what pets government leaders had; and N. G. of Arzamas wanted to know if cats could manage without sex, as he lived on the eighth floor of an apartment building and never let his pet outside the building.[165] What, asked other curious readers, did priests earn? And did prostitutes get pensions?[166] What was President Bush's pension? In which films had Ronald Reagan acted, and where in Russia could they be seen? And had any American states ever tried to become independent?[167] What was a 'computer virus'?[168] Was it true that Michael Jackson had a skin disease, and that he had already died?[169] And that a Russian émigré had designed the US one-dollar bill? (It was.)[170] If there was no longer a USSR, asked still further readers, what was to become of Heroes of the Soviet Union?[171] Was Turkish tea radioactive?[172] Had Lenin magically transmitted his soul to Mikhail Gorbachev?[173] Was Jesus Christ a Jew or not?[174] And when He came again, would He take his believers and, if so, what about the rest?[175]

The life hereafter

Russians had lost a state and a ruling party in 1991. But more than this, they lost a belief system that had defined their entire existence. Whether or not they had internalised its values, Marxism-Leninism explained the place that Russians occupied in the world in which they lived: their place in their own society, and the place of the USSR itself in a wider process of global change. It had been an official ideology for more than two generations, and by 1989, when the last Soviet census was conducted, less than 5 per cent had been born before the October revolution and fewer still had any conscious memory of a different society.[176] Russia, before the revolution, had been an overwhelmingly Orthodox and Christian society; the churches retained their legal existence after 1917, and believers enjoyed the right to practise under successive constitutions. Official theory, however, suggested that 'superstitions' of this kind would gradually disappear along with the attitudes and values that arose from 'pre-socialist socioeconomic formations', and that a materialist world outlook would take their place.[177] Nor, it seemed, was this a misplaced confidence. Studies of religious behaviour found that levels of observance had fallen from 80 per cent at the end of the 1920s to 50 per cent by the late 1930s and to 10–20 per cent by the 1960s;[178] by the end of the 1970s levels of observance had fallen still further, to 8–10 per cent, and skilled workers, farm staff, and the intelligentsia were 'almost entirely free of religious convictions'.[179] There were certainly variations from year to year, researchers found: but the general tendency was clear, and this was the 'elimination of religion as a result of socioeconomic and cultural changes'.[180]

The evidence, in fact, was much less clear than these trends suggested. For a start, it had simply become more difficult to practise, as about two-thirds of the churches that were active before the revolution had been closed (as late as 1997 there were just over 8,000 Orthodox communities for the whole of the Russian Federation but more than 27,000 towns or villages for them to serve, and 'for many Russians, the journey from home to the nearest church took many hours, or even days').[181] Believers who were young and better educated, moreover, had every reason to conceal their faith if they had career ambitions of any kind (this, in part, was the reason for the predominance of women and the elderly among those who attended services). Even so, at least 50 million defined themselves as religious believers,[182] which was three times the membership of the Communist Party. Believers as well as atheists, in fact, had a remarkably diffuse set of personal philosophies. Believers, for a start, had an 'almost 100 per cent ignorance' of the Scriptures, and were quite ready to accept that it was possible to lead a good life without a belief in God; many, indeed, thought religion was positively harmful. At the same time almost half of the atheists who were questioned in the 1960s thought it was impossible to live without a belief in some kind of God, and the same proportion were unwilling to support a campaign against the influence that the various Soviet religions still commanded.[183] Other nonbelievers displayed icons in their homes, marked their graves with crosses, and observed church holidays 'out of habit or respect for their elders and relatives'.[184]

The end of communist rule brought about an end to a situation in which believers had been restricted in their expression of faith, and sometimes penalised. But there had been considerable changes in the public role of religion in the late Soviet years, and in any case there were many respects in which church teaching could find common ground with Marxism-Leninism, including a commitment to family life, to a strong and united Russia, and to peace with other nations and nationalities. The church was bound to favour a greater degree of freedom for its own worshippers; but it was ambiguous about liberal democracy, and hostile to Western influence including that of other churches – 'spiritual aggression', in the words of one of the most outspoken of its leaders, that could result in 'moral degeneration the like of which the much-suffering Russian people have never known before'.[185] At the same time it was the only institution that commanded a high level of public

Plate 6.3   Vespers in the Theological Academy at Zagorsk, Moscow region
(Novosti)

confidence; it offered a belief system that was the only coherent alternative to Marxism-Leninism; it had publications, property, and staff;
and its commitment to a particular leader, or to a particular set of
policies, had enormous potential influence in the unstable circumstances of early postcommunist rule.[186]

There had been few indications at the outset that the Gorbachev
leadership would be one in which there would be a reconciliation
between church and state;[187] the general secretary himself, visiting
Tashkent in November 1986, had called for a 'decisive and uncompromising struggle with religious phenomena', and was particularly
scathing about party officials who campaigned for communist values
but took part themselves in religious ceremonies.[188] But a different line
soon begun to emerge, taking its cue from an unsigned article on
'socialism and religion' that appeared in the party's theoretical journal
Kommunist in March 1988. Ostensibly a reconsideration of church–state
relations in the first years of Soviet rule, the article went on to call for a
much more general reassessment of the place of religion in socialist
society. The existence of millions of believers, it pointed out, was 'a
reality', and everything must be done to avoid 'primitivism' in dealing
with them.[189] The new line became still clearer after a meeting between
Gorbachev and the church hierarchy on the occasion of the millennium

of Orthodoxy, in which the Soviet leader spoke of the 'universal norms and customs' that both sides had in common and invited believers as well as atheists to join together in the 'common great cause of the restructuring and renewal of socialism'.[190] The Patriarch, for his part, described the Party Programme as 'highly humane' and 'close to the Christian ideal'.[191]

It was certainly clear that there had been significant changes in the position of believers and their churches by the late communist period. Gorbachev, it emerged, had himself been baptised, and his mother was a regular worshipper.[192] An early gesture of some importance was the return of the Danilov monastery in Moscow to the Orthodox Church; refurbished, it played a central role in the millennium celebrations a few years later. Other property, including the Kremlin cathedrals, had been returned by the end of the decade, and thousands of new churches had opened all over the country.[193] Another first was the meeting between Gorbachev and the Pope, which took place in December 1989; the following year diplomatic relations were formally established between the USSR and the Holy See.[194] Religious believers, even priests, began to appear in the print and electronic media, the first religious leaders were elected to the Soviet parliament in 1989, and a religious presence began to establish itself in educational and charitable work, including the first prison chaplaincies since 1917.[195] The first religious services took place in the Kremlin cathedrals in January 1990, and the first religious broadcasts went out over state television;[196] a year later, establishing another precedent, the Orthodox Christmas was celebrated as a public holiday.[197]

The last months of communist rule, in 1990 and 1991, extended the liberties of believers through a series of more formal measures. The Law on Property, approved in 1990, gave the churches full rights of ownership,[198] and a Law on Freedom of Conscience, adopted later in the year, affirmed the right of believers to propagate their faith and of parents to give their children a religious upbringing (which had up to this point been illegal if the children were aged less than eighteen). The churches themselves were given the right to take part in public life and to establish their own newspapers, although not political parties; and they were allowed to establish their own schools and colleges.[199] The Communist Party, for its part, changed its rules in 1990 to allow believers to join its ranks;[200] religion, the Secretariat explained, was based on 'general human, moral, and cultural values', and the party's aim was not to offend the susceptibilities of believers but to enlist them in 'joint action for the renewal of socialist society'.[201] The Soviet parliament, in one of its last acts, adopted a 'Declaration of the Rights and Freedoms of the

Individual' that included a guarantee of religious belief and practice;[202] the same guarantees were included in a declaration of rights and freedoms that was approved by the Russian parliament in November 1991;[203] and then in December 1993 the new constitution took matters still further, guaranteeing the 'right to profess individually or jointly with others any religion or to profess none, to freely choose, hold, and propagate religious or other beliefs and to act in accordance with them' in an article that could not be amended by parliamentary vote.

Acting within the framework of this legislation, religious groups and believers more generally had come to play a central role in Russian public life by the early 1990s. The Patriarch was the first to speak at the inauguration of the newly elected president in July 1991, and Yeltsin himself made it known that he attended a religious service 'about once a month'.[204] Both he and the Soviet prime minister, Valentin Pavlov, had attended the Easter service in the Epiphany Cathedral earlier in the year, among a 'gaggle of senior officials who stood gamely, if somewhat sheepishly, at the front of the church, occasionally bowing and fiddling with candles in an attempt to show that they were not totally unfamiliar with the Orthodox rites'.[205] Religious parties had started to form from the late 1980s, and several of them contested the 1993 and 1995 parliamentary elections: in 1995 the Christian-Democratic Union led by Alexander Ogorodnikov and the 'Nur' Muslim movement presented their own lists of candidates, and the Party of the Orthodox, the Russian Christian-Democratic Party, and the Russian Christian Democratic Movement led by Viktor Aksyuchits took part as members of a larger pre-election bloc. Symbolically, the largest change of all was the reappearance in central Moscow of the Church of Christ the Saviour, built in the nineteenth century to commemorate the defeat of Napoleon and destroyed by the Soviet authorities in 1931, but reconstructed on the basis of the original design (it was symbolic in other ways that a new commercial facility was constructed underneath it on an even more impressive scale).[206] 'Never before', commented *Izvestiya* in April 1995, had the church's 'participation in the political life of the country [been] so conspicuous'.[207]

Just as the Soviet system reflected a distinctive blend of Marxism and Russian traditions, so too the Russian Orthodox Church combined more general Christian values with a number of particular characteristics. The Orthodox Church had been a state church that was all but identical with citizenship itself in prerevolutionary Russia, and it was more closely associated with the work of government than was the case in the countries that belonged to the Western Christian tradition. There was a fairly loose concept of 'membership', and religious belief was

Table 6.3. *The main religious communities, 1997*

	Congregations	Seminaries	Monasteries	Missions
Russian Orthodox Church	7,440	38	309	5
Muslims	2,587	103	0	0
Baptists	638	2	0	45
Pentecostalists	379	3	0	43
Evangelicals	296	0	0	38
Seventh Day Adventists	254	1	0	0
Roman Catholic Church	192	3	2	6
Old Believers	177	1	1	1
Lutherans	150	0	0	4
Presbyterian Church	146	0	0	4
Jehovah's Witnesses	143	0	0	0
Buddhists	135	1	2	4
Charismatic churches	126	0	0	15
Hare Krishna	111	0	0	1
Russian Free Orthodox Church	103	0	4	1

Source: Adapted from *Rossiiskii statisticheskii yezhegodnik. Statisticheskii sbornik* (Moscow: Goskomstat Rossii, 1997), pp. 47–9.

more closely associated with participation in a shared community of believers and taking holy communion once a year than with a set of articles of faith.[208] The church stood for values that were not of this world, and it could hardly accept restrictions upon the rights of believers or the sequestration of its property. But there were reconciliations at moments of national crisis, such as the Second World War, and there were associations of several other kinds: the party leadership, in practice, made nominations to leading positions, some members of its hierarchy regarded it as their patriotic duty to report to the KGB,[209] and in the postcommunist period it began to enjoy official favour as the 'national' church as compared with unregistered and, still more so, foreign denominations and sects.[210] It was certainly clear, by the late 1990s, that this was the organised faith of the great majority of Russian believers, and that it was the only one with a genuinely national presence (see table 6.3).

Clearly, there had been a substantial change in the formal position of the churches even before the end of Soviet rule, and more churches were active in postcommunist society – at least seventy separate denominations.[211] But what had been taking place in the wider society? Were there more believers than before, and were they more active in their expression of faith? Levels of religiosity had certainly stabilised by the late 1990s after what some commentators described as an 'explosion' in

Table 6.4. *Levels of religiosity in the 1990s (percentages)*

	Orthodox	Religious
All	75	63
Gender		
Males	67	47
Females	81	75
Age		
Up to 29	76	66
30–59	74	60
60 and over	77	69
Education		
Primary	79	72
Secondary	76	64
Higher	68	51
Income (rubles/year)		
Up to 150,000	75	88
150,000–400,000	81	71
400,000–900,000	77	63
900,000–1.5 million	72	62
Over 1.5 million	66	43
Vote in December 1995		
Our Home Is Russia	80	64
Yabloko	80	64
Liberal Democrats	78	60
Communists	75	62
Nonvoters	75	63

Source: Based on a nationally representative survey conducted by Russian Public Opinion and Market Research in January and February 1996 (n = 1581). Respondents were asked their affiliation, and 'if they were religious'.

the late communist period, but this left more than half the population as self-identified believers, compared with just 10 per cent in the late 1980s.[212] About three-quarters of the society described themselves as 'Orthodox' in a general sense, but not necessarily as believers (see table 6.4); 'believers' were at least 60 per cent according to a variety of investigations;[213] and about 40 per cent had been baptised.[214] Believers, as in other societies, were disproportionately female and somewhat more numerous in the older age groups, although the young were more religious than the middle-aged (two different kinds of religiosity appeared to be involved, a more formal and traditional belief on the part of older generations and a more individual and emotional attachment in the case of younger age groups).[215] Believers, in addition, were likely to have lower levels of education than the average, and lower incomes; surprisingly perhaps, levels of belief were lowest of all in medium-sized towns, rather higher in the countryside, but highest of all in Moscow and St Petersburg.[216]

Patterns of observance were another matter again. On the major church festivals, attendances were high: more than 80 per cent of the entire population at the time of the Orthodox Easter.[217] But there were very few who attended church on a more regular basis. No more than 7 per cent of the adult population attended once a month or more often,[218] a level of attendance that was among the lowest in Europe; it compared with 19 per cent in the United Kingdom, and 48 per cent in the United States.[219] Levels of attendance were indeed so low that for the overwhelming majority they failed to satisfy the normal requirements of church membership.[220] Believers, by the same token, were unlikely to pray on a regular basis; only 30 per cent had taken communion over the two previous years; and just 14 per cent observed Lent.[221]

The beliefs of those who regarded themselves as religious were equally confused. Only a minority, for instance, believed in heaven and hell, or in life after death.[222] Believers, at the same time, were more likely than others to subscribe to a whole series of supernatural phenomena that had no place in their religion. Believers, for instance, were more likely than waverers or atheists to agree that Oriental wisdom played a 'great role in their life'. They were more likely at the same time to believe in the transsubstantiation of souls, and in extrasensory perception. Believers, similarly, were more likely than others to believe in telepathy, astrology, the evil eye, and the abominable snowman; and they were more likely than atheists, although slightly less likely than waverers, to believe in flying saucers.[223] Conversely, atheists were generally 'positive' or 'very positive' in their attitude to Orthodoxy; substantial proportions believed that the church provided answers to moral questions, and that it satisfied man's spiritual needs.[224] 'For the great majority even of those who identify themselves as believers', investigators concluded, their faith had 'practically no real content', and their participation in religious customs like colouring eggs for Easter was a 'sign of their Russianness, not real religiosity'. It was, in other words, a very 'situational religiosity'.[225]

Given these amorphous and contradictory beliefs, it was not surprising that there were few direct associations between religiosity and Russian politics. Of the major parties, Women of Russia and Yabloko attracted the most 'religious' support, but religious believers were even more likely not to vote at all, and their support for the Communist Party was just above the average. Believers, by contrast, were somewhat less likely than the population as a whole to support the Agrarians, the broadly nationalist Congress of Russian Communities and Liberal Democrats, and the pro-government Our Home Is Russia, but the differences were minor. Attendance, again, made little difference to party support, although Communists enjoyed some advantage among those who attended a service at least once a month.[226] Religiosity, equally, exercised little influence on the outcome of the 1996 presidential election. In the first round the most religious electorates were those that supported Vladimir Zhirinovsky and the Yabloko leader Yavlinsky (this mirrored the support the party had received in the Duma election); in the second round the two candidates were equally successful in attracting the religious vote, although Yeltsin did slightly better among 'believers' and Zyuganov among regular attenders.[227]

The Orthodox Church, on the other hand, had some influence in defining the legislative context within which it operated, and to its own advantage. A new law which appeared to discriminate against other religions was vetoed by President Yeltsin in June 1997, but approved by the Duma on a further reading in September and by a majority such that Yeltsin had no alternative but to sign it. The new law[228] excluded 'nontraditional' churches from educational activities, publishing literature, or visiting hospitals and prisons unless they could prove they had operated legally in Russia for more than fifteen years; the law did not state what was to constitute proof in such circumstances, but in practice it applied to Islam, Buddhism, and Judaism as well as Orthodoxy in a manner that appeared to contradict the equality of all religious organisations before the law (Art. 14 of the constitution) and guarantees of freedom of conscience (Art. 28). Several Pentecostalist groups had to revert to practices of the Soviet period, with services in garages and private flats to avoid police harassment; Mormons, similarly, found themselves arrested and 'asked to find another place for their activities'; Jehovah's Witnesses, defined as members of a 'destructive religious organisation of a Western orientation', were put on trial and charged with 'spreading religious hatred'.[229]

Church attenders, it emerged, did in fact have distinctive attitudes on many issues that were part of the postcommunist political agenda. Regular attenders, as in other societies, were typically more 'conservative' than their counterparts outside the church: they were more favourable to law and order, and more likely to believe that children should be taught respect for authority; they were more positive towards Nicholas II, but also Stalin; they were more prepared than others to ban 'harmful' books, and to isolate AIDS victims; and they were less favourable to the market, and to multiparty politics.[230] Believers, equally, were more positive towards a single Slavic state incorporating Russia, Ukraine, and Belarus, and to believe that Russia should be declared an Orthodox state with particular privileges within it for members of the national church.[231] The most religious, across the postcommunist world more generally, were more likely than others to say that 'the new rich should be jailed', and that a woman's place was in the home.[232] Believers, at least in Russia, were more anticommunist than the population as a whole (they were most hostile towards socialism as a doctrine, and to former party officials in government posts); but they were also more likely to favour order above democracy and to support a planned rather than market economy, and they were less committed to the rule of law and human rights.[233] Believers, particularly if they were regular worshippers, were also more likely to express hostility towards groups such as the Chechens and gypsies.[234]

Nonetheless, several circumstances combined to make religion a marginal influence in Russian public life in the postcommunist 1990s. There was a loose association, for a start, between affiliation and belief. In turn, there was a loose association between belief and attendance – generally, in comparative terms, the variable that had the most powerful direct influence on political attitudes and behaviour;[235] and levels of attendance were very low as compared with other European or industrial societies. Many took a positive view of the role of religion in society, and welcomed the more prominent place the churches had been assuming; but there was evidence that the Orthodox Church in particular was losing some of the trust it had earlier enjoyed, and its standing was not improved by reports of its association with the Soviet regime in the past (as the Patriarch, who had his own KGB codename, explained to *Izvestiya*, 'Defending one thing, it was necessary to give something else'),[236] nor by reports of corruption and immorality in the 1990s.[237] For believers and nonbelievers alike there was almost as much faith in Pope John Paul II as in the Patriarch, and the writer Solzhenitsyn carried far more authority in matters of belief and morality than either of them.[238] But it was equally true that very few of the parties had sought to mobilise support on a denominational basis. It was likely, if any attempted to do so, that this would strengthen nationalist and broadly authoritarian opinion within the society, and in public policy; but support for these positions was increasing already for reasons that had nothing to do with religion, and religious belief as such appeared to make little contribution towards them. In a world of rival and often conflicting faiths, the loose association between religious belief and politics in postcommunist Russia was a positive element in a society that was already deeply divided.

For a country of its size and population, the Soviet Union was always rather isolated from the affairs of the rest of the world community. In part, at least, this reflected the influence of geography, and of the patterns of political development that derived from it. With its broad and open frontiers, Russia is a country that has been invaded and occupied many times by outside powers. Its capital, Moscow, was burned down twice by the Tatars, seized by the Poles in the seventeenth century and by Napoleon in the nineteenth, and besieged by the Germans during the Second World War. Foreigners, reflecting this uncertain relationship, were required to live in special residential areas and were treated with a good deal of suspicion by ordinary Russians as well as by government officials; the national heroes were figures like Alexander Nevsky and Mikhail Kutuzov, who had led the struggle against invading armies. Russian liberals were often impressed by Western constitutionalism, as compared with their own autocracy; they travelled abroad, spoke and corresponded in French, and saw their country as a somewhat wayward member of a common European civilisation. Russian socialists, in a similar way, saw themselves as part of a wider movement of working people, and they took part in the Second International, which brought together the labour and socialist parties of Europe during the years before the First World War. Conservatives and nationalists, on the other hand, were more inclined to see Russia as a country with a unique history and culture, and as one that should look to its own traditions for an appropriate form of social organisation; their views were supported by an Orthodox Church that was all but coterminous with Russian nationhood, and which helped to promote a feeling that Russians were a 'special people' with a particular destiny to fulfil in terms of world civilisation.[1]

The Bolshevik leaders, after 1917, could hardly associate themselves with the notion of a divine mission; and yet many of the attitudes towards the outside world that had flourished in the tsarist period were still influential.[2] It had always been a Russian ambition, for instance, to acquire warm-water ports to the south, and to develop a network of client states in Eastern Europe as a means of strengthening the country's defences against other continental powers. Russia, equally, had been an Asian as well as a European power since at least the sixteenth century, when the first of a series of raids began to bring Siberia under imperial control. By the end of the nineteenth century most of Central Asia and the Caucasus had been annexed, together with Sakhalin and the Manchurian coast; there were even ambitions to become the dominant power in the Pacific until the fleet was destroyed in a battle with the Japanese in 1905. The Russian army, reflecting these far-flung responsibilities, was the 'largest on the European continent',[3] and military spending represented a disproportionately heavy burden on the state budget.[4] Feelings of isolation and insecurity, combined with a belief that Russia represented a special and perhaps unique Eurasian civilisation, carried over after 1917 into a Marxist-Leninist ideology that saw the USSR as an embattled champion of world socialism, a view that appeared to be confirmed as foreign governments sought to overthrow Soviet rule immediately after the revolution and then once again invaded in June 1941.

But for all these tendencies towards isolation, the postrevolutionary period saw the USSR integrate itself ever more closely into the common affairs of the world community. The new regime, certainly, might repudiate capitalism; but there was no alternative to a series of agreements within which trade could be conducted in the meantime. Trade agreements led in turn to the establishment of more formal relations, first with the smaller border states such as Finland and Estonia, then, in the 1920s, with Germany, France, Britain, and Japan, and finally, in the early 1930s, with the United States, Belgium, Spain, and the newly established states of Eastern Europe. The USSR maintained diplomatic relations with only thirty-five foreign states as late as the mid-1930s, which was less than half the membership of the international community at the time, but by the end of the Second World War the USSR had diplomatic relations with fifty-two states (which was nearly three-quarters of the total), and by the end of the 1980s there were formal diplomatic relations with 144 foreign states, or 85 per cent of the global total.[5] The USSR, similarly, was not a party to the Versailles peace settlement, but it returned to conference diplomacy when its top-hatted representatives appeared at Genoa in 1922;[6] and although the Soviet government had initially been hostile to the League of Nations, describing it in 1919 as a 'Holy Alliance of capitalists for the suppression of the workers' revolution',[7] the USSR became a member in 1934 and helped to found the United Nations in 1945, with a seat on its Security

Council. The USSR was extending its range of trading partners at the same time, from 45 foreign states in 1950 to 145 in the late 1980s,[8] and there were closer links at a popular level: there were more tourists, sportspeople, and visiting scholars, and more foreign students at Soviet universities than ever before.[9]

The postcommunist Russian government, after 1991, inherited the international associations as well as the debts and treaties of its Soviet predecessor. Russia was the only one of the former Soviet republics to remain a nuclear power, and it was the obvious tenant of the permanent seat on the United Nations Security Council that the USSR had enjoyed since its foundation. But the new Russia had to accommodate itself to a world in which it was no longer a superpower, and in which its economic weakness mattered more than a stockpile of rusting missiles. And there were other challenges, particularly in the relationships that had to be negotiated with the republics of the USSR that had also become independent states and for which the ambiguous term 'near abroad' came into use. Large numbers of Russians found they had become part of the settled population of these new states; many had Russian citizenship, and many more were Russian speakers with a strong association with the country from which they had originated. Clearly, the sovereignty of other states had to be respected; but no Russian government could remain indifferent to the fate of its nationals in these circumstances, particularly when their civil rights were being infringed. Equally, there was a new and apparently more congenial international environment after 1991; but the Western powers were still organised in NATO, and the expansion of the alliance into Eastern Europe that took place in 1999 threatened a new division of the continent that, for many Russians, prejudiced their security almost as seriously as the hostile confrontation of the cold war years.[10]

The Gorbachev revolution in foreign policy

Gorbachev's early pronouncements had given little indication that one of the central features of his administration would be its emphasis on 'new thinking' in international affairs. An address to an ideology conference in December 1984 – in effect a manifesto to the Central Committee members who would soon be deciding on the succession – stressed the need for 'fundamental change through accelerated economic development', and pointed to *glasnost'* and self-management as the most effective means of achieving it. The section on foreign policy was much more orthodox; it spoke of two 'opposing systems', and accused capitalism of resorting to 'wars and terror' in order to further its policy of 'social revenge'.[11] But a different tone was already emerging, and there were signs of it in an address that Gorbachev gave to British members of parliament later the same month. In the speech Gorbachev made clear his wish for renewed dialogue and co-operation, above all in relation to the threat of a nuclear war in which there could be 'no winners'. This, moreover, was just an example of the kind of issue that required the concerted action of states with different social systems. Another was the need to resolve regional issues peacefully; others were the fight against famine and disease, protection of the environment, and the global supply of energy and natural resources. The atomic age, Gorbachev suggested, required a 'new way of political thinking', above all the recognition that the peoples of the world lived in a 'vulnerable, rather fragile but interconnected world'. Whatever divided them, they had to share the same planet; and this dictated a 'constructive dialogue, a search for solutions to key international problems, for areas of agreement'.[12]

Gorbachev's speech on his election as general secretary in March 1985 laid its main emphasis on domestic priorities but also called for better relations with the 'great socialist community', particularly China, and for the continuation of 'peaceful, mutually advantageous co-operation' with the capitalist world, leading if possible to an agreement that would provide for the complete elimination of nuclear arms and with them the threat of nuclear war.[13] His address to the Central Committee in April 1985 – the first full statement of his objectives as party leader – called for 'stable, proper, and, if you like, civilised inter-state relations based on a genuine respect for international law'. The unity of the socialist states and their military-strategic parity with the NATO countries must at all costs be preserved, as the only secure guarantee against the 'aggressive appetites of imperialism'; the Soviet armed forces, in particular, would be provided with everything that was necessary for them to perform their task. But there was no 'fatal inevitability of confrontation' between the USSR and its major capitalist adversaries. On the contrary, neither side wanted a war, and there were 'new progressive and democratic forces' in the capitalist countries that shared the Soviet commitment to the peaceful resolution of their differences.[14] In a speech to French parliamentarians the following October Gorbachev stressed the ever-growing interdependence between countries in environmental as well as military and economic terms; he also emphasised the need to develop cultural contacts, and to avoid extending ideological differences to the conduct of inter-state relations.[15] His address a few days later to the Central Committee balanced these remarks with more familiar assurances about the 'further strengthening

Plate 7.1   Marx and Engels: a 1986 statue in what is still Marx and Engels Square in East Berlin

of the positions of existing socialism' and criticisms of the 'reactionary, aggressive forces of imperialism'.[16]

Gorbachev's address to the 27th Party Congress in February 1986 was relatively short of surprises in terms of foreign policy; there was nothing, at any rate, to compare with the unilateral moratorium on nuclear testing that had been announced just a few weeks earlier. It did, however, make clear the extent to which the Soviet approach to international affairs had changed since the simple dichotomies of the Brezhnev era. Capitalism, certainly, was a system plagued by problems and crises; it was aggressive and interventionist, and based on 'antagonistic contradictions' between social groups and between the various capitalist nations. Beyond these differences, however, lay a further group of contradictions relating to the pollution of the environment, the air, and the oceans, and the depletion of the world's natural resources. These were problems that no group of states could resolve by itself; and there were many others. No single group of states, for instance, could deal with the problem of 'corruption and vandalisation' in the cultural sphere. Nor could capitalist or socialist states deal by themselves with the threat of a nuclear catastrophe, or the difficulties that were facing the developing countries. Gorbachev invited the major capitalist countries to undertake a 'sober, constructive assessment' of problems of this kind, based if nothing else on their common need for self-preservation. The course of history and of social progress, he told the delegates, required the establishment of 'constructive, creative interaction among states and peoples on the scale of the whole planet'; and notwithstanding their competition and confrontation, both capitalist and socialist countries had to appreciate that they lived in an 'interdependent, in many ways integral world' in which they must co-operate for their common benefit.[17]

This 'new thinking' was set out more fully over the months that followed. The 'Delhi declaration' of November 1986, for instance, committed the Soviet leader to a 'nonviolent' as well as nuclear-free world.[18] A new defence doctrine began to take shape at the same time: it was intended to be nonoffensive in character and to give other states no reason to fear for their own security. The Soviet leader had already taken several unilateral initiatives towards this end, among them the decision, in April 1985, to freeze the deployment of SS-20 missiles in Europe, and the moratorium on all underground nuclear testing which began on 6 August 1985, the anniversary of Hiroshima. Gorbachev added a more elaborate proposal in January 1986, calling for the elimination of all nuclear and chemical weapons by the year 2000; a commitment to this objective was written into the new Party Programme, which was adopted shortly afterwards, and a similar commitment was made to 'reasonable sufficiency' in military matters as part of a move towards the establishment of an 'all-embracing system of international security'.[19] Nor were these simply doctrinal changes: there were substantial cuts in Soviet military spending and troop numbers and much more information was made available on the military budget and on troop and weapons deployments, which themselves became more defensive in character.[20]

A still more influential statement of the 'new thinking' came in the Soviet leader's address to the General Assembly of the United Nations in December 1988. In the speech Gorbachev expressed his personal support for the UN as a body that had 'increasingly manifested its ability to act as a unique international centre in the service of peace and security', and he repeated his belief that the most important issues that faced the world community were global rather than regional in character. The French and Russian revolutions, he suggested, had made an enormous contribution to human progress, but they lived today in a different world in which universal human values must have priority. This meant a common search for a new quality of international action, less dependent on military force and free of ideological prejudice. In more practical terms Gorbachev pointed to the need for a greater measure of agreement on the reduction of all forms of armaments and on the elimination of regional conflicts. But the United Nations itself should play a greater role, especially in issues such as Third World development, environmental assistance, and the peaceful use of outer space. And more needed to be done to strengthen international law, particularly in relation to human rights. Most spectacularly of all, the Soviet leader suggested moves to 'convert the armaments economy into a disarmament economy', and he announced himself a reduction of 500,000 in the size of Soviet armed forces over the following two years, together with changes in the structure of the forces that remained (including the withdrawal of a large number of tanks) so that their purposes became more clearly defensive.[21]

In the end, there was virtually no aspect of Soviet foreign policy that remained unchanged. Most notably, there was a steady improvement in relations with the United States after a summit in November 1985 brought Gorbachev face to face with Ronald Reagan, a Republican president who had become notorious for his description of the USSR as an 'evil empire'. Unexpectedly, they established a continuing dialogue, and in December 1987 went on to sign an agreement that eliminated an entire category of nuclear arms – land-based missiles of intermediate and shorter range.[22] In July 1991, meeting in Moscow, Gorbachev and Reagan's successor George Bush went even further, concluding a strategic arms reduction treaty that made the first substantial cuts in the weapons available to each side.[23] Gorbachev had evidently hoped to sustain communist rule in Eastern Europe by encouraging the election of fellow reformers, but in the end he had to accept the defeat of governments throughout the region and the dissolution of the Council for Mutual Economic Assistance and the Warsaw Treaty Organisation, which had provided the economic and military basis for Soviet relations with Eastern Europe throughout the postwar period.[24] Speaking to the Central Committee in December 1989 Gorbachev professed to welcome the 'positive changes' that had taken place, presenting them as a response to *perestroika* in the USSR itself and claiming that they represented 'democratisation' and the 'renewal of socialism'.[25] But in any case, he asked the 28th Party Congress in 1990, what was the alternative? 'Tanks once again'?[26]

The USSR, meanwhile, had moved to normalise its relations with other states. The 'limited contingent' that had been sent to maintain a friendly regime in Afghanistan was withdrawn, after international negotiations, in February 1989.[27] Relations with Cuba underwent a comparable change in September 1991 when 11,000 Soviet troops were brought home after Gorbachev had met the US secretary of state but without any consultation with the Havana government.[28] Gorbachev's speech to the 27th Party Congress in 1986 was the first in modern times to make no reference to the need to assist 'national liberation' movements in the developing countries;[29] the Party Programme that was adopted at the same congress committed the USSR to no more than to 'do what it could' to assist socialist-oriented states in the developing world,[30] and authoritative commentaries made clear that the USSR preferred the peaceful settlement of regional conflicts to the 'export of revolution'.[31] The USSR, meanwhile, established diplomatic relations with the Vatican, with Israel, and with the Afrikaner state in South Africa;[32] it signed a Paris Charter in November 1990 which confirmed that East and West were 'no longer adversaries';[33] and then in 1991 the Soviet government supported international action in the Gulf against an Iraqi regime with which it had for many years sustained a friendship treaty.[34] By the end of the Gorbachev years there were few respects in which the USSR had not become an entirely 'normal' member of the world community it had originally made every effort to overthrow.

Yeltsin and the West

Boris Yeltsin had given little attention to foreign policy in his earlier career, or in his campaign for the Russian presidency in June 1991. He had made a few trips abroad, to Germany, Nicaragua, and Luxembourg, but as a member of an official delegation; and when he visited the United States in September 1989 as a newly elected people's deputy the Bush administration, still supportive of Gorbachev, kept him at arm's length and there was no more than a brief and informal meeting with the US president.[35] Once he had been elected to head the Russian state, however, Yeltsin took an increasingly prominent role on the international scene. Immediately after his victory he made a four-day visit to the United States in which he appeared to have persuaded President Bush that in future he would have to 'deal with Gorbachev, but also with Russia'.[36] And when Bush visited Moscow the following month to sign the strategic arms reduction treaty he held separate talks with Yeltsin as well as the Kazakh president Nazarbaev before travelling on to Kiev to address the Ukrainian parliament. When Secretary of State James Baker visited in mid-December it was clear that Yeltsin had become the dominant figure, and Russian officials were pressing impatiently for full diplomatic relations (a dozen states had recognised the Russian government by 25 December, although the USSR was still formally in existence and Gorbachev was still president).[37] Yeltsin himself referred to the 'former USSR' in the press conference that took place at the end of Baker's visit,[38] and his foreign minister used the same term in an address a few days later.[39]

The Russian government had always included a foreign minister, reflecting the fiction that all the republics were sovereign states that had concluded a voluntary union. But an independent Russian foreign policy had begun to acquire some reality even before the USSR had disappeared, based on the declaration of sovereignty that its parliament had adopted in June 1990. There were agreements with the other Soviet republics, based on a reciprocal recognition of sovereignty, and then in January 1991 a treaty was signed with Estonia that defined both states as 'subjects of international law'.[40] Later in the year, within what was still the USSR, Russian negotiators reached still more far-reaching agreements on the establishment of 'diplomatic relations' with Bulgaria,[41] and on relations with Italy and the Federal Republic of Germany that were based on the 'principles of international law'.[42] By the end of the year, with the agreement of the other republics that had now formed the Commonwealth of Independent States, Russia had taken over the Soviet seat in the United Nations as well as its place on the Security Council, and had also assumed the financial and treaty obligations of the USSR as its successor state under international law. The new head of what had been the Soviet Foreign Ministry was Andrei Kozyrev, who had been Russian foreign minister since October 1990; he directed, as he explained in a New Year's message, 'not a detachment of revolutionary sword-bearers, but a staff of democratically minded people who know and understand well the interests and concerns of their people'.[43]

Yeltsin himself lost no time in underlining the changes that had taken place in what was still the world's largest state. In January 1992 he announced that Russian nuclear weapons would no longer be directed against targets in the United States,[44] and then followed this with a more comprehensive statement in which he announced a series of unilateral reductions in nuclear and conventional arms.[45] At the end of the month Yeltsin visited the United Nations to address a Security Council summit; emphasising that he saw the Western powers 'not just as partners, but as allies', he made clear that the new Russia would play its full part in the maintenance of world peace and put forward his own proposals for a global security system based on the Strategic Defense Initiative and Russia's own military technologies.[46] While Yeltsin was in the United States he held an unofficial meeting with President Bush at which he declared that relations between the two states had 'entered a new era'. Bush himself acknowledged that they had met 'not as adversaries, but as friends',[47] and as the second day of their meeting was Yeltsin's birthday he handed over an autographed pair of cowboy boots to 'my friend Boris' (the boots, it emerged, were too small, but Yeltsin kept them anyway as a souvenir).[48] The 'Camp David declaration' that was issued at the end of their discussions confirmed that relations between the two countries were now based on 'friendship and partnership', and that the two presidents would personally seek to 'eliminate the remains of the hostile period of the "cold war"'.[49] After the UN summit Yeltsin went on to Canada, where he signed a declaration of friendship and co-operation, and then visited France, where he signed a fully fledged treaty.[50]

A new framework of relations began to acquire more definite contours over the months that followed. An agreement on the 'bases of relations' had already been concluded with Russia's close neighbour Finland.[51] In April Yeltsin signed a treaty on friendly relations with Czechoslovakia, and another with Poland, that superseded the alliances of the communist period.[52] In June there was a formal treaty on co-operation with Canada, and in August another treaty on friendly relations with Bulgaria.[53] A treaty on the 'principles of relations' with the United Kingdom followed in November;[54] it was the first treaty of its kind to be concluded between the two states since 1766. Russia and Britain were 'now allies', Yeltsin told the British Parliament in a warmly applauded address; and at a subsequent news conference he announced that the queen had accepted an invitation to visit Russia (a royal visit had been agreed three years earlier but had not taken place). It had, in fact, been Yeltsin himself who had authorised the destruction of the Ipat'ev house in which the tsarist royal family – who were the queen's relatives – had been shot; but they had talked 'like old friends', he told journalists.[55] It was Yeltsin's first official visit to the United Kingdom, and he was the first Russian leader to visit the Stock Exchange rather than the tomb of Karl Marx; his wife, in a 'fashionable emerald green suit with power shoulders', was meanwhile 'stealing the show, a natural in front of the cameras. Hillary Clinton look out!'[56]

The first summit between the Russian president and his US counterpart took place in June 1992 in Washington. 'The abyss has ended', Yeltsin told journalists as he stepped off his plane.[57] Secretary of State Baker, who spoke in reply, described the two nations as united in a 'democratic partnership'.[58] He was not coming across the Atlantic with his hand out, Yeltsin explained, but rather to 'extend a hand to the president', and the summit saw a series of agreements that began to place Russian–American relations on an entirely new footing. The two presidents endorsed the principles of an unprecedented arms reduction agreement which went far beyond the START treaty that Bush and Gorbachev had signed the previous year;[59] they also signed a charter that was designed to establish a 'firm foundation for Russian–American relations of partnership and friendship',[60] and there were more specific agreements on the development of a global nuclear security system and the opening of new consulates in Seattle and Vladivostok (in total, the two presidents signed thirty-five joint documents).[61] Yeltsin, addressing the US Congress on 17 June, obtained an enthusiastic response to his message that the 'communist idol' had 'collapsed for good';[62] it was an occasion to which his speechwriters attached even more importance than to his meeting with President Bush, and they 'worked day and night' to get it right (as *Pravda* reminded its readers, the Russian president had actually played a leading role in the 'communist bondage' to which he had been referring).[63]

A further summit, in Moscow in January 1993, saw the framework agreement of the previous summer develop into the START 2 treaty, under which Russia and the United States each undertook to dismantle two-thirds of their strategic nuclear warheads;[64] the original START treaty, signed in 1991, had called for a cut of just 30 per cent.[65] Yeltsin described the agreement as the most important that had been concluded in the entire history of disarmament, and as a 'Christmas present for the whole of humanity'.[66] It was also, he thought, evidence of a 'real revolution' in Russian–American relations in that it had taken just a few months to agree, as compared with the fifteen years that had been needed to negotiate the original START treaty, because of the 'personal trust' that had developed between the two presidents.[67] The newly elected US president, he noted, was fully committed to the agreement, and Yeltsin invited him to 'take the baton' and visit Russia himself at the earliest opportunity.[68] The treaty had to be approved by the other post-Soviet nuclear powers, as well as by the Russian parliament (the Duma, in fact, was still considering the matter at the end of the decade); but Kazakhstan ratified START 1 in 1992,[69] Belarus did so in 1993,[70] and Ukraine ratified the treaty in 1994 after its prior conditions had been met and also acceded to the Nuclear Nonproliferation Treaty.[71] All nuclear weapons had been removed from Ukrainian territory by the summer of 1996, leaving Russia as the sole nuclear power among the fifteen former Soviet republics.[72]

The first summit between Yeltsin and the new American president, Bill Clinton, took place at Vancouver in April 1993. There was a comprehensive declaration in which both presidents declared their commitment to a 'dynamic and effective Russo-American partnership' – Yeltsin himself suggested their relations were those of 'partners and future allies'[73] – but the main emphasis was upon economic assistance to a new and still fragile Russian democracy. Clinton committed the United States itself to a package of financial aid valued at $1.6 billion, about half of which represented unilateral aid and the other half of which was in the form of credits, and he promised to seek a more substantial response from the leading industrial nations of the Group of Seven.[74] It was the start, Clinton promised, of a 'new democratic partnership'; the Russian president himself spoke of the development of a 'special relationship'.[75] The Canadian prime minister, who also met the Russian president, offered $200 million of unilateral aid;[76] and later in the year, reflecting US pressure as well as the views of its other members, the Group of Seven approved a package of multilateral aid to Russia that was valued at more than $43 billion.[77] A new military doctrine, adopted at the end of the year, consolidated the changes that had taken place in East–West relations by declaring that no country was regarded as an adversary of the new Russia, and that there would be no use of military force unless Russia was itself attacked; the primary role of the armed forces, in these rather different circumstances, was domestic peacekeeping.[78]

President Clinton paid his first official visit to Russia in January 1994, where the two presidents agreed that their relations had become a 'mature strategic partnership'. There were twelve formal agreements, including an undertaking that the strategic missiles held by each side would no longer be targeted against any other party. There was also a

Plate 7.2   At the Soviet war memorial, Treptow Park, East Berlin

public recognition that the rights of Russian speakers in the Baltic republics must be protected.[79] As in Vancouver, Yeltsin called Clinton 'my friend Bill', and Clinton entertained the Russian president and his guests to a recital on the saxophone – 'a simple but agreeable tune' – and was 'genuinely touched' by the response.[80] Yeltsin visited Spain in April and the Italian prime minister visited Moscow in October, in both cases concluding a formal treaty of friendship and co-operation.[81] In June Yeltsin was the guest of the European Union in Corfu, where he signed an agreement on partnership and co-operation[82] (he had concluded a treaty of friendship and co-operation with Greece itself the previous year),[83] and then in late August he was in Berlin with 'my friend Helmut' to take part in a ceremony marking the departure of the last Russian troops from what had originally been the Soviet zone of Germany.[84] Russian troops had already left Lithuania, and the last troops left Latvia and Estonia, ahead of schedule, at the end of August 1994.[85] In September there was another summit meeting with President Clinton, their fifth in eighteen months, at which the two presidents agreed a 'partnership for economic progress' that was designed to reduce the tariff barriers that had been hindering bilateral trade;[86] the Russian president addressed the United Nations in the course of his visit, calling for a 'treaty on nuclear security and strategic stability' that would involve sweeping new cuts in nuclear arms.[87]

Another Russian–United States summit took place in Moscow in May 1995 in connection with the celebration in the Russian capital of the fiftieth anniversary of the Allied victory in Europe.[88] There were six joint declarations, although there was no attempt to disguise the fact that there had been 'differences of approach' to a whole series of questions, among them the sale of nuclear facilities to Iran (Yeltsin insisted on their 'wholly peaceful character'), and the expansion of NATO rather than the development of a more broadly conceived security framework that could extend across the entire Euro-Atlantic region.[89] Yeltsin addressed the UN General Assembly once again on the organisation's fiftieth anniversary in October 1995, where he repeated his call for a more general framework of European security rather than the expansion of existing alliances (if just a single bloc was strengthened, he pointed out, there would be a 'new confrontation').[90] He also met Bill Clinton for their ninth summit, where the main question on the agenda was the deteriorating situation in Bosnia.[91] There were further summits in April 1996[92] and at Helsinki in the spring of 1997, when the two presidents explored the ways in which Russia might be reconciled to the expansion of NATO, and pushed forward disarmament.[93] When they met again in Moscow in September 1998 it was their fourteenth summit, although the least productive because Russia was enmeshed in the governmental crisis that stemmed from the sacking of Kirienko and Clinton himself was engaged in the domestic controversy that led eventually to his impeachment; the two presidents moved forward on disarmament, including the outlines of a START 3, but there were 'no major breakthroughs'.[94]

The early postcommunist years saw not only the establishment of a different relationship with the major Western powers, but also a Russia that was a full member of the international community. Gorbachev, in 1990, had been the first Soviet leader to attend a meeting of the Group of Seven, but not as an equal participant. The Naples meeting of the G-7 in 1994, which Yeltsin attended, was described as a 'political G-8', and at Denver in 1997 there was a 'Summit of the Eight' although not yet a G-8.[95] The Birmingham summit that took place in the summer of 1998 was more generally described as a meeting of the 'Group of Eight', although the day before the summit began the other members held a separate meeting of what was in effect the G-7 that resolved many of the questions on their agenda, underlining Russia's 'honorary' status.[96] Russia had meanwhile led the other former Soviet republics into the World Bank and International Monetary Fund (Soviet membership had been agreed in 1944 but never ratified),[97] and then into the European Bank of Reconstruction and Development. Membership of the Council of Europe was approved in early 1996, confirming Russia's re-entry into the European community of nations,[98] and two years later Russia ratified the European Convention on Human Rights, although capital punishment was still on the statute book.[99] The new Russian government also applied to join the General Agreement on Tariffs and Trade and its successor, the World Trade Organization,[100] and in November 1997 Russia joined another important regional grouping when it became a member of the Asian–Pacific Economic Co-operation Group, in spite of the bitter opposition of some of its members.[101]

The 'Iron Curtain' that Churchill identified in his speech of 1946 divided two irreconcilable ideologies and the states that promoted them. The end of communist rule eliminated some of the causes of that confrontation, but – it became increasingly clear – not all of them. The developed Western countries, in Foreign Minister Kozyrev's earliest policy statements, were 'Russia's natural allies', based on their shared commitment to democracy, human rights, and the market; he looked forward in particular to 'fruitful co-operation' with the United States and saw no reason to fear it would attempt to become the 'sole superpower', imposing its views on other nations.[102] Russian foreign policy, Kozyrev insisted, should avoid 'ideological schemas and messianic ambitions on a global scale in favour of a realistic assessment of Russia's own needs'; their aim should be the 'thoroughgoing transformation of society'[103] and the entry, on this basis, into the 'club of first-class powers of Europe, Asia, and America'.[104] The interests of Russian diplomacy and those of the democratic states, he suggested elsewhere, were 'substantially the same',[105] and he sought to engage them in a broader 'humanisation of international politics' based upon the universal observance of human rights.[106] Russia, Yeltsin himself explained, was 'no longer the main power centre of an enormous communist empire'. They had abandoned earlier thoughts of 'painting the planet red', and rejected the idea that they were surrounded by 'overt or covert enemies' in a struggle they must 'unfailingly win'. In the long run, he believed, Russians would discover that a stable world in which they could engage in 'mutually advantageous co-operation' would serve their interests better than a policy of confrontation.[107]

The new approach was set out more fully in a 'draft concept for the foreign policy of the Russian Federation', approved by President Yeltsin in the spring of 1993. Russia, it pointed out, was still a great power, with a special responsibility for the creation of a new system of relations among the states that were formerly part of the Soviet Union. Russia, moreover, was a state that still needed to defend its vital interests, which meant it should resist the subordinate position it had been accorded in the international economy, and that it should take an interest in local conflicts near its borders. The greatest importance of all was attached to relations with the former Soviet republics, and to the efforts that might be undertaken to encourage their reintegration. These included the establishment of a collective security system, a common boundary, and a special role for Russia in maintaining public order within those boundaries that would legitimise the presence of Russian troops upon the territory of the other republics. Eastern Europe more generally was regarded as a part of Russia's 'historic sphere of interest', and there was a strong case for closer relations with the states of the European Community. Further abroad, Russia and the United States had a common interest in the prevention of regional conflict and nuclear proliferation, although their interests in other respects did not always coincide. And there should be 'balanced and stable relations' with the countries of the Asia–Pacific region, especially China, Japan, and India.[108] At least two features of the new concept attracted attention: the emphasis that was given to the former Soviet republics of the 'near abroad', and the open acknowledgement that Russia had a distinctive set of interests that might not always accord with those of the Western democracies.[109]

Kozyrev was still insisting, in the spring of 1994, that there was 'no sensible alternative to partnership', and he continued to look to the reformers' 'natural friends and allies, the democratic states and governments of the West'.[110] Views of this kind, however, were clearly difficult to reconcile with the 'draft concept' (which reflected the views of the defence and intelligence community as well as the Foreign Ministry), and they were also difficult to reconcile with the views of the Russian electorate, which had given the right-wing Liberal Democratic Party the largest share of the vote in the December 1993 Duma elections and then gave a third of the seats to the Communist Party – also assertively nationalist – in December 1995. Western leaders, in these circumstances, began to take a more cautious view of their relationship with the new government, still more so when Yeltsin launched a war in Chechnya in early December 1994 with what appeared to be an elementary disregard of the human rights to which the regime had made such a public commitment. Already, Kozyrev warned in 1995, the honeymoon in relations with the United States was 'coming to an end', and he moved closer to his nationalist opponents by warning that there might be circumstances in which it was necessary for Russia to use military force to defend its 'compatriots abroad', particularly ethnic Russians in the Baltic republics.[111] He was similarly a strong supporter of the Chechen campaign, siding with the president and abandoning his former colleagues in Russia's Choice.[112] Kozyrev was re-elected to the Duma in December 1995 and chose to resign his ministerial office rather than relinquish his representative duties; but his position had come under heavy attack and Yeltsin had several times made clear his own dissatisfaction (a decree authorising the foreign minister's dismissal had, apparently, already been signed).[113] In the end he became a 'ritual sacrifice' to the new Duma.[114]

At its most radical, Kozyrev's critics accused him of an alliance with the 'prince of darkness', facilitating the efforts of a West that wanted a 'weak and degraded Russia' that was 'easy prey to overseas companies and banks'.[115] Others argued that he had suffered a 'crushing defeat' in the policies he had pursued, such as preventing the expansion of NATO,[116] and that he had subordinated Russia's own interests to a nebulous 'partnership' that had simply allowed the United States to expand its global hegemony without the financial compensation that had originally been promised.[117] These were extreme charges, but there was a much wider degree of support for a more moderate 'pragmatic nationalist' position that was concerned to assert Russia's right of independent action, and to protect domestic industry and culture in the face of the West's overwhelming superiority.[118] This meant, first of all, a multipolar world, not one that was dominated by a single superpower. Yeltsin had already made clear in a speech to senior members of the Foreign Ministry that he was dissatisfied with the heavy emphasis it had been placing on relations with the Western nations, describing it as a 'disbalance'.[119] The United States, he pointed out, was 'not the only country in the world', and it was time to correct what he described as a 'tilt in [their] relations'.[120] Yeltsin himself thought more attention should be given to relations with the former Soviet republics, as well as Russian speakers beyond national boundaries,[121] and there was support within the foreign policy community for a more general shift of orientation towards the 'near abroad' and the neighbouring states of southern and eastern Asia, partly because of the disillusioning experience of their early dealings with the West, but also because of Russia's own 'Eurasianism' and the trading opportunities that appeared to be available in countries with lower levels of technology.[122]

Kozyrev's successor was Yevgenii Primakov, who had been the head of foreign intelligence; a man of a different generation and political formation, he had spent a long career in the service of the Soviet state and had 'never made any secret of his mistrust of the West, above all the United States'.[123] As the new foreign minister made clear in interviews, he would mount a more vigorous defence of Russia's 'national-state interests', and he would be looking for an 'equal' partnership with the Western powers within a foreign policy that would itself be more broadly diversified. Russia, he insisted, had not lost the cold war but shared in a common victory, and there could be no talk of 'victors and vanquished'. Russia, moreover, was still a 'great power', and its foreign policy should 'correspond to its status'.[124] This meant, above all, 'correcting the "bias" towards the West', and emphasising relations with Belarus, with Russian speakers beyond the national boundaries, and with China.[125] Kozyrev had been born to Russian parents in Brussels, spoke Spanish and Portuguese as well as English, and had graduated from the Moscow State Institute of International Affairs – the normal training ground for journalists. Primakov, by contrast, was born in Kiev but grew up in Tbilisi, and knew Arabic as well as Georgian and English; he had graduated from the Moscow Institute of Oriental Studies, and worked for many years as a radio and *Pravda* journalist with a specialisation in foreign and particularly Arab affairs.[126] Primakov moved into academic life in the 1970s as deputy director of the Institute of the World Economy and International Relations and then director of the Institute of Oriental Studies of the Academy of Sciences, moving again in the Gorbachev years to become speaker of the lower house of parliament, a member of the Central Committee, a candidate member of the Politburo, and then (from the end of 1991) the head of Russian foreign intelligence. As commentaries made clear, he was a very different kind of foreign minister, one who reflected the assumptions of the Soviet period in which he had grown up, and one who 'found it much easier to agree with Saddam Hussein than with Clinton'.[127] Primakov himself made clear that Russian relations with the United States would be conducted on a 'completely different basis', and he insisted that it would have to be an 'equal partnership' even if Russia was the weaker participant;[128] the same policies were pursued by his successor and former first deputy, Igor Ivanov, who promised that there would be 'no radical changes' and pointed out that the policies they were now pursuing had the support of the 'broadest possible spectrum of political forces and public opinion'.[129]

There were several issues that divided postcommunist Russia and the Western nations; surprisingly, perhaps, they included espionage and counterintelligence. As early as 1992 four Russian representatives were expelled from Belgium on the grounds that their activities had been 'incompatible with their status',[130] and four were ordered out of France in what was described as the 'biggest espionage case ever in the field of nuclear technology'.[131] Then in January 1993, as Yeltsin and Bush were clinking glasses in the Kremlin, a senior military attaché from the office of the Russian military attaché in Washington was presented with similar charges and forced to leave.[132] Relations with the United States were not improved by the much more serious disclosure in February 1994 that a senior CIA official and his wife, Aldrich and Maria Ames, had been spying for the USSR and then for Russia, betraying the identities of the Americans' top agents and receiving very large payments for doing so (the agents themselves were executed or imprisoned).[133] The Russians themselves announced the arrest of a senior defence official in 1996 on charges of spying for British intelligence and each side eventually expelled four diplomats (two of the British representatives had been about to leave in any case and both sides were trying – newspapers reported – to 'observe decorum').[134] The following year came the arrest of Harold Nicholson, who had been working for the Russians since 1994 in Malaysia and then in the CIA training centre in Virginia and was the 'highest-ranking CIA officer ever charged with espionage'; in 1998 five Russian diplomats in Norway were accused of espionage and obliged to leave.[135] 'After all', as the Federal Bureau of Intelligence told Russian journalists, 'no one has yet abolished spying.'[136]

There were further tensions between Russian and Western approaches towards the conflict in the former Yugoslavia, where Russia's historic ties with the Serbs made it increasingly difficult for even a postcommunist government to accept NATO strikes against their fellow nations in Bosnia. The Western powers, for their part, were more sympathetic towards the Bosnian Muslims because of the Serb aggression that had initiated the conflict, and because of a policy of 'ethnic cleansing' that had led to a series of acknowledged atrocities. The USSR had initially opposed the dissolution of another multinational state – a single, independent Yugoslavia was an 'important element of stability in the Balkans and in Europe as a whole', the Foreign Ministry argued in the summer of 1991[137] – and it supported the UN arms embargo that was imposed the following September. Once the USSR had dissolved into its constituent republics, however, the same considerations no longer applied, and Russia recognised the independent statehood of Slovenia and Croatia in February 1992 ahead of the United States and most European governments.[138] Kozyrev himself made an attempt to mediate after Serb-led forces had invaded Bosnia and Herzegovina in order to prevent them moving towards independence, an action that in its turn precipitated an increasingly bitter struggle for control of the republic. In May the fragile ceasefire broke down and Russia joined the rest of the UN Security Council in voting to impose far-reaching sanctions, including a total ban on trade, the suspension of air links, the withdrawal of diplomats, and the seizure of financial assets.[139] In September the Russian representative chose not to use his veto powers when Serbia and Montenegro were denied the Yugoslav seat in the United Nations and expelled from the organisation itself; and then in November the Security Council voted for the sanctions to be tightened still further.[140]

Sanctions on 'fellow Slavs' were less popular in Russia itself, and there were charges that the country's 'long-standing and traditional ties with the peoples of Yugoslavia' had been 'sacrificed to pro-American interests in Europe'.[141] There were additional grounds for concern when a NATO peacekeeping force under the auspices of the Conference on Security and Co-operation in Europe was despatched to the region. This was an acknowledged extension of the alliance's formal responsibilities, which had hitherto been limited to the territories of its member states, and it raised the possibility that the West might seek to impose its will in various parts of the former USSR – for instance, in Nagorno-Karabakh, or in the conflict between the predominantly Russian enclave of Transdnestria and the majority population in Moldova.[142] The NATO action was nothing less than an 'armed invasion of the Slavic world', warned a group of nationalist politicians and intellectuals; 'if they destroy the Serbs today, they will move against us tomorrow'.[143]

Russian parliamentarians took the same view, voting in a series of resolutions against international intervention and in favour of the lifting of the sanctions that had been imposed on Serbia and Montenegro.[144] Even Mikhail Gorbachev was moved to warn that the West was really seeking to strengthen its influence in the Muslim world and to expand NATO's sphere of operation beyond its 'historical borders', with Russia no more than a 'junior partner'.[145]

There was another crisis in February 1994 when NATO threatened air strikes against the Bosnian Serbs unless they pulled back their artillery from Sarajevo; this time Yeltsin and the newly elected Russian parliament were united in opposing military action, and a breakdown in relations with the Western powers was avoided only when Russian mediators were able to negotiate a ceasefire that brought Russian troops themselves into the peacekeeping force. But in April 1994 NATO launched an air strike against the Bosnian Serbs with no attempt to consult or even inform their Russian counterparts; Yeltsin responded with an angry statement in which he insisted on 'preliminary consultations' in all decisions of this kind and warned that attempts to resolve their differences by force could lead only to an 'endless war'.[146] Nor was there any consultation when further air strikes took place in September 1995 in what Russian commentators described as the 'largest military operation by the North Atlantic Alliance since it was founded in 1949'.[147] Yeltsin warned again that the international community was being drawn into the conflict on the side of one of the contending parties; a ministerial statement a few days later described NATO policies as 'genocide'.[148] The Duma, going still further, demanded the lifting of sanctions and the sacking of Kozyrev, and that NATO be 'called to account for its aggression in Bosnia'.[149] The fighting subsided when a peace agreement brokered by the United States was signed at Dayton in November 1995 and sanctions were eventually lifted in October 1996.

There were further tensions when NATO forces threatened once again to intervene, this time to stop hostilities between Serbs and ethnic Albanians in Kosovo. Any use of force, insisted a Russian statement, would be a violation of the UN Charter, and the Russian foreign minister made clear that he would use his country's veto in the Security Council to block a military option;[150] in the end a crisis was averted in what the Foreign Ministry described as a 'victory for common sense, a victory for forces that want to see world politics in the twenty-first century based on respect for the sovereignty of all states'.[151] But Russian influence was unable to prevent the United States and its allies from attempting to compel Serbian and Kosovan representatives, in talks in Paris early the following year, to reach a settlement or risk

NATO military action; and Russian opinion was ignored when NATO launched a series of air strikes in March 1999 in what President Yeltsin described as an act of 'undisguised aggression' that risked a full-scale Balkan war and perhaps a still wider conflict.[152] There were no obvious Russian interests in the former Yugoslavia, and there had been no military bases there. At the same time there was no way of disguising the fact that Russia had been marginalised in a part of the postcommunist world that had formerly been within its sphere of influence. Nor was there any disguising the difficulty in which Russian diplomats had been placed, torn between their wish to retain a common front with their new Western friends and a commitment to their Slavic and Orthodox brothers that had the support of public and parliament.

A similar conflict of interest arose when the United States and its allies launched air attacks against Iraq in January 1993, without the prior consultation that had taken place before the Gulf War. Kozyrev demanded that any future action of this kind be approved by the UN Security Council; as a senior Russian diplomat remarked, 'We are sick and tired of a situation in which CNN reporters are notified of strikes against Saddam in advance, while Russian leaders are woken up in the middle of the night after an attack has already begun.'[153] The Russian government gave its full support to a further series of air strikes that were launched by the United States, after other members of the Security Council had been informed, in the summer of 1993.[154] But there were further tensions in September 1996 when Saddam Hussein violated UN rules by sending his troops into a Kurdish region in the north of his country and the United States retaliated with two missile attacks against military targets and air defence systems. A Russian deputy foreign minister was in Iraq at the time, attempting to achieve a negotiated solution; Washington, the Russian government complained in an official statement, was 'attempting, in effect, to supplant the Security Council', which under the UN Charter had the 'exclusive right to authorise the use of force'.[155] Russian mediation played some part in averting military action in late 1997, after the American members of the UN weapons inspection team had been expelled, in what Primakov claimed had been a 'great success for Russian diplomacy'.[156] When tensions rose again in early 1998, Russia (in Yeltsin's words) 'from the very beginning advocated a diplomatic resolution of the crisis and opposed the use of force'.[157]

Russia, once again, had interests that diverged from those of the Western countries. There was a long-standing friendship treaty with Iraq, signed originally in 1972. But more than this, there were several thousand Russians living and working in Iraq;[158] and there were substantial Russian investments that would be repaid only if relations were maintained (the Russians, it was estimated, were owed $8 billion).[159] There was also a personal element, in that Primakov had been a friend of Saddam Hussein since the 1960s.[160] But the Foreign Ministry suggested more general grounds of principle for resisting Western action, including the danger that it might encourage Islamic terrorism and increase anti-American feeling in various countries, including Russia.[161] When relations deteriorated once again in December 1998, following Iraq's failure to comply fully with the requirements of UN weapons inspectors, and the United States and Britain launched missile strikes against Iraqi targets, Yeltsin complained that they had 'crudely violated the UN Charter and generally accepted principles of international law and the norms and rules of responsible behaviour of states'.[162] Primakov condemned the American action more directly, and any attempt to 'resolve problems unilaterally from a position of strength'.[163] Underlining the gravity with which it viewed the situation, the Russian government withdrew its ambassadors from London and Washington in a gesture of official dissatisfaction that had not been seen since the worst days of the cold war.[164]

A much larger issue was the security architecture of a postcommunist Europe, and particularly the expansion of NATO.[165] Yeltsin had in fact suggested, as early as December 1991, that Russia might itself join NATO (the USSR had applied for membership in 1954 in rather different circumstances),[166] and in a joint declaration after he visited Warsaw in August 1993 he accepted that a Polish application for membership would 'not be in conflict with the process of European integration, including the interests of Russia'.[167] In October, however, he sent a letter to Western leaders arguing against the early admission of the East European states, suggesting instead that NATO and the Russian government should jointly guarantee the security of the region; he had no objection to admission in principle and the East European states were of course entitled to make their own decisions, but the interests of European security would not (in the president's view) be served by simply extending the alliance in its existing form.[168] It was in these circumstances that the US government proposed a 'Partnership for Peace' that would allow the countries of the region the opportunity to form an association with NATO, but one that stopped short of full membership.[169] A NATO summit in January 1994 approved the Partnership proposal, and ruled at the same time against early NATO admission for the East European countries.[170] Russia, its representatives made clear, would join the Partnership for Peace, but Yeltsin insisted there should be a 'special agreement' that took account of Russia's

Plate 7.3   Yevgenii Primakov, pictured as foreign minister in 1996 (Novosti)

'place and role in world and European affairs and with our country's military power and nuclear status'.[171] In June Kozyrev signed the Partnership agreement on this basis, together with a brief 'protocol' that identified Russia's 'unique and important contribution commensurate with its weight and responsibility as a major European, world, and nuclear power';[172] the NATO foreign ministers made a parallel offer to develop a relationship with Russia in 'appropriate areas outside the Partnership for Peace'.[173]

The possible expansion of NATO itself proved more controversial. Kozyrev insisted in June 1994 that there should be 'no haste' in matters of this kind, and Yeltsin warned in December at a meeting of the Conference on Security and Co-operation in Europe that plans to expand NATO membership raised the danger of a 'cold peace' in place of the 'cold war' that had just concluded. It would be far better, he argued, to establish a new and all-European security structure based on the CSCE, with its own institutions and with responsibility for human rights throughout the continent including the rights of Russian minorities in the newly independent states. It would also have a peacekeeping capacity, in which Russia would play its part. NATO, he pointed out, had been created in the cold war era. But the European states were partners, no longer adversaries, and it would be dangerous to isolate any one of them.[174] Russia, he told journalists, could 'not accept NATO's boundaries moving right up to the border of the Russian Federation', bringing back the system of blocs that had so recently been dissolved; and any move of this kind would be regarded as a 'threat to Russia's security'.[175] The speech was widely seen as 'one of Moscow's toughest international statements since the fall of communism',[176] but in the event the meeting agreed there could be no Russian veto over future admissions, and there was little the Russian authorities could do to resist a process to which the East European countries were themselves very committed.

The prospects for an agreed solution improved in December 1996 when Primakov, speaking in Brussels, let it be known that he would be prepared to start negotiations on a new security treaty without the precondition that the alliance must first suspend its plans for enlargement. Primakov continued to insist that NATO's plans to admit new members from Eastern Europe threatened to establish 'new dividing lines in Europe', but he welcomed NATO's own affirmation that it had no 'intention, plan, or reason' to station nuclear weapons on the territory of new members, and that it was ready to take part in negotiations on a larger East–West security framework.[177] Speaking to the NATO secretary general in January 1997, Primakov emphasised that the establishment of a Russian relationship with the alliance should not be interpreted as a form of 'compensation' for their agreement to its expansion. Russia, he insisted, still took a negative attitude to the expansion for a 'whole complex of political, military-strategic, and moral-psychological reasons'; an expansion of the alliance, in particular, would create the 'danger of new dividing lines in Europe, in other words precisely what the end of the "cold war" was supposed to have eliminated'.[178] Anatolii Chubais, head at this time of the presidential administration and a leading reformer, warned similarly that NATO enlargement would 'inevitably lead to a new dividing line across the whole of Europe', and that it would be the 'biggest mistake in Western foreign policy for fifty years'.[179] Yeltsin himself, at the Helsinki summit in March 1997, reiterated that Russia remained 'consistently opposed' to an expansion that could lead to a 'new confrontation', and he sought formal assurances that would rule out the stationing of nuclear weapons on the territory of new member states as well as a framework for resolving issues of European security in the future.[180]

These rather different perspectives were reconciled in a 'founding act', which was signed in Paris in May 1997 by the Russian president and the leaders of all sixteen NATO states.[181] Yeltsin himself saw the agreement as the 'foundation for an equitable and stable partnership that [took] into account the security interests of each and every signatory', and as another 'victory for common sense'. Russia, he insisted, still took a 'negative view' of NATO expansion, but he appreciated the effort that had been made to 'take our legitimate interests into account' and hoped this would lead to a still more comprehensive 'charter of European security'.[182] For the pro-government *Rossiiskie vesti*, Russian diplomats had managed to prevent an 'anti-Yalta', a 'military and political division of the continent by NATO from a position of brute strength and total disregard for Russian interests';[183] for other commentators the agreement was a logical consequence of Russia's defeat in the cold war and its military and economic weakness, with no firm guarantees from the Western signatories that they would not at some future point move their military infrastructure still closer to Russian borders, or admit former Soviet republics.[184] Alexander Lebed, who had been secretary of the Security Council, went even further, describing the agreement as evidence of the 'complete failure of the policy of Yeltsin and his regime', with the probable result that the country's 'main strategic partners' in the future would be Asian powers like India and China.[185] Yeltsin, adding a flourish, announced after the signing that he had decided to remove the warheads from all the missiles that were targeted at other signatory countries; amid considerable confusion, aides explained that Russian nuclear missiles had not in fact been targeted at the major NATO states for some time, in the case of the United States at least, since 1994.[186]

The NATO summit that took place in Madrid the following July, acting on the basis of this understanding, voted to admit Hungary, Poland, and the Czech Republic, with others to be considered at a later stage. 'Madrid', explained the NATO secretary general, was 'not the end but only the beginning of the alliance's expansion', and he mentioned Slovenia and Romania as strong candidates for future membership with a further more ambiguous reference to the Baltic states.[187] US Secretary of State Albright, after a separate meeting in the Lithuanian capital, emphasised that the decisions taken in Madrid did 'not represent the final state of NATO expansion'.[188] Primakov, for his part, insisted the decision was the 'biggest mistake in Europe since the end of World War II',[189] and Foreign Ministry spokesmen added that it was at odds with the task of creating a 'single security space in the Euro-Atlantic region' within which 'equal security for all states would be guaranteed'; any reference to the Baltic states was particularly unwelcome, although there could be discussions about the security guarantees that might address their legitimate concerns. The way forward, for Russian diplomats, was still the development of the OSCE as a 'model of general and comprehensive security in Europe in the twenty-first century', together with a 'Charter of European Security';[190] East Europeans, by contrast, favoured the guarantees that were already available through the NATO framework, and even former Soviet republics that were not candidates for membership (like Ukraine) began to establish a direct relationship.[191] Russia's isolation was deepened by the decision of the European Union, at its Luxembourg summit in December 1997, to begin talks on the admission of Poland, the Czech Republic, Hungary, Slovenia, and Estonia, with Slovakia, Bulgaria, Romania, Latvia, and Lithuania candidates for admission in a second wave.[192] Even though admission was not an immediate prospect, both of these decisions – above all the expansion of NATO and its assumption of a much broader conception of its legitimate sphere of activity – threatened to recreate some of the divisions that had separated the two halves of the continent over the decades of cold war.

The CIS and the East

Issues of a rather different kind were involved in Russian relations with the other states that had formerly been Soviet republics, and with the 'far abroad' in Asia. The referendum of March 1991, although the three

Baltic republics, Armenia, Georgia, and Moldova refused to participate, had produced a substantial majority in favour of the retention of the USSR as a 'renewed federation' (Gorbachev himself claimed it was a mandate for a 'renewal and strengthening of the union state'),[193] and on 17 June a new version of the union treaty that took account of the vote was sent to the Supreme Soviet and to republican parliaments for their consideration.[194] On 12 July the new treaty was approved by the Supreme Soviet, and on 24 July Gorbachev was able to announce that nine of the fifteen republics had reached a more general agreement.[195] As published in the central press on 15 August it specified that a new 'Union of Sovereign States' would be established in which defence, foreign policy, energy, communications, transport, and budgetary matters would be decided 'jointly' by the centre and the republics, but that in all other matters republican laws would have precedence over those of the union as a whole.[196] Addressing the nation on television at the start of August, Gorbachev confirmed that the new treaty would be signed first by Russia, Kazakhstan, and Uzbekistan at a ceremony later in the month, and went on to describe this as the 'decisive stage' in the transformation of a multinational state into a 'democratic federation of equal soviet sovereign republics' that would continue to be a 'great world power'.[197]

It was this version of the union treaty that was to have been signed by Russian and other representatives on 20 August – a weakening of central authority that the attempted coup, launched the previous day, had apparently been intended to prevent. In the event, the coup discredited the draft treaty and led to a series of declarations of republican independence that by the end of the year had led to the dissolution of the USSR itself. Ukraine was the first to declare its independence, on 24 August; Moldova followed on 27 August, and Azerbaijan on 30 August.[198] The Belorussian president, Nikolai Dementei, who had supported the coup, resigned on 25 August, shortly after which the republican parliament voted to declare the 'political and economic independence of Belorussia'.[199] The Uzbek parliament voted similarly on 31 August; so did Kyrgyzstan; Tajikistan voted for independence on 9 September, Armenia on 23 September, Turkmenistan on 27 October, and Kazakhstan on 16 December.[200] The three Baltic republics had meanwhile been allowed to secede, restoring the independence they had never properly lost;[201] and Georgia had declared its newly independent status in April, following elections in which nationalists had been overwhelmingly successful.[202] By the end of the year Russia was the only republic that had not adopted a declaration of this kind; but it had declared its sovereignty on 12 June 1990, which provided for the precedence of its own laws over those of the USSR as a whole, and had gradually taken over the functions of the all-union government within its own boundaries.[203]

Republican declarations generally took a similar form, including a change of name (they became 'republics' rather than 'Soviet socialist republics') and an assertion of ownership of the property and government institutions located on their respective territories. Their leaders resigned from the CPSU, which by this time had been banned in most of the republics (in some cases, particularly in Central Asia, it continued as a dominant presence in national life under the same leadership but with a change of name and a new-found commitment to democracy).[204] The newly independent republics also became more assertive in matters of defence and foreign policy, applying (in most cases) to join the United Nations and (more generally) seeking to establish their own armed forces. The draft union treaty was clearly superseded by these developments; as the Kazakh president Nursultan Nazarbaev told the Supreme Soviet in early September, only a much looser confederation would satisfy the aspirations of the republics that still wished to conclude some kind of association.[205] In the end, ten of them – including some that had declared independence – agreed a joint statement which indicated that a loose 'union of sovereign states' of the kind Gorbachev had proposed would be established based on the Slavic and Central Asian republics. Gorbachev, for the time being, would remain president, but he would rule through a Council of State on which all the participating republics would be represented. Management of the economy would be entrusted to an inter-republican committee headed by the Russian prime minister, Ivan Silaev; the old Soviet parliament would be replaced by a new two-chamber assembly; and in due course a new constitution would be presented for approval, leading in 1992 to presidential and perhaps more general multiparty elections the following year.[206]

These were intended to be no more than interim arrangements, and further negotiations took place in which Gorbachev sought to establish the basis of a more substantial union. An economic union was established by eight of the former republics on 18 October (Moldova and Ukraine added their signatures the following month),[207] and later, on 14 November, nine of the original fifteen republics (excluding the Baltic republics, Georgia, Armenia, and Moldova) reached agreement on another version of the 'union of sovereign states'. This agreement, like those that had preceded it, envisaged a directly elected presidency and a bicameral legislature. Central authority, however, would be limited to those spheres of activity that had been specifically delegated to it by the members of the union.[208] The draft of this new version of a union treaty, the fifth and final, appeared in the press in late November.[209] Gorbachev announced that it would be sent to republican parliaments for their consideration, and hoped it would be signed by the middle of December;[210] he himself regarded publication of the treaty as a 'collective initialling',[211] and in early December he issued an appeal to the parliaments of the various republics urging them to give it their formal support.[212]

A referendum in Ukraine on 1 December, however, had already resulted in a majority of over 90 per cent in favour of a fully independent status,[213] and this appears to have convinced Yeltsin that it would be unprofitable to pursue the goal of political union any further (he was personally in favour of the Union, but 'could not envisage a Union without Ukraine').[214] The Russian government, in the event, recognised the Ukrainian decision and looked forward to a 'new partnership';[215] and on 8 December, at a country house in the Belovezh forest outside Minsk, the three Slav republics – Russia, Belorussia, and Ukraine – concluded an agreement establishing an entirely new entity, the Commonwealth of Independent States. The new Commonwealth was not a state and it would not have a capital, but it would nonetheless provide for unitary control of nuclear arms, a single currency, and a 'single economic space'. There would be joint action on customs, transport and communications, environment, and organised crime, and a special agreement would be concluded on Chernobyl, which affected all of the signatories. The USSR, as a subject of international law and a geopolitical reality, was declared no longer in existence, and the three republics denounced the 1922 treaty through which it had originally been established.[216] There were considerable questions about the legality of this action, as we have already seen (pp. 32–3); the Committee on Constitutional Supervision ruled the agreement without legal force, as no republic could decide questions that affected the rights and interests of others, and Gorbachev, welcoming some 'positive elements', called for it to be considered by republican parliaments and perhaps to be the subject of another referendum.[217] Andrei Kozyrev, who was one of those present, thought it would be necessary to convene 'some kind of forum of all the union republics' where the new treaty could 'finally' be adopted; but one of Yeltsin's counsellors, lawyer Sergei Shakhrai, persuaded him and others that they could take a decision of this kind without further formality as the three republics had been the founding members of the USSR, together with a Transcaucasian Federation that no longer existed, and must be allowed to reverse their original agreement.[218]

The new Commonwealth declared itself open to other Soviet republics, as well as to states elsewhere that shared its objectives. On 21 December, in the Kazakh capital Alma-Ata, a further agreement was signed by the three original members and by eight of the nine other republics – Armenia, Azerbaijan, Kazakhstan, Kyrgyzstan, Moldova, Tajikistan, Turkmenistan, and Uzbekistan (but not Georgia). The declaration[219] committed those who signed it to recognise the independence and sovereignty of other members, to respect for human rights including those of national minorities, and to observe existing boundaries. Relations among the members of the Commonwealth were to be conducted on an equal, multilateral basis, but it was agreed to endorse the principle of unitary control of strategic nuclear arms and the concept of a 'single economic space'. The USSR as such was held to have 'ended its existence', but the members of the Commonwealth pledged themselves to discharge the obligations that arose from the 15,000 or so international agreements to which the USSR had been a party.[220] In a separate agreement, the heads of member states agreed that Russia should take the seat at the United Nations formerly occupied by the USSR, and a framework of inter-state and inter-governmental consultation was established.[221] Gorbachev resigned as USSR president on 25 December, retaining a salary, a staff of twenty, and two cars;[222] his offices in the Kremlin were occupied by representatives of the Russian government, and on 26 December the upper house of the USSR Supreme Soviet voted a formal end to the original treaty of union (which had not, in fact, provided for any procedure of this kind).[223] The Russian Soviet Federal Socialist Republic, on 25 December, had meanwhile become the Russian Federation, or simply Russia.[224]

The new Commonwealth remained a loose and ambiguous framework. Its intergovernmental institutions provided an opportunity for consultation rather than executive action, its decisions were often of little practical effect, its member states showed little inclination to orient their trade towards other members, and they concluded bilateral agreements among themselves that were often of greater practical significance. Equally, they went to war: most conspicuously when Armenia and Azerbaijan came into conflict over the predominantly Armenian enclave of Nagorno-Karabakh in the late 1980s, in a struggle that had led to 20,000 deaths and over a million refugees by the time a ceasefire was declared in 1994,[225] less dramatically in a continuing civil war in Tajikistan that involved Russian troops as CIS peacemakers in a joint attempt to limit an internecine struggle that had acquired some of the characteristics of Islamic fundamentalism. The member states had originally been committed to a 'single economic space', but there was no formal commitment to the ruble, and in the end all the member states established their own currencies. There were continuing tensions between republics, such as Ukraine, that were suspicious of any form of supranational 'centre', and others – particularly in Central Asia – that favoured a greater degree of integration. The CIS nonetheless survived, and acquired more members;[226] there was even talk of extending membership beyond the Soviet republics, perhaps – its executive secretary himself suggested – to Iran, as a step towards a 'CIS without borders'.[227]

The new Commonwealth, at the same time, began to define its powers and responsibilities more precisely. A collective security treaty was adopted in 1992, initially by six of the member states.[228] A Charter was approved in January 1993, although only seven of the ten states that were present agreed to sign it and only two of them without reservations; it insisted on the 'sovereign equality' of all the CIS members, but at the same time committed them to a variety of forms of co-ordination including human rights, foreign policy, transport and communications, and health and social policy, and to the common maintenance of their external borders. A council of heads of state was the 'supreme organ' of the CIS, with meetings twice a year, but there were other forms of shared decision-making at ministerial level, and an interparliamentary assembly.[229] An economic union was agreed in May 1993, in a treaty initialled by nine of the member states.[230] Primakov took a greater interest in the CIS than his more Western-oriented predecessor, arguing that it would evolve into a fully fledged 'common market';[231] but it remained, in the view of commentators, a 'very sick organism',[232] and in the view of its own executive secretary the CIS was simply a 'mechanism for reconciling interests, nothing more'.[233] Russian relations with the former Soviet republics, in the end, reflected specific sets of circumstances in every case.

Relations with the largest and most important of Russia's CIS partners, Ukraine, were complicated by a dispute over control of the Black Sea fleet, with Yeltsin insisting that the fleet 'was, is, and will continue to be Russian', but with the Ukrainian authorities insisting that all troops in the republic, other than strategic nuclear forces, accept their orders and take an oath of allegiance.[234] Russian relations with Ukraine were also complicated by the issue of the Crimea, whose predominantly Russian population favoured a greater degree of autonomy or even separation; the entire region had become a part of Ukraine as late as 1954, when Khrushchev chose to mark the 300th anniversary of Ukraine's unification with Russia in a transaction that many Russians – including Moscow mayor Yuri Luzhkov – regarded as illegitimate,[235] and which was denounced by the Russian parliament in May 1992.[236]

Nearly a quarter of the entire republican population, including most of eastern Ukraine and the industrial Donbass, was also Russian speaking, and there were as many as 20 million visits a year in each direction.[237] President Kuchma, in an interview in early 1997, blamed Russia's 'prejudiced attitude' for the continuing difficulties in their relationship,[238] and it was not until May 1997 that President Yeltsin was able to make an official state visit. When he did so it was to sign a treaty of friendship, co-operation, and partnership that appeared to place relations between the two countries on a stable and amicable footing.[239] The treaty contained a commitment to the inviolability of the boundaries of the two states (which meant that there would be no Russian encouragement of secessionist movements by fellow nationals), and it ruled out the use of the territory of either state to undermine the security of the other; there were also guarantees for the cultural rights of national minorities, including radio and television transmissions in their respective languages. The Black Sea fleet would consist of a Russian and a Ukrainian section, both of which would use the historic port of Sevastopol; and both states supported the wider framework of security, 'from Vancouver to Vladivostok', for which the Russians had for some time been pressing.[240] When Kuchma, in his turn, visited Moscow in early 1998, the two presidents signed a treaty on economic co-operation that was to last for a further ten years.[241]

Among the other Soviet republics Russia enjoyed particularly close relations with Belarus, as Belorussia was now known, where Alexander Lukashenko had won an overwhelming victory in presidential elections in the summer of 1994.[242] Lukashenko, a former collective farm chairman who had become prominent as an anticorruption campaigner, was a strong supporter of closer relations with Russia, for economic as well as cultural reasons. In February 1995 the two presidents signed a treaty of friendship and co-operation during a state visit by the Russian president to a republic that he described as Russia's 'closest partner'; Lukashenko, for his part, noted that the republic saw its future 'only on the basis of a deeper integration with Russia'.[243] There was a strong emphasis upon economic integration in particular, within the framework of a customs union that had been concluded earlier in the year and to which Kazakhstan had subsequently adhered.[244] In March a statement from President Lukashenko ruled out Belarusian membership of NATO;[245] and in May, a referendum gave overwhelming popular support to the resumption of closer cultural and economic ties with Russia, to the reinstatement of Russian as an official language (together with Belarusian), to the readoption of the Soviet-era flag and national symbol, and to an extension of presidential powers.[246] While insisting that Belarus would 'never lose its sovereignty', Lukashenko called for closer political integration with Russia than had existed even in the Soviet period.[247]

Matters moved much further in March 1996 with the conclusion of a 'treaty of the four' (Russia, Belarus, Kazakhstan, and Kyrgyzstan) which provided for the 'deepening of [their] integration in the economic and humanitarian spheres', and more particularly for the creation of a 'single economic space', the harmonisation of legislation, minimum standards of social assistance across all the member states, and an 'agreed foreign policy', and at some point in the future the creation of a 'community of integrated states'. It was described by the presidents at their signing as an 'epochal' agreement for the four states that were 'joined by a common historical fate', and was to be valid for five years with automatic extension, and open to other states.[248] Then in April Russia and Belarus together concluded a treaty that established a 'deeply integrated . . . Community', with wide-ranging powers including a common foreign policy, shared use of 'military infrastructure', a common power grid, and eventually a common currency.[249] For President Yeltsin, the treaty strengthened his appeal to Russian nationalist opinion in the run-up to the presidential elections of the summer; for President Lukashenko it had obvious economic advantages. Lukashenko was able to secure popular support for an extension of his powers and of his presidential term at a referendum in November 1996;[250] Western governments expressed reservations about the result and about the president's increasingly authoritarian methods, but Prime Minister Chernomyrdin congratulated him on a 'real victory'.[251]

A more far-reaching treaty of union was signed in April 1997, converting a Community of the two states into a Union.[252] The treaty, the two presidents declared, was a 'historic event' that had 'taken to a new level the process of unification of two friendly peoples and the integration of our states'. Both states, they announced, were firm in their resistance to NATO's eastward expansion, which could only lead to a 'dangerous confrontation'. The two presidents undertook to unify their legislation; every effort would be made to synchronise their economic and taxation policies, including the establishment of transnational companies, and with a view to the introduction of a common currency. Social benefits would gradually be equalised so that living standards increasingly converged; and there might be a joint citizenship of the Community that the two states had established.[253] A statute approved the following May, after public discussion, made a series of more specific provisions including a single citizenship of the new Union.[254] And in December 1998 both leaders took a further step, calling for a more far-reaching union but without surrendering their individual sovereignties. Again, many of the more detailed provisions were to be agreed at a future point, and like the other agreements that had been concluded between the two states the rhetoric ran far in advance of the treaty's more practical effect. Yeltsin, nonetheless, declared that it had opened a 'new page' in the history of relations between the two countries; they would 'enter the twenty-first century together', added Lukashenko, 'and God willing, as a unitary state'.[255]

The former Soviet republics had by now divided into a 'two', Russia and Belarus, which were close to a confederal union; a 'four', including Kazakhstan and Kyrgyzstan, which had established a 'common market' and were committed in principle to still closer links; and other groups, such as the 'five' (Azerbaijan, Georgia, Moldova, Ukraine, and from 1999 Uzbekistan), which had established a framework of multilateral co-operation that reflected their regional concerns.[256] Reviewing the whole pattern of Russian relations with the other former Soviet republics in 1998, *Izvestiya* noted that they spanned a wide spectrum. There were 'almost model' relations with Belarus, but 'uncertain' relations with Ukraine in spite of 'encouraging tendencies'. There was 'no convergence' in relations with Georgia, but neighbouring Armenia was 'almost an ally', and the Moldovans were 'well-disposed partners'. In Central Asia, Uzbekistan was 'demonstratively independent' and 'pragmatic', there were 'contradictory' relations with Tajikistan, and 'less and less understanding' with Turkmenistan, but 'more clarity and reliability' in relations with Kazakhstan, and Kyrgyzstan had become a 'loyal and well-meaning partner'.[257] Popular attitudes were equally varied, but there was most support for close relations with the other Slavic republics and particularly Belarus;[258] the same emphases were apparent in patterns of trade, with Ukraine, Belarus, and Kazakhstan providing the largest share of Russian imports and exports of all the CIS members.[259]

The Soviet relationship with Asia was dominated by the relationship with a still communist China, with whom the USSR had shared the world's longest land border as well as an ideology and system of government. The Chinese authorities were clearly distressed by the gradual relaxation of communist control in the USSR and Eastern Europe, but in visits to Beijing by Gorbachev in May 1989, and to Moscow by Premier Li Peng in 1990 and by party leader Jiang Zemin in May 1991, both sides agreed to preserve normal relations and to accept differences in their 'ways and means of pursuing reforms within the framework of the socialist choice'.[260] The collapse of the USSR at the end of 1991 placed Russo-Chinese relations on a new basis, as the postcommunist Russian government was explicitly committed to human rights as they were understood in the West, while the Chinese insisted that human rights were a domestic matter and in any case that they could be understood only in the context of their own history, in which basic human needs had always occupied a more prominent place.[261] Yeltsin made a first visit to China in December 1992, where he called for a 'new era' in relations between the two countries,[262] but his visit was cut short by the need to assist the formation of a new Russian government; and a planned visit to Japan did not take place at all because of continuing differences over the fate of the southern Kurile islands (in the end the two states agreed to 'make every effort' to conclude a peace treaty that would regulate all aspects of their relations by the year 2000).[263]

The Chinese leadership appears to have taken the view that communist rule had come to an end in the USSR because of the weakness and indecision of the Soviet leadership,[264] but they refrained from public criticism of their Russian counterparts; Russian ministers, for their part, made no comment on the state of Chinese human rights (as Gorbachev had remarked about the Tiananmen Square massacre of 1989, 'We cannot interfere or give advice').[265] In September 1994 Jiang Zemin was in Moscow on another official visit but this time to a postcommunist Russia, developing what both countries had agreed to describe as a 'constructive partnership'; as it was defined in a declaration that was signed during the visit, this meant 'equitable, nonideologised relations constructed on the basis of good-neighbourliness, friendship, and mutual advantage'.[266] This, both sides made clear, was not an alliance, but there was a separate and additional agreement that each side would not target the other with its missiles, and there was further progress on defining the Russo-Chinese border and on military co-operation, and a protocol was signed on trade and economic co-operation. Jiang told journalists he had 'reaped a good harvest' during his visit.[267]

Li Peng was in Moscow in 1995 for another round of talks, which took place (according to the communiqué) in a spirit of 'complete political unanimity'; Russia re-emphasised its 'one China' policy, by which relations could be sustained with Taiwan but without conceding that it had any right to China's United Nations representation, and the Chinese supported Yeltsin's Chechen campaign, showing 'complete understanding of the actions taken by the Russian side to preserve the country's unity'.[268] Relations moved to a qualitatively new level during President Yeltsin's visit to Beijing in 1996, as part of a more assertive and less pro-Western orientation in Russian policy more generally. The two countries, it was agreed, had established 'relations of equal partnership, based on trust, that [were] aimed at strategic co-operation in the twenty-first century'.[269] In their joint communiqué Yeltsin committed Russia once again to the Chinese positions on Taiwan and on Tibet, while the Chinese endorsed Russian policy towards Chechnya (an 'internal affair of Russia') and towards the expansion of NATO. Both sides also agreed to deplore the 'hegemonism' of, in effect, the Western powers; and in what was a symbolic as well as a practical move, a 'hot line' was installed between the two capitals.[270]

The Chinese president visited Russia once again in April 1997, signing an elaborate declaration on a 'multipolar world and the forma-tion of a new world order' and concluding an agreement on arms reductions along the common borders of the two countries and of Kazakhstan, Kyrgyzstan, and Tajikistan in which the leaders of those states also took part.[271] A fifth summit between the two presidents took place in November 1997; neither state, it was noted, pursued any 'hegemonistic or expansionist aims', and by this time 'virtually all issues' that related to their common border, still not entirely demarcated, had been agreed.[272] Yeltsin was able to make a friendly visit to the Russian community in Harbin, most of whom had fled their home country in the 1920s, and a Russo-Chinese committee of friendship, peace, and devel-opment was set up to 'strengthen the traditions of Russo-Chinese partnership, trust, and good-neighbourliness'.[273] Reviewing progress at the end of his first full year as foreign minister, Primakov drew particular attention to the 'significant progress' that had been made in relations with China;[274] but while both sides could agree to deplore the 'hege-monism' of a single power, the Chinese remained reluctant to under-write Russian plans for a joint system of Asian security, and bilateral trade remained (in the words of Russian vice-premier Boris Nemtsov) 'laughable for two great countries'.[275]

The USSR had traditionally enjoyed good relations with the other major Asian giant, India; it was, for instance, the only country in the developing world that Leonid Brezhnev had ever visited (and he went there twice).[276] Gorbachev also made two visits, and his 1986 declara-tion on a 'nonviolent' as well as non-nuclear world clearly reflected Indian as well as Soviet thinking.[277] Yeltsin's much-postponed visit, which took place at the start of 1993, was designed to end a 'prolonged interruption' in relations between the two countries, and made signifi-cant progress in dealing with the Indian debt; the USSR had always been India's main arms supplier and there was particular satisfaction that the new Russian government was prepared to supply cryogenic rocket engines, despite strong pressure from the United States. India, for Yeltsin, was a 'faithful partner and reliable ally', and the two countries concluded a new friendship treaty that took the place of the

Soviet agreement of 1971.[278] Primakov, in a visit at the end of 1998, went so far as to call for a 'strategic triangle' that would involve India, China, and Russia in arrangements for regional security, building on the 'strategic partnership' with China and strong ties with India.[279] It was unclear how two traditional adversaries would be persuaded to co-operate in this way, or to accept a place in Primakov's wider framework; but Russian representatives were aware of their limited influence within the postcommunist world order and there was considerable satisfaction that India as well China had been persuaded to share the Russian commitment to a multipolar world order that would 'completely exclude the policy of *diktat*'.[280]

Continuity and change in Russian foreign policy

Just as the Soviet leadership had gradually identified with the foreign policy priorities of its tsarist predecessor, so too the Russian president and his government moved from a 'naïve Westernism' that had assumed a basic community of interest to a vigorous defence of what they took to be the Russian national interest. Like their predecessors, they ruled the world's largest country, spanning Europe and Asia, and one of its most populous. They ruled a nuclear power, and one that was the world's twelfth-largest economy.[281] They were represented among the world's most powerful nations, in the Group of Eight and as a permanent member of the UN Security Council. But if Russia still 'mattered', there was no disguising the fact that it had lost almost a quarter of the territory its Soviet predecessor had occupied, and almost half the population. It had lost its allies in Eastern Europe (some of them, indeed, had changed sides), and it had lost its network of 'fraternal parties' throughout the world. Its economy had contracted almost continuously since the last years of Soviet rule, and so had its armed forces. It was unable to balance its budget, or pay its debts. This meant, unavoidably, that Russia's place in the world order was a very different one from that of its Soviet predecessor: weaker, and often marginal. This gave rise, in turn, to a series of debates, some of them old (was Russia a society that was fundamentally the same as its Western counterparts and therefore a natural partner, or a Eurasian civilisation that had its own characteristics?), and some of them new (including the security architecture that was appropriate to a post-cold war world).

Was Russia, for instance, still a great power, if not an empire? Kozyrev had argued that Russia was 'doomed to be a great power' by virtue of its territory, natural resources, and military might,[282] and this meant that Russia must be an equal, not a junior partnership in the relationship with the other superpower, with every right to promote its own interests as vigorously as necessary. Primakov was still more assertive, insisting that Russia had not lost the cold war and that there must be an 'equal partnership' with other nations. He was aiming, at the same time, to establish Russia as 'one of the influential centres of a multipolar world',[283] and this had become the central objective of Russian foreign policy by the late 1990s. There was no claim to be the 'other superpower', as in the Soviet period, but Russian representatives became increasingly concerned to defend their own interests and to resist what would otherwise be the unchallenged dominance of the United States. This meant an emphasis upon the United Nations, where they commanded a position of formal equality in the Security Council, and upon the OSCE, which provided a framework for European security within which all its nations were represented. It meant a greater emphasis at the same time upon relations with China, and with other states that might help to ensure a more balanced international order. Equally, it meant a determined campaign – even though it was a campaign they were bound to lose – against the expansion of NATO into Eastern Europe, and most of all in the direction of former Soviet republics.

But it was difficult, in the end, to resist the implications of the diminished international status that followed economic decline and the collapse of the network of alliances the USSR had once commanded. As we have seen, there were occasions in Iraq and Yugoslavia when the Western powers took military action without even informing their Russian counterparts, and even when that action was nominally taking place under the auspices of the United Nations. More seriously, there were signs that NATO was becoming the preferred vehicle of Western policy-makers, whether or not their actions had the sanction of the United Nations; and that NATO was increasingly willing to act 'out of area', imposing its will (for instance) in Yugoslavia even though it was not a part of the alliance and had not directly threatened the territory of any of its member nations. Indeed there were indications that NATO was preparing to act in a still broader capacity, keeping peace in the Caucasus, or saving hostages in North Africa,[284] or even (its deputy secretary general told *Krasnaya zvezda*) 'assuming peace-keeping functions the world over'.[285]

There were equally clear signs that Russian opinion mattered less and less to Western policy-makers within this or any other connection. What had once been a 'strategic partnership' with the United States dwindled into a 'pragmatic' and then a 'realistic partnership', and finally to a state of 'candid realism' that appeared to leave no element of partnership at all.[286] The US State Department, by the late 1990s, no longer defined

Russia as even a potential ally, unlike, for instance, Ukraine.[287] And if Russia figured in the speeches of Western and particularly of American politicians, it was less as an emerging democracy and more often as a source of instability, organised crime, and dangerous nuclear power installations. Russia figured in President Clinton's 1999 state of the union address, for instance, only as a dangerous storehouse of badly maintained nuclear weapons. Russia, complained *Kommersant'*, had now 'almost officially been declared to be "Upper Volta with rockets"; but while in the cold war years this was simply a propaganda cliché, now it is treated as reality'.[288]

If Russia could no longer turn to the West, or at least to the United States, where then did Russian interests lie? Was Russia, for instance, destined to become another 'European' power? Russia, after all, shared its Christian heritage with the rest of the continent. It had an Indo-European language. Its monarchy had been related to the other crowned heads of Europe. It had been a part of the international system since at least the seventeenth century, and an ally of the Western democracies in two world wars. Indeed, its ideology had been European, in that it could be traced to Marx and the organised socialist movement before the First World War, a movement to which the Bolsheviks had belonged after they split from more moderate socialists at the congress they held in London in 1903. Russians in the 1990s, on balance, took a positive view of the European Union (the largest number, admittedly, were indifferent), and there was a majority in favour of Russian membership. Other European countries, at the same time, were rarely seen as a threat to Russian security as compared with China, Iran, or the United States.[289] But if there were closer relations, few (7 per cent) thought Russians themselves would benefit; both might benefit (29 per cent took this view), but even more (33 per cent) thought the EU itself would be the beneficiary.[290] And did ordinary Russians think of themselves as 'Europeans' in any case? According to the survey evidence, rarely: 11 per cent did so often and 13 per cent sometimes, but 54 per cent never did so.[291] Substantial majorities, moreover, were convinced Russia should follow its 'own traditions', rather than the West European or any other foreign model.[292]

These questions, in turn, raised complex questions of identity and territoriality. Who, for instance, was a 'Russian', particularly if they lived outside the Russian Federation? And where was the territory that they should properly share: did it extend beyond the borders of the Russian Federation to the former Soviet republics, or at least to the other Slavic states? It was a question that had a particular bearing upon the substantial numbers of Russians that now lived in other states. According to the 1989 census, there were 145.2 million Russians within what were then Soviet borders, but only 119.9 million lived in the Russian Federation. Another 11.4 million lived in Ukraine, where they were 22 per cent of the local population, and the 6.2 million that lived in Kazakhstan represented more than a third of its total population – indeed, until the 1970s there were more Russians in Kazakhstan than Kazakhs themselves. There were fewer Russians in the Baltic republics, but they accounted for a third of the population of Estonia and Latvia, and many more spoke Russian as their native language;[293] no Russian government could be indifferent to their well-being, or regard it as the internal affair of a newly independent foreign state. Under the law on citizenship of 1992, indeed, these 'other Russians' were able to apply for Russian citizenship, and more than 1.5 million had done so by 1997.[294] This was more than a cultural diaspora, these were citizens and fellow nationals who expected the support of their government if their rights were infringed; difficulties of this kind arose most often in the Baltic republics, where substantial numbers were denied the right to vote as well as other forms of participation in public life, and the Russian government occasionally threatened to apply economic sanctions on their behalf.[295]

Just as it was uncertain where 'Russians' came to an end, it was unclear where the state itself had its boundaries. The Crimea, as we have seen, was still 'legally' a part of Russia for the Duma, and for Moscow mayor Yuri Luzhkov. Kaliningrad was universally accepted as a part of Russia, but it was physically separated from the rest of the national territory. Chechnya had declared its independence, a demand that was not accepted by the Russian government, and a resolution of the difference between them had simply been postponed. There were old but unresolved differences with Finland, where part of Karelia had been acquired by the USSR after the Winter War. There were more intractable differences with the Baltic republics; the Potsdam conference of 1945, for instance, had given Klaipeda to the USSR, but it had remained a part of Lithuania. The Russo-Lithuanian border was only a provisional one, the Supreme Soviet resolved in November 1992, and so were Russian borders with the other two Baltic republics.[296] There had been no agreement of any kind with Japan since the Second World War, because of the contested status of the southern Kuriles. Indeed of all the fourteen states that had a common border with postcommunist Russia, only with Norway, Belarus, Mongolia, and Lithuania were the boundaries formally agreed; Ukraine, for instance, had given notice that it would be seeking a new delimitation of the Black and Azov seas.[297]

Beyond these uncertainties, there were still wider issues of geopolitics.

As the Russian foreign minister observed in early 1999, the Asia-Pacific world accounted for 50 per cent of the world's gross domestic product and for 60 per cent of the world's trade.[298] So there was every reason for Primakov to insist that a 'power like Russia, with enormous interests in Asia and the Middle East', could not 'walk on just one – Western – leg'.[299] But there was little sign, at least in patterns of foreign trade, that Russia was turning towards its Asian neighbours. The country's main partners, throughout the postcommunist period, were the developed economies of the capitalist West: China and Japan were important export markets, but less than Germany, the Netherlands, or the United States; China, again, was an important source of Russian imports, but more than five times as much was imported from the United States, and there were also more imports from Italy, Finland, France, the United Kingdom, Poland, and the Netherlands.[300] There was still more disturbing evidence that Russia was being bypassed along its southern borders by the arrangements that were being made for the export of oil and gas from Kazakhstan and Azerbaijan to Western markets. This, it was argued, by a group of Moscow University researchers, could 'fundamentally alter the situation in the regime'; it would be 'comparable to the opening of the sea route to India around Africa and the discovery of the American continent, as a result of which the Italian city-states were consigned to the periphery of European politics'.[301] These were developments that were already shaping the politics of the twenty-first century; they were likely to reduce Russia's geopolitical weight still further, and yet there was little the postcommunist government could do about them.

8   Russia, transition, democracy

Just as the October revolution in 1917 was a landmark in world history, so too the end of communist rule in its country of origin appeared to be a turning point, and not just in Russia. For Boris Yeltsin, speaking just after the attempted coup had collapsed, the Soviet people had 'thrown off the chains of seventy years of slavery'.[1] A 'parliamentary democracy', he claimed later in the year, was 'already being formed'.[2] The defeat of the coup, he wrote in his memoirs, was even more than this: it was the end, not just of communist rule in Russia, but of the twentieth century itself; it had ended, he suggested, 'on 19–21 August 1991', when in just three days 'one century finished and another began'.[3] For Yegor Gaidar, similarly, the end of communist rule had been a 'revolution comparable in its influence on the historical process to the Great French Revolution, the Russian revolution of 1917, and the Chinese revolution of 1949'.[4] *Izvestiya*, writing just after the collapse of the coup, thought democracy itself had 'taught the people not to be silent': a reference to Pushkin's *Boris Godunov*, in which local townspeople had been invited to welcome the False Dmitrii but had refused to respond, and which had served since that time as a metaphor for Russia's long-suffering but (it seemed) eternally passive citizenry.[5] Gorbachev's still larger view was that the society itself had changed: it was more educated, more diverse, and more accustomed to the political freedoms it had acquired during the years of his reforms, and for these reasons it would never accept the reimposition of authoritarian forms of government.[6] For some, indeed, it was the 'end of history' itself, after seventy years in which liberal democracy had faced a real alternative.[7]

The experience of the early postcommunist years suggested a less extravagant verdict. The same people, it appeared, were still in power, even if they no longer called themselves communists. They had very similar privileges, and often the same buildings and facilities. There was little popular control over the actions of government, in spite of elections that were genuinely competitive. Political parties and associations of all kinds were weak and poorly supported; the rule of law was routinely flouted; and the state itself appeared to have dissolved into an agglomeration of powerful interests at the centre and local fiefdoms in the republics and regions, with no ability at any level to collect taxes or maintain public order. This was no longer communism, which had ended in a meaningful sense in the late 1980s; but neither was it democracy, at least in its classic form. It was, some suggested, a new system entirely: a 'military-bureaucratic state with a criminal market economy';[8] or a '*nomenklatura* democracy' that left ordinary people with as little influence as before over those who ruled them;[9] or in Grigorii Yavlinsky's phrase, a 'criminal oligarchy with a monopolistic state'.[10] For Alexander Solzhenitsyn, similarly, the postcommunist Russian system was 'not a democracy but a 'stable and tight oligarchy of 150 or 200 people, including the most cunning representatives of the top and middle strata of the former communist ruling structure, along with *nouveaux riches* who amassed their recent fortunes through banditry'.[11] Equally, others suggested, it might be a state form that paralleled regimes in Latin America, with their social divisions, politicised armies, weak legal systems, and corrupt governments, even if they coexisted with private property, a relatively open press, and competitive elections.[12]

From this perspective there had been a break with communist rule, but not with a much longer-standing pattern in which a strong state had dominated a weak society, with decisive change coming from above and little more than token resistance from ordinary citizens.[13] Russia, it had to be remembered, had always been 'a society apart in the European community'.[14] It had, for a start, established representative government much later than in other European countries or North America. Its first parliament, the State Duma, was elected as late as 1905, with a very limited range of powers. The franchise was much narrower than in other European countries – just 2 or 3 per cent of adults, at a time when 20–30 per cent enjoyed the right to vote in France, Germany, the United Kingdom, and the United States. Political parties and trade unions of any kind were illegal until 1905, and operated thereafter on a severely restricted basis.[15] There was a detailed and intrusive censorship, and even after 1906 the press was treated in a manner that 'would have been considered intolerable in a Western country'.[16] It was difficult, moreover, to defend even these limited rights through the courts, because up to the end of the tsarist period it had been a 'crime in Russia to seek changes in the existing system of government or administration, or even to raise questions about such issues', with politics a 'monopoly of those in power'.[17] From this point of view there had been no radical break, not just between Soviet and postcommunist Russia but between both of them and their tsarist predecessor. There was a new KGB, complained *Izvestiya*; dissidents were still being repressed; former party secretaries were sitting in the same offices but calling themselves governors; and officials were stealing as they would never have dreamed of doing in the Brezhnev years. Was it time to put up a monument to their victory, asked the paper, 'or to our disappointed hopes?'[18]

But if many of the methods of rule had persisted, it was still unclear how a state that had been a going concern for more than seventy years had managed to collapse so suddenly. What were the forces that had sustained communist rule throughout those years, and what were the factors that had brought about its end? What weight should be attached to long-term factors such as 'modernisation', and what to particular and much more short-term circumstances including Western pressure and the choices of the Soviet leadership itself? What, indeed, had 'collapsed' and what had continued after the end of Soviet rule? Had an authoritarian system continued under a different leadership, as *Izvestiya* appeared to be suggesting, or had a recognisable democracy come into being in just a few years, now that a single-party monopoly had been displaced? Were these, indeed, the only choices? And were there explanations that fitted not simply the collapse of communist rule in the USSR, but also its persistence in China, Cuba, and much of South-East Asia? The USSR had been the world's first and most extended experiment in communist rule; it was in turn the most important example of a complex process of change that suggested all kinds of questions for social scientists. What, for instance, were the links between Russia's new institutions of government and popular attitudes? Did democratic institutions reflect a popular commitment of a kind that might help to sustain them, or were values – in Russia and elsewhere – more likely to be shaped by government performance? What, in that connection, were the political implications of a collapsing economy? And could developments of this kind, in any case, be understood in the same terms as democracy in Western Europe, which was informed by a culture that had always valued the rule of law and individual rights?[19]

The end of Soviet rule

The collapse of Soviet rule had been a surprise to the outside world, and indeed to its own citizens. There were many, certainly, for whom there had been few prospects of a change in communist rule during the 1980s, not only in the USSR but throughout Eastern Europe. For Samuel Huntington, writing in 1984, the likelihood of democratic development in Eastern Europe was 'virtually nil'.[20] Eastern Europe,

others argued, had 'faced worse crises before', and there was no reason
to expect radical changes in the 'foreseeable future'.[21] The communist
states of Eastern Europe, another scholar insisted as late as June 1989,
would 'survive, albeit greatly changed'.[22] For Jerry Hough, in 1990,
Soviet difficulties had been 'grossly exaggerated'; the real story of that
year had been the 'further consolidation of Gorbachev's political position', and he was 'almost certain to remain in power at least until the
1995 presidential election'.[23] Gorbachev's position, Hough wrote a year
later, would be 'very strong in the mid-1990s', and the Communist
Party through which he ruled had an 'excellent chance to become a
dominant electoral party in the Slavic areas on the model of Mexico's
Institutional Revolutionary Party . . . [for] the rest of this century'.[24]
This, indeed, was the advice that Western governments were receiving
from their ambassadors at the same time: Gorbachev, Jack Matlock told
Washington, was likely to remain in power 'for at least five (possibly ten)
years';[25] as he concluded later, it seemed likely up to November 1991
that 'some sort of state, if only a transitional one, would be fashioned by
a majority of the twelve republics that had remained in the Soviet Union
when the Baltics seceded'.[26]

There were few who argued that governments of the Soviet type had
secured the active approval of those who nominally elected them. But
there was, it appeared, a basis for stability in the implicit 'social contract'
that had been concluded between the party leadership and the society
over which they ruled, based upon an exchange of political rights for a
stable and assured standard of living (see chapter 4). Many, it was clear,
had gained real advantages from Soviet rule. Incomes were lower, but
they were distributed more equally.[27] There was free and comprehensive
education, and higher levels of enrolment in colleges and universities
than in many of the industrial democracies.[28] There were opportunities
for professional advancement, particularly in the Brezhnev years, and of
a kind that appeared to provide a 'crucial safety valve against discontent
and a key basis for the positive identification of various social strata with
the regime'.[29] Levels of social provision were among the best in the
world, and considerably better than in states at a comparable level of
economic development.[30] Women earned less than men, as we have
seen, but they were the beneficiaries of a form of positive discrimination
that pushed up their representation in elected institutions at all levels,
and gave them generous maternity benefits (see chapter 5). Basic
necessities, at the same time, were made available at low and stable
prices. The rents for public housing, for instance, had remained at the
same level since 1928; foodstuffs were heavily subsidised; and public
transport was extremely cheap (for decades the standard fare on the

Moscow underground had been 5 kopeks, about 6 cents at the prevailing rate of exchange).

For many, indeed, this was a system that had been securely established. It was an 'indigenous' regime, not one that had been imposed by a foreign army, and it had earned the support of the Soviet people when it led the resistance to Nazi occupation throughout a war in which 3 million party members had lost their lives. Nominally at least, it rested upon the participation of millions of citizens at all levels of government. And for some, its longevity was in itself a source of stability. The Soviet authorities themselves claimed that religion, nationalism, and the private-property mentality were all 'survivals' (*perezhitki*) of the previous system, which would gradually disappear as those brought up under capitalism were replaced by those brought up under wholly socialist conditions.[31] Western social scientists were equally persuaded that a regime that had been in existence for two or three generations would become the predominant influence upon the political memories of its adult population, and that it would increasingly be taken for granted by those who reached adult years under its auspices.[32] The Soviet system, by the late 1980s, abundantly satisfied these criteria. It had been in existence for seventy years and more than 95 per cent of the population had been born since its establishment;[33] it should gradually have gained acceptance, on this basis, as those with a conscious recollection of the prerevolutionary order became a small and steadily diminishing proportion of the population as a whole.

Views of this kind, however, were far from universally accepted. And from at least the 1960s there were very different suggestions, for instance that the 'new class was divided' between party officials and a more adaptable group of technocrats.[34] Another influential interpretation was that there would be 'convergence' between the Soviet system and its Western counterparts as both were influenced by the requirements of industrial society;[35] a Trotskyist variation on this theme was that the bureaucracy was 'breeding its own gravediggers', as education and social change undermined the centralised forms of government that had been inherited from late Stalinism.[36] By the late 1970s, as economic growth slowed down, the emphasis shifted away from the pluralising consequences of a maturing society to a deepening tension between the ruling group and the wider population; and by the early 1980s, when growth per head of population had fallen to virtually zero, the prognoses had become extremely bleak. For Marshall Goldman, the USSR was 'in crisis';[37] for Richard Pipes, it already fitted Lenin's description of a 'revolutionary situation';[38] for R. V. Burks, 'all the ingredients for some kind of explosion [were] increasingly in place'.[39] For Martin Malia, writing rather later in a celebrated article that appeared under the pseudonym 'Z', there was no prospect of a viable reform under Gorbachev because the inherent contradictions of the system were 'simply too overwhelming'.[40]

For most of these writers, and for many others, the weakness of Soviet rule was more than a matter of short-term difficulties: it also reflected a much deeper contradiction between communist authoritarianism and the open and bargaining culture that corresponded to its economic maturity. Perhaps the most influential exponent of this view was Talcott Parsons, a sociologist – and member of the Russian Research Center at Harvard University – who drew his inspiration from Darwin and much older theories of social change. All states, for Parsons, had to develop a range of capacities or 'evolutionary universals' that would allow them to adapt to the requirements of modern society, among them a 'democratic association with elective leadership and fully enfranchised membership'.[41] For these reasons, Parsons wrote elsewhere, it was as 'certain as such things can be' that communism would 'prove to be short-lived'. The dictatorship of a single party would be unable to establish its legitimacy; scientific and cultural elites would press for a greater degree of autonomy; and social differentiation would make a centrally dominated system increasingly difficult to sustain. For these and other reasons, Parsons concluded, the communist states would be obliged to move towards the 'restoration – or where it has not yet existed, the institution – of political democracy'; indeed this was the '*only* possible outcome – except for general destruction or breakdown'.[42] Others developed these insights into what was effectively an 'iron law of pluralism', as centralised forms of government became increasingly difficult to reconcile with the pressures for a decentralisation of authority that stemmed from a complex and diverse economy.[43] As their societies and economies developed, in the words of Gabriel Almond, communist systems would face the 'inevitable demands of a healthy, educated, affluent society' for both more material and what he called 'spiritual consumer goods' (such as a share in the decision-making process). 'Already', he wrote, 'Russian success in science, education, technology, economic productivity, and national security have produced some decentralisation of the political process. I fail to see how these decentralising, pluralistic tendencies can be reversed, or how their spread can be prevented.'[44]

There was little evidence, as the Prague Spring was crushed and dissidents were incarcerated in mental hospitals, that pluralistic pressures were in fact exerting the influence that had been so widely expected. There was certainly no sign that elected institutions, still more so the central decision-making bodies of the Communist Party, were evolving into the kind of arena for the resolution of competing claims that pluralists had confidently predicted. And as economic growth slowed down in the late 1970s and early 1980s, the prevailing Western interpretation became increasingly bleak and uncompromising. For Robert Tucker, Brezhnev's Russia was a 'spent state and a swollen society';[45] for Seweryn Bialer, it was an example of 'external expansion, internal decline';[46] for others still, it was a regime that confronted a 'bleak economic and social environment, including severe problems of corruption, ethnic tensions, and social strain'.[47] There was an environmental crisis, and a widening gap between rich and poor;[48] there was also a widening network of privilege and corruption centred around a 'party mafia'.[49] For some, this deepening crisis was evidence that modernisation theory had been right all along, as the East European systems found themselves unable to accommodate the pressures that sprang from the diversity that was a result of the economic development they had sponsored, as well as the spread of international trade and an information revolution that was 'incompatible with centralized authoritarian rule'. For Lucian Pye, these were nothing less than 'inexorable forces of history' and the transition itself was a 'vindication of modernization theory'; for Moshe Lewin, similarly, the changes of the 1980s were evidence that Soviet society needed a state that could 'match its complexity'.[50]

Soviet society, on this interpretation, had outgrown its political system: centralised and authoritarian rule was simply dysfunctional to the requirements of an urban, educated, and differentiated society. But while modernisation theories of this kind were persuasive, at least in retrospect, they raised almost as many questions as they answered. There were states more economically advanced than the USSR that had retained a form of authoritarian politics – for instance, in South-East Asia. At the same time there were poorer states that had sustained democracy – for example, India, Sri Lanka, and postwar Japan.[51] The transition from communist rule, it also became clear, was not necessarily a transition to the kinds of competitive politics that were thought appropriate to a more complex and differentiated society. In the Central Asian republics, at least, the end of communist rule led to more authoritarian and centralised government: local leaderships had been obliged to implement the Gorbachev reforms, including a more open electoral system and opportunities to criticise public officials, but after 1991 they were free to ban opposition parties, to elect presidents in uncontested ballots and then extend their terms by referendum, and to muzzle the press – including reporters from Moscow, if they caused any difficulty. Modernisation theories gave little sense of threshold – how much economic development was needed to sustain a pluralist politics, if indeed it was necessary at all – and they were undiscriminating, compared with culturalist approaches, in that they provided little basis for explaining the very different nature of change in the twenty or thirty states that had emerged from communist rule. Many, indeed, assumed a unilinear movement towards liberal democracy that was all but a mirror image of the old Soviet theory that all societies would inevitably become communist.

Any adequate social scientific explanation of the end of communist rule must also take account of the wider international context, not just of domestic Soviet developments. Unlike most of the East European countries, the USSR was not particularly dependent on foreign trade (it represented no more than 5–6 per cent of national income). Its currency was insulated from global monetary flows because it could not be freely converted. It could veto decisions in the UN Security Council, and had the means of enforcing decisions beyond its national boundaries within a sphere of influence that the West had tacitly accepted since 1945. But it had to compete with the Western nations in military terms, a competition that grew more difficult to sustain as new generations of weapons – like anti-ballistic missile systems and later the Strategic Defense Initiative – were developed and deployed. It had to compete for influence in the developing world, and to spend heavily to retain its foreign allies (like Cuba and Vietnam). Its own society was increasingly exposed to the Western media, to Western youth culture, and to Western commercial pressures. Gorbachev's diplomacy, in these circumstances, was essentially a 'diplomacy of decline',[52] surrendering commitments abroad that could no longer be sustained and making unilateral concessions in arms negotiations; and it was equally a demonstration of the power of globalisation, as it became increasingly difficult to pursue domestic policies that were too radical a departure from the norms of the global marketplace. Gorbachev had pointed out that they lived in an 'interdependent, in many ways integral world' at the 1986 Party Congress;[53] his own regime, in the event, was one of its casualties.

The Russian 'transition'

It was, in fact, a very curious transition. For a start, many of the decisive changes had taken place during the last years of Soviet rule, with a Communist Party still in power. Freedom of conscience, for instance, had been formally secured through the law that was approved in October 1990, which gave parents the right to give their children a religious upbringing and allowed the churches to establish their own schools and publications (see chapter 6). The media law of June 1990 abolished censorship and established the right of all citizens to 'express opinions and beliefs [and] to seek, select, receive, and disseminate information and ideas in any form'; in particular, it confirmed that citizens had the 'right of access to information from foreign sources, including direct television and radio broadcasts, and the press'.[54] A start had been made on ownership through the legislation on property that had been approved in 1990, and a July 1991 law on privatisation and destatification that provided for the transfer of up to half the assets of state-owned industry into private or co-operative hands by the end of the following year (many noncommunist governments also maintained large state sectors, and there had been a mixed economy under communist rule from the revolution until the late 1920s).[55] Above all, there had been competitive elections since the adoption of new legislation in late 1988, and in 1990 the existence of multiparty politics was formally recognised by the reformulation of Article 6 of the constitution and the adoption of a new law on political parties and mass organisations.[56] A more general 'declaration of the rights and freedoms of the individual', adopted by the Soviet parliament in September 1991 and then by the Russian parliament two months later, guaranteed the right to own property and engage in business as well as equality before the law, freedom of movement, and freedom of speech and assembly.[57]

When, in fact, had a communist system become a postcommunist one? There was no doubt about the *Wendepunkt* or turning point in Germany: it was the night of 9 November 1989, when the Berlin Wall was breached in a moment that had enormous symbolic importance for the whole of a divided continent. Nor was there much doubt about the *Wendepunkt* in Romania. As late as November 1989 there had been little obvious threat to party leader Ceausescu at the Romanian Communist Party's 14th Congress, officially dubbed a 'Congress of the Great Socialist Victory'; the leader's own six-hour speech was interrupted no less than 125 times by standing ovations (these owed something to a man in the control room who switched on pre-recorded applause at the appropriate moments), and he was elected to a further five years of office. But on 21 December, as demonstrations spread across the country, Ceausescu was ignominiously shouted down as he attempted to address a rally in the capital. The following day he fled the capital in a helicopter so overloaded that one of the crew had to sit on his lap, but he was captured shortly afterwards, put on trial, and executed with his wife in a grisly exercise that left no doubt the change of government had been irrevocable.[58] Most other East European countries had a reasonably

Plate 8.1   Boris Yeltsin in front of the Russian parliament in August 1991 (Novosti)

clear turning point, such as the moment when a communist government resigned and a largely or entirely postcommunist administration took its place: in Poland in August 1989, in Czechoslovakia the following November. But when was the Russian *Wendepunkt?*

Had it, for instance, been August 1991, when an attempted hard-line coup had been defeated by the Russian parliament and the newly elected Russian president? But the coup had not been led by the CPSU leadership: the conspirators were party members of senior standing, but they headed government agencies rather than the ruling party and included no current members of the Politburo or Secretariat. Their first action, indeed, had been to detain the party's general secretary in his Crimean retreat; the first demand of those who resisted the coup was for the party leader to be released, and for the Soviet constitution and laws to be respected. Yeltsin, no longer a party member by this time, had been joined on a tank in front of the White House by his vice-president, Alexander Rutskoi, who was a Communist, and nearly 90 per cent of the parliament that supported the Russian president against the State Emergency Committee had been Communists at the time of their election. Russians themselves, certainly, were not inclined to see the events around the White House as the decisive moment in the establishment of democratic rule. Just 7 per cent saw the defeat of the coup as the 'victory of the democratic revolution'; for 27 per cent it had simply been a 'tragedy'; but most Russians (53 per cent), at least in retrospect, thought it was no more than an 'episode in the struggle for power within the top leadership'.[59] And had the defeat of the coup seen the end of communist rule? A year later, 41 per cent agreed and 41 per cent disagreed; two years later, opinion was equally divided.[60] What side would they take if there was another coup, Russians were asked in 1997? Just 16 per cent said they would side with Yeltsin, but 21 per cent identified with the Emergency Committee; still larger numbers would have identified with neither side (35 per cent), or had no opinion at all (28 per cent).[61]

There had, in fact, been substantial support for the coup at the time it was taking place. Ordinary workers, according to the press, were 'tired of indiscipline, disorder, and confusion'.[62] According to Gorbachev himself, speaking shortly afterwards to journalists, support for the coup had run as high as 40 per cent.[63] Polls in Kazakhstan, conducted while the coup was taking place, found that it had a 'real social base', with half or more of those surveyed supporting the coup or at least not actively opposing it, with a tendency for this support to increase over time.[64] Representative or otherwise, 60–70 per cent of the letters that were sent to the Russian prosecutor about the arrested conspirators were in their favour;[65] and sentiments of this kind were certainly apparent in some of the letters that were sent to the Soviet press after the coup had been launched but before it had been defeated. 'May your hands be firm and your hearts pure', wrote a Moscow pensioner. 'Force everyone to obey the constitution, and introduce some public order . . . I associate my hopes with you, and my belief in the rebirth of Russia.' Or as thirty automobile workers wrote to *Izvestiya*, 'We welcome order and discipline, we welcome the new leadership.'[66] And what kind of a victory had there been for democracy after the coup had collapsed? Perhaps in Moscow and St Petersburg there had been changes, but in Bashkiriya, wrote V. Beloboky, everything had 'remained as before' except that prices were rising even faster. In Cherepovets, according to another writer, the local 'totalitarian regime' had remained, and even 'strengthened itself'.[67]

Perhaps, then, the decisive moment was the end of the USSR in December 1991? But actually, as a concept, it remained very popular. A very large majority had approved the establishment of a 'renewed federation' in March 1991,[68] and it was to have been inaugurated on 20 August 1991. Those who took action in August 1991 were attempting to retain a union state in what they conceived as their patriotic duty, not to dissolve it. Equally, the coup itself was followed by a series of agreements on various forms of co-operation among the republics that were still committed to a single state. In October, as we have seen, most of the republics concluded an economic union; and in November they established a Union of Sovereign States that would have had a single president, a single parliament, and a single citizenship (see chapter 7). For Boris Yeltsin, at this time, the only question was how many of the republics would join the new association;[69] the Soviet parliament meanwhile approved the treaty that was to bring it into existence, and suggested that it might itself form part of its representative structures.[70] The decisive moment was almost certainly the Ukrainian referendum of 1 December, which led to an overwhelming majority in favour of full independence; this reversed the views that had been expressed in March, and in turn precipitated the formation of the CIS. But the USSR remained immensely popular as a concept, with the support of up to 85 per cent of ordinary Russians,[71] and there was public as well as parliamentary support for the moves that were made in the later 1990s to reconstitute a framework of association between Russia and the other republics, first of all with Belarus, that was intended to lead to the formation of another unitary state.

Was the banning of the Communist Party, then, the *Wendepunkt*? But this was an illegal act, as the Constitutional Court ruled the following year; the Communists, meanwhile, were able to reconstitute their national organisation and went on to win third place in the party-list elections of December 1993, moving up to first place in December 1995. And it was striking, compared with East-Central Europe, how many members of the communist leadership had managed to retain a presence in the new regime. The first postcommunist prime minister in Eastern Europe, Tadeusz Mazowiecki, had been a Solidarity activist and a political prisoner; so had the new Polish president, Lech Walesa. The new Hungarian prime minister Jozsef Antall and the new Czechoslovak president Vaclav Havel had also been political prisoners in the communist period. The Czechoslovak parliamentary speaker was Alexander Dubcek, who had been party leader in 1968 but who was later forced to resign and earn his living as a forestry worker. Russia's postcommunist president, by contrast, had been a party member for thirty years, and a member of its Politburo and Secretariat. Its first postcommunist prime minister, Yegor Gaidar, had worked for *Pravda* and the party theoretical journal *Kommunist*. His successor, Viktor Chernomyrdin, had been a Soviet gas minister and a member of the Central Committee; the man who succeeded him in 1998, Yevgenii Primakov, had been a member of the ruling Politburo as well as of the Central Committee. The speaker of the lower house of the Russian parliament, Gennadii Seleznev, had also been a member of the Central Committee; the chairman of the upper house, Yegor Stroev, had been a member of the Politburo and Secretariat and, before that, a regional first secretary.

Elements of continuity were even stronger at the regional level, where the typical first secretary had become head of the local administration and ran the same region from the same building. Within Yeltsin's presidential administration, about three-quarters had their origins in the communist *nomenklatura*; and within the Russian government it was about the same proportion. At the regional level, more than 80 per cent were former members of the *nomenklatura*.[72] The regional party leadership of the Soviet years were also well represented in the political institutions of the new regime: ten former members of the Central Committee held seats in the Federation Council, one of them Vasilii Starodubtsev, chairman of the V. I. Lenin collective farm in the Tula region but better known as a member of the State Emergency Committee of August 1991. Another twenty-two former Central Committee members were in the Duma, most of them elected on the Communist party list but several on the basis of their success in single-member constituencies. Alexander Dzasokhov, a former North Ossetian first secretary who had also served on the Politburo and Secretariat, took more than half the vote in his district; so did Nikolai Ryzhkov, the former prime minister. Another winner was Sergei Manyakin, formerly first secretary in Omsk and one of those who had taken the floor at the Central Committee meeting in October 1987 at which Yeltsin had delivered his unexpected attack on the Gorbachev leadership. Speaking immediately afterwards, Manyakin had accused the future president of incompetence and 'political immaturity';[73] now a 72-year-old pensioner, he headed the poll in his native region. Others moved into banking and private business, using their party connections and working initially within the 'youth economy' that had developed around the Komsomol in the late Soviet period. Indeed for some the nature of the Russian transition was precisely that it had allowed an elite whose position depended on their control of office, but who were now obliged to seek the support of an unpredictable electorate, to 'convert' their political influence into the more enduring form of advantage that was provided by private property.[74]

In all of these events, moreover, there was very limited popular involvement – compared, at least, with the 'people power' that had been on display in Eastern Europe and in the Baltic republics. Journalists estimated that perhaps 50,000 had ignored the curfew in Moscow and rallied outside the White House in support of the parliamentary resistance (rather more – 9 per cent of the city's entire population of 9 million – 'remembered' having done so a year later).[75] But there was no indefinite strike, as Yeltsin had demanded. There was little action of any kind in the other republics, which took the view that a state of emergency in Russia could have no legal force outside its boundaries. And the numbers involved, even in the Russian capital, were far less than the numbers that had taken part in the popular movements of Eastern Europe: in the Baltic, for instance, 2 million had joined hands in a gesture of defiance in August 1989 on the fiftieth anniversary of the Nazi–Soviet Pact; in Czechoslovakia, an estimated three-quarters of the entire population had taken part in the political strike that was called in November 1989.[76] There was a similar manifestation of 'people power' in the elections that took place in Poland in June 1989 (Solidarity won all the seats it was allowed to contest in the lower house and all but one of the seats in the upper house), and in the demonstrations involving hundreds of thousands that took place on successive Sundays in what was still the GDR. Russians, electing their republican parliament the following spring, returned more Communist Party members than ever before.[77]

A democratic culture?

According to an old but influential literature in comparative politics, democratic institutions were most likely to come into existence and to become consolidated in societies in which they were valued for their own sake. Britain and the United States both had long-established democratic systems, and in both of them there were high levels of commitment to the institutions of government. For Almond and Verba, writing in the 1960s, there was an explanation: it was that in both countries there was a pattern of political and social attitudes that was 'supportive of a stable democratic process', a political culture that in some way 'fitted' their democratic political institutions and one that was 'most congruent with a stable, democratic system'.[78] Clearly, this was a thesis that was open to all kinds of methodological objections.[79] In particular, it was difficult – indeed impossible, given the research design – to establish the causal significance of democratic values. Evidently, they were more likely to be found in countries with stable democratic institutions. But were they the 'cause' of those institutions, or a 'consequence' (or neither)? And how well did the original argument stand up as Britain and the United States suffered a steady loss of confidence in their political institutions, while countries that had originally been authoritarian – like Germany – appeared to have developed the kind of support for democratic institutions they had originally lacked?[80]

It was difficult, in real life rather than a scientific laboratory, to test for the relative importance of country and system, of institutions and values, of sequence, and of international context.[81] It was particularly difficult to discuss causal relations of this kind in the USSR and Eastern Europe when there was very limited access to popular values before the end of communist rule, of a kind that might make it possible to determine if a commitment to democratic principles had preceded or followed the establishment of democratic institutions. But there was an increasing consensus that institutions of this kind were, at least, more likely to be secure where they were valued for their own sake, as well as where they appeared to function effectively. 'Democracy', as Lipset has put it, 'requires a supportive culture, the acceptance by the citizenry and political elites of principles underlying freedom of speech, media, assembly, religion, of the rights of opposition parties, of the rule of law, of human rights, and the like . . . Such norms do not evolve overnight.'[82] Did popular values in the early postcommunist years provide support for those who thought it likely that Russians would be able to extend their formal freedoms into a democratic political culture of this kind? Or was there more support for those who were impressed by the limitations

Table 8.1. *Trust in institutions, 1993–8 (percentages)*

	1993	1994	1995	1996	1997	1998
Churches	48	52	37	39	37	35
Armed forces	39	37	26	25	28	23
President	28	20	6	10	10	11
Mass media	26	27	23	26	24	24
Security services	20	21	13	16	14	15
Government	18	11	4	6	6	8
Courts, police	16	17	9	10	9	10
Local government	13	14	13	14	19	18
Trade unions	13	10	6	8	11	11
Regional government	10	13	9	11	17	17
Parliament	9	5	4	5	5	7
Political parties	–	–	–	–	4	5

Sources: Adapted from *Ekonomicheskie i sotsial'nye peremeny: monitoring obshchestvennogo mneniya*, various issues. The question was 'To what extent do you have confidence in the following?'; responses record those who had 'complete confidence'.

of Russia's postcommunist democracy and by the continuing support for authoritarianism?[83]

It was clear, first of all, that Russians had little trust in the institutions by which they were governed, or in social institutions more generally (see table 8.1). The various churches and the army consistently enjoyed more trust than all other institutions; but confidence in both was steadily declining. Support for the mass media was at a lower level, although it was more stable. All of these institutions, at the same time, commanded more public support than any of the institutions of government. The president, in particular, had suffered a sharp loss of public confidence; by late 1998, after the collapse of the currency, just 2 per cent of Russians were still prepared to trust him.[84] The security services enjoyed a slight strengthening of support, and still more so the institutions of local and regional government; both enjoyed more support than the institutions of central government, especially the government itself, which had the confidence of just 4 per cent of Russians by late 1998 after the currency had been devalued.[85] The most distrusted of all institutions, however, were the political parties: they were trusted less than the trade unions, less than the courts and police, less than central or local government, and more only – in a single investigation – than the investment funds that had been set up after voucher privatisation, and which had in many cases defrauded those who had invested in them;[86] this was true even though the right to form parties and other independent organisations was the most obvious breach in the single-party monopoly that had existed throughout the communist years.

What did Russians themselves make of these changes? To what extent did they think democratisation and then postcommunist rule, with free elections, an independent press, and the rule of law, had given them an effective set of mechanisms to influence the direction of public policy? In many respects, clearly, they thought there had been a substantial and very welcome shift from state control to individual rights, comparing the 'old regime' of the Brezhnev years with the position in the late 1990s. For a start, there was more opportunity to 'say what you think' (73 per cent, according to the survey evidence, thought there had been an improvement in this respect; just 6 per cent took the opposite view). There was more scope to 'join whatever organisation you wish' (75 per cent agreed; just 7 per cent thought things had become worse). Most obviously of all, there had been a great increase in freedom of conscience (79 per cent thought there was 'more freedom of choice in religious matters', and just 5 per cent thought the opposite). There was also a greater degree of freedom to decide whether or not to take part in political life (66 per cent thought there had been an improvement in this respect, and only 7 per cent took the opposite view). In terms of civil liberties, in other words, there had been a great improvement since the Brezhnevite 1970s. But it was less clear that ordinary Russians thought their influence over government had increased, which was critical for assessments of democracy; for most of them, in fact, it was the opposite. Fully 50 per cent, in the late 1990s, thought the postcommunist government was less likely than the Soviet government under Brezhnev to 'treat everyone equally and fairly' (just 8 per cent disagreed). And remarkably, 46 per cent thought they had less influence on government than in the communist years (just 9 per cent thought their influence had increased).[87]

And what about human rights? Were they, for instance, more or less respected than under communist rule, in the view of Russians them-selves? For well over half, surveys suggested, there was 'no difference' (56 per cent); and of those who thought there had been a difference, there were just as many who thought there was less respect for human rights in the postcommunist years as who thought there was more (about 15 per cent in both cases).[88] Nowhere, for obvious reasons, are human rights perfectly respected; among other things, they may often conflict with each other. But Russians, and Ukrainians, were particularly unlikely to believe there had been an improvement since the years of communist rule; Czechs, Slovaks, and Hungarians, asked the same question, were much more likely to believe there had been positive changes.[89] Russians were also more dissatisfied than their counterparts in all the other postcommunist countries with the extent to which they thought there was 'respect for individual human rights nowadays in their country'. Just 15 per cent, according to Eurobarometer, thought individual human rights were broadly respected in their own country; more than five times as many (82 per cent) thought they were not. Ukrainians were almost as dissatisfied as Russians, and respondents in all the former Soviet republics were more likely to be dissatisfied with the state of individual human rights in their country of residence than their counterparts in the other postcommunist nations.[90]

What were the best, and the worst, features of communist and postcommunist rule? For 30 per cent of Russians, the worst feature of the system under which they had formerly been governed was clearly its bureaucracy (see figure 8.1). For an additional 15 per cent it had 'suppressed rights', or practised corruption (14 per cent); nearly 12 per cent, however, thought the former system had no faults at all. The best features of communist rule were more immediately apparent. Nearly 30 per cent praised the 'job security' they had enjoyed (even if the job was poorly paid). For 23 per cent, there had been 'no ethnic conflict' (even if this had been achieved by authoritarian controls). And nearly as many were impressed by the 'stable economy' of the Soviet period (even if it was one that was expanding more slowly than in the past). There was public order, and (at least for some) there was 'equality'.[91] Were the changes that had actually taken place, in fact, welcome or not? For a clear majority (53 per cent), freedom of speech and of the press were clearly changes for the better. The same was true of the rapprochement that had taken place with Western countries, and of the freedom to travel wherever they wished (47 and 45 per cent respectively thought these changes had done more good than harm). But there was much less support for multiparty elections (33 per cent, a plurality, thought they had done more harm than good), and there was still less support for the right to strike (36 per cent, another plurality, thought it had been a change for the worse). The breakup of the USSR was an acknowledged calamity, with 75 per cent convinced it had done more harm than good.[92]

Competitive elections were certainly valued in themselves, but (as these results suggest) there was little belief that they had given ordinary citizens a real degree of influence over those who ruled them or that they had enhanced the quality of Russian public life. Few doubted that, in the abstract, it was important to have 'honest elections that are held regularly' (87 per cent agreed with this view in a 1997 USIA survey). But nearly half those who were asked thought there had been no

What were the worst features of communist rule?

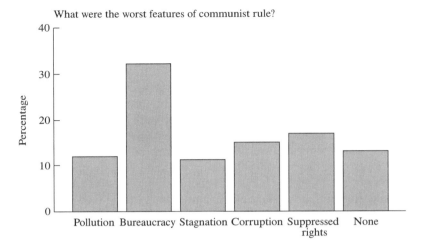

What were the best features of communist rule?

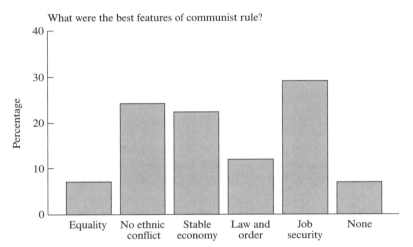

Source: ROMIR survey conducted for the author and associates in December 1993 and January 1994 (n = 2141). Respondents were asked to choose one of the categories shown; 'don't knows' are excluded.

Fig. 8.1   The worst and best features of communist rule

elections of this kind in their own country (45 per cent took this view, 36 per cent were more positive).[93] And did voting (in a question that was routinely asked elsewhere) give 'people like me some say about how the government runs things?' About a third of Russians thought it did (36 per cent), but well over half (56 per cent) took a very different view; competitive elections, in another inquiry, 'lacked a sustained base of public support', and almost half agreed that their main purpose was to 'deceive the people'.[94] Similarly, just 7 per cent thought the national government in Moscow 'looked after the interests of people like me some or nearly all of the time', but 42 per cent took the opposite view. Only 6 per cent thought they could have some influence on the city in which they lived; and just 3 per cent thought they had some opportunity to 'make Russia a better place'.[95]

On the face of it, it was certainly paradoxical that ordinary Russians should feel they had less influence on the political process in a system that provided them with competitive elections, a diversity of newspapers, and a choice of parties. But there were all kinds of reasons that made sense in local terms, if not at the level of abstract principle. For instance, local utilities had become commercial organisations that were responsible to shareholders and not to elected institutions of local government. Similarly, in the Soviet years all kinds of responsibilities, such as the upkeep of roads and street lighting, had been in the hands of local factories. Now services were supposed to be paid for out of taxation, but the resources that were provided by central government were never enough to cover the costs. The political system, meanwhile, had become 'even more opaque and unaccountable', there was no one who could resolve local difficulties in the way party secretaries had been able to resolve them in the past, and there was no longer any point in writing to *Pravda*, which had helped local people to improve their housing conditions in the recent past.[96] The elections that actually took place, in any case, were often reminiscent of the exercises that had taken place in the late Soviet period, with a variety of mechanisms being employed to secure the result the authorities wanted.[97]

A democratic culture needed more than an attachment to institutions of government through which the popular will could be expressed; it also required a willingness to tolerate the views of others. The survey evidence, again, suggested that Russians fell some distance short of the democratic ideal. They were, for instance, very strongly attached to the death penalty: it had the support of the great majority of Russians, and about a quarter thought it should be applied even more frequently than in the past.[98] There was equally little understanding of minority rights, a particularly sensitive indicator of democratic values. A substantial number believed that society should 'liquidate' all prostitutes (18 per cent), and even more thought they should be 'isolated' (23 per cent). Similar proportions favoured the 'liquidation' of homosexuals (22 per cent), or drug addicts (26 per cent), and of children born with birth defects (18 per cent); as these and other findings suggested, Russians were 'considerably more intolerant than citizens in the West'.[99] How, indeed, was democracy itself to be understood? For about a quarter, it meant freedom of speech and conscience; but almost as many thought it meant 'strict legality', or 'order and stability', or (for about a fifth) a 'prospering economy'. Just 7 per cent thought it meant that the leading positions in government should be elected, and only 3 per cent associated democracy with minority rights.[100]

What, finally, about changes over time? Were Russians identifying more strongly with their newly democratic institutions as they became familiar with them? Or had a deepening economic crisis undermined the support that might otherwise have begun to accumulate? Nowhere, obviously, was there complete satisfaction with the development of democracy, but there was certainly more dissatisfaction in the postcommunist countries – including Russia – than in the established democracies of the European Union. And Russians were more dissatisfied than anyone else: more than their counterparts in the other former republics of the USSR, more again than their counterparts in Eastern Europe, and still more so than their counterparts in the European Union, where the same question was routinely asked (see figure 8.2). Russians, in addition, were becoming increasingly dissatisfied with the development of democracy in their country, not increasingly supportive. In 1991, 15 per cent of Russians were 'satisfied with the way democracy [was] developing in their country', but 67 per cent were dissatisfied; five years later, satisfaction was down to 8 per cent and dissatisfaction had reached 82 per cent.[101]

An incomplete democracy

Whether or not a supportive set of values helped to sustain a democratic regime, the establishment of the regime itself was necessarily the action of a political elite: either of incumbents, or of challengers. In Russia the tradition of 'revolution from above' was particularly strong, from Peter the Great up to Gorbachev, and indeed to Yeltsin and his colleagues, who staged what was in effect a state coup in late 1993 that involved the introduction of a new constitution and carefully regulated elections to a new parliament. The comparative literature suggested that the establishment of democratic rule was likely to be particularly successful if the

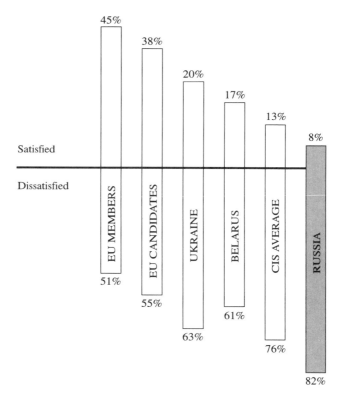

The question asked was 'On the whole are you very satisfied, fairly satisfied, not very satisfied, or not at all satisfied with the way democracy is developing in [country]?

Source: Adapted from the *Central and Eastern Eurobarometer*, 1997; the figure for the twelve EU member states is taken from *Eurobarometer Trends 1974–1992* (Brussels: European Commission, n.d.).

Fig. 8.2   Attitudes to democracy in the 1990s

transition took place through a 'pact' between incumbents and challengers in which both could agree that democracy was (in Giuseppe di Palma's phrase) the 'only game in town';[102] this was hardly the case in postcommunist Russia with the forced resignation of the Soviet president, the suppression of the ruling party, the dissolution of the state itself, and the crushing of political opposition in an armed assault on the elected parliament that was a clear violation of the constitution that was valid at the time.

Formally, at least, the new constitution of December 1993 had marked a step forward. It was a constitution that committed the new state to 'ideological pluralism', 'political diversity', and a multiparty system; and there could be no 'compulsory ideology' (Art. 13). A whole chapter dealt with the rights and freedoms of the individual, including equality before the law, and equal rights for men and women. There were guarantees of personal inviolability and privacy. There was a freedom of information provision, allowing citizens to discover whatever was held about them by any organ of government unless security considerations were involved. There was freedom of movement, within the country and across national boundaries. There was freedom of conscience, of thought and speech, and of association and assembly. Press freedom was guaranteed, and censorship was abolished. There was a more general commitment to the 'generally recognised principles and norms of international law', and in the event of any conflict international agreements would have precedence (Art. 15). And there were economic guarantees: private ownership was explicitly recognised, including private ownership of land and the right of citizens to engage in business. All these rights, moreover, were entrenched: in other words, they could not be amended without a complicated procedure involving a constitutional conference and (normally) a referendum.

At the same time there were grave weaknesses in Russia's new constitutional design. For a start, it had been unilaterally imposed, which meant that it became 'Yeltsin's constitution' rather than a document based on a broader consensus that might have allowed it to provide a framework within which all of Russia's political forces would have been prepared to compete for popular support. Difficult though it would have been to achieve a consensus of this kind, it was beginning to emerge in the summer of 1993 in the workings of the constitutional conference, in a series of drafts that reflected parliamentary as well as presidential opinion. The imposition of a presidential draft after the parliament had been bombed into submission left no scope for a broader agreement of this kind. The constitution, moreover, was itself open to legal challenge. The president, as we have seen in chapter 3, had no authority at the time to call a referendum; the law on the referendum, in any case, made clear that a proposition could be adopted only if a majority of the electorate voted in its favour, not just a majority of those who took part. There were also considerable doubts about the turnout. Yeltsin had specified a minimum of 50 per cent for his 'national vote' to be valid, and informed opinion suggested he had fallen some distance short (see p. 36); the head of the Central Electoral Commission, in a private conversation, was reported to have confirmed that the turnout was in fact 46.7 per cent, which if it had been reported at the time would have rendered the whole exercise invalid.[103]

It was, moreover, a seriously unbalanced constitution. Formally, there was a separation of powers. The president had powers in relation to the Duma, and the Duma had powers in relation to the president, both of them protected from abuse by an independent judicial system. But the president's powers, it became clear, were extraordinarily large in theory and practice: in particular, his power to sack the government, as he did three times in 1998 and 1999 without reference to public or parliamentary opinion (the successful nomination of Primakov in September had emerged from discussions with senators and deputies, but without conceding them any formal authority). Parliament also enjoyed a direct mandate, but its influence over the president was very limited: its 'consent' was needed for the appointment of a new prime minister, but if that consent was withheld it ran the risk of dissolution. Equally, there was no serious prospect that the president could be impeached. Under the arrangements that had been made in 1990, the president could be forced to stand down if he violated the constitution or laws, and if a two-thirds majority in the Congress of People's Deputies voted accordingly. Under the 1993 constitution an action of this kind could be taken only in the event of treason or a crime of similar gravity, and after the Supreme Court and the Constitutional Court had confirmed there was a basis for proceeding. Even when the president was unable to exercise his powers effectively because of bad health or other reasons, he retained a disproportionate concentration of authority; presidential elections, inevitably, became contests for the state itself, the constitution became the rules of the game that the winner found most congenial, and parliamentary elections had only marginal significance – certainly, they had nothing to do with 'winning power'.

Countervailing forces of all kinds were weak in early postcommunist Russia. There were plenty of political parties, but by common consent only one (the Communists) that had achieved a degree of institutionalisation of a kind that made it comparable with parties in other systems. And yet how else were Russian voters to be given an organised choice of alternatives? There were trade unions as well, and they repeatedly made clear that they could bring millions into the streets on 'days of action', but there was little point in striking as the employers, and sometimes entire regional administrations, were often bankrupt themselves. The press was vigorous and often oppositional, but it had increasingly become the plaything of rich financiers and its circulation had fallen dramatically – by more than half between 1992 and 1996;[104] by the late

1990s only a fifth of Russians read a national newspaper regularly, and 'national' papers like *Nezavisimaya gazeta* and *Segodnya* were appearing in just 50,000 copies daily.[105] Judges, in accordance with international practice, were 'independent' and 'inviolable' (Arts. 120 and 122), but the Constitutional Court, which was supposed to regulate the behaviour of the president as well as of the highest levels of government, was appointed on the nomination of the president himself (Art. 128). Under the previous constitution, up to 1993, the Constitutional Court was elected by the Congress of People's Deputies and it had countermanded the president's decisions on several important occasions.

Democracy, for Schumpeter, had famously involved no more than a 'free competition for a free vote'. Many of his examples, indeed, were drawn from Victorian England, when most men and all women were excluded from the franchise.[106] For modern scholars, democracy meant a great deal more than competitive elections. It meant a government that was limited by law, and one that was accountable to the electorate directly or through representative institutions; a country that had elections but lacked the rule of law could only be a 'pseudo-democracy'.[107] It was also important to establish if the rights of ordinary citizens were respected, whether or not they were seeking to influence government. Were they, for instance, able to travel freely, and to express their views in speech and in the printed and electronic media? Did they have freedom of worship, and could they assemble peacefully whenever they chose to do so? And did they have access to public information except where overriding security considerations were involved? Was there, finally, a 'democratic society', including a network of groups and associations, economic institutions that were accountable to those who worked within them as well as to the public, and a 'culture of tolerance and civic responsibility'?[108]

Distinctions of this kind were of central importance in distinguishing between electoral democracy and liberal democracy. Elections, for a start, were sometimes imposed by the US government on foreign states that it wished to support so that it could justify the provision of economic assistance in Congress. But elections of this kind were 'rarely successful', more often providing an opportunity for local elites to engage in a variety of forms of manipulation so that they could retain office.[109] Equally, in non-Western societies without a liberal tradition, elected governments often paid little attention to individual rights, practised discrimination against minorities, restricted press freedom, and sometimes 'tolerate[d] or even encourage[d] police brutality'. Elections in these circumstances could also provide an opportunity for ethnic or religious movements that sought to win power and then establish a political monopoly.[110] Countries like Russia, it was suggested, had elections that were certainly competitive, but there were too many restrictions on political rights and civil liberties to allow them to be classified as more than electoral democracies. As well as elections that were regular and fairly conducted, a liberal democracy must have no 'reserved domains' that were allocated to military or other groups. Government must be accountable 'horizontally' to the courts and other bodies, and there must be political and civic pluralism including a diversity of means by which ordinary citizens could articulate and advance their preferences. There must also be an independent press, and independent courts.[111]

Russia, indeed, was not even an unambiguously 'electoral democracy'. Largely free and fair elections had taken place to a parliament in 1993; they took place with fewer restrictions in 1995, and were scheduled to do so again in December 1999. There had been competitive elections to the presidency in 1991, and again in 1996; a further round was due to take place in the summer of 2000, with Boris Yeltsin no longer an eligible candidate. There had been irregularities in all of these elections, however, and in the 1996 presidential election there had been a very heavy media bias in favour of the incumbent which, combined with almost unlimited campaign spending, gave a clear and improper advantage to the Yeltsin candidature.[112] Elections, again, had been held at the appointed times; but there had been a very real prospect of the cancellation of the 1996 presidential election when it appeared that Yeltsin was likely to lose. In March, just three months before the poll, Yeltsin's legal adviser refused to rule out the possibility that the election might be postponed 'if a crisis emerges in the country'.[113] Yeltsin's bodyguard and close adviser, Alexander Korzhakov, told journalists that elections were 'too risky' and 'a Western idea'; 'why risk everything', he added, 'just to have some people put pieces of paper into something called a ballot box?'[114] When Igor Malashenko, the head of independent television, joined the Yeltsin campaign team, he found it an 'incredible organisation, where half of the members wanted the poll to take place and the other half did not'.[115] Decrees had apparently been drafted dissolving the parliament, banning the Communist Party, and cancelling the whole exercise; Yeltsin's own staff, in private briefings, made clear that he would not leave the presidency if he was defeated by a Communist although he would give way to another candidate.[116] Russia, certainly, was still a long way short of satisfying the 'Huntington test' of a twofold change of regime through the ballot box.[117]

Plate 8.2   Reading *Pravda* on the noticeboard (Novosti)

Democracy also required tolerance by government of its opponents, and not simply tolerance by citizens of each other. There was little sign of this either in early postcommunist Russia. Yeltsin and his supporters, for a start, made every effort to suppress the Communist Party to which they had themselves recently belonged, banning it in a manner the Constitutional Court later found illegal, seizing its property, and appropriating its bank accounts.[118] The bombing of the Russian parliament was another moment that showed how limited was the acceptance of a set of civilised 'rules of the game'. According to the former prosecutor general, Alexei Kazannik, who was a Yeltsin supporter, after the storming of the White House a scenario was outlined to him whereby he would 'investigate the October events for three or four days, charge all those held under Articles 102 and 17, that is, with conspiracy to murder, and then turn them over to the military collegium for criminal cases' rather than to an ordinary court. The case, Kazannik told *Komsomol'skaya pravda*, 'was supposed to last for two or three days and everyone was supposed to be sentenced to death . . . The president's team put a lot of pressure on us'.[119] In the event, there was nothing Yeltsin could do when the Duma voted to exercise its exclusive right to grant an amnesty in February 1994 to all who had been involved in the events of August 1991 and of September–October 1993.

Human rights in postcommunist Russia

Several bodies monitored human rights performance in Russia and other countries, among them Amnesty International and Human Rights Watch. Amnesty, in its reports and recommendations, was particularly concerned to ensure the fair and prompt trial of political prisoners, and to abolish the death penalty as well as the mistreatment of prisoners; it campaigned against extrajudicial executions and 'disappearances', but also against hostage-taking, killings, and other excesses that had been committed by opposition groups. One of Amnesty's concerns in Russia was brutality in the armed forces, including evidence that the physical abuse of conscripts was 'systematic and widespread'. Four sailors in the Pacific Fleet, for instance, had died of malnutrition after being forced to perform heavy manual tasks. Two had been beaten shortly before their death; one of them had his fingers amputated after being compelled to work outdoors in freezing temperatures without gloves, and had been beaten by other recruits with a crowbar.[120] Asylum seekers were routinely deported even if they were likely to face arbitrary arrest in their country of origin, and there were numerous arrests for evading the draft even though the constitution provided for an alternative to military service.[121] Conditions in pre-trial prisons remained 'appalling', with 'gross overcrowding' obliging tens of thousands to sleep in shifts, with their health undermined by inadequate food, a lack of medicines, and even oxygen starvation (more than 5,000 were reported to have died awaiting trial in 1994–6 alone).[122] Other reports found that the torture and ill-treatment of criminal suspects, in at least one of the Russian regions, was 'routine'.[123]

Many of the grossest violations of human rights, in the view of Amnesty, had taken place in the course of the conflict in Chechnya, where there had been 'indiscriminate killings, detention without trial, torture and ill-treatment, and extrajudicial executions' (some were prepared to argue that the indiscriminate use of violence against civilians, the establishment of what were clearly concentration camps and the use of chemical weapons had been paralleled only by Nazi Germany).[124] There were allegations of rape by Russian soldiers, and of torture and ill-treatment of civilians at the detention camps that had been set up in the region.[125] And there were several atrocities, including an incident in the town of Samashki in April 1995 when about 250 civilians, including women and children, were killed by Russian troops who were reported to have burned down houses and thrown grenades into basements where residents were taking cover in what the International Commission of the Red Cross described as 'an indiscriminate attack against civilians and a flagrant violation of humanitarian law', and the bombing of the town of Sernovodsk without any apparent regard for the thousands of civilians that were sheltering there after claiming that armed Chechen groups had set up in the town.[126] The death penalty meanwhile continued to be applied, even after Russia joined the Council of Europe and even though there was evidence of judicial error in about a third of the sentences that were passed.[127]

Human Rights Watch had a wider range of concerns, including freedom of thought and expression and due legal process as well as disappearances, torture, arbitrary imprisonment and the other concerns of Amnesty International.[128] The Russian government, they charged in 1998, had done little to deal with long-standing problems of police torture, prison conditions, and the abuse of conscripts; and there were further restrictions on freedom of information and freedom of conscience, including attempts to regulate use of the internet and email. The Russian provinces, at the same time, had devolved into 'fiefdoms that engage[d] in civil and political rights violations with impunity from Moscow'. In what was apparently an exchange for support of its policies, the central government turned a blind eye to corruption by regional leaders, and refused to investigate the human rights violations for which they were clearly responsible. Regional leaders, for their own part, were making every effort to extend their control over local newspapers and radio stations, and in some cases they were apparently prepared to sanction beatings and even murders to achieve their ends. The editor of an oppositional paper in the Kalmyk republic, for instance, was found stabbed to death beside a pond in the republican capital in June 1998 in what Human Rights Watch described as 'by far the most convincing case of government collusion in the death of a journalist'. The Kalmyk authorities were also involved in a reversion to the worst of Soviet practices when they placed the head of a humanitarian organisation in a psychiatric hospital after she had led a hunger strike of disabled people and mothers of large families.[129]

Human Rights Watch had few objections to the conduct of national elections, but at local level they found Soviet practices continued to prevail. In the elections to the Bashkir presidency in the summer of 1998, for instance, police raided the only independent radio station in the republic after it had broadcast an interview with three opposition candidates, beating and rounding up staff members (the station was later closed). In addition, two of the region's last independent newspapers were harassed, and copies seized as they were brought into the republic (they were printed, of necessity, outside the republic). President Rakhimov easily won the election after three opposition candidates had been struck off the ballot; and although the Supreme Court ruled the Bashkir government's action illegal, neither the local nor the central electoral commission annulled the results. There were further difficulties with freedom of conscience, especially with the terms of the law of September 1997 which allowed local authorities to continue their harassment of 'nontraditional' religious associations, arbitrarily evicting religious groups from public buildings where they had worshipped for years and imposing exorbitant rent increases. Pentecostalists, Catholics, and Jehovah's Witnesses suffered more than others. There were continuing restrictions on movement, particularly through a registration system that had developed in the Soviet period and which was retained even when the Constitutional Court ruled against it. And there were arbitrary arrests and expulsions of members of minority communities, and increasing numbers of racially motivated attacks.[130] Human Rights Watch reported separately on the conflict in Chechnya, which 'from the very beginning' had been characterised by 'massive, appalling violations of humanitarian law', with evidence that Russian troops had 'systematically beaten, tortured, or otherwise mistreated Chechens in captivity' and with a 'systematic failure to punish such abuse'.[131]

Human Rights Watch found that the Russian criminal system in the late 1990s was moving further away from Council of Europe standards, as well as from those that were appropriate to a democracy. Their investigation of police torture, for instance, found that 'corruption and abuse were the rule rather than the exception'. Criminal justice officials solicited and accepted bribes; and crime-solving statistics were 'improbably high, due in part to torture'. Torture, it emerged, was most likely to occur in the early hours of detention when police isolated suspects from family and lawyers; police forcibly extracted confessions using beatings, asphyxiation, electric shock, and other forms of physical and psychological torture. Requests for a lawyer were routinely refused, and 'often resulted in more violence'. Forced confessions were frequently used as the basis for criminal cases, and judges 'frequently used such confessions as the basis for a conviction'. The police, meanwhile, 'tortured with almost complete impunity', intimidating victims who tried to complain about their maltreatment. An 'extreme shortage of judges slowed criminal trials and overwhelmed sitting judges', and acquittal rates were below 1 per cent, 'reminiscent of the Soviet era'. Miscarriages of justice were common under such circumstances, but rarely acknowledged. Human Rights Watch was also concerned by the rising incidence of violence against women, including 'rampant rape and domestic violence'. Meanwhile, human rights activists and even investigative journalists faced restrictions and arrests on trumped-up charges.[132]

In the reports on human rights worldwide that the US State Department had published annually since 1977, Russia continued to be a 'state in transition' with a human rights record that was at best 'uneven'.[133] There were credible reports, for instance, that law enforcement and correctional officials had tortured and severely beaten detainees and inmates. Prison conditions were 'extremely harsh', with between 10,000 and 20,000 detainees dying annually in overcrowded and insanitary facilities. Arbitrary arrest and detention remained problems, with members of ethnic minorities particularly likely to be searched and apprehended. The major print media organisations were 'relatively unhindered by governmental pressure at the national level', but there was less respect for the freedom of the press at lower levels of government, and an increasing concentration of ownership at the national level that led journalists to practise self-censorship. Because the Russian media were generally not financially self-sufficient, newspapers were more easily influenced by government and by private owners; they could exercise their influence in all kinds of ways, through the withdrawal of accreditation or court cases against the journalist concerned, or sometimes more directly, by 'threats, beatings, and even murder'. Outside Moscow and St Petersburg the pressures were 'even more pronounced',

Table 8.2. *The Freedom House classification of the USSR and its successor states*

	1980	1991	1999
Free	UK	UK	UK
	USA	USA	USA
			Estonia
			Latvia
			Lithuania
Partly free		**USSR**	**Russia**
			Armenia
			Georgia
			Kyrgyzstan
			Moldova
			Ukraine
Unfree	**USSR**	China	Azerbaijan
	China		Belarus
			Kazakhstan
			Tajikistan
			Turkmenistan
			Uzbekistan
			China

Source: Derived from *Freedom in the World*, various issues.

with local authorities and criminal groups apparently inclined to believe they had 'absolute power in "their" regions'. The press, overall, was 'free but not independent'.[134]

There were related concerns about the legislation on religion that was adopted in 1997, and which contained provisions that could result in significant restrictions on the activities of minority religious communities, including foreign missionaries. There were 'numerous instances of harassment of religious groups by local authorities', citing the new law, which ironically was more restrictive than the law on freedom of conscience that had been adopted in the Soviet period. Restrictions continued upon freedom of movement, particularly in Moscow, where (as others had noted) the Soviet residence system had been retained even though it had been successfully challenged in the courts. Violence against women and the abuse of children were other problems, as were discrimination against religious and ethnic minorities. There was evidence that women were – illegally – being paid less for the same work, and that they suffered harassment at the workplace from employers who were increasingly inclined to request 'female employees "without complexes", meaning that they should be receptive to liberties taken by their employers'. The courts, meanwhile, were independent of government, but they did 'not yet act as an effective counterweight to other branches of government', and judges remained 'subject to some influence from the executive, military, and security forces, especially in high profile or political cases'. The judiciary also lacked resources and was 'subject to corruption'. Criminal procedures were generally 'heavily weighted in favor of the procurator', with the presumption of innocence 'often disregarded'. There were, however, 'no reports of political prisoners'.[135]

Amnesty, Human Rights Watch, and the US State Department, for the most part deliberately, attempted no relative or (still less) quantitative judgement. Freedom House of New York, however, had produced its Comparative Survey of Freedom since the early 1970s, aiming to provide an 'annual evaluation of political rights and civil liberties everywhere in the world' and to express its judgements in two seven-point scales.[136] It was clear, on their evidence, that the end of communist rule had brought about no dramatic change. Freedom House divided regimes into three groups on the basis of their scores: 'free', 'partly free', and 'unfree'. The USSR, in the Brezhnev years, had been 'unfree', but in 1991, while still under communist rule, it was judged to have become 'partly free'. The new union treaty that was under consideration at this time, Freedom House explained, was based on human rights and the creation of a democratic state based on popular representation and law. All the fifteen republics had declared some form of sovereignty, and the Soviet parliament had adopted laws guaranteeing freedom of the press and freedom of religion.[137] Postcommunist Russia in the late 1990s was given a slightly higher score, but it remained 'partly free', together with Ukraine, below states such as Brazil and India but just above Albania and Uganda.[138]

Freedom House had a series of concerns about democracy and human rights in early postcommunist Russia. Economic life, they pointed out, in an 'alarming trend', was increasingly dominated by the major energy and industrial corporations, which had been privatised by the *nomenklatura* who managed them and who continued to enjoy substantial privileges. By contrast, a nascent private sector of small business and entrepreneurs had had very limited success; and former communists and nationalists were winning a larger share of the vote, often by appealing to ultra-nationalist and anti-Western sentiment in a way that contributed to 'long-term problems that promised to afflict transitions to democracy in many countries of the former Communist world' (these conclusions were based on a field visit, as well as press reports and other sources).[139] The Russian media, in a separate exercise, were considered 'partly free' because of libel laws, harassment, and violence against journalists, and the disproportionate influence of financial and industrial interests connected to the government.[140]

Equally, the Comparative Survey suggested variety (see table 8.2). All the republics of the USSR had a virtually uniform system of government, a single ruling party, and a common framework of law. All of them had been 'unfree' in the 1970s and 1980s, but they had all been classified 'partly free' in the last year of communist rule. Their positions were very different nearly a decade after independence. Two of the former Soviet republics – Tajikistan and Turkmenistan – were among the seventeen least free countries in the world, according to the Survey, together with Iraq, Equatorial Guinea, North Korea, China, and Burundi. The three Baltic republics, at the other extreme, were all considered 'free'. So were nineteen of the twenty-seven countries of the Central and Eastern Europe that had formerly been under communist rule. But of the twelve members of the Commonwealth of Independent States, not a single one was considered 'free'; six, including Russia and Ukraine, were 'partly free'; and the remaining six – including all of the Central Asian republics apart from Kyrgyzstan – were 'unfree' (Belarus, originally 'partly free', became 'unfree' in 1997 because of the 'deteriorating human and political rights climate under the tyrannical President Aleksandr Lukashenka'). The outlook, Freedom House concluded, was 'bleak'.[141]

The cultural limits of transition

Postcommunist Russia was a democracy to the extent that there were competitive elections, the courts were formally independent, government could be criticised, and there was a choice of parties. But it was a very partial democracy, in the terms that have been defined earlier in this chapter. There was little accountability: the government was not directly accountable at all, and the president who appointed it was accountable only to the electorate in a heavily manipulated contest that took place every four years. Secondary associations of all kind were weak, especially political parties. The courts were heavily influenced by government; and government itself, particularly at local level, was based upon the former communist *nomenklatura* and sometimes upon a criminalised mafia. If there was a more general lesson from the Russian experience, it was perhaps that there was no single 'transition to democracy' in the formerly communist world but a variety of outcomes ranging from a stable parliamentary system in the Czech Republic, Hungary, and the Baltic republics to more authoritarian forms of politics in 'Far Eastern Europe',[142] and to personalist dictatorship in the former

Soviet republics in Central Asia. And at least in Russia, it had been less a 'transition to democracy' than a reconfiguration that incorporated many features of the old regime together with some more pluralist elements that had themselves in most cases been introduced before the end of communist rule.

The collapse of Soviet communism, accordingly, suggested a more general conclusion about the process of democratisation. Just as the starting point could be very varied, including societies that had already democratised as well as those that were experiencing democratic politics for the first time, so too the destination could be very different. The outcome could be a stable democracy, particularly in more developed societies that had an earlier history of representative government and the rule of law, where communist rule had normally been an external imposition and where membership of NATO and, eventually, the European Union appeared likely to lock them into the political forms of their Western neighbours. But there was much less change, or even 'regression', in societies that were less prosperous and in which democratic traditions were less firmly established, and which (like the former Soviet republics, the Balkan states, and Central Asia) were excluded from a newly demarcated Europe. The appropriate comparator, in these cases, was less the pluralistic democracy of the developed West and rather more the limited and formal democracy of Latin America with its strongly personalist rule, weak representative institutions, wide social divisions, and passive citizenries. In an influential study of Italian civic traditions, Robert Putnam has suggested that Palermo might be the 'future of Moscow': essentially because of Russia's lack of the kinds of 'networks of civic engagement' that had been established in Italy in medieval times, and which underpinned the practice of democratic politics in later years.[143] This suggested in turn that the construction of democratic institutions in the former Soviet republics would certainly take longer (and might not take place at all) as compared with the former communist countries that had shared the Western experience of co-operation and self-government within the framework of a rule of law.

Moreover, in spite of the hopeful nature of the changes in 1989–91, there was no inevitability about the onward march of democracy. More and more countries, by the late 1990s, were claiming to be democracies, with elected governments. More than 60 per cent of the world's independent states were democracies in this sense, and they accounted for more than half of the world's population. But not all democracies were 'free', in the terms that were employed by Freedom House (about a third were 'partly free', often because they were involved in ethnic or religious strife or faced a legacy of dictatorial rule that held back the development of a civil society and the rule of law). And the distribution of countries and population on this basis showed a much less encouraging trend. At the start of the 1980s, about 36 per cent of the world's population lived in countries that were defined as 'free', and 43 per cent in countries that were 'unfree'. By the late 1990s, the proportion living in 'free' countries was down to 22 per cent (some of the difference, but not all of it, was accounted for by the demotion of India to 'partly free'), while the proportion living in 'unfree' countries was almost as large as it had ever been, at 39 per cent, most of them living in countries that were traditionally Muslim or still communist.[144] There was little evidence here of the 'end of history', or of the worldwide triumph of liberal democracy; indeed, just as the two earlier 'waves of democracy' had fallen back, so too the 'third wave' appeared to be receding in much of Latin America and the Islamic world.[145]

The 'transition' itself lacked an obvious precedent. For a start, it was more than a recapitulation of the experience of the countries of Latin America and the Mediterranean, which were already capitalist and which in some cases were redemocratising after a period of authoritarian rule. There was 'neither model nor precedent for the transition from real socialism to democracy and capitalism', as Bryant and Mokryzcki have pointed out.[146] 'Transition', equally, suggested a kind of unilinearity that was difficult to reconcile with a diverse and open-ended process. There had been changes of political form, but in various directions, and there had also been cases of nontransition that needed explanation, in Cuba, China, and much of the Far East. 'Transition', moreover, suggested a single process, rather than a sequence of change that could take quite different forms at the political and the economic level. There had been capitalism before democracy; and there had been capitalism without democracy, as in Pinochet's Chile. In China, there appeared to be a form of capitalism under communist rule. And 'capitalism' itself needed to be disaggregated. Certainly, it was far more than the transfer of paper ownership from the state to the workforce and management, or to financial institutions. What was crucial for the establishment of a secure democracy was a bourgeoisie, with a 'wide diffusion of property among the population' that could provide a 'social base for independence from the government';[147] and of this there was still little sign in Russia, or in the former Soviet republics.

'Revolution' was equally unhelpful, at least in the sense of the great social revolutions of the past. There had usually been a break of legitimacy, and in some cases – such as the Czech Republic – a far-reaching replacement of ruling elites, which was Pareto's definition of a revolution.[148] But there were no 'simple analogies' between the events of 1989 and the social revolutions that had taken place in Britain, France, or Russia; and some thought it best to answer the question with a 'resounding maybe'.[149] An alternative view, advanced in Hungary, was that there had been a 'power metamorphosis' that had allowed the ruling group to restructure, or what one of Gorbachev's assistants identified as a 'revolution of the second secretaries' in which a first-line leadership had given way to a group of challengers from within the same institutions.[150] There was a still larger argument, as we have seen, which was that the 'transition' had in fact been an exercise by which ruling groups throughout the region had used their political position to secure the kind of ownership rights that could ensure their long-term future. 'Privileges', as Trotsky had pointed out many years earlier, 'have only half their value if they cannot be transmitted to one's children'; and for this reason he thought the ruling group would 'inevitably' seek to consolidate its position by becoming a 'new possessing class'.[151] To the extent to which it had succeeded in doing so, there had been a change of ownership; but it was a change that left ordinary citizens ever further away from the control of their own society.

The changes that were taking place in Eastern Europe, moreover, had to be set within a wider cultural context. Global politics, it was suggested, were being 'reconfigured along cultural lines', and alignments defined by ideology and superpower status were 'giving way to alignments defined by culture and civilisation'.[152] Factors of this kind, research suggested, were 'even more important than economic ones' in the explanation of democracy;[153] and they helped to explain why democratic forms of government had been fragile outside north-western Europe, or lands settled by north-western Europeans (it was of considerable importance in itself whether a country had been a British colony).[154] Russia was a European power, and a Christian one; but democracy had been a product of the West, not of the Eurasian landmass. It was in the West, not in Eurasia, that there had been a separation of spiritual and temporary authority, a rule of law that had laid the basis for constitutionalism and the protection of human rights, a social pluralism that had encouraged the formation of representative institutions, and a 'tradition of individual rights and liberties unique among civilized societies'.[155] Many of these developments had found expression at various times in Russia, but they had rarely been as influential as in Western Europe. There had been no feudalism, at least in the form of a balance of interests regulated by law; social classes were defined by service to the state; the Orthodox Church was an extension of government rather than a rival source of authority; and government itself accepted no legitimate limit to the scope of its decisions.

None of this meant that postcommunist Russia had to be authoritarian. There had, after all, been competitive elections, held on time and with a choice of parties. The press was diverse and often outspoken. There were encouraging moves to introduce trial by jury. The Russian president had even defined 1998 as a 'year of human rights'. But it was equally clear that the attempt to establish democratic forms of government was taking place in unusually difficult circumstances. Economic collapse had brought Russia down to a level of development at which few other states had managed to sustain representative and accountable government. Dissatisfaction with government, and politicians, and with the political system as a whole, were at record levels. Government itself appeared to have lost control of public order, and could no longer pay its own bills. There were mounting national and ethnic tensions, particularly in the predominantly Muslim regions of the northern Caucasus. Russians, it had been suggested at the outset of *perestroika*, would need some time to 'learn democracy'.[156] The evidence of the early postcommunist years was that the educational process might be a lengthy one, that the outcome was still uncertain, and that the establishment of formally democratic institutions would be of limited significance so long as they were not sustained by an active and participatory society and by a commitment to democratic forms of government for their own sake.

Notes

1 FROM BREZHNEV TO YELTSIN

1 Calculated from *Narodnoe khozyaistvo SSSR za 70 let. Yubileinyi statisticheskii sbornik* (Moscow: Finansy i statistika, 1987), various pages.

2 *XXIV S"ezd Kommunisticheskoi partii Sovetskogo Soyuza 30 marta–9 aprelya 1971 goda. Stenograficheskii otchet*, 2 vols. (Moscow: Politizdat, 1971), vol. I, p. 482.

3 A. A. Gromyko and B. N. Ponomarev, eds., *Istoriya vneshnei politiki SSSR, 1917–1980*, 2 vols. (Moscow: Nauka, 1981), vol. II, p. 666. Gromyko expressed very similar views to the 24th Party Congress in 1971: 'There is not a single question of any significance that can be resolved without the Soviet Union or in spite of it' (*XXIV S"ezd*, vol. I, p. 482).

4 *Vestnik MGU: nauchnyi kommunizm*, no. 2, 1990, p. 90.

5 *Voprosy istorii KPSS*, no. 10, 1989, p. 18 (reporting the testimony of K. T. Mazurov).

6 *XXV S"ezd Kommunisticheskoi partii Sovetskogo Soyuza 24 fevralya–5 marta 1976 goda. Stenograficheskii otchet*, 3 vols. (Moscow: Politizdat, 1976), vol. II, pp. 309–10.

7 *Vedomosti Verkhovnogo Soveta SSSR*, no. 19, 1976, item 318; *Pravda*, 7 May 1976, p. 1.

8 *Leonid Il'ich Brezhnev. Kratkii biograficheskii ocherk* (Moscow: Politizdat, 1976), p. 4.

9 *Pravda*, 17 November 1977, p. 1.

10 *Vedomosti Verkhovnogo Soveta SSSR*, no. 8, 1978, art. 117.

11 *Pravda*, 22 April 1979, p. 1, and 26 April 1979, p. 2 (the recipient was Alexander Chakovsky).

12 *XXVI S"ezd Kommunisticheskoi partii Sovetskogo Soyuza 23 fevralya–3 marta 1981 goda. Stenograficheskii otchet*, 3 vols. (Moscow: Politizdat, 1981), vol. I, p. 110 (Viktor Grishin).

13 Yu. V. Aksyutin, ed., *L. I. Brezhnev. Materialy k biografii* (Moscow: Politizdat, 1991), p. 276.

14 *XXVI S"ezd*, vol. II, p. 242.

15 *Pravda*, 20 December 1981, p. 2.

16 Brezhnev had accumulated more state awards than all other Soviet leaders, from Lenin to Gorbachev, according to Dmitrii Volkogonov's estimate in *Sem' vozhdei*, 2 vols. (Moscow: Novosti, 1995), vol. II, p. 69; the comparison

with Zhukov is in Zhores Medvedev, *Andropov: His Life and Death*, rev. edn (Oxford: Blackwell, 1984), pp. 103–4.

17 Roi Medvedev in *Rabochii klass i sovremennyi mir*, no. 6, 1988, p. 155.

18 Roi Medvedev in *Moskovskie novosti*, no. 37, 1988, p. 8. Writing later in a biography of the Soviet leader, Medvedev noted that Brezhnev had suffered several other heart attacks after which he had 'several times' to be brought back to life (*Lichnost' i epokha. Politicheskii portret L. I. Brezhneva*, book 1 [Moscow: Novosti, 1991], pp. 5–6). Another well-placed source, foreign policy adviser Georgii Arbatov, dated Brezhnev's serious illness from December 1974; after that he 'ruled' but did not govern (*Zvezda*, no. 9, 1990, p. 216). Marshal Akhromeev recalled similarly that after his heart attack in 1976 Brezhnev had 'stopped working as head of state and party' (S. F. Akhromeev and G. M. Kornienko, *Glazami marshala i diplomata* [Moscow: Mezhdunarodnye otnosheniya, 1992], p. 15). Brezhnev's doctor, Yevgenii Chazov, ascribed 'fatal influence' to an attractive nurse with whom he had latterly established a 'special relationship': *Zdorov'e i vlast'* (Moscow: Novosti, 1992), p. 117; and (for the 'relationship') Vladimir Medvedev, *Chelovek za spinoi* (Moscow: Russlit, 1994), p. 151. A wider selection of memoirs appears in *Leonid Brezhnev v vospominaniyakh, razmyshleniyakh, suzhdeniyakh* (Rostov on Don: Feniks, 1998).

19 A. S. Chernyaev, *Moya zhizn' i moe vremya* (Moscow: Mezhdunarodnye otnosheniya, 1995), p. 437; and on the Czechoslovakian experience in 1981, Vladimir Medvedev, *Chelovek za spinoi*, pp. 101–2.

20 *Argumenty i fakty*, no. 43, 1996, p. 9.

21 A. M. Aleksandrov-Agentov, *Ot Kollontai do Gorbacheva* (Moscow: Mezhdunarodnye otnosheniya, 1994), p. 273. M. S. Dokuchaev, a member of the KGB division that ensured the security of Soviet leaders, notes that Brezhnev had attempted to resign in 1979: *Moskva. Kreml'. Okhrana* (Moscow: Biznes-Press, 1995), pp. 173–4; so did a member of the Kremlin guard, Sergei Krasikov (*Vozle vozhdei* [Moscow: Sovremennik, 1997], p. 425). Dmitrii Volkogonov, however, suggests that Brezhnev was simply trying to induce his closest colleagues to insist yet again on his 'irreplaceability' (*Sem' vozhdei*, vol. II, p. 79).

22 M. S. Gorbachev, *Zhizn' i reformy*, 2 vols. (Moscow: Novosti, 1995), vol. I, p. 217. Brezhnev's foreign policy adviser A. M. Aleksandrov-Agentov recalled that Politburo meetings 'began to last just an hour, or forty-five minutes' (*Ot Kollontai*, p. 273); so did trade union leader Stepan Shalaev (*Izvestiya TsK KPSS*, no. 2, 1989, p. 246); Pravda editor Viktor Afanas'ev recalled meetings lasting 'an hour or two, not more' (*4-ya vlast' i 4 genseka* [Moscow: Kedr, 1994], p. 38), and Moscow party leader Viktor Grishin meetings that were latterly of an hour and a half's duration (*Ot Khrushcheva do Gorbacheva. Politicheskie portrety pyati gensekov i A. N. Kosygina. Memuary* [Moscow: Askol, 1996], p. 5). Yegor Ligachev, who as Tomsk first secretary occasionally took part in Politburo meetings, recalled that they lasted forty minutes or so in the late Brezhnev years, but 'hours, without a break' under his successor (Ye. K. Ligachev, *Predosterezhenie* [Moscow: Pravda Internashnl, 1998], p. 52). Memoirs agree that the later Brezhnev was very different from the general secretary of earlier years: for Afanas'ev there were

'two Brezhnevs' (*4-ya vlast'*, p. 30); Georgii Arbatov, similarly, knew 'two Brezhnevs – one before and one after his illness' (*Zatyanuvsheesya vyzdorovlenie (1953–1985 gg.). Svidetel'stvo sovremennika* [Moscow: Mezhdunarodnye otnosheniya, 1991], p. 288); and Gromyko noted that Brezhnev was 'not able to work' for the last two or three years of his administration (*Kommunist Belorussii*, no. 4, 1990, p. 51). Even Gorbachev accepted that the Brezhnev of the late 1960s and early 1970s was 'nothing like the cartoon figure' he later became (*Zhizn' i reformy*, vol. I, p. 124).

23 Akhromeev and Kornienko, *Glazami*, p. 15.

24 Yuri Churbanov, *Ya rasskazhu vse, kak bylo . . .*, 2nd edn (Moscow: Nezavisimaya gazeta, 1993), p. 1.

25 Roi Medvedev, *Lichnost' i epokha*, pp. 97–101; for the view that he had become the 'second person in the party', see Vladimir Medvedev, *Chelovek za spinoi*, p. 119 (similarly Roi Medvedev in *Moskovskie novosti*, no. 46, 1997, p. 18).

26 Zhores Medvedev, *Andropov*, pp. 93–6. Tsvigun's obituary appeared in *Pravda*, 21 January 1982, p. 2. Rumours of suicide were strengthened by the fact that Brezhnev, his brother-in-law, was not among the signatories; confirmation that his death was by suicide appears in the memoirs of Brezhnev's bodyguard (Vladimir Medvedev, *Chelovek za spinoi*, p. 148).

27 Zhores Medvedev, *Andropov*, pp. 93–6.

28 Dusko Doder, *Shadows and Whispers. Power Politics Inside the Kremlin from Brezhnev to Gorbachev* (New York: Random House, 1986), p. 62; *Pravda*, 27 April 1982, p. 3.

29 N. I. Ryzhkov, *Desyat' let velikikh potryasenii* (Moscow: Kniga, prosveshchenie, miloserdie, 1995), p. 56.

30 Doder, *Shadows and Whispers*, pp. 94–5 (the report of Medunov's dismissal 'in connection with a transfer to other work' appeared in *Pravda*, 24 July 1982, p. 2); on the dismissal of the manager of Gastronom No. 1, see *Moskovskaya pravda*, 14 April 1983, p. 3 (the arrests had taken place the previous November and December). Brezhnev's daughter found a biographer in Stanley Landau, *Galina Brezhnev and Her Gypsy Lover* (London: Quartet, 1989); she died in the summer of 1998 (*Izvestiya*, 2 July 1998, p. 7). The manager of Gastronom No. 1, with whom she had been associated, was executed in the summer of 1984 (*Vechernyaya Moskva*, 13 July 1984, p. 2).

31 *Pravda*, 12 November 1982, p. 1.

32 Yu. V. Andropov, *Izbrannye rechi i stat'i*, 2nd edn (Moscow: Politizdat, 1983), pp. 209–18. Biographies include Zhores Medvedev, *Andropov*; Roi Medvedev, *Gensek s Lubyanki* (Nizhnii Novgorod: Leta, 1993); and Jonathan Steele and Eric Abraham, *Andropov in Power* (Oxford: Martin Robertson, 1983).

33 Gorbachev discussed their relations during this period in *Zhizn' i reformy*, vol. I, pp. 241–6.

34 *Pravda*, 11 February 1984, p. 1. Andropov's doctor later reported that the general secretary had read about four hundred pages a day although he had the use of only one eye, and that he remained lucid even after his liver, lungs, and kidneys had stopped functioning: *Moskovskie novosti*, no. 8, 1991, p. 11.

35 Gorbachev, *Zhizn' i reformy*, vol. I, pp. 234, 248–9. Viktor Grishin, in his own memoirs, insists that Andropov had 'never included Gorbachev in the inner circle of party leaders', still less identified him as a successor (*Ot Khrushcheva do Gorbacheva*, p. 66, similarly p. 70); Ligachev, however, insists that Gorbachev was seen as a possible leader at this time (*Predosterezhenie*, pp. 57–8).

36 Gorbachev, *Zhizn' i reformy*, vol. I, pp. 248–50.

37 *Pravda*, 14 February 1984, p. 1. There was no real alternative to the election of Chernenko, in the view of Vitalii Vorotnikov, as he was already the 'second person' in the leadership (*A bylo eto tak . . . Iz dnevnika chlena Politbyuro TsK KPSS* [Moscow: Sovet veteranov knigoizdaniya, 1995], p. 37).

38 *Pravda*, 16 February 1984, p. 1.

39 See for instance the *Observer* (London), 19 February 1984, p. 12; Zhores Medvedev, *Andropov*, p. 226. Subsequent memoirs have disputed that Gorbachev had, in fact, a formal position of this kind: Ryzhkov, *Desyat' let*, p. 57, and similarly Vorotnikov, *A bylo eto tak*, pp. 39–40. Ligachev, however, recalled that it was Chernenko's own proposal that Gorbachev should chair the Secretariat during his leadership and that he should occupy on this basis the 'unofficial second post in the upper party hierarchy' (*Predosterezhenie*, p. 65).

40 *Pervaya sessiya Verkhovnogo Soveta SSSR (odinnadtsatyi sozyv) 11–12 aprelya 1984 g. Stenograficheskii otchet* (Moscow: Izvestiya, 1984), pp. 38–42.

41 See particularly the film, *Young Years on the Border*, which recorded Chernenko's 'courage and fortitude' in the border guards service: *Izvestiya*, 1 December 1984, p. 4. Chernenko's lack of personality is noted in Mark Galeotti, *Gorbachev and His Revolution* (London: Macmillan, 1997), p. 41.

42 *Pravda*, 1 March 1985, p. 1.

43 *Trud*, 12 March 1985, p. 2.

44 For the decision, see *Trud*, 12 March 1985, p. 1; and for the views of regional party secretaries, Gorbachev, *Zhizn' i reformy*, vol. I, p. 266. According to a well-placed observer, Grigorii Romanov was Gorbachev's only real challenger at the Politburo meeting that preceded the plenum, not Viktor Grishin (Valerii Legostaev in *Obozrevatel'*, no. 15, 1994, pp. 138–9). Dokuchaev (*Moskva. Kreml'. Okhrana*, pp. 205–6) claims that Romanov had at first proposed Grishin, but this version is not supported by other accounts or by the secretary's minutes (Centre for the Preservation of Contemporary Documentation [TsKhSD], *fond* 89, *perechen'* 36, doc. 16, 11 March 1985). According to Ligachev, Grishin had clearly been angling for the succession, but he had been outmanoeuvred by Foreign Minister Gromyko who stood up at once and proposed Gorbachev, followed by Prime Minister Tikhonov and all the other members (*Predosterezhenie*, p. 109). Gromyko, whose intervention was clearly decisive, had discussed the position with his son Anatolii and Alexander Yakovlev and agreed to take the initiative (Anatolii Gromyko, *V labirintakh Kremlya. Vospominaniya i razmyshleniya syna* [Moscow: Avtor, 1997], pp. 94–6). Ryzhkov (*Desyat' let*, pp. 74–6) confirms that there was no opposition to Gorbachev's election; Kunaev recalls that all including himself were in favour ('O moem vremeni', part 3, *Prostor*, no. 12, 1991, pp. 3–4); so does Vorotnikov (there was 'no

discussion [and] no alternative candidate, still less a struggle': *A bylo eto tak*, p. 57); and so does Gorbachev himself, although he had already told his wife that they 'could not go on living like this' (*Zhizn' i reformy*, vol. I, pp. 265, and more generally 265–72). His wife also recalled this memorable phrase: R. M. Gorbacheva, *Ya nadeyus'* (Moscow: Novosti, 1991), p. 14. According to Ligachev, local party first secretaries were prepared to force the nomination of Gorbachev at the plenum if the Politburo had recommended otherwise (*Predosterezhenie*, pp. 108–9).

45 I owe this anecdote to Archie Brown. Marshal Sokolov commented similarly, leaving the Kremlin: 'at last we have a leader' (Akhromeev and Kornienko, *Glazami*, p. 35).

46 M. S. Gorbachev, *Izbrannye rechi i stat'i*, 7 vols. (Moscow: Politizdat, 1987–90), vol. II, p. 129.

47 For Nikolai Ryzhkov, for instance, the origins of *perestroika* dated 'from the beginning of 1983, when Andropov directed us – a group of Central Committee officials, including myself and Gorbachev – to prepare some basic principles of economic reform' (quoted from the interview in M. Nenashev, *Poslednee pravitel'stvo SSSR* [Moscow: Krom, 1993], p. 23). Andropov, he wrote elsewhere, was the real initiator of *perestroika*, and the word itself had been in use as early as the 1976 Party Congress (*Desyat' let*, pp. 80, 81). For Gorbachev's adviser Georgii Shakhnazarov, on the other hand, Andropov's programme was 'limited to the perfection of the system' (*Tsena svobody. Reformatsiya Gorbacheva glazami yego pomoshchnika* [Moscow: Rossika/Zevs, 1993], p. 34). Gorbachev, too, believed Andropov was a 'man of his time, and one of those who was unable to break through the barrier of old ideas and values' (*Zhizn' i reformy*, vol. I, p. 247).

48 See Mark Zlotnik, 'Chernenko's program', *Problems of Communism*, vol. 31, no. 6 (November–December 1982), pp. 70–5. Chernenko's speech to people's controllers of October 1984 and his election address of February 1985 are especially relevant in this connection: *Pravda*, 6 October 1984, pp. 1–2, and 23 February 1985, pp. 1–2.

49 *Spravochnik partiinogo rabotnika*, vol. XXIII (Moscow: Politizdat, 1983), p. 99; Andrei Kirilenko, a Politburo and Secretariat member who was Brezhnev's exact contemporary, left the leadership at the same time 'for health reasons and at his own request'.

50 Ibid., vol. XXIV, 2 parts (Moscow: Politizdat, 1984), part 1, p. 9. Vorotnikov's subsequent appointment is in *Pravda*, 25 June 1983, p. 1.

51 *Spravochnik partiinogo rabotnika*, vol. XXIV, part 1, p. 63. M. S. Solomentsev moved at the same time to full Politburo membership, and KGB head Viktor Chebrikov became a candidate.

52 His obituary appeared in *Pravda*, 22 December 1984, p. 1.

53 These biographical details have been drawn from *Sostav tsentral'nykh organov KPSS, izbrannykh XXVI s"ezdom partii* (Moscow: Politizdat, 1982), and *Izvestiya TsK KPSS*, no. 1, 1989, pp. 9–31.

54 *Pravda*, 18 December 1982, p. 2.

55 *Literaturnaya gazeta*, 18 May 1988, p. 13.

56 *Spravochnik partiinogo rabotnika*, vol. XXIV, part 1, p. 9. Medunov was later expelled from the CPSU itself: *Pravda*, 24 March 1989, p. 2.

57 *Izvestiya*, 9 November 1984, p. 6.
58 *Literaturnaya gazeta*, 18 May 1988, p. 11; his wife's suicide is reported in T. Gdlyan and E. Dodolev, *Mafiya vremen bezzakoniya* (Yerevan: Izdatel'stvo AN Armenii, 1991), p. 113, and his son's loss of position in *Dokumenty TsK VLKSM 1983* (Moscow: Molodaya gvardiya, 1984), p. 13.
59 Zhores Medvedev, *Andropov*, pp. 97–8.
60 *Pravda*, 31 December 1988, p. 3; and for his loss of state honours, *Izvestiya*, 25 July 1989, p. 8. On the Uzbek cotton scandal, see Arkadii Vaksberg, *The Soviet Mafia* (London: Weidenfeld and Nicolson, 1991), and T. Gdlyan and N. Ivanov, *Kremlevskoe delo*, 2nd edn (Moscow: Gramota, 1996).
61 *Izvestiya*, 16 January 1988, p. 3.
62 *Istochnik*, no. 2, 1994, pp. 71–3.
63 *Izvestiya*, 25 July 1989, p. 8, and 29 September 1989, p. 3.
64 *Pravda*, 7 January 1988, p. 1.
65 Brezhnev was assessed 'negatively' or 'very negatively' by 89 per cent of respondents and positively by just 7 per cent, in a Moscow telephone poll; Stalin was assessed positively by 13 per cent, and negatively by 37 per cent (Lenin, at this time, was evaluated positively by 94 per cent and negatively by just 1 per cent: *Argumenty i fakty*, no. 5, 1989, p. 4). Similar results were reported in *Soviet Weekly*, 18 February 1989, p. 6, and in *Dialog*, no. 2, 1990, p. 5. Brezhnev's grandson is quoted from *Moskovskie novosti*, no. 38, 1988, p. 10.
66 *Radio Liberty Research Report*, RL 92 (21 February 1983), and *Pravda*, 28 December 1982, p. 3.
67 *Spravochnik partiinogo rabotnika*, vol. XXIV, pt. 2, pp. 95–9.
68 For instance *Pravda*, 7 January 1985, p. 1. Gorbachev himself paid tribute in December 1984: *Izbrannye rechi i stat'i*, vol. II, p. 92.
69 *Trud*, 31 August 1988, pp. 1–2. Stakhanov's obituary appeared in *Pravda*, 6 November 1977, p. 8.
70 *Pravda*, 6 May 1984, pp. 1–2; *Literaturnaya gazeta*, 13 June 1984, p. 2.
71 *The Times*, 4 September 1982, p. 4.
72 The new law on the Soviet frontier was published in *Pravda*, 26 November 1982, pp. 1–3; on postal restrictions, see *The Times*, 19 November 1982, p. 8.
73 *The Times*, 22 May 1983, p. 7 (Vladimov's deprivation of citizenship was reported in *Vedomosti Verkhovnogo Soveta SSSR*, no. 33, 1983, item 520); and *The Times*, 20 January 1983, p. 5.
74 *Vedomosti Verkhovnogo Soveta SSSR*, no. 29, 1984, item 515, and no. 51, 1983, item 797.
75 *Keesing's Contemporary Archives*, 1984, p. 33120; *The Observer*, 10 February 1985, p. 19.
76 The first such report appeared in *Pravda*, 11 December 1982, p. 1. For a detailed analysis of such reports up to 1988, see John Löwenhardt, 'Politbyuro zasedaet: reported and secret meetings of the Politburo of the CPSU', *Nordic Journal of Soviet and East European Studies*, vol. 5, no. 2 (1988), pp. 157–74.
77 *Pravda*, 1 February 1983, pp. 1–2, and 30 April 1984, pp. 1–2.
78 Ibid., 19 June 1983, pp. 1, 3. For a full study, see Darrell P. Slider,

'Reforming the workplace: the 1983 Soviet Law on Labour Collectives', *Soviet Studies*, vol. 37, no. 2 (April 1985), pp. 173–83.

79 *Pravda*, 21 October 1984, p. 2.

80 Ibid., 15 June 1983, p. 3, and 16 June 1983, p. 3. (The All-Russian Public Opinion Centre, VTsIOM, came into existence at the end of 1987: see ch. 6.)

81 See *Plenum Tsentral'nogo komiteta KPSS 14–15 iyunya 1983 goda. Stenografificheskii otchet* (Moscow: Politizdat, 1983).

82 *Pravda*, 11 December 1982, p. 1, and 9 January 1983, p. 3.

83 *The Times*, 14 February 1983, p. 10.

84 Yu. Korolev, *Kremlevskii sovetnik* (Moscow: Olimp, 1995), p. 226.

85 Andropov, *Izbrannye rechi i stat'i*, pp. 245–6. For a full discussion of these and related changes, see Alfred B. Evans, *Soviet Marxism-Leninism: The Decline of an Ideology* (Westport, CT: Praeger, 1993).

86 Andropov, *Izbrannye rechi i stat'i*, pp. 286–7, 212 (November 1982).

87 K. U. Chernenko, *Narod i partiya yediny. Izbrannye rechi i stat'i* (Moscow: Politizdat, 1984), p. 246. Chernenko expressed similar sentiments in his 'Na uroven' trebovanii razvitogo sotsializma', *Kommunist*, no. 18, 1984, pp. 3–21.

88 See Chernenko's articles in *Voprosy filosofii*, no. 10, 1982, pp. 16–29, and no. 2, 1984, pp. 116–23.

89 Gorbachev, *Izbrannye rechi i stat'i*, vol. III, p. 269. For further discussion of this important debate, see Ernst Kux, 'Contradictions in Soviet socialism', *Problems of Communism*, vol. 33, no. 6 (November–December 1984), pp. 1–27; and Stephen White and Alex Pravda, eds., *Ideology and Soviet Politics* (London: Macmillan, 1988), chs. 1 and 5.

90 *Materialy vneocherednogo Plenuma TsK KPSS 11 marta 1985 goda* (Moscow: Politizdat, 1985), pp. 7–8.

91 TsKhSD, Moscow, *fond* 89, *perechen'* 36, doc. 16, 11 March 1985 (also published in *Istochnik*, no. 0 [trial issue], 1993, pp. 66–75); Gorbachev provided the same assurance on matters of foreign policy at the Politburo meeting that took place on 21 March 1985 (Vorotnikov, *A bylo eto tak*, p. 60).

92 *Materialy vneocherednogo Plenuma*, p. 9.

93 Gorbachev referred to the 20th Congress as the starting point of reform in his opening speech at the 28th Party Congress in 1990 (*XXVIII S"ezd Kommunisticheskoi partii Sovetskogo Soyuza , 2–13 iyulya 1990 g. Stenograficheskii otchet*, 2 vols. [Moscow: Politizdat, 1991], vol. I, p. 87) and stressed its impact in his memoirs (*Zhizn' i reformy*, vol. I, pp. 83–5). A more general consideration of the flow of political generations is provided in Evan Mawdsley and Stephen White, *The Soviet Elite: The CPSU Central Committee and Its Members, 1917–1991* (Oxford: Oxford University Press, forthcoming).

94 Gorbachev, *Zhizn' i reformy*, vol. I, pp. 42–51. Gorbachev travelled frequently between the south and Moscow at the end of the 1940s; 'with my own eyes', as he recalled, 'I saw the destruction of Stalingrad, Rostov, Khar'kov, Orel, Kursk, Voronezh' (*Perestroika i novoe myshlenie dlya nashei strany i dlya vsego mira* [Moscow: Politizdat, 1987], pp. 37–8).

95 Gorbachev, *Zhizn' i reformy*, vol. I, pp. 37–8.
96 Ibid., p. 62.
97 Zdenek Mlynar, 'Il mio compagno di studi Mikhail Gorbaciov', *L'Unità*, 9 April 1985, p. 9.
98 Gorbachev, *Zhizn' i reformy*, vol. I, pp. 64–5.
99 The fullest available biography is Archie Brown, *The Gorbachev Factor* (Oxford: Oxford University Press, 1996). See also Zhores Medvedev, *Gorbachev*, rev. edn (Oxford: Blackwell, 1988); Christian Schmidt-Hauer, *Gorbachev: The Road to Power* (London: Tauris, 1986); Michel Tatu, *Gorbatchev. L'URSS va-t-elle changer?* (Paris: Le Centurion, 1987); Dev Murarka, *Gorbachev* (London: Hutchinson, 1988); *Mikhail S. Gorbachev: An Intimate Biography* (New York, Time, 1988); Dusko Doder and Louise Branson, *Gorbachev: Heretic in the Kremlin* (London: Macdonald, 1990); and Gerd Ruge, *Gorbachev: A Biography* (London: Chatto and Windus, 1991). The possibility that Gorbachev might have found a position in the KGB on graduation is reported in *Argumenty i fakty*, no. 41, 1992, p. 4; nothing came of it because his family had spent some time under German occupation during the Second World War.
100 Gorbachev, *Zhizn' i reformy*, vol. I, pp. 67–71.
101 Ibid., pp. 38–42; Gorbachev's paternal grandfather had spent two years in prison. Gorbachev first referred to his family's experience of Stalinism in *Pravda*, 1 December 1990, p. 4.
102 *Gorbachev: An Intimate Biography*, pp. 198–202. Raisa's memoirs were published as *Ya nadeyus'* (see n. 44 above); for a biography, see Urda Juergens, *Raisa* (London: Weidenfeld and Nicolson, 1990).
103 Gorbachev, *Izbrannye rechi i stat'i*, vol. V, p. 486; Vladimir Medvedev, *Chelovek za spinoi*, p. 272.
104 Gorbachev, *Izbrannye rechi i stat'i*, vol. V, pp. 58–9.
105 *Izvestiya*, 24 March 1989, p. 3.
106 *Izvestiya TsK KPSS*, no. 5, 1989, pp. 57–60.
107 Ibid., no. 8, 1989, p. 66.
108 *Pravda*, 11 December 1984, pp. 1–2 (full text in *Izbrannye rechi i stat'i*, vol. II, pp. 75–108).
109 *Pravda*, 21 February 1985, p. 2 (full text in *Izbrannye rechi i stat'i*, vol. II, pp. 117–28).
110 Gorbachev, *Izbrannye rechi i stat'i*, vol. II, pp. 152–67.
111 *Spravochnik partiinogo rabotnika*, vol. XXVI (Moscow: Politizdat, 1986), pp. 15–16. KGB chairman Viktor Chebrikov moved at the same time from candidate to full Politburo membership.
112 Ibid., p. 38. The other new Central Committee secretary was Lev Zaikov, first secretary of the Leningrad regional party organisation.
113 *III sessiya Verkhovnogo Soveta SSSR (odinnadtsatyi sozyv) 2–3 iyulya 1985 goda. Stenograficheskii otchet* (Moscow: Izvestiya, 1985), pp. 8, 12. Outgoing foreign minister Gromyko was shocked by the appointment: Gromyko, *V labirintakh Kremlya*, p. 101.
114 *Vedomosti Verkhovnogo Soveta SSSR*, 1985, no. 48, item 907. Tikhonov retired from the Politburo the following month: *Spravochnik partiinogo rabotnika*, vol. XXVI, p. 39. Two other Brezhnevites, Viktor Grishin and

Konstantin Rusakov, retired from the Politburo and Secretariat respectively early the following year: ibid., vol. XXVII (Moscow: Politizdat, 1987), p. 121.

115 These and other details are taken from *Izvestiya TsK KPSS*, no. 1, 1989, pp. 9–31.

116 Roi Medvedev in *Pravda*, 30 May 1989, p. 2.

117 *Spravochnik partiinogo rabotnika*, vol. XXVIII (Moscow: Politizdat, 1988), p. 32; the circumstances of Kunaev's expulsion are set out in *Izvestiya TsK KPSS*, no. 2, 1989, p. 44.

118 *Spravochnik partiinogo rabotnika*, vol. XXVIII, p. 31.

119 *Izvestiya TsK KPSS*, no. 8, 1990, p. 4. There was no republican party organisation at this time in the Russian Republic.

120 *Kommunist*, no. 13, 1988, p. 11.

121 *I s''ezd narodnykh deputatov SSSR 25 maya–9 iyunya 1989 g. Stenograficheskii otchet*, 3 vols. (Moscow: Izdanie Verkhovnogo Soveta SSSR, 1989), vol. I, p. 44.

122 *Pravda*, 31 March 1989, p. 2.

123 The term had already been employed in the 1977 'Brezhnev' constitution and had been used as early as 1874 by the radical writer Nikolai Chernyshevsky, who noted, accurately, that it was a 'bureaucratic expression thought up to replace "freedom of speech"' (*Arkhiv Marksa i Engel'sa*, vol. XI [Moscow: Ogiz/Gospolitizdat, 1948], pp. 190–1 [I owe this reference to Dr James White]). For a full account, see Stephen White, *After Gorbachev*, rev. 4th edn (Cambridge: Cambridge University Press, 1994), ch. 3; Alec Nove, *Glasnost' and After* (Boston: Unwin Hyman, 1989); Anna Lawton, *Kinoglasnost: Soviet Cinema in Our Time* (Cambridge: Cambridge University Press, 1992); on television, Ellen Mickiewicz, *Split Signals* (New York: Oxford University Press, 1988); David Wedgwood Benn, *From Glasnost to Freedom of Speech* (London: Pinter, 1992); and Walter Laqueur, *The Long Road to Freedom: Russia and Glasnost* (London: Unwin Hyman, 1989).

124 Gorbachev, *Izbrannye rechi i stat'i*, vol. II, p. 131.

125 *Sovetskaya Rossiya*, 24 November 1985, p. 1.

126 Ibid., 5 January 1986, p. 3.

127 Gorbachev, *Izbrannye rechi i stat'i*, vol. III, p. 181.

128 Ibid., vol. V, p. 408.

129 Ibid., vol. III, p. 162, and vol. V, p. 401 (November 1987).

130 Ibid., vol. IV, p. 373.

131 Ibid., vol. V, pp. 397–402.

132 *Pravda*, 6 February 1988, p. 1 (a copy of the Court's decision appeared in *Izvestiya TsK KPSS*, no. 1, 1989, p. 121); Bukharin's readmission into the Communist Party was reported in *Pravda*, 10 July 1988, p. 1, and into the Academy of Sciences, *Pravda*, 21 October 1988, p. 2.

133 An early reassessment by V. Ivanov in *Sovetskaya Rossiya*, 27 September 1987, p. 4, noted Trotsky's willpower and personal courage but also emphasised his arrogance and lack of principle. A fuller account by N. A. Vasetsky, 'L. D. Trotsky: politicheskii portret', *Novaya i noveishaya istoriya*, no. 3, 1989, emphasised Trotsky's 'contradictory' character, valuable where he had acted as a party and state leader, but not where his 'personal

ambitions' led him into conflict with the party line (p. 165). The first of Trotsky's writings to be reprinted were, predictably, his studies of Lenin (*Ogonek*, no. 17, 1989, pp. 3–7); for a full bibliography, see Ian D. Thatcher, 'Recent Soviet writings on Leon Trotsky', *Coexistence*, vol. 27, no. 3 (September 1990), pp. 141–67.

134 Yuri Polyakov as quoted in the *Guardian* (London), 10 October 1987, p. 7; *Moskovskie novosti*, no. 48, 1988, pp. 8–9 (Medvedev gave a figure of 40 million 'victims of Stalinism' in an interview in *Argumenty i fakty*, no. 5, 1989, p. 6). The official KGB figures were 3.8 million 'victims' of Stalinism between 1930 and 1953, of whom 786,098 were shot (*Pravitel'stvennyi vestnik*, no. 7, 1990, p. 11); this is close to the figure of 3.1 million sentenced on political grounds – of whom 749,421 were condemned to death – that is reported from state archives in *Sotsiologicheskie issledovaniya*, no. 7, 1996, p. 6. The current state of research is considered in J. Arch Getty and Robert T. Manning, eds., *Stalinist Terror: New Perspectives* (Cambridge: Cambridge University Press, 1993), and R. W. Davies, *Soviet History in the Yeltsin Era* (London: Macmillan, 1997).

135 *Izvestiya*, 12 September 1988, p. 4, 27 November 1988, p. 3, and 25 January 1989, p. 1 (number of victims); and more generally, David R. Marples, 'Kuropaty: the investigation of a Stalinist historical controversy', *Slavic Review*, vol. 53, no. 2 (Summer 1994), pp. 513–23.

136 On the Memorial Society and popular memory, see Nanci Adler, *Victims of Soviet Terror: The Story of the Memorial Movement* (Westport, CT: Praeger, 1993), and Kathleen E. Smith, *Remembering Stalin's Victims: Popular Memory and the End of the USSR* (Ithaca, NY: Cornell University Press, 1996).

137 See Vladimir Treml, 'Perestroika and Soviet statistics', *Soviet Economy*, vol. 4, no. 1 (January–March 1988), pp. 65–94, and Tim Heleniak and Albert Motivans, 'A note on glasnost' and the Soviet statistical system', *Soviet Studies*, vol. 43, no. 3 (1991), pp. 473–90.

138 For the text of the law, see *Vedomosti S''ezda narodnykh deputatov SSSR i Verkhovnogo Soveta SSSR*, no. 29, 1990, art. 492; on the operation of censorship, see A. V. Blyum, 'Zakat glavlita. Kak razrushalas' sistema sovetskoi tsenzury: dokumental'naya khronika 1985–1991 gg.', *Kniga: issledovaniya i materialy*, vol. 71 (1995), pp. 168–87, and T. M. Goryacheva, et al., eds., *Istoriya sovetskoi politicheskoi tsenzury. Dokumenty i kommentarii* (Moscow: ROSSPEN, 1997).

139 *Izvestiya*, 22 April 1989, p. 6.

140 *Materialy XIX Vsesoyuznoi konferentsii Kommunisticheskoi partii Sovetskogo Soyuza 28 iyunya–1 iyulya 1988 goda* (Moscow: Politizdat, 1988), pp. 35–7. On democratisation the most satisfactory account is Michael E. Urban with Vyacheslav Igrunov and Sergei Mitrokhin, *The Rebirth of Politics in Russia* (Cambridge: Cambridge University Press, 1997).

141 For the text of the law, see *Vedomosti Verkhovnogo Soveta SSSR*, no. 49, 1988, art. 729.

142 *Materialy XIX Vsesoyuznoi konferentsii*, pp. 145–8.

143 *XIX Vsesoyuznaya konferentsiya Kommunisticheskoi partii Sovetskogo Soyuza, 28 iyunya–1 iyulya 1988 g. Stenograficheskii otchet*, 2 vols. (Moscow:

Politizdat, 1988), vol. I, p. 337 (G. I. Zagainov); on the membership, see *Izvestiya TsK KPSS*, no. 7, 1989, p. 113. Developments in the party more generally are considered in Ronald J. Hill, 'The CPSU: from monolith to pluralist?', *Soviet Studies*, vol. 43, no. 2 (1991), pp. 217–35; Stephen White, 'Rethinking the CPSU', *Soviet Studies*, vol. 43, no. 3 (1991), pp. 405–28; E. A. Rees, ed., *The Soviet Communist Party in Disarray* (London: Macmillan, 1992); Graeme Gill, *The Collapse of a Single-Party System* (Cambridge: Cambridge University Press, 1994); White, 'Communists and their Party in the late Soviet period', *Slavonic and East European Review*, vol. 72, no. 4 (October 1994), pp. 644–63; and White, 'The failure of CPSU democratization', *Slavonic and East European Review*, vol. 75, no. 4 (October 1997), pp. 681–97.

144 Gorbachev, *Zhizn' i reformy*, vol. I, p. 270; Gorbachev did employ the term in his address to the April 1985 Central Committee plenum (ibid., p. 279) and it was incorporated into the Programme and Rules that were adopted at the 27th Party Congress in 1986 (*Materialy XXVII S"ezda Kommunisticheskoi partii Sovetskogo Soyuza* [Moscow: Politizdat, 1986], pp. 122, 188).

145 For this term, see for instance Gorbachev, *Izbrannye rechi i stat'i*, vol. IV, p. 110.

146 *Materialy Plenuma Tsentral'nogo Komiteta KPSS, 5–7 fevralya 1990 g.* (Moscow: Politizdat, 1990), p. 125 (I. I. Mel'nikov). The text of the declaration as adopted at the Plenum is ibid., pp. 353–82, and as adopted at the Congress in *Materialy XXVIII S"ezda Kommunisticheskoi partii Sovetskogo Soyuza* (Moscow: Politizdat, 1990), pp. 77–98.

147 To quote the Leningrad party leader, Boris Gidaspov, in *Pravda*, 27 July 1991, p. 4; the text of the new draft Programme appeared ibid., 8 August 1991, pp. 3–4, and also in *Kommunist*, no. 12, 1991, pp. 3–15. According to Valerii Tishkov, the reference to a 'communist perspective' had originally been omitted entirely and was included in the interests of compromise (*Izvestiya*, 8 August 1991, p. 4). For a discussion, see Mark Sandle, 'The final word: the draft Party Programme of July/August 1991', *Europe–Asia Studies*, vol. 48, no. 7 (November 1996), pp. 1131–50.

148 *Pravda*, 26 July 1991, p. 2.

149 *XXVIII S"ezd*, vol. II, pp. 196–7 (*Short Course*); *Pravda*, 26 October 1990, p. 2 (railway timetables). Gorbachev, his adviser Anatolii Chernyaev explained, 'genuinely believed in the formula: socialism is the creation of the masses. Let them create it. And we'll see what happens' (A. S. Chernyaev, *1991 god. Dnevnik pomoshchnika Prezidenta SSSR* [Moscow: Terra/Respublika, 1997], p. 24).

150 Gorbachev, *Izbrannye rechi i stat'i*, vol. IV, pp. 308–9.

151 Ibid., vol. II, p. 154.

152 Ibid., vol. III, pp. 181–3.

153 *Pravda*, 26 June 1990, p. 2.

154 Ibid., 9 October 1990, p. 1.

155 Ibid., 16 November 1990, p. 3.

156 See Mikhail Gorbachev, *Avgustovskii putch. Prichiny i sledstviya* (Moscow: Novosti, 1991), p. 9 (Gorbachev spoke here of his 'betrayal'); Raisa Gorbacheva is quoted on Boldin from Chernyaev, *1991 god*, p. 189.

157 *Izvestiya*, 20 December 1990, p. 6.
158 *Komsomol'skaya pravda*, 3 August 1991, p. 3.
159 *Sovetskaya Rossiya*, 23 July 1991, p. 1.
160 *Pravda*, 13 August 1989, p. 4, and *Izvestiya*, 16 August 1991, p. 2. Yakovlev expressed similar views in an interview the same day that appeared in *Literaturnaya gazeta*, 28 August 1991, p. 2.
161 Anatolii Sobchak noted his 'complete surprise' in his *Khozhdenie vo vlast'*, 2nd edn (Moscow: Novosti, 1991), p. 275. Gorbachev may possibly have given reason to believe that he would support the introduction of a state of emergency (see for instance Amy Knight, 'The coup that never was: Gorbachev and the forces of reaction', *Problems of Communism*, vol. 40, no. 6 [November–December 1991], pp. 36–44, at pp. 39–40); about 6 per cent of the Soviet public, indeed, saw him as the 'chief instigator' of the coup (*Argumenty i fakty*, no. 36, 1991, p. 1). A detailed chronology and documentation of the coup is available in *Putch. Khronika trevozhnykh dnei* (Moscow: Progress, 1991); *Avgust-91* (Moscow: Politizdat, 1991), which is more 'Gorbachevian' in tone; M. K. Gorshkov and V. V. Zhuravlev, eds., *Krasnoe ili beloe? (Drama avgusta-91: fakty, gipotesy, stolknoveniya mnenii)* (Moscow: Terra, 1992); and in Yu. Kazarin and B. Yakovlev, eds., *Smert' zagovora: belaya kniga* (Moscow: Novosti, 1992), which reflects the position of the Moscow city administration. There are also several journalists' accounts: Martin Sixsmith, *Moscow Coup* (London: Simon and Schuster, 1991); Giulietto Chiesa, *Cronaca del golpe rosso* (Milan: Baldini and Castoldi, 1991); and the relevant chapters of David Remnick, *Lenin's Tomb* (New York: Random House, 1993). Contemporary testimony is collected in Victoria Bonnell, et al., *Russia at the Barricades: Eyewitness Accounts of the August Coup* (Armonk, NY: Sharpe, 1993) and in V. Maslyukov and K. Truevtsev, eds., *V avguste 91-go. Rossiya glazami ochevidtsev* (Moscow and St Petersburg: Limbus-Press, 1993). Gorbachev's own account is his *Avgustovskii putch*. For discussions, see Richard Sakwa, 'The revolution of 1991 in Russia: interpretations of the Moscow coup', *Coexistence*, vol. 29, no. 4 (December 1992), pp. 335–75, and John B. Dunlop, *The Rise of Russia and the Fall of the Soviet Empire* (Princeton, NJ: Princeton University Press, 1993).
162 Gorbachev, *Avgustovskii putch*, pp. 9–10.
163 *Izvestiya*, 20 August 1991, p. 1.
164 *Pravda*, 20 August 1991, pp. 1–2.
165 *Izvestiya*, 20 August 1991, p. 1.
166 Ibid.
167 Ibid., 29 August 1991, pp. 4, 8 (Pavlov admitted later that he 'probably had a sip': ibid., 10 October 1991, p. 7).
168 *Avgustovskii putch*, pp. 19–20.
169 *Izvestiya*, 21 August 1991, pp. 1–2.
170 Ibid., 26 August 1991, p. 6 (whether an order was actually given to attack remains unclear: see Knight, 'The coup that never was', p. 40).
171 On Luk'yanov as 'chief ideologist', see *Izvestiya*, 22 August 1991, p. 4; his arrest is reported ibid., 2 September 1991, p. 1. For Luk'yanov, writing subsequently, this was not a coup but a 'desperate attempt to save the

social order that was established by the USSR constitution' (*Perevorot mnimyi i nastoyashchii* [Moscow: Manuskript, 1993], p. 12). Bessmertny-kh's unconvincing press conference is in *Pravda*, 22 August 1991, p. 5.

172 Gorbachev's initial assessment appeared in *Pravda*, 23 August 1991, p. 2; he later named three Central Committee secretaries, Andrei Girenko, Galina Semenova, and Yegor Stroev, who had refused their support to the conspirators and emerged as 'mature politicians and honest people': *Zhizn' i reformy*, vol. II, p. 575.

173 *Izvestiya*, 26 August 1991, p. 2.

174 *Vedomosti S"ezda narodnykh deputatov RSFSR i Verkhovnogo Soveta RSFSR*, no. 35, 1991, art. 1149, 23 August 1991.

175 Ibid., no. 35, 1991, art. 1164, 25 August 1991.

176 Ibid., no. 45, 1991, art. 1537, 6 November 1991.

177 The declaration establishing the CIS appeared in *Rossiiskaya gazeta*, 10 December 1991, p. 1; the text of the agreement is ibid., 11 December 1991, p. 1.

178 *Vedomosti S"ezda narodnykh deputatov RSFSR i Verkhovnogo Soveta RSFSR*, no. 51, 1991, arts. 1798 and 1799, 12 December 1991. For the view that the full Congress of People's Deputies should have considered the matter, see Boris Lazarev in *Vestnik Rossiiskoi Akademii nauk*, no, 7, 1993, p. 612; for the view that there should have been a referendum, A. S. Tsipko in G. A. Bordyugov, ed., *Rossiiskaya imperiya, SSSR, Rossiiskaya Federatsiya: istoriya odnoi strany?* (Moscow: Rossiya molodaya, 1993), p. 95. The jurist and deputy Viktor Sheinis commented that the December 1991 agreement between the three Slavic leaders was 'outside any constitutional procedure' and that the decision to end the USSR was 'ratified by a Supreme Soviet that had no competence to decide accordingly' (*Gosudarstvo i pravo*, no. 12, 1997, p. 65).

179 *Rossiiskaya gazeta*, 24 December 1991, p. 1.

180 *Pravda*, 20 December 1991, p. 5.

2 PARTIES, VOTERS, AND GOVERNMENT

1 This chapter draws in part upon visits to Russia as an official election observer in December 1995 and in June 1996, and upon a collection of ephemera and video recordings relating to the December 1995 election kindly made available by Sarah Oates. The fullest available discussion of Soviet and Russian electoral behaviour is Stephen White, Richard Rose, and Ian McAllister, *How Russia Votes* (Chatham, NJ: Chatham House, 1997); the postcommunist period and particularly the elections of 1995 and 1996 are given close and rigorous attention in Timothy J. Colton, *Transitional Citizenship: Voting in Post-Soviet Russia* (Cambridge, MA: Harvard University Press, forthcoming). The development of the electoral system itself is considered in Yu. A. Novikov, *Izbiratel'naya sistema Rossii. 90 let istorii* (Moscow: Manuskript, 1996), which reprints the relevant legislation.

2 *Izvestiya*, 10 February 1987, p. 1.

3 *Pravda*, 5 March 1989, p. 1; *Izvestiya*, 13 July 1992, p. 3.

4 See Stephen White, 'Reforming the electoral system', in Walter Joyce, et al., *Gorbachev and Gorbachevism* (London: Cass, 1989), pp. 1–17; and Jeffrey Hahn, 'An experiment in competition: the 1987 elections to the local soviets', *Slavic Review*, vol. 47, no. 2 (Fall 1988), pp. 434–47.

5 For the text, see *Vedomosti Verkhovnogo Soveta SSSR*, no. 49, 1988, art. 729.

6 For Ligachev's view, see his *Zagadka Gorbacheva* (Novosibirsk: Interbuk, 1992), p. 75. The number of defeats of first secretaries was reported in *Argumenty i fakty*, no. 21, 1989, p. 8; Yeltsin's victory in Moscow (with 89.4 per cent of the vote) was reported in *Moskovskaya pravda*, 28 March 1989, p. 2. Gorbachev told his Politburo colleagues the election was a 'major step in . . . the further democratisation of society', and Alexander Yakovlev argued similarly that it had been a 'referendum for *perestroika*'; but Yuri Solov'ev (who had lost his seat) thought a 'struggle for power' was in progress, and Alexander Luk'yanov called for measures against Memorial and Pamyat', which were 'close to anti-Soviet organisations' (Politburo minutes, 28 March 1989, Chernyaev papers, Gorbachev Foundation, Moscow). Nikolai Ryzhkov recalled Gorbachev's 'delight' but warned for his own part that the party had 'lost the elections' (*Perestroika. Istoriya predatel'stv* [Moscow: Novosti, 1992], pp. 284–5).

7 For the casualties, see *Izvestiya*, 28 December 1993, p. 1. Yeltsin's 'appeal to the citizens of Russia' appeared in *Rossiiskie vesti*, 5 October 1993, p. 1; Gaidar is quoted from his *Dni porazhenii i pobed* (Moscow: Vagrius, 1996), p. 294. There are several documentary accounts of the confrontation: N. L. Zheleznova, et al., eds., *Moskva. Osen'-93. Khronika protivosostoyaniya* (Moscow: Respublika, 1994), favour the presidential position; more critical are A. V. Buzgalin and A. I. Kolganov, eds., *Krovavyi oktyabr' v Moskve. Khronika, svidetel'stva, analiz sobytii 21 sentyabrya–4 oktyabrya 1993 goda* (Moscow: Erebus, 1993), and V. Ya. Vasil'ev, Buzgalin, and Kolganov, eds., *Ploshchad' svobodnoi Rossii. Sbornik svidetel'stv o sentyabr'skikh–oktyabr'skikh dnyakh 1993 goda v stolitse Rossii* (Moscow: Erebus, 1994). A chronology and commentary is provided in A. Zevelev and Yu. Pavlov, eds., *Raskolotaya vlast'* (Moscow: Rosspen, 1995); there is also a chronology in *Svobodnaya mysl'*, no. 15, 1993, pp. 12–42.

8 The views of Gaidar and Yeltsin's press secretary Sergei Filatov are reported in Gaidar, *Dni*, pp. 274–5; Filatov, in tears, had begged Yeltsin's bodyguard to persuade the president to withdraw his decree, describing it as a 'catastrophe' (Alexander Korzhakov, *Boris Yel'tsin. Ot rassveta do zakata* [Moscow: Interbuk, 1997], p. 157).

9 Korzhakov, *Boris Yel'tsin*, p. 170.

10 B. N. Yeltsin, *Zapiski Prezidenta* (Moscow: Ogonek, 1994), p. 347.

11 Korzhakov, *Boris Yel'tsin*, pp. 158–9.

12 *Rossiiskie vesti*, 4 March 1993, p. 1.

13 For the referendum result, see ibid., 25 December 1993, p. 1; independent observers estimated the real level of turnout at between 38 and 43 per cent (O. G. Rumyantsev, *Osnovy konstitutsionnogo stroya Rossii* [Moscow: Yurist, 1994], pp. 216–17), or in another estimate 46.1 per cent (*Sovetskaya Rossiya*, 7 May 1994, p. 2). Yeltsin's press secretary, Vyacheslav Kostikov, himself witnessed the alteration of the results by the chairman of the Central

Electoral Commission, Nikolai Ryabov, a defector from the parliamentary camp who was 'universally regarded as cunning and treacherous' (*Roman s prezidentom* [Moscow: Vagrius, 1997], pp. 266–7).

14 The full text of the constitutional amendments appears in *Vneocherednoi III s"ezd narodnykh deputatov SSSR 12–15 marta 1990 g. Stenograficheskii otchet,* 3 vols. (Moscow: Izdanie Verkhovnogo Soveta SSSR, 1990), vol. III, pp. 192–207.

15 *Materialy Plenuma Tsentral'nogo Komiteta KPSS, 5–7 fevralya 1990 g.* (Moscow: Politizdat, 1990), pp. 9–10; the Platform for the 28th Party Congress that was approved at the plenum, 'Towards a humane, democratic socialism', made clear that elections should be a 'terrain of honest competition of the representatives of all sections of society', and that the development of society did 'not exclude the creation of parties' (ibid., p. 365).

16 For the text of the law, see *Vedomosti S"ezda narodnykh deputatov SSSR i Verkhovnogo Soveta SSSR,* no. 42, 1990, art. 840.

17 *Argumenty i fakty,* no. 24, 1992, p. 8; the number of activists is estimated in *Izvestiya,* 20 April 1992, p. 2. There were an estimated 1,200 parties or movements at this time: ibid., 11 June 1992, p. 2.

18 *Sobranie zakonodatel'stva Rossiiskoi Federatsii,* no. 21, 1995, art. 1930. By 1998 'over three thousand' parties had registered under its auspices (*Argumenty i fakty,* no. 20, 1998, p. 24); there were 95 parties that were organised on a national basis, and 154 public movements (*Nezavisimaya gazeta,* 20 November 1998, p. 1).

19 *Nezavisimaya gazeta,* 7 October 1993, p. 2, and Yu. G. Korgunyuk and S. Ye. Zaslavsky, *Rossiiskaya mnogopartiinost' (stanovlenie, funktionirovanie, razvitie)* (Moscow: Indem, 1996), pp. 191–2. For a full account of the 1993 elections, see White, Rose, and McAllister, *How Russia Votes,* chs. 6 and 7; Jerry F. Hough, 'The Russian election of 1993: public attitudes toward economic reforms and democratization', *Post-Soviet Affairs,* vol. 10, no. 1 (January–March 1994), pp. 1–37; Stephen Whitefield and Geoffrey Evans, 'The Russian election of 1993: public opinion and the transition experience', *Post-Soviet Affairs,* vol. 10, no. 1 (January–March 1994), pp. 38–60; Richard Sakwa, 'The Russian elections of December 1993', *Europe–Asia Studies,* vol. 47, no. 2 (March 1995), pp. 195–227; Matthew Wyman, Stephen White, Bill Miller, and Paul Heywood, 'Public opinion, parties and voters in the December 1993 Russian elections', *Europe–Asia Studies,* vol. 47, no. 4 (June 1995), pp. 591–614; Peter Lentini, ed., *Elections and Political Order in Russia* (Budapest: Central European University Press, 1995); and Jerry F. Hough and Timothy J. Colton, eds., *Growing Pains: The 1993 Russian Duma Election* (Washington, DC: Brookings, 1998).

20 Boris Grushin, 'Fiasko sotsial'noi mysli', *Mir mnenii i mneniya o mire,* no. 5, 1994, p. 9; VTsIOM's last published poll appeared in *Segodnya,* 30 November 1993, p. 1. Russia's senior pollster, Yuri Levada, explained later that his own organisation had 'underestimated the influence of the opposition and the role of provincial attitudes (of the "backwoods") in the overall results' (*Sotsiologicheskii zhurnal,* no. 4, 1997, p. 225).

21 *Izvestiya,* 15 December 1993, p. 2; *Vechernyaya Moskva,* 13 December 1993, p. 1.

22 See A. G. Beloborodov, et al., *Vybory deputatov Gosudarstvennoi Dumy. 1995. Elektoral'naya statistika* (Moscow: Ves' mir, 1996), p. 11. The possibility of a 'world record' was suggested in *Segodnya*, 18 August 1995, p. 2.

23 Beloborodov, et al., *Vybory*, pp. 154, 152.

24 Ibid., p. 80 (there were 329 fewer candidates by the day of the election).

25 Ibid., p. 11.

26 *Izvestiya*, 14 October 1995, p. 4; for the increasing cost, see ibid., 18 October 1995, p. 2.

27 Ibid., 18 October 1995, p. 2.

28 Any classification is necessarily arbitrary. The fourfold scheme employed in this discussion is based upon Beloborodov, et al., *Vybory*, p. 242. Five separate groups were identified by the *Financial Times*, 11 December 1995, p. 2; Colton, *Transitional Citizenship*, identifies six; and Vladimir Pribylovsky, *43 linii spektra. Kratkoe opisanie vsekh predvybornykh blokov* (Moscow: Panorama, 1995), identifies seven. See also Michael McFaul and Nikolai Petrov, eds., *Previewing Russia's 1995 Parliamentary Elections* (Washington, DC: Carnegie Endowment, 1995), which identifies five blocs and five 'special interest groups'; Sergei Markov, 'Izbiratel'nye ob"edineniya v Rossii v preddverii parlamentskikh vyborov 1995 goda', in A. I. Ioffe, ed., *Analiz elektorata politicheskikh sil Rossii* (Moscow: Komtekh, 1995), pp. 62–91; and White, Rose, and McAllister, *How Russia Votes*, ch. 10, on which I have drawn for this part of the discussion. The Central Electoral Commission produced a guide to all the electoral associations and blocs: *Izbiratel'nye ob"edineniya, izbiratel'nye bloki na vyborakh – 95* (supplement to *Vestnik Tsentral'noi izbiratel'noi komissii Rossiiskoi Federatsii*, 1995). See also *Politicheskie partii Rossii* (Moscow: Fond prava, 1995); V. I. Timoshenko and S. Ye. Zaslavsky, *Rossiiskie partii, dvizheniya i bloki na vyborakh v Gosudarstvennuyu Dumu 17 dekabrya 1995 goda. Opyt, problemy, perspektivy* (Moscow: Znanie, 1996); Korgunyuk and Zaslavsky, *Rossiiskaya mnogopartiinost'*; and V. A. Oleshchuk and V. B. Pavlenko, *Politicheskaya Rossiya. Partii, bloki, lidery. God 1997. Spravochnik* (Moscow: Ves' mir, 1997). The early development of Russian multiparty politics is considered in A. M. Salmin, et al., *Partiinaya sistema v Rossii v 1989–1993 godakh. Opyt stanovleniya* (Moscow: Nachala Press, 1994), and V. N. Krasnov, *Sistema mnogopartiinosti v sovremennoi Rossii* (Moscow: Obozrevatel', 1995); for the subsequent period, see John Löwenhardt, ed., *Party Politics in Post-Communist Russia* (London: Cass, 1998), and Matthew Wyman, Stephen White, and Sarah Oates, eds., *Elections and Voters in Post-Communist Russia* (Cheltenham and Northampton, MA: Edward Elgar, 1998).

29 Korgunyuk and Zaslavsky, *Rossiiskaya mnogopartiinost'*, p. 67.

30 See *Izvestiya*, 28 October 1995, p. 5.

31 *Predvybornaya programma partii 'Demokraticheskii vybor Rossii'* (Moscow: DVR, 1995), pp. 26–7.

32 Korgunyuk and Zaslavsky, *Rossiiskaya mnogopartiinost'*, p. 70.

33 Ibid., p. 73.

34 Yavlinsky set out his views in *Izvestiya*, 12 July 1995, p. 2, and 13 July 1995, p. 2.

35 See *Deklaratsiya obshchestvennogo dvizheniya 'Yabloko'* (Moscow: Yabloko,

September 1995); their political platform and economic programme were included in *Reformy dlya bol'shinstva* (Moscow: Yabloko, 1995). There is a further discussion in V. Ya. Gel'man, '"Yabloko": opyt politicheskoi al'ternativy', *Kentavr*, no. 6, 1995, pp. 43–57.

36 Korgunyuk and Zaslavsky, *Rossiiskaya mnogopartiinost'*, pp. 72, 73 (emphasis added).

37 See *Liberal'nyi plan dlya Rossii*, 2nd edn (Moscow: Vpered, Rossiya, 1995).

38 Korgunyuk and Zaslavsky, *Rossiiskaya mnogopartiinost'*, p. 204; for the split, see *Argumenty i fakty*, no. 14, 1995, p. 16.

39 Svyatoslav Fedorov, *Mne obidno, chto lyudi, kotorym ya vernul zrenie, vidyat razvalennuyu stranu* (Moscow: Partiya samoupravleniya trudyashchikhsya, 1995). See more generally Fedorov, *Put' istseleniya* (Moscow: Fedorov, 1995); for the view that they should be separately categorised, see Korgunyuk and Zaslavsky, *Rossiiskaya mnogopartiinost'*, p. 201.

40 *Trud*, 19 December 1998, p. 2.

41 *Segodnya*, 21 December 1998, p. 1.

42 *Materialy II s"ezda Vserossiiskogo obshchestvenno-politicheskogo dvizheniya 'Nash dom – Rossiya' (vtoroi etap) 2–3 sentyabrya 1995 g.* (Moscow: NDR, 1995), p. 61.

43 *Predvybornaya platforma Vserossiiskogo obshchestvenno-politicheskogo dvizheniya 'Nash dom – Rossiya'. Utverzhdena Vtorym s"ezdom Dvizheniya 12 avgusta 1995 g.* (Moscow: NDR, 1995).

44 *Izvestiya*, 28 April 1998, p. 2.

45 Ibid., 5 November 1995, p. 4.

46 *Sovetskaya Rossiya*, 11 November 1995, p. 4.

47 See respectively K. Kholodkovsky, 'Rossiiskie partii i problema politicheskogo strukturirovaniya obshchestva', *Mirovaya ekonomika i mezhdunarodnye otnosheniya*, no. 10, 1995, p. 87; Yekaterina Lakhova, *Moi put' v politiku* (Moscow: Aurika, 1995), p. 237.

48 See *Programma politicheskogo dvizheniya 'Zhenshchiny Rossii'* (Moscow: Zhenshchiny Rossii, 1995).

49 Lakhova, *Moi put'*, p. 207 (20 October 1993).

50 *Argumenty i fakty*, 1995, no. 36, p. 2; *Kommersant'-daily*, 7 July 1995, p. 3, placed him first among a list of possible presidential candidates, and so did a September 1996 poll (*USIA Opinion Analysis* M-205-96, 7 October 1996, p. 2).

51 *Financial Times*, 3 June 1995, p. 8.

52 See Alexander Lebed, *Za derzhavu obidno . . .* (Moscow: Moskovskaya pravda, 1995), pp. 423 (church, army, and people) and 432 (for his reference to 'political chatter about reforms, democracy, [and] human rights'). Lebed did however defer to his wife at home: he was the 'lieutenant-general', she the 'colonel-general' (*Komsomol'skaya pravda*, 17 September 1996, p. 3). There is a study of Lebed by his former press secretary (Alexander Barkhatov, *General Lebed', ili moya lebedinnaya pesnya* [Moscow: Politbyuro, 1998]) and a Western biography (Harold Elletson, *The General Against the Kremlin. Alexander Lebed: Power and Illusion* [London: Little, Brown, 1998]).

53 For the Congress's programme, see *Bud'te s nami* (Moscow: Kongress

russkikh obshchin, 1995); it also appeared in *Dialog*, 1995, no. 11–12, pp. 32–9. The Congress's 'Appeal to voters' was in *Trud*, 11 November 1995, p. 2.

54 *Obshchaya gazeta*, 29 June 1995, p. 8; Lebed's win in Krasnoyarsk was reported in *Izvestiya*, 19 May 1998, p. 1.

55 See Vladimir Zhirinovsky, *Programmnyi manifest Liberal'noi-demokraticheskoi partii Rossii* (Moscow: LDPR, 1995). Zhirinovsky identified the LDPR's ideals as freedom, democracy, justice, law and order, and patriotism (*LDPR. Ideologiya i praktika* [Moscow: LDPR, 1995]), p. 37.

56 *Izvestiya*, 12 February 1992, p. 3.

57 Korgunyuk and Zaslavsky, *Rossiiskaya mnogopartiinost'*, pp. 129–30. The Liberal Democrats' first programme had been printed with the support of the CPSU Central Committee, in an attempt (it appeared) to establish an alternative party that the CPSU itself could control (*Izvestiya*, 14 April 1994, p. 2). The former KGB chairman Vladimir Kryuchkov, however, denied the direct assistance of his own organisation (*Lichnoe delo*, 2 vols. [Moscow: Olimp/Ast, 1996], vol. II, p. 13).

58 The Liberal Democrats' support in the armed forces was reported in, for instance, *Argumenty i fakty*, no. 38, 1995, p. 2. They claimed a national membership of half a million (ibid., no. 20, 1998, p. 24), and distributed two national and forty regional newspapers with a total print of 2 million copies a month (*Programma Liberal'no-demokraticheskoi partii Rossii (proekt)* (Moscow, 1998).

59 *Guardian*, 29 December 1998, p. 14. Zhirinovsky's more serious pretensions were recognised in the award of a doctorate by Moscow University: *Izvestiya*, 28 April 1998, p. 2 (the event was also reported in *Moskovskie novosti*, no. 15, 1998, pp. 1, 3).

60 Korgunyuk and Zaslavsky, *Rossiiskaya mnogopartiinost'*, pp. 127–8, 130.

61 Viktor Sheinis quoted in *Argumenty i fakty*, no. 36, 1997, p. 5.

62 See *Za nashu sovetskuyu rodinu! Predvybornaya platforma Kommunisticheskoi partii Rossiiskoi Federatsii* (Moscow: Informpechat', 1995); it also appeared in *Sovetskaya Rossiya*, 31 August 1995, p. 3, and in *Dialog*, no. 10, 1995, pp. 3–9. For a full account of the development of the CPRF, see Joan Barth Urban and Valerii D. Solovei, *Russia's Communists at the Crossroads* (Boulder, CO: Westview, 1997); and Richard Sakwa, 'Left or right? The CPRF and the problem of democratic consolidation in Russia', in Löwenhardt, *Party Politics*, pp. 128–58.

63 Korgunyuk and Zaslavsky, *Rossiiskaya mnogopartiinost'*, p. 95.

64 The party programme adopted in January 1995 appeared in *III S"ezd Kommunisticheskoi partii Rossiiskoi Federatsii 21–2 yanvarya 1995 goda* (Moscow: Informpechat', 1995), pp. 96–118. It was modified in minor respects at the party's fourth congress in 1997 (*IV S"ezd Kommunisticheskoi partii Rossiiskoi Federatsii 19–20 aprelya 1997 goda (Materialy i dokumenty)* [Moscow, 1997], pp. 74–92); a report of the congress itself appeared in *Nezavisimaya gazeta*, 22 April 1997, pp. 1–2.

65 Korgunyuk and Zaslavsky, *Rossiiskaya mnogopartiinost'*, p. 97.

66 *Agrarnaya partiya Rossii. Dokumenty, sobytiya, litsa* (Moscow: Paleya, 1994), pp. 10–11, 15, 16.

67 *Materialy IV (vneocherednogo) S''ezda Agrarnoi partii Rossii* (Moscow: APR, 1995), pp. 25, 22, 24.

68 See *Programma. Ustav Agrarnoi partii Rossii* (Moscow: APR, 1995); the party's pre-election programme also appeared in *Dialog*, 1995, no. 11–12, pp. 13–18. Minor changes in the programme were made at the party's fifth congress in March 1997: *Agrarnaya partiya Rossii* (Moscow: APR, 1997).

69 *Predvybornaya platforma Izbiratel'nogo bloka 'Vlast' narodu'* (Moscow: Vlast' narodu, 1995); the pre-election platform also appeared in *Pravda*, 12 September 1995, p. 2.

70 These comments are based on the party's election flyers; for its programme, see *Predvybornaya pozitsiya izbiratel'nogo bloka 'Kommunisty–Trudovaya Rossiya–Za Sovetskii Soyuz'* (mimeo., 1995), and *Pravda*, 25 November 1995, p. 2.

71 Korgunyuk and Zaslavsky, *Rossiiskaya mnogopartiinost'*, p. 208.

72 *Izvestiya*, 23 December 1995, p. 1. On the 1995 Duma election see White, Rose, and McAllister, *How Russia Votes*, chs. 10–11; Stephen White, Matthew Wyman, and Sarah Oates, 'Parties and voters in the 1995 Russian Duma election', *Europe–Asia Studies*, vol. 49, no. 5 (July 1997), pp. 767–98; and Laura Belin and Robert Orttung, *The Russian Parliamentary Elections of 1995: The Battle for the Duma* (Armonk, NY: Sharpe, 1997).

73 Beloborodov, et al., *Vybory*, pp. 95–6.

74 I draw at this point upon the results of a nationally representative survey conducted by Russian Public Opinion and Market Research (ROMIR) in January 1996, reported more fully in William L. Miller, Stephen White, and Paul Heywood, *Values and Political Change in Postcommunist Europe* (London: Macmillan, 1998).

75 See for instance Wyman, et al., 'Public opinion, parties and voters'.

76 Seymour M. Lipset and Stein Rokkan, eds., *Party Systems and Voter Alignments: Cross-National Perspectives* (New York: Free Press, 1967).

77 Mair, for instance, has argued that the democratisation process in Russia and Eastern Europe is 'sui generis', in that it is the 'first case of European democratization occurring in the effective absence of a real civil society'; the electorate, as a consequence, is 'substantially more open and more available than those of the established democracies', and the parties 'lack an established standing, status, and legitimacy within the electorate at large' (Peter Mair, *Party System Change: Approaches and Interpretations* [Oxford: Clarendon Press, 1997], pp. 178, 187, 181).

78 This multiple regression performed on our January 1996 survey data is not separately reported.

79 The following is based on White, et al., 'Parties and voters', which draws on a nationally representative survey conducted for the authors by VTsIOM in late December 1995 (n=1568).

80 Similar data are reported in Kholodkovsky, 'Rossiiskie partii': 61.3 per cent of 1995 Communist voters had voted Communist in 1993, but only 15.7 per cent of those who had voted for Russia's Choice (p. 85).

81 Beloborodov, et al., *Vybory*, pp. 91–6; the effects of area as such are considered in Matthew Wyman, Stephen White, Ian McAllister, and Sarah Oates, 'How Russia's regions vote: mapping electoral change in a new

democracy', a paper presented to the 1997 Annual Meeting of the American Political Science Association, Washington, DC.

82 See respectively Oleshchuk and Pavlenko, *Politicheskaya Rossiya*, pp. 151, 48, 28.

83 *Izvestiya*, 28 January 1997, p. 2.

84 Oleshchuk and Pavlenko, *Politicheskaya Rossiya*, p. 57.

85 New legislation on the 'basic guarantees of electoral rights and the right to participate in a referendum' was adopted by the Duma on 5 September 1997; it defined an electoral association as a body whose statute included as a principal objective the nomination of candidates at elections (*Rossiiskaya gazeta*, 25 September 1997, pp. 4–6, and 30 September 1997, pp. 3–6). The early evidence, however, suggested that other bodies would simply modify their statutes to include this purpose, as the Automobilists' Club had done (*Izvestiya*, 18 February 1998, p. 2).

86 Radio Free Europe/Radio Liberty, *Research Report*, vol. 1, no. 4 (26 January 1992), p. 3; Korgunyuk and Zaslavsky, *Rossiiskaya mnogopartiinost'*, p. 154.

87 Oleshchuk and Pavlenko, *Politicheskaya Rossiya*, p. 43; *Izvestiya*, 2 April 1997, p. 2.

88 *Izvestiya*, 14 October 1991, p. 1.

89 Gaidar particularly noted the 'organisational weakness and tendency to split' of the pro-reform parties; more and more little democratic groups were appearing, 'reflecting only the ambitions of their little leaders'; and the intelligentsia generally appeared to find the concept of organised politics an alien one (*Dni*, pp. 301–2).

90 Oleshchuk and Pavlenko, *Politicheskaya Rossiya*, p. 42.

91 *Politicheskoe obrazovanie*, no. 18, 1990, p. 6; the head of the party's Central Control Commission himself identified ten distinct tendencies (*Pravda*, 29 July 1991, p. 3).

92 Oleshchuk and Pavlenko, *Politicheskaya Rossiya*, pp. 58, 116.

93 Ibid., pp. 123–4.

94 *Izvestiya*, 10 January 1992, p. 3.

95 *Argumenty i fakty*, no. 7, 1993, p. 2 (slightly adapted).

96 White, Rose, and McAllister, *How Russia Votes*, p. 135. Other inquiries have found still lower levels of party identification: Salmin, et al., *Partiinaya sistema*, report a level of 6 per cent (p. 30).

97 Levels of trust ranged, in one representative investigation, from 1 per cent for political parties to 74 per cent for the armed forces: *Argumenty i fakty*, no. 22, 1994, p. 1.

98 Membership levels varied from 1.5 and 1.7 per cent respectively in Ukraine and Russia to 5.7 and 6.1 per cent respectively in Slovakia and the Czech Republic (based on nationally representative surveys conducted in 1993 and reported more fully in Miller, et al., *Values and Political Change*). On volatility, see Matthew Wyman, 'Developments in Russian voting behaviour: 1993 and 1995 compared', *Journal of Communist Studies and Transition Politics*, vol. 12, no. 3 (September 1996), p. 278.

99 Paul Webb and Paul G. Lewis, 'The lessons of comparative politics: Russian political parties as independent variables?', in Löwenhardt, *Party Politics*, pp. 255–6.

100 See ch. 3.

101 *Segodnya*, 20 December 1995, p. 1.

102 *Argumenty i fakty*, no. 36, 1997, p. 5.

103 Beloborodov, et al., *Vybory*, p. 207.

104 Vladimir Shumeiko, for instance, the former Federation Council chairman, made clear that his purpose in establishing 'Reformy – novyi kurs' was at least in part to sustain a subsequent presidential bid (*Izvestiya*, 18 May 1998, p. 2).

105 Yuri Korolev, *Kremlevskii sovetnik* (Moscow: Olimp, 1995), p. 160.

106 *Moskovskie novosti*, no. 50, 1988, p. 4.

107 See Stephen White, 'The USSR Supreme Soviet: a developmental perspective', in Daniel N. Nelson and White, eds., *Communist Legislatures in Comparative Perspective* (Albany: State University of New York Press, 1982), ch. 6. On turnover particularly, see Ronald J. Hill, 'Continuity and change in USSR Supreme Soviet elections', *British Journal of Political Science*, vol. 2, no. 1 (January 1972), pp. 47–67 (men, older deputies, and party members were disproportionately likely to be re-elected).

108 For the decision, see *Pravda*, 20 August 1986, p. 1. Reformer Yuri Chernicheniko claimed that a 'victory' had been achieved in public life with this and a decision to abandon an unpopular plan for a memorial to the Second World War: 'public opinion has won and official opinion has been forced to retreat' (*Sovetskaya kul'tura*, 16 August 1986, p. 3).

109 *Izvestiya*, 19 June 1989, p. 5.

110 *Materialy XIX Vsesoyuznoi konferentsii Kommunisticheskoi partii Sovetskogo Soyuza 28 iyunya–1 iyulya 1988 goda* (Moscow: Politizdat, 1988), pp. 35–7.

111 *Sovet Federatsii pervogo sozyva* (Moscow: Izdatel'stvo Soveta Federatsii, 1994), pp. 27–8.

112 Ibid., p. 6. The standing orders of the Federation Council are in *Sobranie zakonodatel'stva Rossiiskoi Federatsii*, no. 7, 1996, art. 655. Article 99 of the constitution specified that the Federal Assembly was a 'permanently working body'; it had been directly elected in December 1993, but the law of December 1995 on the formation of the Federation Council specified that it was made up on an *ex officio* basis of the heads of the executive and legislative branches in each of the republics and regions, who were clearly in full-time employment (*Sobranie zakonodatel'stva*, no. 50, 1995, art. 4869).

113 Understandably, there were calls for the Federation Council to be elected and to work on a full-time basis (see for instance Viktor Sheinis in *Gosudarstvo i pravo*, no. 12, 1997, p. 72, and Gennadii Seleznev in *Izvestiya*, 4 March 1998, p. 2), or at least for this inconsistency to be resolved (S. A. Avak'yan, *Konstitutsiya Rossii. Priroda, evolyutsiya, sovremennost'* [Moscow: Rossiiskii yuridicheskii izdatel'skii dom, 1997], p. 216).

114 *Izvestiya*, 15 January 1998, p. 4.

115 Ibid., 26 September 1997, p. 1, and 15 May 1997, p. 1.

116 *Gosudarstvo i pravo*, no. 9, 1998, p. 97.

117 Calculated from Ivan Rybkin, ed., *Pyataya Gosudarstvennaya Duma* (Moscow: Izdanie Gosudarstvennoi Dumy, 1994).

118 Beloborodov, et al., *Vybory*, pp. 204–5, 233–4.
119 Ye. P. Ishchenko, ed., *Gosudarstvennaya Duma Rossiiskoi Federatsii vtorogo sozyva. Spravochnik* (Moscow: Ves' mir, 1996), p. 4.
120 Beloborodov, et al., *Vybory*, p. 205. The Duma's standing orders appear in *Sobranie zakonodatel'stva*, no. 7, 1998, art. 801.
121 *Moskovskie novosti*, no. 7, 1998, pp. 2–3.
122 V. N. Krasnov, ed., *Rossiya. Partii, vybory, vlast'* (Moscow: Obozrevatel', 1996), pp. 187–8. For a further and more positive discussion of the role of parties in the Duma, see Thomas F. Remington and Steven S. Smith, 'The development of parliamentary parties in Russia', *Legislative Studies Quarterly*, vol. 20, no. 4 (November 1995), pp. 457–89, and Remington, 'Political conflict and institutional design: paths of party development in Russia', in Löwenhardt, *Party Politics*, pp. 201–23.
123 *New York Times*, 19 January 1997, section 4, p. 3 (I am grateful to Mark Thompson for drawing my attention to this item).
124 *New Statesman and Society*, 22 September 1995, pp. 22–3.
125 *Moskovskie novosti*, no. 10, 1998, pp. 1, 5; another report appeared in *Segodnya*, 12 March 1998, pp. 1, 3.
126 *New York Times*, 19 January 1997, section 4, p. 3.
127 *Izvestiya*, 30 May 1997, p. 1 (two large Duma fractions alone were reported to have received $27 million for adoption of the budget). According to a former member of the Communist fraction, members were being 'bought for a variety of objectives: to pass amendments to a law or approve a certain wording of a law'; a vote in favour of Chernomyrdin's nomination was worth an immediate $10,000, and the budgetary vote was also a 'time to reap fruit' (*Komsomol'skaya pravda*, 1 December 1998, pp. 1–2).
128 *Izvestiya*, 1 March 1997, p. 1.
129 *Vlast'*, no. 7, 1997, p. 56 (a May 1997 survey, n=1500). In another survey, only 4 per cent believed the Duma was working actively and taking the decisions that were necessary: *Izvestiya*, 3 February 1998, p. 1.
130 *Ekonomicheskie i sotsial'nye peremeny: monitoring obshchestvennogo mneniya*, no. 1, January–February 1998, pp. 66, 70, 74.

3 PRESIDENTIAL GOVERNMENT

1 N. A. Sakharov, *Institut prezidentstva v sovremennom mire* (Moscow: Yuridicheskaya literatura, 1994), notes that 130 of the United Nation's 183 members in 1993 had a presidential form of government (p. 3). On Russia's 'leadership', see Dinmukhamed Kunaev in *Prostor*, no. 12, 1991, p. 39.
2 M. F. Nenashev, *Poslednee pravitel'stvo SSSR* (Moscow: Krom, 1993), p. 26. Yeltsin's first deputy head of staff, Oleg Sysuev, rejected the idea that Yeltsin would be willing to be a 'Queen of England' in a later interview (*Moskovskii komsomolets*, 10 November 1998, p. 2).
3 *Izvestiya*, 15 November 1993, p. 4.
4 Ibid., 6 April 1991, p. 1.
5 This is the central thesis of Stephen Whitefield, *Industrial Power and the Soviet State* (Oxford: Clarendon Press, 1993).

6 L. A. Okun'kov, *Prezident Rossiiskoi Federatsii. Konstitutsiya i politicheskaya praktika* (Moscow: Infra.M-Norma, 1996), p. 27.

7 See Philip G. Roeder, 'Varieties of post-Soviet authoritarian regimes', *Post-Soviet Affairs*, vol. 10, no. 1 (January–March 1994), pp. 61–101; and more particularly John Anderson, 'Authoritarian political development in Central Asia: the case of Turkmenistan', *Central Asian Survey*, vol. 14, no. 4 (December 1995), pp. 509–27.

8 The classification adopted here is based on Sakharov, *Institut prezidentstva*. For a fuller discussion of presidentialism in the postcommunist context, see Ray Taras, ed., *Postcommunist Presidents* (Cambridge: Cambridge University Press, 1997), and Gerald M. Easter, 'Preference for presidentialism: postcommunist regime change in Russia and the NIS', *World Politics*, vol. 49, no. 2 (January 1997), pp. 184–211. Of the Baltic republics, Estonia and Latvia had parliamentary rather than presidential systems, while Lithuania had a directly elected executive presidency.

9 For a representative selection of views, see for instance Arend Lijphart, ed., *Parliamentary Versus Presidential Government* (Oxford: Oxford University Press, 1992); Giovanni Sartori, *Comparative Constitutional Engineering* (London: Macmillan, 1994), part 2; and Juan J. Linz and Arturo Valenzuela, eds., *The Failure of Presidential Democracy: Comparative Perspectives* (Baltimore: Johns Hopkins University Press, 1994).

10 *Materialy Plenuma Tsentral'nogo Komiteta KPSS, 5–7 fevralya 1990 goda* (Moscow: Politizdat, 1990), p. 19. Speaking to a working group on 19 February 1990 Gorbachev argued similarly for a 'power which can react rapidly' and for a 'strong executive mechanism': *Demokratizatsiya*, vol. 2, no. 2 (Spring 1994), p. 331. A more general discussion of the Russian presidency is available in Okun'kov, *Prezident*, and in S. A. Avak'yan, 'Prezident Rossiiskoi Federatsii: evolyutsiya konstitutsionno-pravovogo statusa', *Vestnik Moskovskogo Universiteta: Pravo*, no. 1, 1998, pp. 8–40.

11 I. V. Stalin, *Sochineniya*, vol. I (XIV) (Stanford, CA: Hoover Institution, 1967), p. 177 (the Supreme Soviet, in his view, could be regarded as a 'collective presidency').

12 *Sovetskoe gosudarstvo i pravo*, no. 7, 1990, p. 4.

13 Gorbachev as quoted by Vadim Medvedev in Ye. L. Kuznetsov, 'Iz istorii sozdaniya instituta Prezidenta SSSR', *Gosudarstvo i pravo*, no. 5, 1996, p. 95.

14 *XIX Vsesoyuznaya konferentsiya Kommunisticheskoi partii Sovetskogo Soyuza 28 iyunya–1 iyulya 1988 g. Stenograficheskii otchet*, 2 vols. (Moscow: Politizdat, 1988), vol. I, p. 59 (Gorbachev), and vol. II, pp. 129 ('undue concentration') and 138 (resolution).

15 *Izvestiya*, 24 October 1989, p. 4.

16 See A. D. Sakharov, *Trevoga i nadezhda* (Moscow: Interverso, 1990), pp. 258–9, 272, 274. Proposals for a 'firm hand' at the top in any transition from totalitarian to democratic rule had a similar logic: see for instance A. Migranyan in *Novyi mir*, no. 7, 1990, pp. 166–84, and Migranyan and I. Klyamkin in *Literaturnaya gazeta*, 16 August 1989, p. 10.

17 See Kuznetsov, 'Iz istorii', p. 96.

18 Ibid. Medvedev and Shakhnazarov's memorandum of 29 November 1989

appears with other documents in *Demokratizatsiya*, vol. 2, no. 2 (Spring 1994), pp. 317–22.

19 Kuznetsov, 'Iz istorii', pp. 96–7, 104. The lack of an agreed procedure was also identified by Boris Lazarev in *Sovetskoe gosudarstvo i pravo*, no. 7, 1990, p. 9.

20 Burlatsky, editor at this time of the weekly *Literaturnaya gazeta*, was identified as the author of a Soviet presidency by Boris Kurashvili, *Strana na pereput'e* (Moscow: Yuridicheskaya literatura, 1990), p. 105; and also in Dusko Doder and Louise Branson, *Gorbachev: Heretic in the Kremlin* (New York: Viking, 1990), pp. 279–80.

21 Kuznetsov, 'Iz istorii', pp. 98–9.

22 *Vneocherednoi III S"ezd narodnykh deputatov SSSR 12–15 marta 1990 g. Stenograficheskii otchet*, 3 vols. (Moscow: Izdanie Verkhovnogo Soveta SSSR, 1990), vol. I, pp. 17–18.

23 Ibid., vol. I, pp. 126–7 (N. T. Dabizha), 45–6 (Yuri Afanas'ev, speaking for the radical Inter-Regional Group of deputies), 58–61 (the Georgian party first secretary G. G. Gumbaridze, one of those who advanced republican arguments), and 395–6 (vote).

24 Ibid., p. 193.

25 Ibid., vol. III, p. 55.

26 Ibid., vol. II, pp. 385–6.

27 For the text of the law, see *Vedomosti S"ezda narodnykh deputatov SSSR i Verkhovnogo Soveta SSSR*, no. 12, 1990, art. 189.

28 Ibid., no. 40, art. 802.

29 For the text of the constitutional changes, see ibid., 1991, no. 1, art. 3.

30 *IV S"ezd narodnykh deputatov SSSR 17–27 dekabrya 1990 g. Stenograficheskii otchet*, 4 vols. (Moscow: Izdanie Verkhovnogo Soveta SSSR), vol. I, p. 582 (V. K. Chernyak).

31 Ibid., p. 296.

32 *Pravda*, 1 December 1990, p. 4.

33 *IV S"ezd*, vol. I, pp. 12, 34.

34 *Izvestiya*, 6 April 1991, p. 1.

35 On these developments, see Michael E. Urban, 'Boris El'tsin, Democratic Russia and the campaign for the Russian presidency', *Soviet Studies*, vol. 44, no. 2 (1991), pp. 187–208.

36 *Vedomosti S"ezda narodnykh deputatov RSFSR i Verkhovnogo Soveta RSFSR*, no. 2, 1990, art. 22.

37 *II (vneocherednoi) S"ezd narodnykh deputatov RSFSR 27 noyabrya–15 dekabrya 1990 g. Stenograficheskii otchet*, 6 vols. (Moscow: Respublika, 1992), vol. VI, pp. 242–3 (15 December 1990).

38 *Izvestiya*, 26 March 1991, p. 2.

39 *III (vneocherednoi) S"ezd narodnykh deputatov RSFSR 28 marta–5 aprelya 1991 goda. Stenograficheskii otchet*, 5 vols. (Moscow: Respublika, 1992), vol. V, pp. 154–5 (5 April 1991); and *Izvestiya*, 6 April 1991, p. 3.

40 For the text of the law, see *Vedomosti S"ezda narodnykh deputatov RSFSR i Verkhovnogo Soveta RSFSR*, no. 17, 1991, art. 512.

41 Ibid., no. 22, 1991, art. 776.

42 Ibid., no. 34, 1991, art. 1125, 21 August 1991.

43 *VI S"ezd narodnykh deputatov Rossiiskoi Federatsii 6–21 aprelya 1992 goda. Stenograficheskii otchet*, 5 vols. (Moscow: Respublika, 1992), vol. I, pp. 30–1 (the voting on 6 April was 412 in favour but 447 against placing a vote of confidence on the agenda), and for the resolution vol. II, pp. 289–94 (11 April 1992).

44 *VII S"ezd narodnykh deputatov Rossiiskoi Federatsii 1–14 dekabrya 1992 goda. Stenograficheskii otchet*, 4 vols. (Moscow: Respublika, 1993), vol. I, pp. 536–42, 5 December 1992. The president's powers were further weakened by amendments to the constitution: *Vedomosti S"ezda narodnykh deputatov Rossiiskoi Federatsii i Verkhovnogo Soveta Rossiiskoi Federatsii*, no. 2, 1993, art. 55, 9 December 1992.

45 *VIII (vneocherednoi) S"ezd narodnykh deputatov Rossiiskoi Federatsii 10–13 marta 1993 goda. Stenograficheskii otchet* (Moscow: Respublika, 1993), pp. 414–15 and 415–17, 11 and 12 March 1993.

46 For the broadcast, see *Delovoi mir*, 23 March 1993, p. 1; the published version contained no reference to a 'special form of administration' (*Rossiiskaya gazeta*, 25 March 1993, p. 1).

47 *Rossiiskaya gazeta*, 1 April 1993, p. 3. For the text of the resolution, which included the wording of the questions, see *Vedomosti S"ezda narodnykh deputatov Rossiiskoi Federatsii i Verkhovnogo Soveta Rossiiskoi Federatsii*, no. 14, 1993, art. 501, 29 March 1993.

48 The full results appeared in *Rossiiskaya gazeta*, 19 May 1993, pp. 2–3. For a discussion, see Marie Mendras, 'Les trois Russie. Analyse du référendum du 25 avril 1993', *Revue française de science politique*, vol. 43, no. 6 (December 1993), pp. 897–939.

49 *VII S"ezd*, vol. III, pp. 126–31, 10 December 1992. It was 'inevitable', he reflected later, that at the end of the Soviet period there would be a conflict between 'two systems of power' (*Izvestiya*, 10 December 1994, p. 1).

50 *Narodnyi deputat*, no. 12, 1992, pp. 13–14, and no. 13, pp. 7–8. For an extended statement of his views, see R. I. Khasbulatov, *Vybor sud'by* (Moscow: Respublika, 1993); and Khasbulatov, *Velikaya rossiiskaya tragediya*, 2 vols. (Moscow: SIMS, 1994).

51 *Izvestiya*, 12 March 1993, p. 1.

52 Ibid., 9 February 1993, p. 1, and (for the 'collective Rasputin') 10 April 1993, p. 1.

53 Ibid., 5 June 1993, pp. 1–2; similarly *Rossiiskaya gazeta*, 2 June 1993, pp. 3–4.

54 *Rossiiskie vesti*, 14 July 1993, p. 1. The presidential draft appeared in *Izvestiya* and *Rossiiskie vesti*, 30 April 1993, pp. 3–5 and 3–6 respectively, and in *Konstitutsionnyi vestnik*, no. 16, 1993, pp. 65–106, with a discussion; the version agreed by the constitutional conference on 12 July appeared in *Rossiiskie vesti*, 15 July 1993, pp. 3–6. A number of drafts are conveniently reprinted in *Konstitutsii Rossiiskoi Federatsii (al'ternativnye proekty)*, 2 vols. (Moscow: Obozrevatel', 1993), and in S. A. Avak'yan, *Konstitutsiya Rossii. Priroda, evolyutsiya, sovremennost'* (Moscow: Rossiiskii yuridicheskii izdatel'skii dom, 1997), pp. 305–512.

55 For the text, see *Izvestiya*, 10 November 1993, pp. 3–5.

56 Rita Moore, 'The path to the new Russian constitution', *Demokratizatsiya*, vol. 3, no. 1 (Winter 1995), pp. 55–6.

57 *Izvestiya*, 12 October 1994, p. 4 (similarly ibid., 19 March 1998, p. 2); the 'monarchical' label was used, for instance, by Alexander Rutskoi in *Nezavisimaya gazeta*, 8 May 1993, p. 2.

58 *Nezavisimaya gazeta*, 13 October 1993, as cited in Robert V. Daniels, *Russia's Transformation: Snapshots of a Crumbling System* (Lanham, MD: Rowman and Littlefield, 1998), p. 191; Gorbachev's opinion is cited in *The Times*, 29 November 1993, p. 16.

59 *Pravda*, 19 January 1994, p. 1; and for the comparison with Napoleon III, Anatolii Luk'yanov, ibid., 10 December 1993, p. 3.

60 Under legislation that was adopted in 1995, a referendum could be initiated by 2 million citizens or by a constitutional convention (*Sobranie zakonodatel'stva Rossiiskoi Federatsii*, no. 42, 1995, art. 3921).

61 For the text, see *Konstitutsiya Rossiiskoi Federatsii. Prinyata vsenarodnym golosovaniem 12 dekabrya 1993 goda* (Moscow: Yuridicheskaya literatura, 1993).

62 Staffing levels were reduced to 1,945 at the time of this reorganisation (*Izvestiya*, 14 February 1998, p. 2). The senior presidential staff were listed and their functions discussed in *Argumenty i fakty*, no. 49, 1997, p. 5.

63 *Sobranie zakonodatel'stva Rossiiskoi Federatsii*, no. 5, 1999, art. 652.

64 *Kto yest' kto v Rossii. Spravochnoe izdanie* (Moscow: Olimp/EKSMO-Press, 1998), p. 742; his appointment was reported in *Izvestiya*, 12 March 1997, p. 1, and his replacement by Nikolai Bordyuzha in *Rossiiskaya gazeta*, 8 December 1998, p. 1; Bordyuzha was replaced in his turn by Alexander Voloshin in the spring of 1999 (*Segodnya*, 20 March 1999, p. 1). Yumashev's influence made him 'effectively equal to the premier' in the view of commentators (*Segodnya*, 3 October 1998, p. 1).

65 *Segodnya*, 20 December 1995, p. 1.

66 *Sobranie zakonodatel'stva Rossiiskoi Federatsii*, no. 1, 1998, art. 1.

67 Ibid., no. 22, 1999, art. 2727.

68 *Kommersant'-daily*, 24 March 1998, p. 1.

69 *Rossiiskaya gazeta*, 24 March 1998, p. 1.

70 *Moscow News*, no. 11, 1998, p. 1.

71 *Rossiiskaya gazeta*, 28 March 1998, p. 1.

72 Ibid., 3 April 1998, p. 2.

73 The voting was 251 in favour, 25 against: ibid., 25 April 1998, p. 2.

74 Ibid., 15 August 1998, p. 1; Kirienko's interview was in *Moskovskii komsomolets*, 5 August 1998, pp. 1–2 (as the paper noted, Napoleon, who inaugurated the 'first hundred days' transition, had come to a 'bad end').

75 Yeltsin's own health, it appears, was a crucial element in this decision: in the event of incapacity his powers would pass to the prime minister, and there was concern within the Kremlin 'inner circle' that Kirienko would be 'too weak and inexperienced to handle all that' (*Newsweek*, 18 January 1999, p. 35).

76 Chernomyrdin's appointment and Yeltsin's broadcast were both reported in *Rossiiskaya gazeta*, 25 August 1998, p. 1.

77 *Segodnya*, 1 September 1998, p. 1 (the voting was 94 in favour, 257 against); ibid., 8 September 1998, p. 1 (this time there were 138 votes in favour).

78 *Rossiiskaya gazeta*, 2 September 1998, p. 1. A report in *Nezavisimaya gazeta* earlier in the year suggested that Our Home Is Russia and the Communist Party would both have gained slightly, but that Yabloko would nearly have

trebled its vote (22 April 1998, p. 8); another survey reported that the Communist Party would have jumped from the 22.3 per cent it had achieved in the 1995 election to 37.9 per cent (*Argumenty i fakty*, no. 16, 1998, p. 7).

79 *Segodnya*, 12 September 1998, p. 1 (315 were in favour, 63 against).

80 *Obshchaya gazeta*, no. 36, 1998, p. 7.

81 *Segodnya*, 8 September 1998, p. 2.

82 *Rossiiskaya gazeta*, 12 September 1998, p. 1.

83 For the vote, see *Segodnya*, 22 August 1998, p. 1. In the end, five impeachment charges were tabled in May 1999, including the break-up of the USSR and the Chechen war, but none secured a sufficient majority (*Segodnya*, 17 May 1999, p. 1).

84 *Kommersant'-daily*, 29 August 1998, p. 1.

85 Oleg Sysuev in *Segodnya*, 28 October 1998, pp. 1–2.

86 Yeltsin's statement on Primakov's dismissal appeared in *Nezavisimaya gazeta*, 13 May 1999, pp. 1, 3. Stepashin, in the event, was confirmed on the first vote with 301 votes in favour, 55 against and 14 abstentions (*Izvestiya*, 20 May 1999, p. 1). Yeltsin explained his dismissal of Stepashin in a morning television address; the new prime minister, he believed, was a man who was 'capable of consolidating society', and who could be a presidential candidate a year later (*Rossiiskaya gazeta*, 10 August 1999, p. 1); *Izvestiya*'s reaction was in its issue of 14 August 1999, p. 1.

87 *Izvestiya*, 28 September 1993, p. 4; the incident was also reported in B. N. Yeltsin, *Zapiski Prezidenta* (Moscow: Ogonek, 1994), pp. 121–5.

88 Alexander Korzhakov, *Boris Yel'tsin. Ot rassveta do zakata* (Moscow: Interbuk, 1997), p. 78.

89 B. N. Yeltsin, *Ispoved' na zadannuyu temu* (Leningrad: Chas pik, 1990), pp. 17–18 (baptism) and elsewhere; Naina Yeltsin explained how they had met in *Moskovskie novosti*, no. 7, 1997, p. 4. For biographical accounts, see John Morrison, *Boris Yeltsin: From Bolshevik to Democrat* (Harmondsworth: Penguin, 1991); and Timothy J. Colton, 'Boris Yeltsin: Russia's all-thumbs democrat', in Colton and Robert C. Tucker, eds., *Patterns in Post-Soviet Leadership* (Boulder, CO: Westview, 1995), pp. 49–74.

90 Yeltsin, *Ispoved'*, p. 58. Yeltsin's speech at the burial was reported in *Izvestiya*, 18 July 1998, p. 1; the Orthodox Church retained some doubts about the authenticity of the 'Yekaterinburg remains' and the Patriarch remained in Moscow.

91 Yeltsin, *Ispoved'*, p. 63; Korzhakov, *Boris Yel'tsin*, p. 49.

92 His appointment was reported in *Pravda*, 25 December 1985, p. 2.

93 *XXVII S"ezd Kommunisticheskoi partii Sovetskogo Soyuza 25 fevralya–6 marta 1986 goda. Stenograficheskii otchet*, 3 vols. (Moscow: Politizdat, 1986), vol. I, pp. 140–5.

94 V. I. Vorotnikov, *A bylo eto tak . . . Iz dnevnika chlena Politbyuro TsK KPSS* (Moscow: Sovet veteranov knigoizdaniya, 1995), p. 167. Ten years later Yeltsin recalled his own action as the 'result of prolonged reflection', based on a belief that *perestroika* would 'make sense only if it affected the party' (*Segodnya*, 28 October 1997, p. 1).

95 *Izvestiya TsK KPSS*, no. 2, 1989, pp. 239–41; for the unauthorised version, see *Le monde*, 2 February 1988, p. 6. Yeltsin referred to his preparation for

the speech in *Ispoved'*, p. 134. Many different versions of the speech were circulated as a kind of 'samizdat of the *glasnost'* era', and its purported author became a 'hero' (Yekaterina Lakhova, *Moi put' v politiku* [Moscow: Aurika, 1995], pp. 97, 98).

96 Yeltsin, *Ispoved'*, p. 137.

97 *Izvestiya TsK KPSS*, no. 2, 1989, p. 287; Yeltsin, *Ispoved'*, p. 99.

98 Yeltsin, *Ispoved'*, p. 143 ('barely conscious'); *Pravda*, 13 November 1987, pp. 1–3. Yeltsin, it appeared to Gorbachev, had simulated a suicide, although he later claimed it had been a hooligan attack (M. S. Gorbachev, *Zhizn' i reformy*, 2 vols. [Moscow: Novosti, 1995], vol. I, p. 374).

99 Korzhakov, *Boris Yel'tsin*, pp. 65, 66.

100 Yeltsin, *Ispoved'*, p. 175.

101 *Materialy Plenuma Tsentral'nogo komiteta KPSS, 15–16 marta 1989 goda* (Moscow: Politizdat, 1989), pp. 5–6.

102 *Moskovskaya pravda*, 28 March 1989, p. 2.

103 *Izvestiya*, 5 March 1990, p. 2.

104 *Materialy Plenuma . . . 5–7 fevralya 1990 goda*, pp. 68–9.

105 *Argumenty i fakty*, no. 22, 1990, p. 3.

106 *Rossiiskaya gazeta*, 4 November 1993, p. 4; Yeltsin referred again to Peter the Great in his interview in *Argumenty i fakty*, no. 16, 1993, p. 3.

107 *Izvestiya*, 11 June 1992, p. 3.

108 *Pravda*, 10 June 1991, p. 2; *Mir mnenii i mneniya o mire*, no. 11 (November 1992), p. 8.

109 Yeltsin, *Zapiski Prezidenta*, p. 181.

110 Lev Sukhanov, *Tri goda s Yel'tsinym* (Riga: Vaga, 1992), pp. 143–50.

111 Viktor Yaroshenko, *Yel'tsin. Ya otvechu za vse* (Moscow: Vokrug sveta, 1997), pp. 32–3.

112 Her appointment was reported in *Izvestiya*, 1 July 1997, p. 1; Korzhakov left no doubt of her influence in his *Boris Yel'tsin*, pp. 353–60.

113 Korzhakov, *Boris Yel'tsin*, p. 126.

114 See for instance *Argumenty i fakty*, no. 3, 1995, p. 3, and no. 44, 1995, p. 1.

115 *Izvestiya*, 22 December 1995, p. 1; Korzhakov replied ibid., 28 December 1995, p. 2.

116 See ibid., 6 May 1996, p. 1.

117 Korzhakov, *Boris Yel'tsin*, pp. 359, 360.

118 *Argumenty i fakty*, no. 49, 1997, p. 2. Berezovsky's direct access to the Yeltsin family could be exaggerated, even before his dismissal as CIS executive secretary in 1999: Mrs Yeltsin, interviewed in late 1998, had not seen him since the presidential elections, and insisted he had 'never visited them at home' (*Argumenty i fakty*, no. 41, 1998, p. 3).

119 Yavlinsky quoted in *Dialog*, no. 9, 1998, p. 17; and *Izvestiya*, 1 November 1995, p. 1.

120 *Moskovskie novosti*, no. 36, 1995, p. 5.

121 *Kommersant'-daily*, 4 November 1995, p. 1.

122 Vyacheslav Kostikov, *Roman s prezidentom* (Moscow: Vagrius, 1997), pp. 10–11, 16. Boris Nemtsov, while first deputy premier, was another who believed his telephone was tapped (*Izvestiya*, 11 September 1997, p. 1, and similarly ibid., 20 January 1998, p. 5).

123 Kostikov, *Roman*, pp. 14–15, 20–1.

124 Korzhakov, *Boris Yel'tsin*, p. 253.
125 Ibid., pp. 252–3.
126 *New York Review of Books*, 9 April 1998, p. 10.
127 Lakhova, *Moi put'*, p. 146.
128 Kostikov, *Roman*, pp. 65, 84, 128, 300–1, 130, 317, 339, 347.
129 Yegor Gaidar, *Dni porazhenii i pobed* (Moscow: Vagrius, 1996), pp. 60–2, 105–6.
130 Korzhakov, *Boris Yel'tsin*.
131 *Argumenty i fakty*, no. 16, 1994, p. 1 (the other Aquarians were Shevardnadze, Karimov, and Niyazov).
132 *Nezavisimaya gazeta*, 28 February 1991, p. 2.
133 *Sem' s plyusom*, no. 12 (March 1991), p. 4.
134 *Nezavisimaya gazeta*, 28 February 1991, p. 2; similarly *Moskovskie novosti*, no. 15, 1991, p. 10.
135 *Argumenty i fakty*, no. 38, 1993, p. 2.
136 *Ekonomicheskie i sotsial'nye peremeny: monitoring obshchestvennogo mneniya*, no. 1, 1995, p. 5.
137 *Izvestiya*, 14 December 1994, p. 3.
138 *Kommersant'-daily*, 10 March 1995, p. 3.
139 *Moskovskie novosti*, no. 33, 1993, p. 11A. Another survey found that the 'ideal' president was a man (71 per cent), a Russian (61 per cent), and with 'a great deal of management experience' (71 per cent) (V. K. Levashov et al., *Kak zhivesh, Rossiya?* (Moscow: ISPI RAN, 1998), pp. 38, 39, 41).
140 Kostikov, *Roman*, p. 313.
141 *Ekonomicheskie i sotsial'nye peremeny*, no. 3, 1996, pp. 10, 43 (resignation).
142 *Nezavisimaya gazeta*, 7 September 1996, p. 1.
143 See for instance *Izvestiya*, 18 May 1996, pp. 1–2 (conscription and service in Chechnya). Yeltsin's success is largely explained in these terms in Daniel Treisman, 'Why Yeltsin won', *Foreign Affairs*, vol. 75, no. 5 (September–October 1996), pp. 64–77.
144 *International Herald Tribune*, 8 July 1996, p. 1. As in the case of other candidates, Yeltsin's election expenses were reported in the bulletin of the Central Electoral Commission: *Vestnik Tsentral'noi izbiratel'noi komissii Rossiiskoi Federatsii*, no. 18 (38), 1996, pp. 20–2. For a more general discussion, see Daniel Treisman, 'Dollars and democratization: the role and power of money in Russia's transitional elections', *Comparative Politics*, vol. 31, no. 1 (October 1998), pp. 1–21.
145 *Nezavisimaya gazeta*, 7 September 1996, p. 1.
146 *Argumenty i fakty*, no. 22, 1996, p. 1; *International Herald Tribune*, 8 July 1996, p. 1.
147 For the flow of votes between the two rounds, see *Argumenty i fakty*, no. 28, 1996, p. 2.
148 Tsentral'naya izbiratel'naya komissiya Rossiiskoi Federatsii, *Vybory Prezidenta Rossiiskoi Federatsii. 1996. Elektoral'naya statistika* (Moscow: Ves' mir, 1996), pp. 190, 192.
149 Ibid., pp. 193–4, 130, 135.
150 Sakharov, *Institut prezidentstva*, p. 89.
151 *Moskovskie novosti*, no. 75, 1995, p. 5.

152 Kostikov, *Roman,* pp. 53–6; for the calls for a medical inspection, see for instance *Moskovskie novosti,* no. 38, 1996, p. 6, and *Kommersant'-daily,* 11 June 1998, p. 3 (which noted that there had been demands of this kind since May 1992).

153 *Kommersant'-daily,* 7 September 1996, p. 1. A decree of 19 September 1996 provided for the 'temporary performance of the duties of the president of the Russian Federation' in such circumstances: *Sobranie zakonodatel'stva Rossiiskoi Federatsii,* no. 39, 1996, art. 4533.

154 *Izvestiya,* 26 March 1994, p. 1.

155 Ibid., 5 July 1996, p. 2.

156 Stanislav Govorukhin quoted in the *Guardian,* 2 July 1996, p. 2.

157 *Rossiiskie vesti,* 10 November 1996, p. 3.

158 *Izvestiya,* 10 January 1997, p. 1.

159 Ibid., 11 January 1997, p. 1.

160 *Kommersant'-daily,* 15 February 1997, p. 3.

161 *Argumenty i fakty,* no. 16, 1993, p. 3.

162 *Nezavisimaya gazeta,* 16 May 1992, p. 2.

163 *Guardian,* 29 March 1993, p. 18.

164 Korzhakov, *Boris Yel'tsin,* pp. 213–18.

165 *Guardian,* 9 September 1994, p. 12.

166 Korzhakov, *Boris Yel'tsin,* pp. 219–20.

167 *Lipetskaya gazeta,* 2 March 1995, p. 2. Yeltsin told voters during the 1996 presidential election that he could 'take a drink' but didn't 'go too far' (*Izvestiya,* 22 May 1996, p. 2). Yeltsin had not emerged at Shannon airport, in fact, because of a heart attack, following which Korzhakov refused to allow him to leave the aircraft (*Boris Yel'tsin,* pp. 209–10).

168 *Izvestiya,* 3 December 1997, p. 2.

169 *Financial Times,* 3 December 1997, p. 2.

170 *Izvestiya,* 4 December 1997, p. 1.

171 Ibid., p. 3; *The Times,* 4 December 1997, p. 15; *Moskovskii komsomolets,* 4 December 1997, p. 1.

172 *Izvestiya,* 14 March 1998, p. 1, and 18 March 1998, p. 1 (postponement).

173 *Financial Times,* 27 March 1998, p. 2.

174 *Izvestiya,* 13 October 1998, p. 1.

175 Interview on Russian television, 14 March 1996, as quoted in the *OMRI Daily Digest,* no. 54, part 1, 15 March 1996.

176 For Yeltsin's sympathetic interest in a restoration of the monarchy, see for instance the *Guardian,* 15 October 1994, p. 13, based on statements made during his visit to China in 1992; Yeltsin's interest was shared by the historian Yuri Afanas'ev in *Izvestiya,* 20 June 1997, p. 5.

177 *Segodnya,* 26 December 1997, p. 3. Yeltsin made clear elsewhere that he could 'not agree with proposals for amending the existing constitution'; in his opinion it had 'proved its viability' and they must 'all learn to live under the present constitution and make full use of its potential, and only then consider the question of changing it – unhurriedly and with cool heads' (ibid., 1 February 1997, p. 1). Yeltsin, in other statements, remained opposed to any amendment that might 'infringe the president's authority'; he was willing to hold discussions, but intended that any working group should 'keep working for as long as possible, and preferably without

results'; and there could be no question of changes in the 'basic principles' of the constitution, or of 'disproportionate powers' for the government (*Izvestiya*, 31 October 1998, p. 1). Yeltsin's refusal to contemplate any reduction in his constitutional powers was reiterated by his press spokesman the following year: ibid., 28 January 1999, p. 1.

178 *Politicheskaya platforma* (Moscow: Yabloko, 1995), p. 12.
179 *Izvestiya*, 31 January 1997, pp. 1–2.
180 Gennadii Seleznev, ibid., 11 April 1996, p. 1; Zyuganov suggested that the power vested in the president be redistributed to other branches of government: ibid., 10 April 1996, p. 1. Under its 1997 Programme the party was committed to the 'restoration of the soviets and other forms of people's power' (*IV S"ezd Kommunisticheskoi partii Rossiiskoi Federatsii 19–20 aprelya 1997 goda (materialy i dokumenty)* (Moscow, 1997), p. 87.
181 *Nezavisimaya gazeta*, 17 November 1998, p. 3.
182 *Rossiiskaya gazeta*, 11 December 1997, p. 2.
183 *Moskovskie novosti*, no. 3, 1997, p. 2. The constitution, he argued similarly in early 1999, 'is not an icon that cannot be touched' (*Rossiiskaya gazeta*, 5 January 1999, p. 2).
184 *Nezavisimaya gazeta*, 14 January 1997, p. 2.
185 *Moskovskie novosti*, no. 3, 1997, p. 2.
186 *Argumenty i fakty*, no. 3, 1997, p. 3; Stroev was also interviewed in *Izvestiya*, 28 January 1997, pp. 1, 5.
187 *Rossiiskaya gazeta*, 11 December 1997, p. 2.
188 *Nezavisimaya gazeta*, 11 April 1998, p. 3.
189 Ibid., 24 October 1998, p. 1.
190 Stroev in *Izvestiya*, 17 October 1998, p. 1; similarly Zyuganov, ibid., 28 October 1998, p. 1, and Duma speaker Seleznev in *Segodnya*, 29 October 1998, p. 2 (the proposal was opposed, among others, by Yabloko).
191 *Obshchaya gazeta*, no. 5, 1997, p. 10.
192 Avak'yan, *Konstitutsiya Rossii*, pp. 215–16, 221.
193 *Rossiiskaya Federatsiya*, no. 14, 1997, pp. 54–5; the opportunity to vote a lack of confidence in individual ministers and the desirability of an easier process of impeachment were proposed in *Gosudarstvo i pravo*, no. 4, 1998, p. 7, and a simpler process of impeachment also no. 12, 1997, p. 73.
194 *Gosudarstvo i pravo*, no. 12, 1997, pp. 69–72.
195 Boris Strashun in Strashun, ed., *Konstitutsiya Rossiiskoi Federatsii* (Moscow: Infra.M-Norma, 1997), p. 93.
196 *Gosudarstvo i pravo*, no. 4, 1998, p. 6; for the lack of a 'clear idea', see *Izvestiya*, 31 January 1997, p. 2.
197 *Izvestiya*, 30 December 1997, p. 2; and for the 'cleavage', *Rossiiskaya Federatsiya*, no. 14, 1997, p. 55.
198 Maurice Duverger, 'A new political system model: semi-presidential government', *European Journal of Political Research*, vol. 8, no. 2 (June 1980), pp. 165–87, identifies three distinct subtypes. For a fuller discussion, see Horst Bahro, Bernhard H. Bayerlein, and Ernst Veser, 'Duverger's concept: semi-presidential government revisited', *European Journal of Political Research*, vol. 34, no. 2 (October 1998), pp. 201–24, and Robert Elgie, ed., *Semi-Presidentialism in Europe* (Oxford: Oxford University Press, forthcoming).

4 REFORMING THE ECONOMY

1 V. I. Lenin, *Polnoe sobranie sochinenii*, 5th edn, 55 vols. (Moscow: Politizdat, 1958–65), vol. XXXIX, p. 21.
2 M. S. Gorbachev, *Izbrannye rechi i stat'i*, 7 vols. (Moscow: Politizdat, 1987–90), vol. V, p. 301.
3 Ibid.
4 Ibid., p. 482.
5 Ibid., vol. II, p. 93.
6 Ibid., p. 154.
7 Valeria Bunce and John M. Echols III in Donald R. Kelley, ed., *Soviet Politics in the Brezhnev Era* (New York: Praeger, 1980), pp. 1–26. For a fuller discussion, see Peter Hauslohner, 'Gorbachev's social contract', in Ferenc Feher and Andrew Arato, eds., *Gorbachev: The Debate* (Cambridge: Polity, 1989), pp. 84–123, and Linda J. Cook, *The Soviet Social Contract and Why It Failed* (Cambridge, MA: Harvard University Press, 1993).
8 *I S''ezd narodnykh deputatov SSSR 25 maya–9 iyunya 1989 g. Stenograficheskii otchet*, 6 vols. (Moscow: Izdanie Verkhovnogo Soveta SSSR, 1989), vol. II, p. 290.
9 Oleg Bogomolov in *Soviet Weekly*, 4 November 1989, p. 15.
10 *Izvestiya TsK KPSS*, no. 8, 1989, p. 64.
11 See for instance Michael Ellman and Vladimir Kontorovich, 'The collapse of the Soviet system and the memoir literature', *Europe–Asia Studies*, vol. 49, no. 2 (March 1997), pp. 259–79, and Ellman and Kontorovich, eds., *The Destruction of the Soviet Economic System: An Insiders' History* (Armonk, NY: Sharpe, 1998).
12 See for instance Peter Nolan, *China's Rise, Russia's Fall: Politics, Economics and Planning in the Transition from Stalinism* (London: Macmillan, 1995).
13 S. N. Prokopovich, ed., *Opyt ischisleniya narodnogo dokhoda 50 gubernii Yevropeiskoi Rossii v 1900–1913 gg.* (Moscow: Sovet vserossiiskikh kooperativnykh s''ezdov, 1918), p. 26.
14 A. P. Korelin, ed., *Rossiya 1913 god. Statistiko-dokumental'nyi spravochnik* (St Petersburg: Blits, 1995), p. 51.
15 Ibid., p. 327; for the US figure of 89.3 per cent in 1900, see *Historical Statistics of the United States: From Colonial Times to 1970*, 2 vols. (Washington, DC: Bureau of the Census, 1975), vol. I, p. 382; for the UK, see Juliet Gardiner and Neil Wenborn, eds., *The Columbia Companion to British History* (New York: Columbia University Press, 1997), p. 473.
16 Calculated from B. R. Mitchell, ed., *International Historical Statistics: Europe, 1750–1993*, 4th edn (London: Macmillan, 1998), and Mitchell, ed., *International Historical Statistics: The Americas, 1750–1993*, 4th edn (London: Macmillan, 1998), various pages.
17 Korelin, *Rossiya 1913 god*, pp. 148, 150.
18 These data are taken from *Narodnoe khozyaistvo SSSR v 1987 godu* (Moscow: Finansy i statistika, 1988), pp. 5, 8, 13, 14, and 666 (international comparisons).
19 More recent research suggests a loss of 26.6 million lives (Yu. A. Polyakov, et al., *Lyudskie poteri SSSR v period vtoroi mirovoi voiny. Sbornik statei* (St Petersburg: Institut rossiiskoi istorii RAN, 1995), p. 41). Chernomyrdin

officially confirmed a loss of 27 million in *Izvestiya*, 19 April 1995, p. 1; it
had earlier been reported in *Vestnik statistiki*, no. 10, 1990, p. 27.

20 M. S. Gorbachev, *Perestroika i novoe myshlenie dlya nashei strany i dlya vsego mira* (Moscow: Politizdat, 1987), pp. 37–8.

21 Gorbachev, *Izbrannye rechi i stat'i*, vol. II, pp. 352–3.

22 *Kommunist*, no. 1, 1991, p. 74; for a recent comparison of growth rates, see R. W. Davies, *Soviet Economic Development from Lenin to Khrushchev* (Cambridge: Cambridge University Press, 1998), ch. 5.

23 *Narodnoe khozyaistvo SSSR v 1987 godu*, pp. 58–9.

24 N. Shmelev and V. Popov, *Na perelome. Ekonomichskaya perestroika v SSSR* (Moscow: Novosti, 1989), p. 131.

25 *EKO*, no. 11, 1987, pp. 50–2; Shmelev and Popov, *Na perelome*, pp. 169–71, 181–204. The steady fall in relative plan fulfilment is noted on p. 131.

26 Shmelev and Popov, *Na perelome*, p. 44.

Voprosy ekonomiki, no. 3, 1991, p. 59 (there were similar losses of fruit and vegetables; losses of grain ran at 20 per cent, compared with 2 per cent in the USA: ibid.).

28 Abel Aganbegyan, *The Challenge: Economics of Perestroika* (London: Hutchinson, 1988), p. 2.

29 *Novyi mir*, no. 2, 1987, pp. 181–201. Khanin published slightly different figures in *Kommunist*, no. 17, 1988, pp. 83–90, and in his book *Dinamika ekonomicheskogo razvitiya SSSR* (Novosibirsk: Nauka, 1991); his analysis of Western estimates appeared in Khanin, *Sovetskii ekonomicheskii rost. Analiz zapadnykh otsenok* (Novosibirsk: Ekor, 1993). Khanin's estimates were found to be 'for the most part, consistent and well grounded' by Mark Harrison, 'Soviet economic growth since 1928: the alternative statistics of G. I. Khanin', *Europe–Asia Studies*, vol. 45, no. 12 (1993), p. 159; they were found 'very crude' in *Voprosy ekonomiki*, no. 10, 1995, p. 112, and plausible but 'intuitive' in *Voprosy statistiki*, no. 5, 1996, pp. 84–8. A secret working group that was established within the Institute of the World Economy and International Relations in 1967 reached conclusions at the time that were close to those of the CIA, and which suggested that Soviet utilised national income was 41.1 per cent of that of the United States (*Mirovaya ekonomika i mezhdunarodnye otnosheniya*, no. 2, 1997, pp. 139–45, and no. 3, 1997, p. 148). Another working group within the State Statistics Committee calculated that Soviet GNP at the end of the 1980s was actually 37 per cent of that of the United States, not the 64 per cent reported in official sources, and that at the end of its existence it was 'not more than 30 per cent' of the American figure (*Voprosy statistiki*, no. 9, 1996, p. 10).

30 S. S. Shatalin and Ye. T. Gaidar, *Ekonomicheskaya reforma. Prichiny, napravleniya, problemy* (Moscow: Ekonomika, 1989), p. 16; Gorbachev in *Pravda*, 16 March 1989, p. 3.

31 Aganbegyan in *Izvestiya*, 25 August 1987, p. 2, and in *Literaturnaya gazeta*, 18 February 1987, p. 13.

32 Shmelev and Popov, *Na perelome*, p. 50; *Narodnoe khozyaistvo SSSR v 1988 g.* (Moscow: Finansy i statistika, 1989), p. 680.

33 *Voprosy statistiki*, no. 9, 1996, p. 10.

34 V. Perevedentsev in *Rabochii klass i sovremennyi mir*, no. 4, 1988, pp. 57–67.

35 Aganbegyan, *The Challenge*, p. 69.
36 *Vestnik statistiki*, no. 10, 1990, p. 41.
37 G. M. Sorokin, ed., *Intensifikatsiya i effektivnost' sotsialisticheskogo proiz-vodstva* (Moscow: Nauka, 1988), p. 10.
38 Aganbegyan, *The Challenge*, p. 71.
39 Ibid., p. 72, and on the Noyabr'skoe field, Sorokin, *Intensifikatsiya*, p. 11.
40 *XXVII S''ezd Kommunisticheskoi partii Sovetskogo Soyuza, 25 fevralya–6 marta 1986 goda. Stenograficheskii otchet*, 3 vols. (Moscow: Politizdat, 1986), vol. I, p. 236, and vol. II, p. 298. These apprehensions were noted at the time by Peter Frank, 'Gorbachev's dilemma: social justice or political instability?', *The World Today*, vol. 42, no. 6 (June 1986), pp. 93–5.
41 Gorbachev, *Izbrannye rechi i stat'i*, vol. II, pp. 86 and 154–5.
42 Leonid Abalkin on Moscow radio in the BBC Summary of World Broadcasts, 10 February 1989, SU/0386 B/6; Nikolai Shmelev in *Znamya*, no. 7, 1988, p. 179.
43 Gorbachev, *Izbrannye rechi i stat'i*, vol. III, p. 182.
44 Ibid., pp. 199–202.
45 Ibid., pp. 202–23. For the text of the five year plan, as adopted, see *Vedomosti Verkhovnogo Soveta SSSR*, no. 26, 1986, art. 481.
46 Gorbachev, *Izbrannye rechi i stat'i*, vol. V, pp. 157–9.
47 For the text of the law, see *Vedomosti Verkhovnogo Soveta SSSR*, no. 26, 1987, art. 385.
48 Gorbachev's speech appeared in *Pravda*, 16 March 1989, pp. 1–4; the Central Committee's resolution on leaseholding is ibid., 1 April 1989, pp. 1–2.
49 For the text of the law, see *Vedomosti Verkhovnogo Soveta SSSR*, no. 47, 1986, art. 964; the numbers employed – 673,800 – are reported in *Narodnoe khozyaistvo SSSR v 1990 g.* (Moscow: Finansy i statistika, 1991), p. 65.
50 For the text of the law, see *Vedomosti Verkhovnogo Soveta SSSR*, no. 22, 1988, art. 355. It was described as the 'first major step away from the totally state-controlled economy' by F. J. M. Feldbrugge (*Russian Law: The End of the Soviet System and the Role of Law* [Dordrecht: Nijhoff, 1993], p. 267); Yevgenii Yasin, who became minister of economics in the Chernomyrdin government, commented later that 'Literally within a year or two, under the guise of co-operatives, private enterprise was born' (Ellman and Kontorovich, *The Destruction of the Soviet Economic System*, p. 151).
51 *Narodnoe khozyaistvo v 1990 g.*, p. 55 (for a third of those employed it was a second job); future projections appeared in V. F. Yakovlev, ed., *Kooperativy segodnya i v budushchem* (Moscow: Yuridicheskaya literatura, 1989), p. 62, and Leonid Abalkin in *Sovetskaya Rossiya*, 27 July 1988, p. 3.
52 *Spravochnik partiinogo rabotnika*, vol. XXVIII (Moscow: Politizdat, 1988), p. 50.
53 Ryzhkov, in his report to the Party Congress, specified a growth rate of 5 per cent in the last years of the century and a more modest rate of between 3.5 and 4 per cent in the course of the five year plan that was to begin that year; the 'Basic Guidelines of the Economic and Social Development of the USSR for 1986–1990 and for the Period to 2000' and the new edition of the Party Programme both promised that national income would 'almost

double' by the end of the century. See *XXVII S''ezd*, vol. II, pp. 11 and 14 (Ryzhkov); for the 'Basic Guidelines', see ibid., pp. 221–92 (at p. 228), and for the Programme, vol. I, pp. 554–623 (at p. 574). The 12th Five Year Plan specified an increase of 22.1 per cent in national income between 1985 and 1990, which represented an annual rate of 4.2 per cent as compared with the 3.6 per cent that had been achieved in 1981–5 (*Narodnoe khozyaistvo SSSR za 70 let. Yubileinyi statisticheskii sbornik* [Moscow: Finansy i statistika, 1987], p. 55).

54 *Narodnoe khozyaistvo v 1990 g.*, p. 7.

55 *Ekonomika i zhizn'*, no. 5, 1991, p. 9.

56 Ibid., no. 6, 1992, pp. 13–16. For a discussion of these results, see *Vestnik statistiki*, no. 3, 1992, pp. 4–12.

57 *Voprosy ekonomiki*, no. 3, 1991, p. 36.

58 *Materialy Plenuma Tsentral'nogo komiteta KPSS 25 aprelya 1989 goda* (Moscow: Politizdat, 1989), p. 89.

59 *Pravda*, 26 January 1991, p. 1.

60 Ibid., 2 January 1991, p. 2.

61 Yegor Gaidar, *Dni porazhenii i pobed* (Moscow: Vagrius, 1996), p. 96. Other estimates suggested a budgetary deficit of 22–3 per cent for the former USSR as a whole (*Svobodnaya mysl'*, no. 6, 1992, p. 56); a subsequent and more precise figure for the Russian Federation alone was 31.9 per cent (*Voprosy ekonomiki*, no. 7, 1995, p. 23).

62 For the national debt estimate (of 60 per cent), see *Izvestiya*, 23 January 1992, p. 2.

63 *Pravda*, 8 May 1989, p. 1.

64 Ibid., 16 January 1989, p. 1.

65 Ibid., 21 September 1987, p. 3 (sugar), 23 November 1987, p. 1 (bread), and 22 August 1991, p. 3 (medicine).

66 *Izvestiya*, 30 October 1991, p. 2 (Novosibirsk), and 31 January 1991, p. 2 (sales staff).

67 *Pravda*, 27 April 1989, p. 3.

68 Ibid., 11 July 1989, p. 2.

69 *Izvestiya TsK KPSS*, no. 2, 1991, p. 92.

70 According to the trade union paper *Trud*, the black market already accounted for about 30 per cent of the value of services provided by the state (12 August 1988, p. 2); the appearance of the coupons themselves on the black market was reported in *Pravda*, 1 September 1988, p. 3. For a more general discussion, see *Voprosy ekonomiki*, no. 3, 1990, pp. 110–33, and A. P. Bunich, et al., *Tenevaya ekonomika* (Moscow: Ekonomika, 1991).

71 *Klinicheskaya meditsina*, vol. 66, no. 8 (August 1988), pp. 155–7 ('significant exposure'); *Nezavisimaya gazeta*, 26 April 1991, p. 1 (deaths over following decade); *Izvestiya*, 25 April 1996, p. 5 (survivors). For a more general discussion, see David R. Marples, *Chernobyl and Nuclear Power in the USSR* (London: Macmillan, 1987), and Zhores Medvedev, *The Legacy of Chernobyl* (Oxford: Basil Blackwell, 1990). The party leadership's attempt to play down the incident was subsequently documented from the archives: see Alla Yaroshinskaya, *Chernobyl'. Sovershenno sekretno* (Moscow: Drugie berega, 1992).

72 *Izvestiya*, 24 April 1996, p. 5 (resettlement), and 25 April 1996, p. 5 (land).

73 Zhores Medvedev in the *Times Higher Education Supplement*, 22 March 1996, p. 20 (economic costs); *Izvestiya*, 25 April 1996, p. 5 (costs for Ukraine). The long-term effects are considered in A. I. Ionov, et al., *10-letnii period v issledovanii Chernobyl'skoi avarii. Analiticheskii obzor* (Moscow: Nauchno-issledovatel'skii i konstruktorskii institut energotekhniki, 1997).

74 These details were communicated to journalists by Nikolai Ryzhkov, who headed an emergency commission (*Pravda*, 14 December 1988, pp. 1–2); the eighty-year comparison is ibid., 8 December 1988, p. 12.

75 *Narodnoe khozyaistvo v 1990 g.*, pp. 397, 644–62.

76 *Izvestiya*, 29 July 1991, p. 7 (there were also threats of 'state bankruptcy', ibid., 27 August 1991, p. 2).

77 *Molodoi kommunist*, no. 2, 1980, p. 69. For a full account of the campaign, see Stephen White, *Russia Goes Dry: Alcohol, State and Society* (Cambridge: Cambridge University Press, 1996).

78 Ye. K. Ligachev, *Zagadka Gorbacheva* (Novosibirsk: Interbuk, 1992), pp. 286–7.

79 V. I. Vorotnikov, Second Russian Revolution interview transcript, British Library of Political and Economic Science, London, 26 May 1990.

80 M. S. Solomentsev, Soviet Elites Project interview transcript, in author's possession, May 1993.

81 M. S. Gorbachev, *Zhizn' i reformy*, 2 vols. (Moscow: Novosti, 1995), vol. I, p. 340.

82 The budgetary loss was estimated to represent about a tenth of all indirect taxation (Aganbegyan in *Pravda*, 6 February 1989, p. 3); Nikolai Shmelev later dated the collapse of the economy itself to the 'mindless, idiotic anti-alcohol campaign' (ibid., 31 October 1992, p. 2).

83 KGB chairman Vladimir Kryuchkov had already presented a dossier of evidence to Gorbachev that appeared to implicate Alexander Yakovlev, the Politburo's leading reformer, as an American agent, recruited when he was an exchange student at Columbia University in the late 1950s. It was clear, he wrote later, that the system could have been reformed, but 'certain forces' had wanted its destruction and they had used all kinds of methods, including financial support for its domestic opponents, to achieve their ends: *Lichnoe delo*, 2 vols. (Moscow: Olimp), vol. I, pp. 294–309, 264 ('certain forces'), and vol. II, ch. 1. For a further discussion, see Jerry F. Hough, *Democratization and Revolution in the USSR 1985–1991* (Washington, DC: Brookings, 1997), pp. 368–9.

84 Gaidar, *Dni*, pp. 42, 56, 59, 60.

85 *Vedomosti S"ezda narodnykh deputatov SSSR i Verkhovnogo Soveta SSSR*, no. 11, 1990, art. 164, 6 March 1990.

86 *Sobranie postanovlenii pravitel'stva SSSR*, no. 19, 1990, art. 101, 8 August 1990, and no. 24, 1990, art. 114, 16 August 1990.

87 *Vedomosti S"ezda narodnykh deputatov SSSR i Verkhnovnogo Soveta SSSR*, no. 32, 1991, art. 904, 1 July 1991.

88 Ibid., no. 16, 1991, art. 442, 2 April 1991.

89 *Pravda*, 4 July 1991, p. 3.

90 Nikolai Ryzhkov, *Perestroika. Istoriya predatel'stv* (Moscow: Novosti, 1992),

p. 311; he had gone to the tribune in May 1990, he told *Pravda*, 'as to the scaffold' (4 March 1991, p. 4).

91 *VI S''ezd narodnykh deputatov Rossiiskoi Federatsii 6–21 aprelya 1992 goda. Stenograficheskii otchet*, 5 vols. (Moscow: Respublika, 1993), vol. I, p. 122.

92 *V (vneocherednoi) S''ezd narodnykh deputatov RSFSR 10–17 iyulya, 28 oktyabrya–2 noyabrya 1991 goda. Stenograficheskii otchet*, 3 vols. (Moscow: Respublika, 1992), vol. II, pp. 4–29, esp. pp. 4–18. The development of the postcommunist economy is considered more fully in Rose Brady, *Kapitalizm: How Russia Freed Its Economy* (New Haven, CT: Yale University Press, 1999), and in Thane Gustafson, *Capitalism Russian-Style* (Cambridge: Cambridge University Press, 1999).

93 *Vedomosti S''ezda narodnykh deputatov RSFSR i Verkhovnogo Soveta RSFSR*, no. 44, 1991, art. 1456, 1 November 1991; for the measures, see ibid., no. 47, 1991, art. 1609, 15 November 1991; no. 46, art. 1612, 15 November 1991; and no. 48, art. 1675, 25 November 1991.

94 Ibid., no. 52, 1991, art. 1878, 3 December 1991.

95 *Ekonomicheskaya gazeta*, no. 4, 1993, p. 13.

96 *Rossiiskaya gazeta*, 17 January 1992, p. 1.

97 *Izvestiya*, 28 February 1992, pp. 1–2.

98 *Programma uglubleniya ekonomicheskikh reform v Rossii* (Moscow: Respublika, 1992); it was also carried in full in *Voprosy ekonomiki*, no. 8, 1992.

99 Roman Frydman, Andrzej Rapaczynski, and John S. Earle, et al., *The Privatization Process in Russia, Ukraine and the Baltic States* (Budapest: Central European University Press, 1993), p. 39. The same authors identify a 'plethora of often overlapping and conflicting laws and decrees emanating from a number of jurisdictions' (p. 15), some of which are conveniently collected in *Voprosy ekonomiki*, no. 9, 1992, pp. 75–153. See also Maxim Boycko, Andrei Shleifer, and Robert Vishny, *Privatizing Russia* (Cambridge, MA: MIT Press, 1995), and Joseph R. Blasi, Maya Kroumova, and Douglas Kruse, *Kremlin Capitalism: The Privatization of the Russian Economy* (Ithaca, NY: Cornell University Press, 1997), both of which are strongly supportive of the policies followed, and which in turn reflected the authors' own advice; a more critical view is presented in Lynn D. Nelson and Irina Y. Kuzes, *Property to the People: The Struggle for Radical Economic Reform in Russia* (Armonk, NY: Sharpe, 1994), and Nelson and Kuzes, *Radical Reform in Yeltsin's Russia: Political, Economic and Social Dimensions* (Armonk, NY: Sharpe, 1995).

100 *Vedomosti S''ezda narodnykh deputatov RSFSR i Verkhovnogo Soveta RSFSR*, no. 27, 1991, art. 927; it was amended on 5 June 1992: ibid., no. 28, 1992, art. 1614.

101 Ibid., no. 27, 1991, art. 925.

102 Ibid., no. 3, 1992, art. 92, 28 December 1991.

103 Ibid., art. 93, 29 December 1991.

104 Ibid., no. 28, 1992, art. 1617, 11 June 1992.

105 Ibid., no. 35, 1992, art. 2001; a presidential decree of April 1992 had announced that a system of 'personal privatisation accounts' would be introduced in the fourth quarter of the year (ibid., no. 15, 1992, art. 825, 2 April 1992).

106 Gaidar, *Dni*, pp. 201–2.
107 *Vedomosti S"ezda narodnykh deputatov RSFSR i Verkhnovnogo Soveta RSFSR*, no. 35, 1992, art. 2001.
108 *Izvestiya*, 1 October 1992, p. 1.
109 Ibid., 25 August 1992, p. 1; Boycko, et al., *Privatizing Russia*, p. 108.
110 *Vedomosti S"ezda narodnykh deputatov Rossiiskoi Federatsii i Verkhovnogo Soveta Rossiiskoi Federatsii*, no. 28, 1992, art. 1617, 11 June 1992.
111 The second option was selected by 73 per cent of all the firms concerned, and the first by 25 per cent: Boycko, et al., *Privatizing Russia*, p. 98.
112 Ibid., p. 79.
113 *Izvestiya*, 20 August 1992, p. 2; speaking to the Congress of People's Deputies earlier in the year he had called similarly for 'millions of owners, not hundreds of millionaires' (*VI S"ezd*, vol. I, p. 127).
114 *Rossiiskaya gazeta*, 20 January 1993, p. 6.
115 *Izvestiya*, 6 January 1993, p. 2 (Tyumen'); ibid., 24 December 1992, p. 1 (Yaroslavl').
116 For counterfeiting, see for instance ibid., 11 March 1993, p. 1; for theft, *Nezavisimaya gazeta*, 8 October 1992, p. 1; for their interception, *Moskovskaya pravda*, 20 March 1993, p. 2.
117 *Nezavisimaya gazeta*, 11 August 1992, p. 4.
118 Gaidar, *Dni*, p. 201.
119 Roi Medvedev, *Chubais i vaucher* (Moscow: Impeto, 1997), p. 9.
120 The regulations for investment funds are in *Vedomosti S"ezda narodnykh deputatov Rossiiskoi Federatsii i Verkhovnogo Soveta Rossiiskoi Federatsii*, no. 42, 1992, art. 2370, 7 October 1992.
121 *Izvestiya*, 20 February 1993, p. 5, and 24 February 1993, p. 2.
122 Boycko, et al., *Privatizing Russia*, p. 101; *Izvestiya*, 10 September 1996, p. 1.
123 *Argumenty i fakty*, no. 49, 1996, p. 5; later estimates suggested there had been fewer victims (ibid., no. 10, 1997, p. 12).
124 Mavrodi had sent an estimated 70 per cent of the money abroad: ibid., no. 38, 1997, p. 8; he had been officially declared bankrupt by the time (*Izvestiya*, 4 September 1997, pp. 1–2).
125 *Izvestiya*, 8 February 1995, p. 13.
126 Ibid., 30 June 1994, p. 1.
127 Michael Kaser, *Privatization in the CIS* (London: RIIA, 1995), p. 15; *Izvestiya*, 30 June 1994, p. 1.
128 *Sobranie zakonodatel'stva Rossiiskoi Federatsii*, no. 13, 22 July 1994, art. 1478.
129 *Ekonomika i zhizn'*, no. 7, 1999, p. 1.
130 *Rossiiskii statisticheskii yezhegodnik. Statisticheskii sbornik* (Moscow: Goskomstat Rossii, 1997; hereafter *RSYe97*), p. 335.
131 *Segodnya*, 2 July 1994, p. 2.
132 See for instance Anders Aslund, *How Russia Became a Market Economy* (Washington, DC: Brookings, 1995), pp. 266, 223.
133 V. Belotserkovsky in *Svobodnaya mysl'*, no. 6, 1996, pp. 25–6.
134 Sergei Glaz'ev, *Genotsid. Rossiya i novyi mirovoi poryadok. Strategiya ekonomicheskogo rosta na poroge XXI veka* (Moscow: Astra sem', 1997), p. 29.
135 *Pravda*, 27 September 1997, p. 1.
136 According to Roi Medvedev, there were 'almost two hundred' foreign

advisers and heads of section in the State Property Committee alone, provided with exorbitant salaries on the basis of an unpublished decree (*Chubais i vaucher*, p. 8).

137 *Nezavisimaya gazeta*, 13 November 1997, pp. 1–2 (the authors had gained nearly half a million dollars among them).

138 Ibid., 18 November 1997, pp. 1–2; the investigation of Al'fred Kokh, the former chairman of the State Property Committee, was reported in *Izvestiya*, 2 October 1997, p. 1.

139 Tat'yana Zaslavskaya in *Obshchestvo i ekonomika*, no. 9, 1995, p. 10.

140 Richard Rose and Evgeny Tikhomirov, *Trends in the New Russia Barometer, 1992–1995* (Glasgow: Centre for the Study of Public Policy, University of Strathclyde, SPP 256, 1995), pp. 48–9.

141 Ibid., p. 33.

142 *Vestnik Moskovskogo universiteta: sotsiologiya i politika*, no. 3, 1995, p. 7 (based on a Russia-wide survey of late 1994).

143 Richard B. Dobson, *Is Russia Turning the Corner? Changing Russian Public Opinion, 1991–1996* (Washington, DC: USIA, 1996), p. 62.

144 *Obshchestvo i ekonomika*, no. 9, 1995, p. 5.

145 *Voprosy ekonomiki*, no. 6, 1996, p. 128 (labour productivity had fallen by 1995 to 69.7 per cent of its 1990 level, and in industry to 66.6 per cent of its 1990 level).

146 *Rossiiskii statisticheskii yezhegodnik. Statisticheskii sbornik* (Moscow: Goskomstat Rossii, 1998, hereafter RSYe 98), p. 387.

147 Glaz'ev, *Genotsid*, p. 29.

148 Blasi, et al., *Kremlin Capitalism*, pp. 179, 180–1.

149 M. A. Deryabina, ed., *Privatizatsiya* (Moscow: IMEMO, 1992), p. 3.

150 See respectively *Vedomosti S"ezda narodnykh deputatov Rossiiskoi Federatsii i Verkhovnogo Soveta Rossiiskoi Federatsii*, no. 11, 1992, art. 56, March 1992; and no. 25, 1992, art. 1427, 14 June 1992. For a well-informed discussion of developments in agriculture at this time, see Stephen K. Wegren, *Agriculture and the State in Soviet and Post-Soviet Russia* (Pittsburgh: University of Pittsburgh Press, 1998).

151 *Nezavisimaya gazeta*, 29 October 1993, p. 1.

152 *Sobranie aktov Prezidenta i pravitel'stva Rossiiskoi Federatsii*, no. 44, 1993, art. 4181, 27 October 1993.

153 *RSYe98*, pp. 443, 450.

154 Ibid., p. 381.

155 *Kommersant'-daily*, 2 September 1995, p. 2.

156 *Argumenty i fakty*, no. 8, 1997, p. 5.

157 *Kommersant'-daily*, 12 March 1996, p. 8.

158 Ibid.

159 *Trud*, 13 March 1996, p. 1.

160 *RSYe98*, p. 480, and *Rossiya '99. Statisticheskii sbornik* (Moscow: Goskomstat Rossii, 1999), p. 33; for livestock; *RSYe98*, p. 459, and *Rossiya '99*, p. 31, for grain; *RSYe98*, p. 481, for meat and milk (which fell less sharply); and *RSYe98*, pp. 459, 481 (flax and wool). Potatoes and vegetables sustained their output levels, but eggs also fell substantially (*RSYe98*, p. 481).

161 *Pravda*, 27 March 1991, p. 1; *Izvestiya*, 7 October 1991, p. 1.
162 *Vedomosti S"ezda narodnykh deputatov SSSR i Verkhovnogo Soveta SSSR*, no. 31, 1991, art. 880, 5 July 1991.
163 *Izvestiya*, 18 July 1991, p. 1.
164 Ibid., 28 April 1991, p. 1 (membership of the IMF had been agreed in 1944 but never ratified); ibid., 17 June 1992, p. 5.
165 Ibid., 30 April 1992, pp. 1–2.
166 Ibid., 16 April 1993, pp. 1, 3.
167 Ibid., 6 April 1993, p. 3.
168 *Argumenty i fakty*, no. 5, 1993, p. 1; the IMF itself insisted that a larger sum was involved (*Financial Times*, 4 February 1993, p. 8).
169 *Izvestiya*, 5 June 1997, p. 4; *Ekonomika i zhizn'*, no. 43, 1998, p. 4.
170 *Finansovye izvestiya*, 17 April 1997, p. 1; *Izvestiya*, 27 November 1998, p. 1.
171 *Izvestiya*, 6 March 1996, p. 7. On other calculations, about $140 billion had been exported since 1992; this was more than Brazil, Venezuela, Mexico, and Peru had lost, taken together, in the course of their financial crises in the 1970s and 1980s (*Rossiiskaya gazeta*, 6 October 1998, p. 2). For other estimates, see Vladimir Tikhomirov, 'Capital flight from post-Soviet Russia', *Europe–Asia Studies*, vol. 49, no. 4 (June 1997), pp. 591–615; Leonid Abalkin, 'Begstvo kapitala. Priroda, formy, metody bor'by', *Voprosy ekonomiki*, no. 7, 1998, pp. 33–41; and A. Abalkin and J. Whalley, 'The problem of capital flight from Russia', *World Economy*, vol. 22, no. 3 (May 1999), pp. 421–44.
172 *Segodnya*, 30 December 1998, p. 1; *Financial Times*, 12 February 1999, p. 2.
173 See respectively *Izvestiya*, 25 April 1997, p. 5, 11 July 1997, p. 2, and 1 August 1997, p. 2.
174 *Nedvizhimost' za rubezhom*, no. 13–14 (August–September 1996), p. 1.
175 *Izvestiya*, 15 August 1997, p. 8; *The Times*, 6 January 1998, p. 9.
176 *Izvestiya*, 22 May 1998, p. 3.
177 *Sunday Telegraph*, 20 September 1998, p. 28.
178 *Izvestiya*, 6 July 1996, p. 1.
179 *Argumenty i fakty*, no. 51, 1996, p. 16.
180 *Finansovye izvestiya*, 6 May 1997, p. 5.
181 *RSYe98*, pp. 696, 710.
182 Ibid., p. 335.
183 *Argumenty i fakty*, no. 17, 1995, p. 5.
184 *Izvestiya: ot pyatnitsy do pyatnitsy*, 29 May 1998, p. 1.
185 Quoted in Jerrold L. Schecter, *Russian Negotiating Behavior: Continuity and Transition* (Washington, DC: United States Institute of Peace Press, 1998), p. 146.
186 *Izvestiya*, 11 December 1996, p. 4; similarly *Voprosy ekonomiki*, no. 3, 1997, pp. 129–30.
187 Grigorii Khanin in *Izvestiya*, 7 April 1998, p. 4; see also the critique by Grigorii Yavlinsky, *Finansovye izvestiya*, 5 February 1998, p. 2.
188 *Izvestiya*, 10 June 1998, p. 1, and 11 June 1998, p. 1.
189 See *Finansovye izvestiya*, no. 70, 29 September 1995, p. 2.
190 Khanin in *Izvestiya*, 7 April 1998, p. 4; the World Bank estimate was 40 per cent (*Argumenty i fakty*, no. 1–2, 1998, p. 7).

191 *RSYe98*, pp. 398–404, 413–14, 693 (investment).

192 *Argumenty i fakty*, no. 48, 1996, p. 7 (from 34.5 to 20.7 per cent).

193 *Ekonomika i zhizn'*, no. 4, 1999, p. 1 (between the start of the decade and 1998).

194 *World Development Report 1998/99: Knowledge for Development* (New York: Oxford University Press for the World Bank, 1999), pp. 190–1; for other purchasing power parity comparisons, see *Voprosy ekonomiki*, no. 3, 1997, pp. 128–44.

195 *Izvestiya*, 11 December 1996, p. 4. World Bank figures, expressed in terms of purchasing power parity, also put Russian GNP per capita in 1997 below that of Peru, Namibia, and Gabon, but above that of Jordan; no figures for Iraq were reported (*World Development Report 1998/99*, pp. 190–1).

196 *RSYe97*, p. 578.

197 *Argumenty i fakty*, no. 32, 1996, p. 7.

198 *Izvestiya*, 9 January 1998, p. 1; *Trud*, 22 November 1996, p. 6 (cheese, tinned meat, and pasta). Up to 60 per cent of all meat and 80 per cent of poultry was imported (*Izvestiya*, 4 November 1998, p. 1).

199 *Rossiya v tsifrakh*, pp. 373–6.

200 Dzhul'etto K'eza, *Proshchai, Rossiya!* (Moscow: Geya, 1997), p. 141.

201 *RSYe97*, p. 552; *Rossiya v tsifrakh*, p. 345.

202 *Izvestiya*, 30 October 1998, p. 4.

203 Ibid., 17 October 1996, p. 1.

204 *Moskovskie novosti*, no. 44, 1996, p. 4.

205 *Izvestiya*, 9 October 1996, p. 2.

206 *Argumenty i fakty*, no. 22, 1998, p. 7.

207 *Izvestiya*, 4 November 1997, p. 1.

208 Ibid., 18 July 1997, p. 2, 26 July 1997, p. 2, and 2 April 1997, p. 2.

209 See respectively ibid., 1 February 1994, p. 1; *Argumenty i fakty*, no. 47, 1996, p. 1 (and *Izvestiya*, 21 January 1997, p. 1); *Izvestiya*, 15 February 1997, p. 2; *Herald*, 7 September 1998, p. 8 (coffins); *Guardian*, 23 September 1998, p. 15 (Altai).

210 *Izvestiya*, 2 August 1996, p. 2.

211 *Argumenty i fakty*, no. 9, 1997, p. 6.

212 *Izvestiya*, 22 October 1996, p. 1.

213 Ibid., 19 September 1996, p. 1, and 8 February 1996, p. 1.

214 *Moskovskie novosti*, no. 36, 1996, p. 9.

215 *Rossiiskaya gazeta*, 15 January 1997, pp. 1, 3.

216 *Kommersant'-daily*, 1 November 1996, p. 10; *Izvestiya*, 15 February 1996, p. 1.

217 *Izvestiya*, 22 May 1999, p. 1; *Rossiya v tsifrakh*, p. 47 (proportion registered); *RSYe97*, p. 120 (long-term unemployed).

218 *Financial Times*, 6 February 1997, p. 2.

219 *Ekonomika i zhizn'*, no. 15, 1998, p. 28; *RSYe98*, pp. 174–7 (regional differences).

220 *Nezavisimaya gazeta*, 15 August 1998, p. 1.

221 Ibid., p. 3.

222 *Rossiiskaya gazeta*, 18 August 1998, p. 1.

223 *Rossiya '99*, p. 58.

224 *Izvestiya*, 30 October 1998, p. 4.
225 'All my money is gone', he told the West German magazine *Bunte*: *Guardian*, 30 December 1998, p. 2.
226 *Kommersant'-daily*, 15 September 1998, p. 8; a fuller version appeared in *Voprosy ekonomiki*, no. 6, 1998, pp. 10–67. A set of related proposals was approved by the Council of the Federation, involving an increase in state regulation, a state alcohol monopoly, and a limited currency emission (*Nezavisimaya gazeta*, 25 July 1998, p. 3).
227 *Izvestiya*, 20 November 1998, p. 1.
228 *Segodnya*, 29 October 1998, p. 5.
229 *Izvestiya*, 7 October 1998, p. 1.
230 Aslund, *How Russia Became a Market Economy*, pp. 279, 284, 311, 312. Writing elsewhere, Aslund hailed Russia as a 'success story' (*Foreign Affairs*, vol. 73, no. 5 [September–October 1994], pp. 58–71); the outcome was similarly a 'Russian success story' for Brigitte Granville, *The Success of Russian Economic Reforms* (London: RIIA, 1996), p. 105. A more sceptical view was expressed at the time by Harvard economist Marshall Goldman, who pointed to the 'growing mafia presence', the 'grabitization' rather than privatisation of property, the export of capital, and rising unemployment. New economic and legal institutions, in his view, should have had greater priority (*Foreign Affairs*, vol. 73, no. 6 [November–December 1994], p. 196).
231 Richard Layard and John Parker, *The Coming Russian Boom: A Guide to New Markets and Politics* (New York: Free Press, 1996), pp. 335.
232 *Izvestiya*, 14 May 1994, p. 1.
233 *Literaturnaya gazeta*, no. 21, 1995, p. 1.
234 *Izvestiya*, 31 December 1991, p. 2; there was a further assurance in the spring that their economic difficulties would be resolved 'by the autumn' (ibid., 27 May 1992, p. 1). The promise to 'lie on the rails' was recalled by Alexander Solzhenitsyn, *Rossiya v obvale* (Moscow: Russkii put', 1998), p. 21.
235 *Izvestiya*, 20 February 1992, p. 1.
236 Aslund, *How Russia Became a Market Economy*, p. 312.
237 Boycko, et al., *Privatizing Russia*, p. 9.
238 *Nezavisimaya gazeta*, 27 February 1992, p. 5.
239 *Times Higher Education Supplement*, 23 October 1998, p. 16.
240 *Trud*, 29 September 1998, Delovoi vtornik, p. 3. Several of those associated with the Harvard Institute for International Development were investigated for possible insider dealing, and one of them was dismissed from his university post (*Financial Times*, 18 January 1999, p. 3). For a vigorous polemic on this subject, see Janine R. Wedel, *Collision and Collusion* (London: Macmillan, 1998).
241 Cited in *Sotsiologicheskii zhurnal*, no. 4, 1997, p. 7.
242 Gaidar, *Dni*, p. 9.
243 *Izvestiya*, 28 June 1995, p. 5.
244 See respectively *Segodnya*, 30 July 1997, p. 1; *Nezavisimaya gazeta*, 17 March 1998, p. 8 (also *Kommersant'-daily*, 27 August 1998, p. 3); and *Argumenty i fakty*, no. 12, 1998, p. 3.
245 Peter Rutland, quoted in the Kennan Institute's *Meeting Report*, vol. 13, no. 9 (1996).

246 See respectively Anatolii Buzgalin in the *Times Higher Education Supplement*, 25 December 1998, p. 10; *New Statesman*, 21 August 1998, p. 14; and Michael Ellman in *Economic and Political Weekly*, 26 December 1998, p. 3317. For a broader discussion of some of these issues, see Philip Hanson, 'What sort of capitalism is developing in Russia?', *Communist Economies and Economic Transformation*, vol. 9, no. 1 (March 1997), pp. 27–42.

247 *Voprosy ekonomiki*, no. 3, 1996, pp. 74–83.

248 Ibid., no. 4, 1995, p. 58.

249 Glaz'ev, *Genotsid*, pp. 52, 77–8.

250 *Nezavisimaya gazeta*, 21 March 1993, p. 5.

251 Glaz'ev, *Genotsid*, pp. 45, 52, 78–9, 97.

252 G. V. Osipov, et al., eds., *Rossiya – novyi etap liberal'nykh reform* (Moscow: Respublika, 1997), p. 7.

253 *Argumenty i fakty*, no. 3, 1995, p. 5; his impressions were reported in *Rossiya v obvale*, pp. 5–12.

254 *Nezavisimaya gazeta*, 20 June 1992, p. 2.

255 *Voprosy ekonomiki*, no. 3, 1997, p. 4.

256 Ibid., no. 9, 1998, p. 150.

257 Ibid., no. 6, 1998, p. 7. Among the distinctive features of the Soviet economy were its high levels of specialisation and (accordingly) monopoly, and the dependence of many small towns on one or two often loss-making factories (ibid., no. 7, 1995, pp. 54–5). There was also a quite specific 'Russian economic mentality' that was a product of historical circumstances, among them the very late ending of serfdom (ibid., no. 9, 1996, pp. 158–60).

258 *Svobodnaya mysl'*, no. 7, 1993, p. 57.

259 *Nezavisimaya gazeta*, 20 February 1998, p. 3.

260 *Financial Times*, 30 November 1998, p. 2.

261 A point made in V. P. Loginov, et al., eds., *Ekonomicheskie reformy v Rossii. Itogi pervykh let 1991–1996* (Moscow: Nauka, 1997), p. 6.

262 *Nezavisimaya gazeta*, 1 July 1996, pp. 1, 4.

263 To quote Peter Murrell in the *Journal of Economic Literature*, vol. 33, no. 1 (March 1995), p. 175.

264 As two Nobel laureates pointed out, it made 'little sense for economists to discuss the process of exchange without specifying the institutional setting within which the trading takes place', as developments in Eastern Europe had made 'crystal clear' (R. H. Coase in *American Economic Review*, vol. 82, no. 4 (September 1992), p. 718; or as Douglass C. North pointed out, 'transferring the formal political and economic rules of Western market economies to third-world and East European economies is not a sufficient condition for good economic performance' (*American Economic Review*, vol. 84, no. 3 [June 1994], p. 366). A broader perspective is presented in Alice H. Amsden, et al., *The Market Meets Its Match: Restructuring the Economies of Eastern Europe* (Cambridge, MA: Harvard University Press, 1994).

265 *World Development Report 1997: The State in a Changing World* (New York: Oxford University Press for the World Bank, 1997), pp. 29–38; the quotation is on p. 38.

5 A DIVIDED SOCIETY

1 *Voprosy istorii*, no. 6, 1989, p. 134.
2 A. M. Prokhorov, ed., *SSSR. Entsiklopedicheskii spravochnik* (Moscow: Sovetskaya entsiklopediya, 1982), p. 20.
3 According to the 1977 constitution, the USSR was a 'multinational state' which had been formed 'as a result of the free self-determination of nations and the voluntary association of equal Soviet socialist republics' (Art. 70).
4 This wording disappeared in 1977 when the 'Brezhnev' constitution was adopted. Borrowings of this kind were not uncommon in the early Soviet period: see Jay Bergman, 'The image of Jesus in the Russian revolutionary movement', *International Review of Social History*, vol. 25, no. 2 (1990), pp. 220–48.
5 F. J. M. Feldbrugge, *Russian Law: The End of the Soviet System and the Role of Law* (Dordrecht: Nijhoff, 1993), p. 301.
6 Yu. V. Andropov, *Izbrannye rechi i stat'i*, 2nd edn (Moscow: Politizdat, 1983), pp. 194–5.
7 M. S. Gorbachev, *Izbrannye rechi i stat'i*, 7 vols. (Moscow: Politizdat, 1987–90), vol. V, p. 219 (socialist pluralism), vol. VI, p. 205 (pluralism of opinions), 212 (pluralism of interests). There had already been a reference to political pluralism in *Pravda* on 18 January 1985, shortly before Gorbachev's accession (Vadim Pechenev, *Gorbachev. K vershinam vlasti* [Moscow: Gospodin narod, 1991]), p. 71.
8 *Narodnoe khozyaistvo SSSR v 1990 g.* (Moscow: Finansy i statistika, 1991), p. 97.
9 *Rossiiskii statisticheskii yezhegodnik. Statisticheskii sbornik* (Moscow: Goskomstat Rossii, 1997; hereafter *RSYe97*), p. 109. Somewhat different but equally authoritative figures are presented in *Rossiya v tsifrakh. Kratkii statisticheskii sbornik* (Moscow: Goskomstat Rossii, 1998), p. 42; according to this source, the state and municipal sector was still substantially larger, at 42 per cent in 1997 as compared with 36.2 per cent working in the private sector.
10 *RSYe97*, p. 142, and *Rossiya v tsifrakh*, p. 67; for the ownership of wealth, *Argumenty i fakty*, no. 18, 1998, p. 7.
11 *RSYe97*, p. 138 (for 1990); *Rossiya v tsifrakh*, p. 67 (for 1997); and for international comparisons, *World Development Report 1998/99: Knowledge for Development* (New York: Oxford University Press for the World Bank, 1999), pp. 198–9. A degree of inequality of this kind was 'unprecedented' in the experience of Western countries: *Sotsiologicheskie issledovaniya*, no. 6, 1997, p. 57.
12 *Rossiya v tsifrakh*, p. 61.
13 Respectively 37.6 and 19.3 per cent: *Rossiiskii statisticheskii yezhegodnik. Statisticheskii sbornik* (Moscow: Logos, 1996; hereafter *RSYe96*), p. 811). For a fuller discussion of emerging inequalities, see Bertram Silverman and Murray Yanowitch, *New Rich, New Poor, New Russia: Winners and Losers on the Russian Road to Capitalism* (Armonk, NY: Sharpe, 1997); according to a World Bank study, as many as 20 per cent of the population would be living in extreme poverty – earning less than half the subsistence minimum – by early 2000 (*Financial Times*, 30 April 1999, Russia, p. v).

14 Richard Rose and Ian McAllister, 'Is money the measure of welfare in Russia?', *Review of Income and Wealth*, vol. 42, no. 1 (March 1996), pp. 75–90.

15 Calculated from *RSYe97*, p. 139.

16 Ibid., p. 161.

17 Ibid., p. 172.

18 Ibid., p. 175.

19 Ibid., p. 176. The poor, surveys suggested, spent about 70 per cent of their income on food; parents with large families, and pensioners, spent up to 90 per cent of their income in this way (*Sotsiologicheskie issledovaniya*, no. 3, 1994, p. 66).

20 *Rossiya v tsifrakh*, p. 79 (224 per cent).

21 *Rossiiskii statisticheskii yezhegodnik. Statisticheskii sbornik* (Moscow: Goskomstat Rossii, 1995; hereafter *RSYe95*), pp. 583–5; similarly *Izvestiya*, 25 October 1997, p. 5.

22 *RSYe96*, pp. 808–10.

23 Ibid., pp. 811–13. Tyva also had the highest levels of tuberculosis and syphilis among the Russian regions: *Izvestiya*, 11 March 1998, p. 5.

24 *RSYe97*, p. 145.

25 VTsIOM surveys found that 44 per cent had an 'allotment where they [grew] vegetables and fruit' (*Ekonomicheskie i sotsial'nye peremeny: monitoring obshchestvennogo mneniya*, no. 3, 1998, p. 67); USIA found that Russia had become a 'country of partial subsistence farmers', with 54 per cent reporting that they grew half or more of their own food (*USIA Opinion Analysis* M-4-99, 12 January 1999), p. 5.

26 *Argumenty i fakty*, no. 11, 1997, p. 2.

27 *Voprosy statistiki*, no. 2, 1997, pp. 30–6; similarly Rimashevskaya in *Sotsiologicheskie issledovaniya*, no. 6, 1997, p. 59.

28 *Ekonomicheskie i sotsial'nye peremeny*, no. 4, 1998, p. 58, and no. 3, 1998, p. 31 (earning the most); a similar point is made in *Sotsiologicheskie issledovaniya*, no. 6, 1997, p. 58. USIA surveys found that only 10 per cent of working Russians had a second job or a second source of income, and another 6 per cent that they sometimes had additional income of this kind (*USIA Opinion Analysis* M-4-99, 12 January 1999, p. 10). Surveys in Samara, Kemerovo, Lyubertsy, and Syktyvar found similarly that the poorest households did not have access to agricultural land, and had neither the time nor the money to grow their own crops; those who did so were richer than average, and still spent considerable sums on buying food (*Financial Times*, 11 December 1998, p. 3).

29 *Izvestiya*, 26 January 1996, p. 4; according to another survey, 71 per cent of families had incomes below subsistence level (*Vestnik MGU: sotsiologiya i politologiya*, no. 3, 1996, p. 19).

30 *Izvestiya*, 22 April 1998, p. 6.

31 *Obshchestvo i ekonomika*, no. 1–2, 1997, pp. 54–5.

32 *Izvestiya*, 12 August 1995, p. 5.

33 Ibid., 27 December 1995, p. 7.

34 *Ekonomicheskie i sotsial'nye peremeny*, no. 2, 1997, pp. 78–9; another survey found that 'connections' counted most of all, then 'personal qualities', but

after that 'position occupied before reform' including previous employment in the party apparatus (*Izvestiya*, 22 April 1998, p. 6).

35 Olga Kryshtanovskaya, 'Rich and poor in post-communist Russia', *Journal of Communist Studies and Transition Politics*, vol. 10, no. 1 (March 1994), p. 12. According to a later survey, 64 per cent of Russians were unsure who the oligarchs were: 23 per cent named Boris Berezovsky, 18 per cent Chubais, 17 per cent Chernomyrdin, and 8 per cent Yeltsin (*Izvestiya*, 16 June 1998, p. 1).

36 For biographies, see *Kto yest' kto v Rossii. Spravochnoe izdanie* (Moscow: Olimp/EKSMO Press, 1998). Vyakhirev was rated the 'most important figure in Russian business' in a reputational study (*Izvestiya: ot pyatnitsy do pyatnitsy*, 29 May 1998, p. 5).

37 Berezovsky was rated first as a 'professional lobbyist' in a reputational study reported in *Nezavisimaya gazeta*, 11 April 1998, p. 1; see also ch. 3. His wealth was estimated by *Forbes* magazine at $3 billion in 1997: *Argumenty i fakty*, no. 30, 1997, p. 8. Berezovsky's dismissal from his CIS post, in connection with an anti-corruption drive by the Primakov government, was reported in *Kommersant'*, 5 March 1999, p. 1.

38 *Economist*, 4 April 1998, p. 40, and *Moskovskie novosti*, no. 38, 1997, p. 7.

39 Quoted in Dzhul'etto K'eza, *Proshchai, Rossiya!* (Moscow: Geya, 1997), p. 198.

40 *Argumenty i fakty*, no. 40, 1998, p. 3.

41 *Nezavisimaya gazeta*, 3 June 1998, p. 8.

42 *Argumenty i fakty*, no. 44, 1996, p. 6.

43 Ibid.

44 *Sunday Times*, 30 August 1998, News Review, p. 2; *Daily Telegraph*, 10 April 1999, p. P4.

45 *Argumenty i fakty*, no. 44, 1996, p. 6.

46 *Izvestiya*, 22 April 1998, p. 6.

47 Ibid., 13 March 1996, p. 7.

48 Ibid., 12 April 1997, p. 4 (cost); *Argumenty i fakty*, no. 20, 1998, p. 7 (competition).

49 *Scotland on Sunday*, 28 December 1997, p. 17.

50 Yeltsin's grandson – also called Boris – was at Winchester and started at Oxford in 1999; on Berezovsky's family, see *Kto yest' kto v Rossii*, p. 63.

51 *Izvestiya*, 5 August 1997, p. 3; British aristocratic titles were being advertised in the daily press at this time (see for instance ibid., 1 October 1997, p. 5).

52 *Living Here*, no. 5, 1996.

53 *Prospect*, no. 43 (July 1999), pp. 49–50.

54 *Newsweek*, 19 December 1994, pp. 34–6.

55 *Guardian*, 5 March 1998, Section 2, p. 19.

56 *Argumenty i fakty*, no. 30, 1996, p. 9.

57 *Sunday Times*, 14 May 1995, Section 1, p. 17.

58 *Izvestiya*, 5 August 1997, p. 3.

59 *Sunday Times*, 14 May 1995, Section 1, p. 17.

60 *RSYe97*, p. 153; *Segodnya*, 16 June 1997, p. 5.

61 *Izvestiya*, 20 February 1997, p. 1.

62 *Guardian*, 18 April 1997, p. 10.

63 *Izvestiya*, 20 February 1997, p. 5.

64 Ibid., 24 October 1997, p. 5.
65 Ibid., 23 October 1997, p. 5.
66 *Argumenty i fakty*, no. 17, 1997, p. 5.
67 *Sunday Telegraph*, 12 October 1997, p. 31.
68 *Izvestiya*, 9 April 1996, p. 1.
69 *Guardian*, 11 July 1998, p. 15; *Izvestiya*, 3 April 1996, p. 5.
70 *Herald*, 9 November 1998, p. 13.
71 *Guardian*, 11 July 1998, p. 15.
72 *Literaturnaya gazeta*, no. 49, 1996, p. 10; see also more generally S. A. Stivenson, *Bezdomnye v sotsial'noi strukture bol'shogo goroda* (Moscow: INION RAN, 1997).
73 *Izvestiya*, 12 April 1996, pp. 1–2, and (for Moscow) ibid., 25 February 1995, p. 1.
74 *Sunday Telegraph*, 12 October 1997, p. 31.
75 *RSYe96*, p. 125, and (for 1996) *RSYe97*, pp. 148, 170–1; *Rossiya v tsifrakh*, pp. 70–3. For a more general discussion, see *Svobodnaya mysl'*, no. 5, 1997, pp. 37–50.
76 *Argumenty i fakty*, no. 46, 1996, p. 5.
77 *Izvestiya*, 6 May 1993, p. 6.
78 Ibid., 27 January 1993, p. 5.
79 *Rossiya v tsifrakh*, p. 79. For Rimashevskaya, for instance, the poor were about 40 per cent of the total population at this time, including two-thirds of all children, and they were an increasing rather than diminishing proportion of the population (*Sotsiologicheskie issledovaniya*, no. 6, 1997, p. 56).
80 *Sotsiologicheskie issledovaniya*, no. 6, 1997, pp. 56–7.
81 *Nezavisimaya gazeta*, 25 November 1998, p. 8.
82 *Izvestiya*, 30 October 1998, p. 4.
83 Ibid., 1 October 1998, p. 1.
84 Ibid., 30 October 1998, p. 4.
85 Ibid., 24 October 1998, p. 2.
86 *Novye izvestiya*, 19 September 1998, p. 4.
87 *Trud*, 31 October 1998, p. 1.
88 Ibid., 28 October 1998, p. 2.
89 *Izvestiya*, 18 October 1994, p. 5. For a further discussion, see for instance Stephen Handelman, *Comrade Criminal: Russia's New Mafia* (New Haven, CT: Yale University Press, 1995); Phil Williams, ed., *Russian Organized Crime* (London: Cass, 1997); and Tanya Frisby, 'The rise of organised crime in Russia: its roots and social significance', *Europe–Asia Studies*, vol. 50, no. 1 (January 1998), pp. 27–49. There is a well-informed survey in Alexander Maksimov, *Rossiiskaya prestupnost'. Kto yest' kto?* (Moscow: EKSMO-Press, 1998).
90 TsKhSD, Moscow, *fond* 89, *opis'* 11, doc. 131, 14 July 1987.
91 *Narodnoe khozyaistvo SSSR v 1988 g.* (Moscow: Finansy i statistika, 1989), p. 253.
92 *Materialy XXII S''ezda Kommunisticheskoi partii Sovetskogo Soyuza* (Moscow: Gosudarstvennoe izdatel'stvo, 1961), p. 400.
93 *Izvestiya*, 18 October 1994, p. 5.
94 A. I. Dolgova, ed., *Kriminal'naya situatsiya v Rossii i yee izmerenie* (Moscow:

Kriminologicheskaya assotsiatsiya, 1996), pp. 4, 13–14 (the number of criminals had doubled over the same period: p. 5). Other inquiries suggested that more than 60 per cent of the victims of serious crime did not bother to report it (*Izvestiya*, 2 April 1997, p. 1).

95 On arson, see *Prestupnost' i pravonarusheniya (1992–1996). Statisticheskii sbornik* (Moscow: MVD RF, 1997), p. 148; on criminal groupings, see V. I. Gladkikh, *Prestupnost' v sverkhkrupnom gorode i yee preduprezhdenie organami vnutrennykh del* (Moscow: VNII MID Rossii, 1996), p. 54.

96 *Prestupnost' v Rossii* (Moscow: Tsentr kompleksnykh sotsial'nykh issledo-vanii i marketinga, 1997), p. 5.

97 *Rossiya v tsifrakh*, p. 123.

98 *RSYe97*, p. 270. Not only were there more murders: there were more unidentified bodies, and nearly twice as many who were 'lost without trace' (Dolgova, *Kriminal'naya situatsiya*, pp. 14–15).

99 Derived from *RSYe97*, p. 270.

100 Ibid., pp. 245, 247.

101 Ibid., p. 270.

102 *Nezavisimaya gazeta*, 9 April 1997, p. 6; these figures were not included in the sentencing statistics in *RSYe97*, p. 272.

103 Public executions in Chechnya were reported in *Izvestiya*, 5 September 1997, p. 1, and 19 September 1997, p. 1. The death penalty was retained for 'exceptionally grave and life-threatening crimes' in Article 59 of the new Code, but not for women, the young, or the old: *Ugolovnyi kodeks Rossiiskoi Federatsii* (Moscow: Infra.M-Norma, 1997). There were 143 executions in 1995 and 153 in 1996 (*Prestupnost' i pravonarusheniya*, p. 159), but death sentences were suspended in the spring of that year in deference to Russia's obligations as a member of the Council of Europe (*Kommersant'-daily*, 13 January 1998, p. 1) and the sentence was effectively abolished in early 1999 (ibid., 3 February 1999, p. 2).

104 Boris Kagarlitsky, *Restoration in Russia* (London: Verso, 1995), p. 23.

105 *Argumenty i fakty*, no. 30, 1996, p. 8.

106 *Prestupnost' i pravonarusheniya*, pp. 16–17, 31–2, 36–7.

107 Ibid., pp. 31–2, 62–3.

108 *Voprosy statistiki*, no. 3, 1997, p. 63; its high levels of poverty and ill-health have already been noted (above, p. 147).

109 *Komsomol'skaya pravda*, 10 November 1994, p. 3.

110 *Problemy bor'by s prestupnost'yu (regional'nyi aspekt)* (Moscow: VNII MVD Rossii, 1996), pp. 34–40.

111 *Prestupnost' i pravonarusheniya*, p. 18.

112 *Izvestiya*, 9 February 1994, p. 5.

113 *Argumenty i fakty*, no. 36, 1996, p. 16.

114 See respectively *Izvestiya*, 18 October 1994, p. 5, and *Financial Times*, 20 March 1997, p. 2.

115 This was the estimate of the Ministry of Internal Affairs (*Izvestiya*, 6 February 1997, p. 1); Ivan Rybkin, for instance, estimated 45–50 per cent, and Grigorii Yavlinsky 70 per cent (ibid., 23 October 1997, p. 4).

116 *Nezavisimaya gazeta*, 1 October 1997, p. 1.

117 *Izvestiya*, 1 March 1997, p. 1. On these parallels, see for instance Federico

Varese, 'Is Sicily the future of Russia? Private protection and the rise of the Russian mafia', *European Journal of Sociology*, vol. 35, no. 2 (1994), pp. 224–58; Stefan Hedlund and Niclas Sundstrom, 'Does Palermo represent the future for Moscow?', *Journal of Public Policy*, vol. 16, no. 2 (May–August 1996), pp. 113–55.

118 *RSYe97*, p. 270.

119 Yu. M. Antonyan, *Prestupnost' sredi zhenshchin* (Moscow: Rossiiskoe pravo, 1992), p. 26.

120 Ibid., p. 25.

121 *Prestupnost' i pravonarusheniya*, p. 8.

122 *Izvestiya*, 31 January 1996, p. 2.

123 Ibid., 20 October 1994, p. 5.

124 More than 6,000 such guards had registered their services by April 1994, and 26,000 had obtained licences allowing them to take on security guard or detective duties: ibid., 18 October 1994, p. 5.

125 Ibid., 20 October 1994, p. 5.

126 Ibid., 5 November 1993, p. 3.

127 *The Times*, 26 August 1998, p. 10; *Argumenty i fakty*, no. 22, 1992, p. 8.

128 *Izvestiya*, 7 December 1993, p. 6.

129 Ibid., 14 September 1993, p. 5.

130 *Nezavisimaya gazeta*, 9 October 1998, p. 12.

131 *Izvestiya*, 12 April 1997, p. 1 (38,000 and 1,700 respectively).

132 *Daily Telegraph*, 5 November 1998, p. 21; *Guardian*, 19 October 1998, p. 11.

133 There were 'graveyard wars' in St Petersburg in this connection: *Izvestiya*, 17 February 1994, p. 7.

134 Ibid., 18 December 1993, p. 10.

135 Ibid., 21 September 1995, p. 5; similar figures were presented by the Ministry of Internal Affairs: ibid., 6 February 1997, p. 1.

136 Ibid., 6 February 1997, p. 1.

137 Ibid., 9 April 1996, p. 1.

138 *Guardian*, 1 August 1997, p. 13.

139 Ibid., 6 May 1998, p. 14.

140 See for instance *Izvestiya*, 5 August 1992, p. 1.

141 *Guardian*, 22 October 1998, p. 18.

142 *Argumenty i fakty*, no. 30, 1996, p. 8.

143 *Izvestiya*, 21 October 1994, p. 5.

144 *Kommersant'-daily*, 15 December 1994, p. 14; *Rossiiskaya gazeta*, 10 January 1995, p. 3.

145 *Izvestiya*, 31 March 1998, p. 2, commenting on the election of a former criminal, A. Kliment'ev, to the mayoralty; Kliment'ev was subsequently arrested and sentenced (ibid., 28 May 1998, p. 1). The elected mayor of Leninsk-Kuznetskii in the Kemerovo region had a criminal record and was believed to be implicated in a 'series of murders' (ibid., 19 September 1997, p. 1).

146 General accounts include Georgii Podlesskikh and Andrei Tereshonok, *Vory v zakone. Brosok k vlasti* (Moscow: Khudozhestvennaya literatura, 1994); Alexander Kirpichnikov, *Vzyatka i korruptsiya v Rossii* (Moscow:

Al'fa, 1997); Federico Varese, 'The transition to the market and corruption in post-socialist Russia', *Political Studies*, vol. 45, no. 3 (1997), pp. 579–96.

147 *Moskovskie novosti*, no. 5, 1997, p. 15.

148 *Guardian*, 4 November 1997, p. 20.

149 *Argumenty i fakty*, no. 30, 1996, p. 8.

150 See respectively *Izvestiya*, 17 February 1996, p. 1, and *Segodnya*, 4 February 1999, p. 1. A first deputy finance minister was also charged with bribe-taking: *Kommersant'-daily*, 10 September 1998, p. 5.

151 *Ekonomicheskie i sotsial'nye peremeny*, no. 4, 1998, pp. 78–9 (the figure related to respondents themselves or their family members).

152 *Izvestiya*, 6 January 1996, p. 5.

153 The fourth was reported in *Segodnya*, 28 November 1995, p. 1; Starovoitova (see below) was the sixth.

154 *Izvestiya*, 4 July 1998, p. 1.

155 *Nezavisimaya gazeta*, 15 March 1994, p. 2.

156 *Segodnya*, 22 November 1998, p. 1.

157 *Izvestiya*, 19 March 1997, p. 1.

158 Ibid., 25 March 1997, pp. 1–2.

159 Ibid., 1 March 1997, p. 1.

160 *Segodnya*, 24 May 1996, p. 1.

161 *Kommersant'-daily*, 5 July 1996, p. 14.

162 See respectively *Izvestiya*, 14 June 1996, p. 1, 10 April 1996, p. 2, and 6 June 1997, p. 8.

163 Ibid., 19 August 1997, p. 1, and 2 August 1997, p. 2.

164 Among those who suffered an attempt on their lives were the governors of Bryansk (ibid., 7 December 1996, p. 1), Vologda (ibid., 30 August 1996, p. 1), and Sverdlovsk regions (*Segodnya*, 15 January 1998, p. 1).

165 See for instance *Izvestiya*, 31 August 1996, p. 1.

166 Ibid., 27 June 1998, p. 1.

167 Ibid., 4 December 1993, p. 2.

168 Ibid., 5 August 1995, p. 1.

169 Ibid., 20 March 1996, p. 1.

170 See respectively ibid., 7 December 1993, p. 1, and *Argumenty i fakty*, no. 48, 1996, p. 7 (there were 118 such killings).

171 *The Times*, 28 August 1997, p. 12.

172 *Izvestiya*, 28 October 1997, p. 1.

173 See respectively *Segodnya*, 3 August 1998, p. 1, and *Izvestiya*, 10 January 1998, p. 1.

174 *Segodnya*, 17 June 1997, p. 1.

175 *Izvestiya*, 22 April 1997, p. 1.

176 Ibid., 21 September 1995, p. 5.

177 Ibid., 7 April 1994, pp. 1–2; the funeral was described in *Segodnya*, 9 April 1994, p. 7.

178 *Izvestiya*, 12 November 1994, p. 2. Likhodei had been elected chairman in 1993 in place of the former head of Soviet military intelligence: *Kommersant'-daily*, 11 November 1996, pp. 1, 10.

179 *Segodnya*, 11 November 1996, p. 1.

180 *Rossiiskaya gazeta*, 12 November 1996, p. 8.

181 *Kommersant'-daily*, 11 November 1996, pp. 1, 10.
182 *Segodnya*, 2 November 1996, p. 5 (the chairman of the Moscow Society of the Deaf had been shot the previous September).
183 *Izvestiya*, 4 May 1995, p. 1.
184 *Moskovskii komsomolets*, 18 October 1994, p. 1.
185 *Segodnya*, 3 March 1995, p. 1; Yeltsin's message was reported in *Rossiiskaya gazeta*, 3 March 1995, p. 2.
186 Some twenty-four had died over the two previous years: *Izvestiya*, 11 January 1997, p. 1.
187 *Segodnya*, 26 August 1998, p. 7.
188 *Izvestiya*, 10 June 1998, p. 2, and 11 June 1998, pp. 1–2.
189 *Argumenty i fakty*, no. 6, 1997, p. 4.
190 The trial was reported in *Izvestiya*, 15 April 1992, p. 8, and 16 October 1992, p. 3.
191 See Lyudmila Vinnikova, *Man'yak yavlyaetsya v dozhd'. Dokumental'naya povest' o prestupnike-man'yake Chikatilo* (Moscow: Argumenty i fakty, 1992); and Richard Lourie, *Hunting for the Devil: The Search for the Russian Ripper* (London: Grafton, 1993). Chikatilo's son was later arrested for rape: *Argumenty i fakty*, no. 9, 1997, p. 13.
192 *Argumenty i fakty*, no. 7, 1997, p. 13.
193 Ibid., no. 9, 1997, p. 13.
194 *Scotland on Sunday*, 19 October 1997, pp. 16–17.
195 *Kuranty*, 12 May 1994, p. 1.
196 *Scotland on Sunday*, 2 November 1997, p. 20.
197 *Herald*, 27 October 1997, p. 10.
198 *Evening Times* (Glasgow), 21 July 1997, p. 3.
199 *Herald*, 10 March 1998, p. 10.
200 *Guardian*, 14 July 1997, p. 11.
201 *Ekonomika i zhizn'*, no. 47, 1998, p. 6 (all crime was up by 4.1 per cent in the first nine months of 1998 compared with the year before, but assaults by twice as much).
202 *Sotsiologicheskie issledovaniya*, no. 8, 1995, p. 105.
203 *Sunday Telegraph*, 5 October 1997, p. 29.
204 *Izvestiya*, 1 September 1995, p. 3.
205 *Independent*, 2 February 1998, p. 10.
206 *Izvestiya*, 2 June 1998, p. 3.
207 *Transition*, vol. 3, no. 6 (4 April 1997), p. 40.
208 *Sotsiologicheskie issledovaniya*, no. 8, 1995, p. 99.
209 *The Times Magazine*, 31 January 1998, p. 27 (the second phrase was Yavlinsky's).
210 *Izvestiya*, 26 January 1994, p. 2.
211 *Vestnik statistiki*, no. 1, 1992, p. 65.
212 Gorbachev, *Izbrannye rechi i stat'i*, vol. III, p. 266. Statistics on the position of women and the family were reported annually in *Vestnik statistiki*, and as a separate serial publication, *Zhenshchiny i deti v SSSR*; many are conveniently available in Peter Lentini, *Statistical Data on Women in the USSR* (Glasgow: Lorton House, 1994). Fuller discussions include Mary Buckley, *Women and Ideology in the Soviet Union* (Hemel Hempstead: Harvester

Wheatsheaf, 1989); Buckley, ed., *Perestroika and Soviet Women* (Cambridge: Cambridge University Press, 1992); Rosalind Marsh, ed., *Women in Russia and Ukraine* (Cambridge: Cambridge University Press, 1996); Sue Bridger, Rebecca Kay, and Kathryn Pinnick, *No More Heroines? Russia, Women and the Market* (London: Routledge, 1996); and Buckley, ed., *Post-Soviet Women: From the Baltic to Central Asia* (Cambridge: Cambridge University Press, 1997).

213 *Vestnik statistiki*, no. 1, 1992, p. 53.
214 Ibid., pp. 65, 64.
215 *Pravda*, 13 April 1984, pp. 1, 4 (there were no women among the ninety-nine listed members of the new government).
216 A. D. Chernev, *229 kremlevskikh vozhdei. Politbyuro, Orgbyuro, Sekretariata TsK Kommunisticheskoi partii v litsakh i tsifrakh* (Moscow: Rodina/Russika, 1996), p. 82. Women were 30.5 per cent of the mass membership of the CPSU, and 8 per cent of its Central Committee: *Izvestiya TsK KPSS*, no. 6, 1991, pp. 27, 28.
217 *Izvestiya TsK KPSS*, no. 6, 1991, p. 28.
218 *Pravda*, 2 June 1989, p. 2.
219 *XIX Vsesoyuznaya konferentsiya Kommunisticheskoi partii Sovetskogo Soyuza, 28 iyunya–1 iyulya 1988 g. Stenograficheskii otchet*, 2 vols. (Moscow: Politizdat, 1988), vol. II, pp. 78–80.
220 *Pravda*, 9 March 1989, p. 2; see also ibid., 5 March 1988, p. 1.
221 *Izvestiya TsK KPSS*, no. 6, 1991, p. 33.
222 Ibid., pp. 34, 32, 37, 38.
223 Gorbachev, *Izbrannye rechi i stat'i*, vol. III, p. 232.
224 M. S. Gorbachev, *Perestroika i novoe myshlenie dlya nashei strany i dlya vsego mira* (Moscow: Politizdat, 1987), pp. 116–17. Addressing the 19th Party Conference in 1988, Gorbachev called for a 'broad road to be opened to women into ruling bodies from top to bottom', but this was so that 'questions that directly affected the interests of women' – not, apparently, more general issues – were 'not resolved without their participation' (*Izbrannye rechi i stat'i*, vol. VI, p. 380).
225 *XIX Vsesoyuznaya konferentsiya*, vol. II, p. 81. A rather different set of figures, suggesting that economic reasons were primary, was reported in *Vestnik statistiki*, no. 1, 1992, p. 52.
226 *Soviet Weekly*, 29 July 1989, p. 5.
227 Ibid., 25 November 1988, p. 15.
228 N. Zakharova, A. Posadskaya, and N. Rimashevskaya in *Kommunist*, no. 4, 1989, pp. 56–65.
229 See respectively *Vestnik statistiki*, no. 1, 1990, p. 47 (women were a somewhat higher 18.5 per cent of the working parliament, the Supreme Soviet), and *Izvestiya TsK KPSS*, no. 6, 1991, p. 38.
230 *Moskovskie novosti*, no. 10, 1989, p. 14.
231 *Izvestiya TsK KPSS*, no. 12, 1990, p. 134.
232 *Soviet Weekly*, 26 November 1988, p. 15.
233 *Izvestiya TsK KPSS*, no. 6, 1991, pp. 25–7.
234 Ibid., no. 12, 1990, p. 134; see similarly *Pravda*, 25 June 1990, p. 5, and *Izvestiya*, 25 November 1990, p. 2.

235 See *Pravda*, 15 August 1990, p. 4, and *Izvestiya*, 13 May 1990, p. 1.

236 *Pravda*, 9 December 1990, p. 3; the proposal was supported ibid., 11 February 1991, p. 4, and in *Izvestiya*, 22 March 1991, p. 7.

237 *Pravda*, 9 April 1991, p. 1.

238 *Rossiiskaya gazeta*, 2 October 1998, p. 3.

239 *Izvestiya*, 25 October 1995, p. 7.

240 *Nezavisimaya gazeta*, 27 March 1997, p. 6.

241 *Izvestiya*, 25 September 1995, p. 7.

242 *RSYe97*, p. 117.

243 See respectively *Segodnya*, 18 February 1998, p. 3; *Rossiya v tsifrakh*, p. 47; and *Ekonomika i zhizn'*, no. 10, 1998, p. 1 (8.6 as compared with 7.9 months).

244 *RSYe97*, p. 112; *Ekonomika i zhizn'*, no. 10, 1998, p. 1.

245 *Izvestiya*, 19 February 1998, p. 5.

246 *RSYe97*, p. 184.

247 Ibid., p. 255.

248 Ibid., pp. 235 (beds), 186–7 (orphanages).

249 *Trud*, 31 May 1996, p. 4.

250 *Izvestiya*, 14 September 1993, p. 5.

251 *Nezavisimaya gazeta*, 9 April 1997, p. 6; other estimates went up to 4 million (*Segodnya*, 24 May 1997, p. 2).

252 *Segodnya*, 24 May 1997, p. 2.

253 *Trud*, 29 May 1996, p. 8.

254 *RSYe97*, p. 93.

255 Ibid., pp. 84, 236.

256 *Rossiiskii statisticheskii yezhegodnik. Statisticheskii sbornik* (Moscow: Goskomstat Rossii, 1998), p. 157.

257 See respectively *Rossiiskaya gazeta*, 31 May 1996, p. 27; *Izvestiya*, 25 October 1995, p. 7.

258 *Rossiiskaya gazeta*, 31 May 1996, p. 27. For a further discussion, see Natalia Khodyreva, 'Sexism and sexual abuse in Russia', in Chris Corrin, ed., *Women in a Violent World: Feminist Analyses and Resistance Across 'Europe'* (Edinburgh: Edinburgh University Press, 1996), pp. 27–43, and Lynne Attwood, '"She was asking for it": rape and domestic violence against women', in Buckley, *Post-Soviet Women*, pp. 99–118.

259 *Nezavisimaya gazeta*, 28 November 1996, p. 6.

260 *Izvestiya*, 30 August 1988, p. 6. For a further discussion, see Elizabeth Waters, 'Restructuring and the "woman question": perestroika and prostitution', *Feminist Review*, no. 33 (Autumn 1989), pp. 3–19.

261 *Sovetskaya Rossiya*, 13 March 1987, p. 4.

262 *Trud*, 31 July 1987, p. 4; and on the question of legislation, *Sovetskoe gosudarstvo i pravo*, no. 2, 1991, p. 71.

263 *Izvestiya*, 14 August 1996, p. 5.

264 Locations in Moscow, and typical charges, were set out in *Argumenty i fakty: Moskva*, no. 24, 1997, p. 14.

265 *Ekspress-gazeta*, no. 41, 1998, p. 1 (I thank Ronald J. Hill for this reference).

266 *Segodnya*, 4 February 1998, p. 7. Doctors in Moscow, in a mass screening in 1997, found that one prostitute in five was in a position to provide her client 'not only with unforgettable memories but also with a couple of

venereal diseases', most often 'the later stages of syphilis' (*Moskovskii komsomolets*, 27 September 1997, p. 1).
267 *Sobesednik*, no. 36, 1997, pp. 2–3.
268 *Izvestiya*, 14 August 1996, p. 5.
269 *Komsomol'skaya pravda*, 10 October 1992, pp. 1, 3 (there were 'over a thousand' child prostitutes in Moscow at this time, p. 3).
270 *Argumenty i fakty*, no. 31, 1996, p. 4.
271 *Segodnya*, 24 May 1997, p. 2. There was another report in *Argumenty i fakty*, no. 36, 1996, p. 7.
272 *Komsomol'skaya pravda*, 12 May 1993, p. 3.
273 *Argumenty i fakty*, no. 9, 1997, p. 9.
274 *Komsomol'skaya pravda*, 12 May 1993, p. 3.
275 *Sunday Telegraph*, 11 January 1998, p. 28.
276 *RSYe97*, p. 243.
277 See respectively *Argumenty i fakty*, no. 29, 1990, p. 5; *Segodnya*, 28 January 1997, p. 7; and *Nezavisimaya gazeta*, 15 May 1997, pp. 1–2 (projection).
278 *Argumenty i fakty*, no. 9, 1997, p. 5; a similar report appeared in *Obshchaya gazeta*, no. 11, 1997, p. 8.

6 CHANGING TIMES, CHANGING VALUES

1 L. A. Onikov and N. V. Shishlin, eds., *Kratkii politicheskii slovar'* (Moscow: Politizdat, 1978), p. 264.
2 L. F. Il'ichev, ed., *Filosofskii entsiklopedicheskii slovar'* (Moscow: Sovetskaya entsiklopediya, 1983), p. 449.
3 L. A. Onikov and N. V. Shishlin, eds., *Kratkii politicheskii slovar'*, 6th edn (Moscow: Politizdat, 1989), p. 350.
4 Onikov and Shishlin, *Kratkii politicheskii slovar'* (1978), pp. 289 and 308–9.
5 Ibid., pp. 159–62.
6 B. A. Grushin, *Mneniya o mire i mir mnenii* (Moscow: Politizdat, 1967), p. 175. The full report appeared as Grushin and V. V. Chikin, *Ispoved' pokoleniya* (Moscow: Moldaya gvardiya, 1962), based on the 17,466 responses that were received (p. 5). For a more general account, see Elizabeth Ann Weinberg, *The Development of Sociology in the Soviet Union* (London: Routledge, 1974), ch. 6.
7 *Kto yest' kto v Rossii. Spravochnoe izdanie* (Moscow: Olimp/EKSMO-Press, 1998), pp. 183–4.
8 *Sotsiologicheskie issledovaniya*, no. 7, 1993, p. 7.
9 On these developments, see M. G. Pugacheva, 'Institut konkretnykh sotsiologicheskikh issledovanii Akademii nauk SSSR, 1968–1972 gody', *Sotsiologicheskii zhurnal*, no. 2, 1994, pp. 158–72, and more generally Vladimir Shlapentokh, *The Politics of Sociology in the Soviet Union* (Boulder, CO: Westview, 1987).
10 *Ogonek*, no. 12, 1988, p. 20.
11 B. Grushin and L. A. Onikov, *Massovaya informatsiya v sovetskom promyshlennom gorode* (Moscow: Politizdat, 1980), p. 414 (67 per cent of letters to the local paper were largely or entirely negative, but 69 per cent of the articles it published were largely or entirely positive).

12 R. A. Safarov, *Obshchestvennoe mnenie i gosudarstvennoe upravlenie* (Moscow: Yuridicheskaya literatura, 1975), pp. 145, 121, 159.

13 See for instance Murray Yanowitch, ed., *Soviet Work Attitudes: The Issue of Participation in Management* (White Plains, NY: Sharpe, 1979).

14 See Darrell P. Slider, 'Party-sponsored public opinion research in the Soviet Union', *Journal of Politics*, vol. 47, no. 1 (February 1985), pp. 209–27.

15 V. S. Korobeinikov, *Piramida mnenii* (Moscow: Molodaya gvardiya, 1981), pp. 176, 173, 182. The establishment of an institute of this kind was proposed in a letter to the party and state leadership from Andrei Sakharov and others (*Posev*, no. 7, 1970, p. 40); Safarov also called for a greater degree of attention to public opinion, and to its systematic investigation (*Pravda*, 25 September 1981, pp. 2–3).

16 M. S. Gorbachev, *Izbrannye rechi i stat'i*, 7 vols. (Moscow: Politizdat, 1987–90), vol. III, p. 241. Legislation on 'national discussion of important questions of state life' was approved the following year: *Vedomosti Verkhovnogo Soveta SSSR*, no. 26, 1987, 30 June 1987.

17 *Spravochnik partiinogo rabotnika*, vol. XXIX (Moscow: Politizdat, 1989), pp. 322–5.

18 Onikov and Shishlin, *Kratkii politicheskii slovar'* (1989), p. 378.

19 *Plenum Tsentral'nogo Komiteta KPSS 14–15 iyunya 1983 goda. Stenograficheskii otchet* (Moscow: Politizdat, 1983), pp. 40, 200. The Centre, it was agreed in a July 1987 resolution adopted jointly by the Central Committee, the Soviet government, and the All-Union Council of Trade Unions, would in fact be established under the auspices of the All-Union Council and the State Committee on Labour and Social Questions, and it would 'systematically conduct surveys of the population on the most important social-economic themes' (*O korennoi perestroike upravleniya ekonomikoi. Sbornik dokumentov* [Moscow: Politizdat, 1988], p. 242).

20 *Détente*, no. 8 (Winter 1987), pp. 11–12.

21 *Materialy XIX Vsesoyuznoi konferentsii Kommunisticheskoi partii Sovetskogo Soyuza, 28 iyunya–1 iyulya 1988 g.* (Moscow: Politizdat, 1988), pp. 69, 26, 144.

22 In spite of the changes that had taken place in official thinking, Levada recalled, it was only Zaslavskaya's 'enormous scholarly and public authority' together with the 'organisational talent and enthusiasm' of Grushin that had made it possible: *Sotsiologicheskii zhurnal*, no. 4, 1997, p. 220. Zaslavskaya herself had been greatly impressed by the Institut für Demoskopie in West Germany, which she had visited in 1972 and again in 1989, but refused to take on the organisational responsibility unless Boris Grushin was her deputy (he left within two years to establish his own service): *Ekonomicheskie i sotsial'nye peremeny: monitoring obshchestvennogo mneniya*, no. 1, 1998, pp. 8–9.

23 *Pravda*, 18 March 1988, p. 4.

24 *Moskovskie novosti*, no. 35, 1988, p. 10.

25 *Ekonomicheskie i sotsial'nye peremeny*, no. 5, 1998, p. 45. For two inventories of the Centre's early findings, see Yu. A. Levada, ed., *Yest' mnenie! Itogi sotsiologicheskogo oprosa* (Moscow: Progress, 1990), and Levada, ed., *Sovetskii prostoi chelovek. Opyt sotsial'nogo portreta na rubezhe 90-kh* (Moscow: Mirovoi okean, 1993). For a convenient guide, see *A Catalogue of VCIOM*

Surveys, 1989–1996 (Glasgow: University of Strathclyde, Centre for the Study of Public Policy, SPP 281, 1997).

26 *Mir mnenii i mneniya o mire*, no. 6, 1994, p. 11.

27 For an overview, see Richard Rose and Evgeny Tikhomirov, *Trends in the New Russia Barometer, 1992–1995* (Glasgow: University of Strathclyde, Centre for the Study of Public Policy, SPP 256, 1995).

28 See *Central and Eastern Eurobarometer*, 8 issues to date (Brussels: European Commission Directorate General X for Information, Communication, Culture, Audiovisual, 1991–8); Eurobarometer surveys have been conducted in the European Union member countries themselves since 1973.

29 For a retrospective survey of its findings, see Richard B. Dobson, *Is Russia Turning the Corner? Changing Russian Public Opinion, 1991–1996* (Washington, DC: USIA, 1996).

30 *Sotsiologicheskie issledovaniya*, no. 6, 1993, p. 39.

31 *Segodnya*, 28 December 1995, p. 3. The 1993 result, for Boris Grushin, was nothing less than a 'fiasco' (*Mir mnenii i mneniya o mire*, no. 5, 1994, p. 9). A fuller discussion is available in A. V. Dmitriev and Zh. T. Toshchenko, 'Sotsiologicheskii opros i politika', *Sotsiologicheskie issledovaniya*, no. 5, 1994, pp. 42–51; Vladimir Shlapentokh, 'The 1993 Russian election polls', *Public Opinion Quarterly*, vol. 58, no. 4 (Winter 1994), pp. 579–602; and William L. Miller, Stephen White, and Paul Heywood, 'Twenty-five days to go: measuring and interpreting the trends in public opinion during the 1993 Russian election campaign', *Public Opinion Quarterly*, vol. 60, no. 1 (Spring 1996), pp. 106–27. The 1995 election is considered in the same context in Ye. G. Andryushchenko, et al., 'Oprosy i vybory 1995 goda', *Sotsiologicheskie issledovaniya*, no. 6, 1996, pp. 3–17.

32 For a comprehensive review of survey findings, see Matthew Wyman, *Public Opinion in Postcommunist Russia* (London: Macmillan, 1997). There are several critical discussions of the experience of polling in the Russian context, including James Alexander, 'Surveying attitudes in Russia: a representation of formlessness', *Communist and Post-Communist Studies*, vol. 30, no. 2 (June 1997), pp. 107–27; James L. Gibson, 'Survey research in the past and future USSR: reflections on the methodology of mass opinion surveys', *Research in Micropolitics*, vol. 4 (1994), pp. 87–114; John P. Willerton and Lee Sigelman, 'Public opinion research in the USSR: opportunities and pitfalls', *Journal of Communist Studies*, vol. 7, no. 2 (June 1991), pp. 217–34; and Frederic J. Fleron Jr and Richard Ahl, 'Does the public matter for democratization in Russia? What we have learned from "third wave" transitions and public opinion surveys', in Harry Eckstein, et al., eds., *Can Democracy Take Root in Post-Soviet Russia? Explorations in State–Society Relations* (Lanham, MA: Rowman & Littlefield, 1998), pp. 287–327.

33 *Ekonomicheskie i sotsial'nye peremeny*, no. 2, 1999, p. 67.

34 Ibid., p. 56.

35 Ibid., no. 2, 1997, pp. 72 and 87.

36 *Ekonomicheskie i sotsial'nye peremeny*, no. 3, 1997, p. 79.

37 *Central and Eastern Eurobarometer*, no. 7, Annex Fig. 3. Similar figures were reported in the New Russia Barometer: Richard Rose, *Getting Things Done*

With Social Capital: New Russia Barometer VIII (Glasgow: University of Strathclyde, Centre for the Study of Public Policy, SPP 303, 1998), p. 30 (52 per cent thought 'state control [was] the best way to run an enterprise', 24 per cent thought it was 'best run by private entrepreneurs'). A rather different conclusion emerges from William L. Miller, Stephen White, and Paul Heywood, *Values and Political Change in Postcommunist Europe* (London: Macmillan, 1998), pp. 109–10, but support was 'neither unqualified nor enthusiastic' and it reflected opinion in 1993 when the practical implications of a market economy were less obvious.

38 See *Ekonomicheskie i sotsial'nye peremeny*, no. 3, 1997, p. 78 (91.2 and 88.3 per cent respectively were in favour).

39 Ibid., no. 2, 1997, p. 81 (51.2 per cent agreed, 17.6 per cent disagreed).

40 Ibid., no. 5, 1998, p. 56.

41 James L. Gibson, 'Political and economic markets: changes in the connections between attitudes toward political democracy and a market economy within the mass culture of Russia and Ukraine', *Journal of Politics*, vol. 58, no. 4 (November 1996), pp. 965–6.

42 *Ekonomicheskie i sotsial'nye peremeny*, no. 5, 1998, p. 54.

43 Ibid. (37 per cent, by contrast, were prepared to tolerate their situation).

44 Ibid.

45 Ibid. (13.1 per cent thought there would be an improvement in the coming year but 63.6 per cent took the opposite view).

46 Ibid., no. 4, 1997, p. 56. The USIA found similarly that 20 per cent in 1998 thought the most difficult times were behind them, but that 64 per cent thought they were still to come (15 per cent were unsure): *USIA Opinion Analysis* M-165-98, 5 February 1998.

47 Richard Rose, *New Russia Barometer VI: After the Presidential Election* (Glasgow: University of Strathclyde, Centre for the Study of Public Policy, SPP 272, 1996), p. 12.

48 *Ekonomicheskie i sotsial'nye peremeny*, no. 4, 1998, p. 74.

49 Ibid., no. 5, 1998, p. 56. In a separate inquiry, 52.6 per cent found the political situation 'critical' and 32.4 per cent found it 'catastrophic' (*Nezavisimaya gazeta*, 22 April 1998, p. 8).

50 Ibid., no. 3, 1998, p. 61.

51 Ibid., no. 4, 1997, p. 56.

52 Dobson, *Is Russia Turning the Corner?*, p. 31.

53 *Central and Eastern Eurobarometer*, no. 7, Annex Fig. 6.

54 *Moskovskii komsomolets*, 11 March 1998, p. 3.

55 *Argumenty i fakty*, no. 45, 1997, p. 10.

56 Miller, et al., *Values and Political Change*, p. 90; similar results were reported in *Segodnya*, 30 January 1999, p. 2.

57 *Vek*, no. 42, 1997, p. 10.

58 There were 51 per cent in favour, 39 per cent against: *Moskovskii komsomolets*, 11 March 1998, p. 3.

59 *Ekonomicheskie i sotsial'nye peremeny*, no. 2, 1997, p. 81.

60 See respectively Rose, *Getting Things Done*, p. 44 (41 per cent were in favour, 59 per cent opposed), and *Moskovskii komsomolets*, 11 March 1998, p. 3.

61 Dobson, *Is Russia Turning the Corner?*, p. 32; similarly *Izvestiya*, 13 March

1998, p. 1. In a later survey, as many as 85 per cent regretted the demise of the USSR (*Novye izvestiya*, 30 January 1999, p. 1).

62 Richard Rose and Christian Haerpfer, *New Russia Barometer III: The Results* (Glasgow: University of Strathclyde, Centre for the Study of Public Policy, SPP 228, 1994), p. 41 (4 per cent thought the disintegration of the USSR had affected their living standards for the better, but 76 per cent thought they had been affected for the worse).

63 *Argumenty i fakty*, no. 12, 1996, p. 1.

64 *USIA Opinion Analysis* M-000-96, 23 December 1996, pp. 1–3.

65 Miller, et al., *Values and Political Change*, pp. 86–7 (see also ch. 8).

66 *Ekonomicheskie i sotsial'nye peremeny*, no. 3, 1998, p. 57.

67 Ibid., no. 4, 1998, pp. 76–7.

68 Richard Rose and Christian Haerpfer, *Trends in Democracies and Markets: New Democracies Barometer 1991–1998* (Glasgow: University of Strathclyde, Centre for the Study of Public Policy, SPP 308, 1998), p. 50; Rose, *Getting Things Done*, pp. 22–5.

69 Rose and Haerpfer, *Trends*, p. 31; Rose, *Getting Things Done*, pp. 40–3.

70 Rose and Haerpfer, *Trends*, pp. 26, 28.

71 *Ekonomicheskie i sotsial'nye peremeny*, no. 3, 1997, p. 78.

72 Ibid., no. 5, 1998, pp. 54–5.

73 Ibid., no. 3, 1998, pp. 65–6. Similar findings are reported in Dobson, *Is Russia Turning the Corner?*, p. 32 (a time series); Rose, *Getting Things Done*, pp. 58–9; and *Argumenty i fakty*, no. 29, 1997, p. 2.

74 *Ekonomicheskie i sotsial'nye peremeny*, no. 1, 1998, pp. 80–1.

75 *The Times*, 12 July 1982, p. 1. For a fuller discussion of the evolution of letter-writing and petitioning over the Soviet period, see Gregory L. Freeze, *From Supplication to Revolution: A Documentary Social History of Imperial Russia* (Oxford: Oxford University Press, 1988); Sheila Fitzpatrick, ed., 'Petitions and denunciations in Russia from Muscovy to the Stalin era', *Russian History*, vol. 24, no. 1–2 (Spring–Summer 1997); A. K. Sokolov, ed., *Golos naroda. Pis'ma i otkliki ryadovykh sovetskikh grazhdan o sobytiyakh 1918–1932 gg.* (Moscow: Rosspen, 1997); and I. B. Orlov and A. Ya. Livshin, 'Sotsiologicheskii analiz "pisem vo vlast'"' (1917–1927-e gody)', *Sotsiologicheskie issledovaniya*, no. 2, 1999, pp. 79–87.

76 Ye. N. Roshchepkina, 'O rabote s pis'mami grazhdan v pervye gody sovetskoi vlasti (1917–1924 gg.)', *Sovetskie arkhivy*, no. 6, 1979, p. 23.

77 See particularly *Novyi mir*, no. 6, 1992, pp. 281–300.

78 Lev Karpinsky in *Vospominaniya o V. I. Lenine*, vol. IV (Moscow: Politizdat, 1969), p. 283.

79 *Neizvestnaya Rossiya. XX vek*, vol. III (Moscow: Istoricheskoe nasledie, 1993), pp. 200, 222.

80 Regional party first secretaries, in fact, 'were often quite responsive to appeals from ordinary people' at this time (Sheila Fitzpatrick, 'Supplicants and citizens: public letter-writing in Soviet Russia in the 1930s', *Slavic Review*, vol. 55, no. 1 [Spring 1996], p. 104). For a more general account, see V. K. Romanovsky, 'Pis'ma rabochikh kak istochnik dlya izucheniya sotsial'nogo oblika rabochego klassa 20-kh godov', *Vspomogatel'nye istoricheskie distsipliny*, vol. 21 (1990), pp. 54–65.

81 E. B. Pashukanis and P. V. Tumanov, eds., *Vsenarodnoe obsuzhdenie proekta Konstitutsii Soyuza SSR* (Moscow: Partizdat, 1936), p. 5. See further Ellen Wimberg, 'Socialism, democratism and criticism: the Soviet press and the national discussion of the 1936 draft constitution', *Soviet Studies*, vol. 44, no. 2 (1992), pp. 313–32; and V. A. Syrkin, 'Massovyi istochnik po istorii sovetskoi derevni', *Otechestvennye arkhivy*, no. 5, 1996, pp. 54–7.

82 Robert C. Tucker, *Stalin in Power: The Revolution from Above, 1928–1941* (New York: Norton, 1990), pp. 357–8.

83 For the text, see *Partiinaya zhizn'*, no. 18, 1967, p. 8.

84 For the text, see *Vedomosti Verkhovnogo Soveta SSSR*, no. 17, 1968, art. 144, 12 April 1988; the decree was expanded in scope in 1980 (ibid., no. 11, 1980, art. 192, 4 March 1980).

85 See respectively Arts. 49 and 58. Another resolution on the party's own 'work with letters' was adopted after the 26th Party Congress in 1981: *Partiinaya zhizn'*, no. 8, 1981, pp. 9–11.

86 L. I. Brezhnev, *Leninskim kursom. Rechi i stat'i*, vol. VI (Moscow: Politizdat, 1978), p. 518.

87 *Voprosy istorii KPSS*, no. 10, 1990, pp. 73–7. For the same author's earlier study, see V. P. Smirnov, *Referendum v pechati* (Moscow: Mysl', 1978). The number of proposals that had been received in the course of the discussion was rather arbitrarily determined: Supreme Soviet staff thought it was about 300,000, Central Committee staff thought it had been 600,000, and Brezhnev simply decided 'let's say 400,000' (Yuri Korolev, *Kremlevskii sovetnik* [Moscow: Olimp, 1995], p. 197).

88 Gorbachev, *Izbrannye rechi i stat'i*, vol. II, p. 164.

89 *Pravda*, 24 February 1989, p. 2.

90 Ibid., 13 October 1987, p. 1.

91 *Izvestiya*, 7 August 1991, p. 1.

92 Lloyd S. Fischel, ed., *Dear Mr Gorbachev* (Edinburgh: Canongate, 1990), p. 187; V. Korotich and S. Koen, intr. to V. Ye. Kachanov, ed., *Amerikantsy pishut Gorbachevu* (Moscow: Progress, 1988), pp. 247, 102, 300.

93 Gorbachev, *Izbrannye rechi i stat'i*, vol. V, p. 497.

94 Fischel, *Dear Mr Gorbachev*, pp. xv–xvi, 6.

95 Diego Cordovez and Selig S. Harrison, *Out of Afghanistan: The Inside Story of the Soviet Withdrawal* (New York: Oxford University Press, 1995), p. 247.

96 *Narodnyi deputat*, no. 1, 1992, pp. 118–23.

97 *Pravda*, 19 September 1990, p. 2.

98 *Izvestiya*, 7 August 1991, p. 1. Staff found he 'lost interest' as his post became increasingly hostile, but the head of his staff still placed 'a couple of dozen' on his desk every day: V. I. Boldin, *Krushenie p'edestala. Shtrikhi k portretu M. S. Gorbacheva* (Moscow: Respublika, 1995), p. 254.

99 S. M. Gurevich, *Rabota s pis'mami v redaktsii* (Moscow: Vysshaya shkola, 1991), p. 7.

100 *Spravochnik partiinogo rabotnika*, vol. 21, pp. 503–4; and for 1988, *Izvestiya TsK KPSS*, no. 4, 1990, p. 157.

101 See *Partiinaya zhizn'*, no. 17, 1979, pp. 22–30.

102 Ibid., pp. 26–7.

103 See for instance *Izvestiya TsK KPSS*, no. 4, 1990, pp. 157–62, and no. 9,

1990, pp. 35–54 (which quotes numerous extracts from the letters themselves); both surveys noted the 'politicisation' of the party's postbag (pp. 157 and 35 respectively).

104 Ibid., no. 9, 1990, pp. 133, 134.

105 Ibid., no. 7, 1990, p. 21.

106 Ibid.

107 Ibid.

108 Ibid.

109 Ibid., p. 22.

110 Ibid., no. 9, 1990, p. 39.

111 Ibid.

112 Ibid., p. 40.

113 Ibid., p. 41.

114 *Pravda*, 25 May 1989, p. 1.

115 Gurevich, *Rabota s pis'mami*, pp. 35, 24, 25, 23. *Pravda*'s postbag was 473,201 in 1989: *Pravda*, 6 January 1990, p. 3.

116 Gurevich, *Rabota s pis'mami*, p. 23.

117 Ibid., p. 45.

118 Ibid., p. 46; for the 'main correspondent', see Yu. Rytov, ed., *Komandirovka po pros'be chitatelei* (Moscow: Izvestiya, 1985), p. 6. A selection of letters to the paper since 1917 appeared in L. Tolkunov, ed., *Ot glavnogo korrespondenta* (Moscow: Izvestiya, 1970).

119 *Knizhnoe obozrenie*, no. 32, 1988, p. 15 (there were further letters of support in the following issue); *Pravda*, 23 March 1985, p. 3 (the campaign itself is considered in Stephen White, *Russia Goes Dry: Alcohol, State and Society* [Cambridge: Cambridge University Press, 1996]).

120 *Argumenty i fakty*, no. 24, 1996, p. 12. A survey of letters to a range of newspapers and journals in the late 1980s found that there had in fact been a general belief that the society needed 'not radical reform, but only a few changes' (*Svobodnaya mysl'*, no. 7, 1993, p. 80). Equally, the archives suggested, there had been 'few' letters in support of Solzhenitsyn after the 1974 decision to expel him: *Svobodnaya mysl'*, no. 6, 1992, p. 81.

121 Gurevich, *Rabota s pis'mami*, p. 54; *Pravda*, for instance, received over 3,000 visitors in 1990: *Pravda*, 4 January 1991, p. 4.

122 *Izvestiya*, 11 June 1992, p. 3.

123 *Rossiiskie vesti*, 16 March 1994, p. 2.

124 See for instance *Argumenty i fakty*, no. 42, 1992, pp. 1–2; *Trud*, 6 October 1992, pp. 1–2.

125 There were 300 letters in 1996–7 that secured a response of this kind: *Argumenty i fakty*, no. 3, 1998, p. 5.

126 Ibid.

127 *Izvestiya*, however, made clear that it would be giving less prominence to its postbag in future: 2 January 1992, p. 3.

128 *Argumenty i fakty*, no. 37, 1996, p. 2.

129 Ibid., no. 38–9, 1992, p. 1.

130 Ibid., no. 47, 1993, p. 12.

131 Ibid., no. 24, 1996, p. 16.

132 Ibid., no. 9, 1995, p. 16.

133 Ibid., no. 34, 1993, p. 8.
134 Ibid., no. 2, 1994, p. 16.
135 Ibid., no. 9, 1993, p. 16.
136 Ibid., no. 43, 1993, p. 8.
137 Ibid., no. 10, 1993, p. 12.
138 Ibid., no. 8, 1993, p. 12.
139 Ibid., no. 23, 1993, p. 12.
140 Ibid., no. 38–9, 1992, p. 13; no. 41, 1992, p. 1; no. 38–9, p. 2; and no. 41, 1992, p. 5.
141 Ibid., no. 43, 1993, p. 8.
142 ibid., no. 39, 1991, p. 6, and no. 10, 1993, p. 10.
143 Ibid., no. 10, 1992, p. 8.
144 Ibid., no. 51, 1991, p. 12.
145 Ibid., no. 14, 1993, p. 8.
146 *The Times*, 22 September 1992, p. 10.
147 *Argumenty i fakty*, no. 39, 1993, p. 8.
148 Ibid., no. 38–9, 1992, p. 9.
149 Ibid., no. 15, 1998, p. 24.
150 Ibid., no. 9, 1993, p. 16.
151 Ibid., no. 43, 1993, p. 8.
152 Ibid., no. 48, 1995, p. 12; similarly no. 4, 1996, p. 1.
153 Ibid., no. 15, 1996, p. 13, and no. 43, 1993, p. 8.
154 Ibid., no. 6, 1996, p. 1.
155 Ibid., no. 30, 1994, p. 13.
156 Ibid., no. 3, 1993, p. 8.
157 Ibid., no. 38, 1994, p. 13.
158 Ibid., no. 4, 1993, p. 6.
159 Ibid., no. 37, 1993, p. 5.
160 Ibid., no. 6, 1996, p. 16.
161 Ibid., no. 6, 1992, p. 8.
162 Ibid., no. 5, 1995, p. 16.
163 Ibid., no. 13, 1995, p. 16.
164 Ibid., no. 38–9, 1992, p. 15.
165 Ibid., no. 41, 1994, p. 16, and no. 34, 1993, p. 13.
166 Ibid., no. 43, 1993, p. 4, and no. 43, 1993, p. 8.
167 Ibid., no. 6, 1993, p. 12, no. 41, 1992, p. 5, and no. 38–9, 1992, p. 3.
168 Ibid., no. 17, 1993, p. 8.
169 Ibid., p. 12.
170 Ibid., no. 14, 1993, p. 12.
171 Ibid., no. 38–9, 1992, p. 2.
172 Ibid., no. 3, 1993, p. 12.
173 Ibid., no. 38–9, 1992, p. 11.
174 Ibid., no. 17, 1993, p. 5; similarly no. 38–9, 1992, p. 3.
175 Ibid., no. 17, 1993, p. 12.
176 Calculated from *Itogi Vsesoyuznoi perepisi naseleniya 1989 goda* (Minneapolis: EastView, 1992), vol. II, part 1, pp. 13–14.
177 See for instance V. T. Syzrantsev, ed., *Kratkii slovar'–spravochnik agitatora i politinformatora* (Moscow: Politizdat, 1977), p. 225.

178 V. D. Kobetsky, 'Issledovanie dinamiki religioznosti naseleniya v SSSR', in V. D. Sherdakov, ed., *Ateizm. Religiya. Sovremennost'* (Leningrad: Nauka, 1973), pp. 126–7, 129. According to the census that was conducted in 1937 but whose results were suppressed at the time, 42.9 per cent of the population aged over sixteen were atheist, 42.3 per cent were Orthodox, and 14.8 per cent subscribed to other faiths (calculated from Yu. A. Polyakov, ed., *Vsesoyuznaya perepis' naseleniya 1937 g. Kratkie itogi* [Moscow: Institut istorii AN SSSR, 1991], pp. 106–7).

179 *Pravda*, 30 March 1979, pp. 2–3.

180 Sherdakov, *Ateizm*, p. 129.

181 *Rossiiskii statisticheskii yezhegodnik. Statisticheskii sbornik* (Moscow: Goskomstat Rossii, 1997, pp. 47, 50–1; Nathaniel Davis, *A Long Walk to Church: A Contemporary History of Russian Orthodoxy* (Boulder, CO: Westview, 1995), p. xi.

182 See Raymond E. Zickel, ed., *Soviet Union: A Country Study*, 2nd edn (Washington, DC: US Government Publishing Office, 1991), p. 188.

183 *Materialy mezhvuzovskoi nauchnoi konferentsii po probleme vozrastaniya aktivnosti obshchestvennogo soznaniya v period stroitel'stva kommunizma* (Kursk: Kurskii gosudarstvennyi pedagogicheskii institut, 1968), pp. 361–2.

184 S. I. Tereshchenko, et al., *Gor'kaya balka. Kompleksnoe sotsiologicheskoe issledovanie kolkhoza imeni V. I. Lenina* (Stavropol': Stravropol'skoe knizhnoe izdatel'stvo, 1972), pp. 114–16.

185 *Sovetskaya Rossiya*, 29 August 1992, p. 2.

186 For a fuller discussion, see for instance Sabrina Petra Ramet, ed., *Religious Policy in the Soviet Union* (Cambridge: Cambridge University Press, 1993); John Anderson, *Religion, State and Politics in the Soviet Union and Successor States* (Cambridge: Cambridge University Press, 1994); Davis, *A Long Walk*; and Jane Ellis, *The Russian Orthodox Church: Triumphalism and Defensiveness* (London: Macmillan, 1996). The survey evidence is considered further in Stephen White and Ian McAllister, 'The politics of religion in postcommunist Russia', *Religion, State and Society*, vol. 25, no. 3 (September 1997), pp. 235–52, and in White and McAllister, 'Orthodoxy and political behavior in postcommunist Russia', *Review of Religious Research*, forthcoming.

187 See for instance the two-page article on 'increasing the effectiveness of atheistic propaganda' in *Pravda*, 13 September 1985, pp. 2–3.

188 *Pravda Vostoka*, 25 November 1986, p. 1.

189 *Kommunist*, no. 4, 1988, pp. 121–2.

190 Gorbachev, *Izbrannye rechi i stat'i*, vol. VI, pp. 201–3.

191 *Izvestiya*, 9 April 1988, p. 3.

192 For Gorbachev's baptism, see *Izvestiya TsK KPSS*, no. 8, 1989, p. 66; for his mother's church attendance, see Michael Bordeaux, *Gorbachev, Glasnost and the Gospel* (London: Hodder and Stoughton, 1990), p. 24. A different account is provided by Davis, *A Long Walk*, who visited Privol'noe in 1991 and noted that the village church had been destroyed many years earlier (p. 253).

193 *Pravda*, 29 November 1991, p. 1 (Kremlin cathedrals), and *Izvestiya*, 7 February 1991, p. 3 (return of monasteries). Over 4,000 new Orthodox

churches were opened between 1985 and 1990: *Otechestvennye arkhivy*, no. 1, 1995, p. 61.

194 *Pravda*, 16 March 1990, p. 6.

195 *Izvestiya*, 7 June 1994, p. 5. On charity work, see Anne White, 'Charity, self-help and politics in Russia, 1985–1991', *Europe–Asia Studies*, vol. 45, no. 5 (1993), pp. 787–810.

196 *Pravda*, 30 December 1989, p. 3, and 4 February 1991, p. 6.

197 *Izvestiya*, 7 January 1991, p. 1.

198 For the text, see *Vedomosti S"ezda narodnykh deputatov SSSR i Verkhovnogo Soveta SSSR*, no. 11, 1990, item 164.

199 Ibid., no. 41, 1990, item 813. A corresponding Russian law was adopted on 25 October 1990: *Vedomosti S"ezda narodnykh deputatov RSFSR i Verkhovnogo Soveta RSFSR*, no. 21, 1990, item 240.

200 *Materialy XXVIII S"ezda Kommunisticheskoi partii Sovetskogo Soyuza* (Moscow: Politizdat, 1990), rule 2, pp. 108–9.

201 TsKhSD, Moscow, *fond* 89, *perechen'* 20, doc. 66, April 1991.

202 *Vedomosti S"ezda narodnykh deputatov SSSR*, no. 37, 1991, item 1083.

203 *Vedomosti S"ezda narodnykh deputatov RSFSR*, no. 52, 1991, item 1865.

204 *Izvestiya*, 10 July 1991, p. 1, and 11 June 1992, p. 3 (Yeltsin).

205 *New York Times*, 8 April 1991, p. A6.

206 *Nezavisimaya gazeta*, 31 December 1994, p. 13. For a further discussion, see Andrew Gentes, 'The life, death and resurrection of the Cathedral of Christ the Saviour', *History Workshop Journal*, no. 46 (Autumn 1998), pp. 63–95.

207 *Izvestiya*, 4 April 1995, p. 5.

208 For a clear presentation of Orthodox teaching, see for instance Timothy Ware, *The Orthodox Church*, new edn (Harmondsworth: Penguin, 1993).

209 According to documents that are now available, three metropolitans played a key role in the Kremlin's ideological battle with the West, reporting directly to KGB handlers. Metropolitan Yuvenalii of Krutitsy, former head of the Orthodox Church's external relations department, worked under the codename Adamant, using his influential position within the World Council of Churches to attack as 'falsehoods and lies' reports of the arrests of Orthodox priests and the destruction of churches in the Soviet Union. Filaret of Kiev was another church leader with a KGB codename, and who was active (for instance) during the Gorbachev–Reagan summit at Iceland in 1987 where, as his KGB handler reported, he 'fulfilled the task of providing religious circles in the West with objective information and impressed upon them the need for positive action in support of the peaceful initiatives of the Soviet Union' (*Scotland on Sunday*, 5 July 1998, p. 11). According to M. V. Shkarovsky, the CPSU had been conducting a 'cadres policy' in the Orthodox Church since the 1950s: *Russkaya pravoslavnaya tserkov' i sovetskoe gosudarstvo v 1943–1964 godakh* (St Petersburg: Dean + Adia-M, 1995), p. 11. Relations between the 'last Soviet Patriarch' (Pimen, who died in 1990) and the party and state leadership are examined in the light of archival sources in *Otechestvennye arkhivy*, no. 1, 1995, pp. 27–66. On the current Patriarch, see below, p. 212.

210 For perceptions of the 'privileged' position of the Orthodox Church, see

for instance *Sotsiologicheskie issledovaniya*, no. 5, 1994, p. 10 (17 per cent of Orthodox believers themselves agreed with this view).

211 *Moskovskie novosti*, no. 11, 1996, p. 34.

212 For the 'explosion', see Levada, ed., *Sovetskii prostoi chelovek*, p. 217; a figure of 10 per cent of believers in 1988 is reported in L. M. Mitrokhin, ed., *Religiya i politika v postkommunisticheskoi Rossii* (Moscow: Institut filosofii RAN, 1994), p. 35. The stabilisation of levels of religious belief is suggested in for instance *Svobodnaya mysl'*, no. 11, 1998, p. 95, and levels of trust were falling after 1993 (p. 96; see also table 8.1), although there is evidence of a continuing increase in levels of Orthodox affiliation (White and McAllister, 'Politics of religion', p. 242, based on survey data between 1991 and 1996).

213 See V. I. Garadzha, *Sotsiologiya religii* (Moscow: Aspekt Press, 1996), p. 226. Somewhat lower figures for 'believers' are reported in *Nauka i religiya*, no. 1, p. 33 (49.6 per cent), and in *Ekonomicheskie i sotsial'nye peremeny*, no. 1, 1999, p. 86 (52.5 per cent).

214 Ibid. (37 per cent had been christened and 5.7 per cent had christened themselves).

215 Boris Dubin, ibid., no. 6, 1996, pp. 15–16.

216 Our 1996 survey findings accord in this respect with VTsIOM data reported in *Svobodnaya mysl'*, no. 11, 1998, p. 99.

217 Ibid., p. 103.

218 Based on a nationally representative survey conducted by Russian Public Opinion and Market Research in January–February 1996 (n=1581), reported more fully in Miller, et al., *Values and Political Change*; similar results for 1997 are reported in *Ekonomicheskie i sotsial'nye peremeny*, no. 1, 1999, p. 86 (5.7 per cent).

219 For the United Kingdom, see *Social Trends*, no. 28 (London: Stationery Office, 1998), p. 228, reporting a 1996 survey. For the United States, the figures are derived from the General Social Survey, National Public Opinion Research Center, University of Chicago, reporting a 1994 survey. There were lower levels of attendance only in Belarus and Latvia, in Europe-wide surveys (*Svobodnaya mysl'*, no. 1, 1997, p. 80).

220 *Svobodnaya mysl'*, no. 11, 1998, p. 99.

221 Mitrokhin, *Religiya i politika*, p. 49 (22 per cent of self-identified believers reported praying on a regular basis).

222 Ibid., p. 49 (just 25 per cent believed in heaven and hell); only 45 per cent of believers, in another survey, believed in life after death (*Svobodnaya mysl'*, no. 1, 1997, p. 80).

223 Mitrokhin, *Religiya i politika*, p. 50. For the evil eye and abominable snowman, see Filatov and Furman in *Religion, State and Society*, vol. 22, no. 1 (March 1994), pp. 89–90.

224 *Svobodnaya mysl'*, no. 1, 1997, p. 81.

225 See respectively Mitrokhin, *Religiya i politika*, p. 49, and *Segodnya*, 7 May 1994, p. 11. For 'situational religiosity', see Garadzha, *Sotsiologiya religii*, p. 227.

226 *Ekonomicheskie i sotsial'nye peremeny*, no. 6, 1996, p. 18. White and McAllister found similarly that Yabloko and the Liberal Democrats had a slight

advantage among the self-identified Orthodox, and Yabloko among those who indicated that they were 'religious', but the differences were very small ('Orthodoxy and political behavior').

227 *Ekonomicheskie i sotsial'nye peremeny*, no. 6, 1996, pp. 17–18.
228 *Rossiiskaya gazeta*, 1 October 1997, pp. 3–4.
229 *Guardian*, 23 March 1998, p. 12, and 12 February 1999, p. 17.
230 See for instance Mark Rhodes, 'Religious believers in Russia', *RFE/RL Research Report*, vol. 1, no. 14, 3 April 1992, pp. 60–4.
231 *Svobodnaya mysl'*, no. 8, 1996, p. 118.
232 Miller, et al., *Values and Political Change*, pp. 260–3.
233 *Polis*, no. 3, 1993, pp. 144–5.
234 *Ekonomicheskie i sotsial'nye peremeny*, no. 6, 1996, p. 17; believers were similarly persuaded that non-Russians 'had too much influence'.
235 Anthony Heath, Bridget Taylor, and Gabor Toka, 'Religion, morality and politics', in Roger Jowell, et al., eds., *International Social Attitudes: The 10th BSA report* (Aldershot: Dartmouth, 1993), pp. 57–8.
236 *Independent*, 7 January 1998, p. 12. Subsequent reports, based upon KGB documents left behind in Estonian archives, identified the Patriarch as a 'fully fledged KGB spy' who had used his connections to secure his rapid advancement (*Guardian*, 12 February 1999, p. 18).
237 See for instance the reported homosexual murder in *Moskovskii komsomolets*, 27 September 1997, p. 1; or the controversies reported in *Sovershenno sekretno*, no. 5, 1999, pp. 3–5, and in *Nezavisimaya gaseta*, 2 June 1999, pp. 9, 11.
238 *Svobodnaya mysl'*, no. 5, 1994, p. 54.

7 RUSSIA AND THE WIDER WORLD

1 Russians, as Isaiah Berlin put it, combined a sense of the West as 'enviably self-restrained, clever, efficient, and successful: but also as being cramped, cold, mean, calculating, and fenced in, without capacity for large views or generous emotion' (*Russian Thinkers* [London: Hogarth Press, 1978], p. 181). For the wider context, see for instance Paul Dukes, *October and the World* (London: Macmillan, 1979).
2 See for instance Ivo J. Lederer, ed., *Russian Foreign Policy: Essays in Perspective* (New Haven, CT: Yale University Press, 1962); Robert H. Donaldson and Joseph L. Nogee begin their study of *The Foreign Policy of Russia: Changing Systems, Enduring Interests* with a chapter on 'the tsarist roots of Russia's foreign policy' (Armonk, NY: Sharpe, 1998), ch. 1.
3 John L. H. Keep, *Soldiers of the Tsar. Army and Society in Russia, 1462–1874* (Oxford: Clarendon Press, 1985), p. 145.
4 Walter M. Pinter, 'The burden of defense in Imperial Russia, 1725–1914', *Russian Review*, vol. 43, no. 3 (October 1984), pp. 231–59.
5 Stephen White and Stephen Revell, 'Revolution and integration in Soviet international diplomacy 1917–1991', *Review of International Studies*, forthcoming.
6 See Stephen White, *The Origins of Detente: The Genoa Conference and*

Soviet–Western relations, 1921–1922 (Cambridge: Cambridge University Press, 1985).

7 *Pervyi kongress Kominterna* (Moscow: Partiinoe izdatel'stvo, 1933), p. 199.

8 *Vneshnyaya torgovlya SSSR v 1987 g. Statisticheskii sbornik* (Moscow: Finansy i statistika, 1988), p. 4.

9 Half a million tourists visited the USSR in 1950, for instance, but there were over 5 million in the late 1980s (*Pravda*, 24 September 1988, p. 3).

10 For more comprehensive accounts of Russian foreign policy, see Peter Shearman, ed., *Russian Foreign Policy Since 1990* (Boulder, CO: Westview, 1995); Mette Skak, *From Empire to Anarchy: Postcommunist Foreign Policy and International Relations* (London: Hurst, 1996); Neil Malcolm, Alex Pravda, Roy Allison, and Margot Light, *Internal Factors in Russian Foreign Policy* (Oxford: Oxford University Press for the RIIA, 1996); Mark Webber, *The International Politics of Russia and the Successor States* (Manchester: Manchester University Press, 1996); Mike Bowker, *Russian Foreign Policy and the End of the Cold War* (Aldershot: Dartmouth, 1997); Donaldson and Nogee, *The Foreign Policy of Russia*; and Michael Mandelbaum, ed., *The New Russian Foreign Policy* (New York: Council on Foreign Relations, 1998).

11 M. S. Gorbachev, *Izbrannye rechi i stat'i*, 7 vols. (Moscow: Politizdat, 1987–90), vol. II, p. 99 and 99–103 passim.

12 Ibid., pp. 109–16.

13 Ibid., p. 131.

14 Ibid., pp. 167–72.

15 Ibid., pp. 460, 466–7.

16 Ibid., vol. III, p. 9.

17 Ibid., pp. 183–96.

18 For the text, see *Spravochnik partiinogo rabotnika*, vol. XXVII (Moscow: Politizdat, 1987), pp. 342–4.

19 *Materialy XXVII S"ezda Kommunisticheskoi partii Sovetskogo Soyuza* (Moscow: Politizdat, 1986), p. 179; Gorbachev spoke of 'reasonable sufficiency' at the 27th Party Congress (*Izbrannye rechi i stat'i*, vol. III, p. 248) and the Warsaw Treaty Organisation made its commitment shortly afterwards: *Pravda*, 12 June 1986, pp. 1–2.

20 Cuts in military spending and personnel were approved by the Supreme Soviet Presidium in March 1989 (*Pravda*, 22 March 1989, p. 1); the first useful figures for Soviet and WTO troop and weapons numbers were reported in early 1989 (ibid., 30 January 1989, p. 5, and 19 April 1989, p. 4), and the first meaningful figures for Soviet defence expenditure in May 1989 (ibid., 30 May 1989, p. 2).

21 Gorbachev, *Izbrannye rechi i stat'i*, vol. VII, pp. 184–202.

22 For the text, see *Sbornik mezhdunarodnykh dogovorov SSSR*, vol. XLIII (Moscow: Mezhdunarodnye otnosheniya, 1990), no. 4413, pp. 58–137.

23 For the text, see Ministerstvo inostrannykh del Rossiiskoi Federatsii, *Vneshnyaya politika Rossii. Sbornik dokumentov, 1990–1992* (Moscow: Mezhdunarodnye otnosheniya, 1996), no. 23, pp. 65–105.

24 The dissolution of the CMEA was reported in *Izvestiya*, 28 June 1991, p. 6, and of the WTO, ibid., 2 July 1991, p. 5.

25 *Materialy Plenuma Tsentral'nogo Komiteta KPSS, 9 dekabrya 1989 goda* (Moscow: Politizdat, 1989), pp. 18–19.

26 *XXVIII S"ezd Kommunisticheskoi partii Sovetskogo Soyuza, 2–13 iyulya 1990 g. Stenograficheskii otchet*, 2 vols. (Moscow: Politizdat, 1991), vol. II, p. 199. A substantial literature, much of it drawing upon archives or interviews, includes (on Soviet–American relations) Michael Beschloss and Strobe Talbott, *At the Highest Levels: The Inside Story of the End of the Cold War* (London: Little, Brown, 1993); Raymond L. Garthoff, *Détente and Confrontation: American–Soviet Relations from Nixon to Reagan*, rev. edn (Washington, DC: Brookings, 1994); Garthoff, *The Great Transformation: American–Soviet Relations and the End of the Cold War* (Washington, DC: Brookings, 1994); and Don Oberdorfer, *From the Cold War to a New Era: The United States and the Soviet Union, 1983–1991* (Baltimore: Johns Hopkins University Press, 1998); on Soviet relations with Eastern Europe, Jacques Levesque, *The Enigma of 1989: The USSR and the Liberation of Eastern Europe* (Berkeley: University of California Press, 1997); and on relations with Germany and the rest of Europe, Philip Zelikow, and Condoleezza Rice, *Germany Unified and Europe Transformed: A Study in Statecraft* (Cambridge, MA: Harvard University Press, 1995); Hannes Adomeit, *Imperial Overstretch: Germany in Soviet Policy from Stalin to Gorbachev* (Baden-Baden: Nomos, 1998); and Angela Stent, *Russia and Germany Reborn: Unification, the Soviet Collapse, and the New Europe* (Princeton, NJ: Princeton University Press, 1999).

27 *Pravda*, 16 February 1989, p. 1; the background to the decision is considered in Diego Cordovez and Selig S. Harrison, *Out of Afghanistan: The Inside Story of the Soviet withdrawal* (New York: Oxford University Press, 1995).

28 *Izvestiya*, 12 September 1991, p. 1.

29 Gorbachev, *Izbrannye rechi i stat'i*, vol. III, pp. 256–7.

30 *Materialy XXVII S"ezda*, p. 174.

31 See for instance *Pravda*, 14 November 1986, pp. 2–3, and 10 July 1987, p. 4.

32 Ambassadorial relations with the Vatican were established in 1990 (*Pravda*, 16 March 1990, p. 6) and were restored with Israel in 1991 (*Izvestiya*, 19 October 1991, p. 1); consular relations with South Africa were restored the following month (ibid., 11 November 1991, p. 1).

33 The signatories were the thirty-four members of the Conference for Security and Co-operation in Europe (*Pravda*, 22 November 1990, pp. 1, 3); there was also a treaty on conventional forces in Europe: ibid., 24 November 1990, pp. 3–4.

34 Why, asked Gorbachev, had the United States, which had itself invaded Grenada and Panama, been allowed to expatiate about the rights of man (*Pravda*, 28 February 1991, p. 2)? His statement on the outbreak of the war, however, emphasised that everything must be done to bring it to an end in co-operation with other governments and the UN (ibid., 18 January 1991, p. 1), and Foreign Ministry statements took the same line (see for instance ibid., 13 December 1990, p. 5).

35 *Izvestiya*, 14 September 1989, p. 4.

36 Ibid., 21 June 1991, p. 4.

37 *Diplomaticheskii vestnik*, no. 1, 1992, p. 36. In addition, the United Kingdom had recognised the new Russian government on 24 December (ibid., p. 33); by 10 January, 116 states had done so (ibid., no. 2–3, 1992, p. 33).

38 Ibid., no. 1, 1992, pp. 24–5, 15–16 December 1991.

39 Ibid., p. 28, 23 December 1991; Russia took over the USSR's seat in the United Nations, also prematurely, on 24 December: ibid., p. 13.

40 *Vneshnyaya politika Rossii 1990–92*, no. 8, pp. 29–33.

41 Ibid., no. 28, p. 111.

42 See respectively *Diplomaticheskii vestnik*, no. 1, 1992, pp. 14–18; *Vestnik ministerstva vneshnykh snoshenii*, no. 24, 1991, p. 13.

43 *Izvestiya*, 2 January 1992, p. 3; also in *Diplomaticheskii vestnik*, no. 2–3, 1992, pp. 3–5.

44 *Pravda*, 29 January 1992, p. 5.

45 *Vneshnyaya politika Rossii 1990–92*, no. 80, pp. 185–90.

46 Ibid., no. 91, pp. 214–18.

47 *Rossiiskaya gazeta*, 3 February 1992, p. 3.

48 *Izvestiya*, 3 February 1992, p. 4; on the boots, see Alexander Korzhakov, *Boris Yel'tsin. Ot rassveta do zakata* (Moscow: Interbuk, 1997), p. 60.

49 The declaration was printed in *Rossiiskaya gazeta*, 3 February 1992, p. 3, and also in *Diplomaticheskii vestnik*, no. 4–5, 1992, p. 12, 1 February 1992.

50 See respectively *Vneshnyaya politika Rossii 1990–92*, no. 95, pp. 226–8, and no. 106, pp. 248–55.

51 Ibid., no. 73, pp. 173–6.

52 See respectively ibid., no. 149, pp. 329–35, and no. 175, pp. 381–7.

53 See respectively ibid., no. 201, pp. 445–51, and no. 223, pp. 495–9.

54 Ibid., no. 256, pp. 555–60.

55 *Izvestiya*, 11 November 1992, p. 1. When the visit took place two years later – the first by a reigning British monarch since 1917 – the Russian president and his assistants all wore dinner jackets for the first time in their lives (Vyacheslav Kostikov, *Roman s prezidentom* [Moscow: Vagrius, 1997], p. 131); the visit was reported in *Izvestiya*, 19 October 1994, p. 1.

56 *The Times*, 10 November 1992, p. 1.

57 *Izvestiya*, 16 June 1992, p. 1.

58 Ibid.

59 *Vneshnyaya politika Rossii 1990–92*, no. 196, pp. 437–8 (it was ratified by the Supreme Soviet later in the year: *Pravda*, 5 November 1992, p. 1).

60 *Vneshnyaya politika Rossii 1990–92*, no. 195, pp. 431–7.

61 See respectively ibid., no. 197, pp. 438–9, and no. 198, pp. 439–40; the total number of agreements is given in *Diplomaticheskii vestnik*, no. 13–14, 1992, p. 3.

62 *Vneshnyaya politika Rossii 1990–92*, no. 194, pp. 426–7.

63 Kostikov, *Roman s prezidentom*, pp. 51, 57 (they hoped particularly to eclipse the influence that Gorbachev had enjoyed); *Pravda*, 3 February 1992, p. 4.

64 For the text, see *Diplomaticheskii vestnik*, no. 1–2, 1993, pp. 19–24.

65 *Izvestiya*, 5 January 1993, pp. 1, 5.

66 *Diplomaticheskii vestnik*, no. 1–2, 1993, pp. 25, 18.

67 Ibid., pp. 25–6.

68 Ibid., pp. 26, 19.

69 *Izvestiya*, 20 November 1993, p. 1.
70 Belarus also ratified the Nuclear Non-Proliferation Treaty: ibid., 6 February 1993, p. 2.
71 *Segodnya*, 5 February 1994, p. 4; *Nezavisimaya gazeta*, 18 November 1994, p. 1.
72 *Segodnya*, 4 June 1996, p. 1.
73 *Diplomaticheskii vestnik*, no. 7–8, 1993, p. 18.
74 See respectively ibid., p. 17, and *Izvestiya*, 6 April 1993, p. 1.
75 *Izvestiya*, 6 April 1993, p. 3.
76 *Diplomaticheskii vestnik*, no. 7–8, 1993, p. 18.
77 *Nezavisimaya gazeta*, 10 July 1993, p. 1.
78 *Diplomaticheskii vestnik*, no. 23–4, 1993, pp. 6–16.
79 Ibid., no. 3–4, 1994, pp. 11–18.
80 Korzhakov, *Boris Yel'tsin*, p. 236.
81 See respectively *Diplomaticheskii vestnik*, no. 9–10, 1994, pp. 7–11, and no. 21–2, 1994, pp. 9–14.
82 Ibid., no. 15–16, 1994, pp. 29–59; it eventually came into force in December 1997: *Finansovye izvestiya*, 2 December 1997, p. 1.
83 *Diplomaticheskii vestnik*, no. 13–14, 1993, pp. 4–6 (the text was not reproduced).
84 Ibid., no. 19–20, 1994, pp. 3–6; Yeltsin referred in these familiar terms only to his American and German counterparts (Korzhakov, *Boris Yel'tsin*, p. 339).
85 *Keesing's Record of World Events*, August 1993, p. 39610, and August 1994, p. 40153.
86 *Diplomaticheskii vestnik*, no. 19–20, 1994, pp. 10–19.
87 Ibid., p. 9.
88 Ibid., no. 6, 1995, pp. 9–15.
89 Ibid., p. 9.
90 Ibid., no. 11, 1995, pp. 55–6.
91 Ibid., p. 10.
92 Ibid., no. 5, 1996, p. 15.
93 Ibid., no. 4, 1997, pp. 4–11.
94 *Nezavisimaya gazeta*, 3 September 1998, p. 1. The documents adopted at the summit were published in *Diplomaticheskii vestnik*, no. 10, 1998, pp. 12–23.
95 *Segodnya*, 21 June 1997, p. 3.
96 *Izvestiya*, 12 May 1998, p. 7; for the previous day's meeting, see *Nezavisimaya gazeta*, 19 May 1998, pp. 1–2.
97 *Izvestiya*, 17 January 1992, p. 5, and 28 April 1992, p. 1.
98 Membership was approved by 164 votes to 35 with 15 abstentions: ibid., 27 January 1996, p. 1.
99 Ibid., 2 June 1998, p. 3.
100 In June 1993 and December 1994 respectively: *Mirovaya ekonomika i mezhdunarodnye otnosheniya*, no. 8, 1998, p. 13.
101 *Izvestiya*, 27 November 1997, p. 1.
102 Ibid., 2 January 1992, p. 3.
103 *Voprosy istorii*, no. 1, 1994, p. 4
104 *Rossiiskie vesti*, 3 December 1992, p. 2.

105 *Slavic Review*, vol. 51, no. 2 (Summer 1989), p. 289; he had advocated this view as early as August 1995: Andrei Kozyrev, *Preobrazhenie* (Moscow: Mezhdunarodnye otnosheniya, 1995), p. 211.

106 *Slavic Review*, vol. 51, no. 2 (Summer 1989), p. 293.

107 *Izvestiya*, 22 February 1992, p. 3.

108 *Nezavisimaya gazeta*, 29 April 1993, pp. 1, 3; the 'concept' itself was not officially published.

109 Margot Light, 'Foreign policy thinking', in Malcolm, et al., *Internal Factors*, p. 62, and more generally pp. 61–70.

110 *Izvestiya*, 11 March 1994, p. 3.

111 *Nezavisimaya gazeta*, 19 April 1995, p. 1; journalists claimed to distinguish a 'late Kozyrev' in these speeches as compared with the 'early' and more pro-Western Kozyrev: *Preobrazhenie*, p. 53.

112 *Moskovskie novosti*, no. 63, 1994, p. 6.

113 For the decree, see *Kto yest' kto v Rossii. Spravochnoe izdanie* (Moscow: Olimp/EKSMO-Press, 1998). Kozyrev had been criticised by Yeltsin at a press conference (*Rossiiskie vesti*, 9 September 1995, p. 3); the following month the president was 'still dissatisfied' with the performance of the Foreign Ministry, but had not found a 'fitting candidate' to replace the minister himself: ibid., 21 October 1995, p. 9.

114 Kostikov, *Roman s prezidentom*, p. 71.

115 *Zavtra*, no. 1, November 1993, p. 1.

116 *Nezavisimaya gazeta*, 10 December 1994, p. 1.

117 Ibid., 16 November 1995, pp. 1, 5.

118 For these distinctions, see Light, 'Foreign policy thinking'.

119 This term was referred to in the course of Primakov's first press conference (*Diplomaticheskii vestnik*, no. 2, 1996, p. 4); there is no reference to it in the report of Yeltsin's address to the Foreign Ministry (ibid., no. 1, 1996, p. 4).

120 *Rabochaya tribuna*, 9 December 1997, Delovoi vtornik, p. 3.

121 *Diplomaticheskii vestnik*, no. 4, 1995, p. 3.

122 See for instance *Segodnya*, 20 October 1995, p. 3.

123 *Izvestiya*, 11 September 1998, p. 1.

124 *Diplomaticheskii vestnik*, no. 2, 1996, pp. 3, 4.

125 *Rossiiskaya gazeta*, 10 January 1997, p. 2.

126 See respectively *Kto yest' kto v Rossii*, pp. 320, 523; an official biography of Primakov appeared in *Diplomaticheskii vestnik*, no. 1, 1996, p. 3. He had been a committed supporter of *perestroika* in the Gorbachev years but was already in disagreement with the 'Americanocentrism' by which its success was to be judged by the extent to which the US government approved of it (*Znamya*, no. 6, 1989, pp. 185, 192).

127 *Kto yest' kto v Rossii*, p. 523.

128 *Izvestiya*, 23 December 1997, p. 3.

129 Ibid., 28 October 1998, pp. 1, 6.

130 Ibid., 13 April 1992, p. 4.

131 Ibid., 26 October 1992, p. 4.

132 Ibid., 5 January 1993, p. 3.

133 *Nezavisimaya gazeta*, 24 February 1994, p. 1.

134 *Kommersant'-daily*, 21 May 1996, p. 4.

135 *Guardian*, 10 March 1999, Section 2, p. 3; *Rossiiskie vesti*, 14 March 1998, p. 12.
136 *Nezavisimaya gazeta*, 24 February 1994, p. 1.
137 *Pravda*, 29 June 1991, p. 1.
138 *Vneshnyaya politika Rossii 1990–92*, nos. 119 and 120, pp. 285–6.
139 *Izvestiya*, 1 June 1992, p. 1.
140 *Pravda*, 24 September 1992, p. 3; *The Times*, 18 November 1992, p. 13.
141 See respectively *Pravda*, 21 January 1993, p. 5 ('fellow Slavs'), and *Sovetskaya Rossiya*, 6 June 1992, p. 1.
142 *Izvestiya*, 5 June 1992, pp. 1, 5.
143 *Pravda*, 21 January 1994, p. 5.
144 In a resolution that was adopted by an overwhelming majority on 17 December 1992, for instance, the Supreme Soviet called for the Russian representative in the UN to veto military intervention (*Izvestiya*, 18 December 1992, p. 4); a resolution of 18 February 1993 called for UN sanctions to be imposed on Croatia and for those on Serbia and Montenegro to be lifted.
145 *Nezavisimaya gazeta*, 22 February 1994, p. 2.
146 *Izvestiya*, 12 April 1994, p. 1, and *Rossiiskie vesti*, 13 April 1994, pp. 1, 3.
147 *Izvestiya*, 31 August 1995 pp. 1, 3.
148 *Diplomaticheskii vestnik*, no. 10, 1995, p. 7.
149 *Rossiiskaya gazeta*, 12 September 1995, p. 1.
150 *Izvestiya*, 6 October 1998, p. 2.
151 *Rossiiskaya gazeta*, 15 October 1998, p. 1.
152 Ibid., 26 March 1999, p. 2.
153 Ibid., 23 January 1993, p. 7.
154 *Izvestiya*, 29 June 1993, p. 1.
155 *Diplomaticheskii vestnik*, no. 10, 1996, pp. 3–4.
156 *Rossiiskaya gazeta*, 21 November 1997, p. 4.
157 *Rossiiskie vesti*, 24 February 1998, p. 1. The tensions related to the inspection of eight 'presidential sites'; the immediate crisis was resolved by the personal intervention of the UN secretary general.
158 About 5,000, according to *Nezavisimaya gazeta*, 30 December 1997, p. 1.
159 *Economist*, 9 May 1998, p. 27; on Russian investment, see *Izvestiya*, 4 July 1997, p. 2.
160 *Nezavisimaya gazeta*, 30 December 1997, p. 5.
161 Ibid., 17 March 1998, p. 6.
162 *Rossiiskaya gazeta*, 18 December 1998, p. 3.
163 Ibid., 19 December 1998, p. 1.
164 The Soviet ambassador to the UK had last been withdrawn in 1971, and the ambassador to the USA not since the Second World War: *Guardian*, 19 December 1998, p. 2.
165 For a general discussion, see for instance Richard L. Krugler and Marianna V. Kozintseva, *Enlarging NATO: The Russia Factor* (Santa Monica, CA: Rand, 1996), and Gerald B. Solomon, *The NATO Enlargement Debate, 1990–1997* (Westport, CT: Praeger, 1998). The Russian position is considered in *Mirovaya ekonomika i mezhdunarodnye otnosheniya*, no. 8, 1997, pp. 17–31, and no. 9, 1997, pp. 42–51.

166 *Diplomaticheskii vestnik*, no. 1, 1992, pp. 12–13.
167 *Segodnya*, 27 August 1993, p. 1 (Yeltsin's statement was quickly disowned by his staff and Foreign Ministry officials).
168 *Izvestiya*, 2 October 1993, p. 4.
169 *Segodnya*, 26 October 1993, p. 5.
170 *Diplomaticheskii vestnik*, no. 13–14, 1994, pp. 32–3.
171 *Nezavisimaya gazeta*, 7 April 1994, p. 1.
172 *Diplomaticheskii vestnik*, no. 13–14, 1994, pp. 30–1.
173 *Keesing's*, p. 40081.
174 *Diplomaticheskii vestnik*, no. 1, 1995, pp. 4–5, 5 December 1994.
175 *Rossiiskaya gazeta*, 8 December 1994, pp. 1–2.
176 *Nezavisimaya gazeta*, 7 December 1994, p. 1.
177 *Diplomaticheskii vestnik*, no. 1, 1997, pp. 9–10, Brussels, 11 December 1996.
178 His remarks were paraphrased ibid., no. 2, 1997, p. 11.
179 *Rossiiskie vesti*, 5 February 1997, p. 1.
180 *Rossiiskaya gazeta*, 18 March 1997, pp. 1–2.
181 *Diplomaticheskii vestnik*, no. 6, 1997, pp. 4–10.
182 Ibid., pp. 3–4.
183 *Rossiiskie vesti*, 28 May 1997, p. 3.
184 Andranik Migranyan in *Nezavisimaya gazeta*, 27 May 1997, pp. 1–2.
185 *Izvestiya*, 28 May 1997, p. 4.
186 *Nezavisimaya gazeta*, 28 May 1997, pp. 1–2; *Izvestiya*, 28 May 1997, p. 1.
187 *Segodnya*, 10 July 1997, p. 4.
188 *Izvestiya*, 15 July 1997, p. 3.
189 *Keesing's*, p. 41756.
190 *Rossiiskaya gazeta*, 11 July 1997, p. 4.
191 *Kommersant'-daily*, 10 July 1997, p. 2.
192 For a discussion of the background to the decision, see Heather Grabbe and Kirsty Hughes, *Enlarging the European Union Eastwards* (London: RIIA, 1998); Graham Avery and Fraser Cameron, *The Enlargement of the European Union* (Sheffield: Sheffield Academic Press, 1998); and Karen Henderson, ed., *Back to Europe: Central and Eastern Europe and the European Union* (London: UCL Press, 1999).
193 *Izvestiya*, 10 April 1991, p. 1. The results appeared ibid., 27 March 1991, pp. 1, 3.
194 For the text, see *Pravda*, 27 June 1991, p. 3.
195 See respectively ibid., 13 July 1991, p. 2, and 25 July 1991, p. 1; an Armenian representative was also in attendance. All that remained, according to the Soviet president, was the question of federal taxation.
196 Ibid., 15 August 1991, p. 2, and also *Izvestiya*, 15 August 1991, pp. 1–2. The text, with a substantial body of documentation drawn in part from the Gorbachev archives, is reproduced in *Soyuz mozhno bylo sokhranit'. Belaya kniga* (Moscow: Aprel'-85, 1995), pp. 186–99.
197 *Pravda*, 3 August 1991, p. 1. Moldova subsequently announced that it would not be signing the union treaty (*Izvestiya*, 9 August 1991, p. 2), but Belarus and Kazakhstan confirmed that they would do so (ibid., 10 August 1991, p. 1).

198 See respectively *Pravda*, 26 August 1991, p. 2 (Ukraine); *Izvestiya*, 27 August 1991, p. 3 (Moldova); and *Pravda*, 31 August 1991, p. 1 (the Azerbaijani Supreme Soviet confirmed the vote in October [ibid., 19 October 1991, p. 1], and it was endorsed by a referendum with 99.6 per cent in favour at the end of the year [*Izvestiya*, 8 January 1992, p. 2]).

199 *Nezavisimaya gazeta*, 27 August 1991, p. 3.

200 See respectively *Pravda*, 2 September 1991, p. 2 (Uzbekistan and Kyrgyzstan; in a referendum in Uzbekistan later in the year there was over 98 per cent support for independence: *Izvestiya*, 31 December 1991, p. 1); *Narodnaya gazeta*, 10 September 1991, p. 1 (Tajikistan); Armenia voted in the same sense on 23 September following a referendum in which independence was approved by 99.3 per cent (*Pravda*, 24 September 1991, p. 1); so did Turkmenistan on 27 October (*Pravda*, 28 October 1991, p. 1), and Kazakhstan on 16 December (*Izvestiya*, 17 December 1991, p. 1).

201 *Izvestiya*, 6 September 1991, pp. 1–2.

202 There was a 98.9 per cent vote in a 30 March 1991 referendum in favour of the restoration of full independence, which had been proclaimed by the Georgian parliament on 9 April 1991 (ibid., 2 April 1991, p. 1, and 9 April 1991, p. 1).

203 *Vedomosti S"ezda narodnykh deputatov RSFSR i Verkhovnogo Soveta RSFSR*, no. 2, 1990, art. 22.

204 In Uzbekistan, for instance, the Communist Party became the People's Democratic Party, with the Communist leader Islam Karimov unanimously elected its new leader: *Pravda*, 2 November 1991, p. 1.

205 Ibid., 3 September 1991, p. 1.

206 *Vedomosti S"ezda narodnykh deputatov SSSR i Verkhovnogo Soveta SSSR*, no. 37, 1991, art. 1082, 5 September 1991.

207 *Izvestiya*, 19 October 1991, p. 1; the text was published in *Rossiiskaya gazeta*, 22 October 1991, p. 2. Moldova and Ukraine initialled it as well on 6 November 1991: *Izvestiya*, 7 November 1991, p. 1.

208 *Izvestiya*, 15 November 1991, p. 1. Georgia and Armenia later announced they would not be taking part (ibid., 18 November 1991, p. 1, and 23 November 1991, p. 1). Yeltsin, however, was 'firmly convinced' there would be a union; the only question was how many of the republics would belong to it (M. S. Gorbachev, *Dekabr'-91. Moya pozitsiya* [Moscow: Novosti, 1992], p. 9).

209 *Izvestiya*, 25 November 1991, p. 3.

210 *Pravda*, 26 November 1991, p. 1.

211 Ibid., 27 November 1991, p. 1; the USSR Supreme Soviet approved the draft but suggested that the president not be directly elected: *Izvestiya*, 5 December 1991, p. 2.

212 *Izvestiya*, 3 December 1991, p. 2.

213 The vote in favour was 90.3 per cent: *Pravda*, 6 December 1991, p. 1.

214 *Izvestiya*, 29 November 1991, p. 3.

215 Ibid., 5 December 1991, p. 1.

216 The declaration establishing the CIS appeared in *Rossiiskaya gazeta*, 10 December 1991, p. 1; the text of the agreement is ibid., 11 December 1991, p. 1. The agreement was ratified by Ukraine but with significant

amendments (for instance, there would be 'consultation' rather than 'co-ordination' in foreign policy: *Izvestiya*, 12 December 1991, p. 1); it was also ratified by Belorussia (ibid.) and by Russia (ibid., 13 December 1991, p. 1).

217 *Pravda*, 13 December 1991, p. 1; Gorbachev's television address of the evening of 9 December was published in *Izvestiya*, 10 December 1991, p. 2.

218 Kozyrev, *Preobrazhenie*, pp. 171–2.

219 *Rossiiskaya gazeta*, 24 December 1991, p. 1. Gorbachev, in a letter to the participants, had proposed a 'Commonwealth of European and Asian States', and emphasised the need for common citizenship and economic co-ordination (*Izvestiya*, 20 December 1991, pp. 1–2).

220 *Izvestiya*, 19 December 1991, p. 1.

221 Ibid., 23 December 1991, p. 2.

222 Ibid., 25 December 1991, p. 1.

223 *Pravda*, 27 December 1991, p. 1. The union treaty provided for with-drawal, but not for dissolution, and any changes were the 'exclusive competence of a Congress of Soviets of the Union of Soviet Socialist Republics' (S. S. Studenikin, ed., *Istoriya sovetskoi konstitutsii (v dokumen-takh) 1917–1956* [Moscow: Gosudarstvennoe izdatel'stvo yuridicheskoi literatury, 1957], p. 398).

224 *Pravda*, 26 December 1991, p. 1.

225 *Izvestiya*, 5 May 1994, p. 1.

226 Georgia adhered by a presidential decree in October 1993, which was ratified by the Georgian parliament the following March: *Keesing's*, pp. 39695, 39931. Azerbaijan formally became a member of the CIS in 1993 (*Segodnya*, 23 September 1993, p. 5; membership had not previously been ratified by the Azerbaijani parliament); the Moldovan parliament ratified membership of the CIS on 8 April 1994.

227 *Kommersant'-daily*, 17 September 1998, p. 3. For a fuller discussion, see Mark Webber, *CIS Integration Trends: Russia and the Former Soviet South* (London: RIIA, 1997); a comprehensive collection of documents is available in Zbigniew Brzezinski and Paige Sullivan, eds., *Russia and the Commonwealth of Independent States: Documents, Data and Analysis* (Armonk, NY: Sharpe, 1997).

228 *Izvestiya*, 16 May 1992, p. 1.

229 Ibid., 23 January 1993, p. 1; the text of the Charter was printed in *Rossiiskaya gazeta*, 12 February 1993, p. 6.

230 *Izvestiya*, 8 May 1993, p. 1, and (for the initialling) 25 September 1993, p. 1.

231 Ibid., 23 December 1997, p. 3.

232 Ibid., 23 July 1998, p. 1.

233 Ibid., 17 September 1998, p. 1.

234 *Rossiiskaya gazeta*, 10 January 1992, p. 1.

235 Luzhkov set out his views in *Argumenty i fakty*, no. 50, 1996, p. 3, and no. 51, p. 5.

236 *Rossiiskaya gazeta*, 25 May 1992, p. 1.

237 *Diplomaticheskii vestnik*, no. 7, 1997, p. 42.

238 *Nezavisimaya gazeta*, 20 February 1997, p. 3.

239 *Diplomaticheskii vestnik*, no. 7, 1997, pp. 35–41.

240 Ibid., pp. 41 and 42; Russia was to lease Sevastopol for twenty years, with the possibility of extension; the wider security framework, in line with Russian preferences, was to be based on the OSCE.

241 *Izvestiya*, 28 February 1998, p. 1; for the text, see *Diplomaticheskii vestnik*, no. 4, 1998, pp. 37–8, and an associated programme of co-operation, pp. 38–43.

242 He won 80.1 per cent of the vote in the second round: *Izvestiya*, 12 July 1994, p. 1.

243 *Diplomaticheskii vestnik*, no. 3, 1995, p. 37.

244 Ibid., p. 37; the treaty appeared on pp. 38–42.

245 *Keesing's*, p. 40464.

246 *Nezavisimaya gazeta*, 16 May 1995, p. 1.

247 *Keesing's*, p. 40567. For a full account of the relationship from a Belarusian perspective, see David R. Marples, *Belarus: A Denationalized Nation* (London: Harwood, 1999), ch. 6.

248 *Izvestiya*, 30 March 1996, p. 1; for the text, see *Diplomaticheskii vestnik*, no. 4, 1996, pp. 56–60.

249 For the text, see *Diplomaticheskii vestnik*, no. 5, 1996, pp. 39–42.

250 *Izvestiya*, 26 November 1996, p. 2 (about 70 per cent had voted for the new constitution).

251 *Nezavisimaya gazeta*, 29 November 1996, p. 3.

252 *Diplomaticheskii vestnik*, no. 4, 1997, pp. 41–3.

253 Ibid., pp. 40–1. Other states could join the new Community and it was of indefinite duration (p. 42).

254 Ibid., no. 6, 1997, pp. 30–9.

255 *Rossiiskaya gazeta*, 26 December 1998, p. 1.

256 *Izvestiya*, 29 March 1997, p. 1.

257 Ibid., 29 April 1998, p. 2.

258 Two-thirds of those who were asked, in a USIA investigation, supported integration with Belarus, most of them 'strongly' (*USIA Opinion Analysis* M-87-97, 27 May 1997, p. 4). See further L. Sedov, 'SSSR i SNG v obshchestvennom mnenii Rossii', *Ekonomicheskie i sotsial'nye peremeny: monitoring obshchestvennogo mneniya*, no. 1, 1997, pp. 12–14.

259 *Rossiya v tsifrakh. Kratkii statisticheskii sbornik* (Moscow: Goskomstat Rossii, 1998), p. 372.

260 The communiqué issued at the end of Gorbachev's visit emphasised 'noninterference in each other's internal affairs' (*Pravda*, 19 May 1989, p. 1); Li Peng's visit was reported ibid., 27 April 1990, p. 6, and Jiang Zemin's ibid., 16 May 1991, pp. 1, 5 (the final communiqué was ibid., 20 May 1991, p. 5). For a more general account of Russian–Chinese relations, see V. G. Gel'bras, 'Kitai v vostochnoi politike Rossii (suzhdeniya i ottsenki)', *Polis*, no. 4, 1997, pp. 166–73, and no. 5, pp. 170–8; and Gilbert Roszman, 'Sino-Russian relations in the 1990s: a balance sheet', *Post-Soviet Affairs*, vol. 14, no. 2 (April–June 1998), pp. 93–113.

261 *Izvestiya*, 18 March 1992, p. 4.

262 Ibid., 17 December 1992, p. 1.

263 Ibid., 4 November 1997, pp. 2, 3; the Moscow declaration on Russo-Japanese relations was published in *Rossiiskaya gazeta*, 14 November 1998, p. 2.

264 *Izvestiya*, 1 February 1994, p. 5.

265 *Pravda*, 6 July 1989, p. 2.

266 *Segodnya*, 2 September 1994, p. 3.

267 Ibid., 6 September 1994, p. 2.

268 *Segodnya*, 28 June 1995, p. 2. The final communiqué was published in *Diplomaticheskii vestnik*, no. 7, 1995, pp. 4–5, and the documents that were agreed ibid., pp. 5–12.

269 *Diplomaticheskii vestnik*, no. 5, 1996, p. 18.

270 Ibid., pp. 16–21.

271 Ibid., no. 5, 1997, pp. 19–21 (declaration), p. 18 (arms agreement).

272 Ibid., no. 12, 1997, pp. 9–10.

273 *Izvestiya*, 12 November 1997, p. 3 (Harbin); *Diplomaticheskii vestnik*, no. 12, 1997, pp. 17–19.

274 *Rossiiskaya gazeta*, 10 January 1997, p. 2.

275 *Izvestiya*, 26 June 1997, p. 1.

276 For a more general study of the development of Soviet–Indian relations, see Peter J. S. Duncan, *The Soviet Union and India* (London: Routledge/RIIA, 1989).

277 For the text, see *Spravochnik partiinogo rabotnika*, vol. XXVII, pp. 342–4.

278 *Rossiiskaya gazeta*, 30 January 1993, pp. 1, 7. The friendship treaty was published in *Diplomaticheskii vestnik*, no. 3–4, 1993, pp. 19–23.

279 *Rossiiskaya gazeta*, 22 December 1998, p. 7.

280 See Ivanov's interview in *Nezavisimaya gazeta*, 23 February 1999, p. 6.

281 According to World Bank data: *World Development Report 1998/99: Knowledge for Development* (New York: Oxford University Press for the World Bank, 1999), pp. 190–1.

282 *Izvestiya*, 11 March 1994, p. 3.

283 *Rossiiskaya gazeta*, 10 January 1997, p. 2.

284 *Pravda*, 22–5 January 1999, p. 3.

285 *Krasnaya zvezda*, 3 November 1998, p. 3.

286 *Segodnya*, 12 November 1998, p. 2.

287 *Kommersant'*, 21 January 1999, p. 1.

288 Ibid.

289 Richard Rose and Christian Haerpfer, *New Russia Barometer III: The Results* (Glasgow: University of Strathclyde, Centre for the Study of Public Policy, SPP 228, 1994), pp. 42–3 (attitude towards the EU and possible membership); on foreign threats, see Richard Rose, *Getting Things Done with Social Capital: New Russia Barometer VII* (Glasgow: University of Strathclyde, Centre for the Study of Public Policy, SPP 303, 1998), pp. 36–7.

290 *Central and Eastern European Barometer 7* (Brussels: European Commission, 1997), Annex Fig. 60. The EU's image was the least positive in postcommunist Europe, apart from Ukraine, and it was deteriorating further (ibid., Text Fig. 4 and Annex Fig. 45).

291 Rose, *Getting Things Done*, p. 69.

292 Just 21 per cent thought Russians had 'much the same values and interests as people in the West', and 78 per cent thought their values and interests were different: Richard Rose, *New Russia Barometer IV: Survey Results* (Glasgow: University of Strathclyde, Centre for the Study of Public Policy, SPP 250, 1995), p. 50. The complex relationship between Russia and Europe is considered in Iver B. Neumann, *Russia and the Idea of Europe* (London: Routledge, 1996); wider issues of identity are considered in Ilya Prizel, *National Identity and Foreign Policy: Nationalism and Leadership in Poland, Russia, and Ukraine* (Cambridge: Cambridge University Press, 1998), and Neumann, *Uses of the Other: 'The East' in European Identity Formation* (Manchester: Manchester University Press, 1999).

293 These figures are derived from *Natsional'nyi sostav naseleniya SSSR po dannym vsesoyuznoi perepisi naseleniya 1989 g.* (Moscow: Finansy i statistika, 1991).

294 Of these, about 900,000 lived outside Russia, and about 100,000 in the 'far abroad'; 40,000 had relinquished Russian citizenship, usually because they had been obliged to do so (*Diplomaticheskii vestnik*, no. 2, 1997, p. 41).

295 Kozyrev, for instance, argued that discrimination was evidenced by the steady flow of emigration from the former Soviet republics back to Russia, as well as in 'limitations on the use of the Russian language and reduced opportunities for Russian speakers to secure leading positions in the state apparatus and in government' (ibid., no. 5, 1995, p. 53). A presidential decree on 'state policy towards fellow nationals living abroad' was approved in 1994: *Sobranie zakonodatel'stva Rossiiskoi Federatsii*, no. 21, 1994, art. 2383, 11 August 1994.

296 *Gosudarstvo i pravo*, no. 11, 1996, p. 5; on the Russo-Estonian border dispute, see *Nezavisimaya gazeta*, 18 March 1992, p. 2.

297 *Izvestiya*, 19 March 1998, pp. 1–2. There is a full discussion of these and other border issues in A. Barsenkov, V. Koretsky, and A. Ostapenko, 'The borders of the Russian Federation', *Russia and the Successor States Briefing Service*, 2 parts, vol. 2, no. 2, April 1994, pp. 23–31, and no. 3, June 1994, pp. 3–19.

298 *Nezavisimaya gazeta*, 23 February 1999, p. 6.

299 *Rossiiskaya gazeta*, 10 January 1997, p. 2.

300 *Rossiya v tsifrakh*, pp. 370–1.

301 *Izvestiya*, 19 October 1994, p. 13. A broader geopolitical perspective is available in Zbigniew Brzezinski, *The Grand Chessboard: American Primacy and Its Geostrategic Imperatives* (New York: BasicBooks, 1997).

8 RUSSIA, TRANSITION, DEMOCRACY

1 *Izvestiya*, 23 August 1991, p. 1.

2 Ibid., 12 November 1991, p. 1.

3 B. N. Yeltsin, *Zapiski Prezidenta* (Moscow: Ogonek, 1994), p. 67; the apparent reference to Eric Hobsbawm's *Age of Extremes: The Short Twentieth Century 1914–1991* (London: Michael Joseph, 1994) was no doubt unintended.

4 Yegor Gaidar, *Dni porazhenii i pobed* (Moscow: Vagrius, 1996), p. 8.

5 *Izvestiya*, 22 August 1991, p. 1. This was not, in fact, the ending to the play that Pushkin had originally intended: see John Bayley, *Pushkin: A Comparative Commentary* (Cambridge: Cambridge University Press, 1971), pp. 176–7.

6 As he explained in a speech on 9 September 1991, the August events had confirmed the 'irrevocable character of the changes to which democratisation and *glasnost'* had led' (M. S. Gorbachev, *Gody trudnykh reshenii* [Moscow: Al'fa-print, 1993], p. 282).

7 An extract from Francis Fukuyama's controversial 'end of history' article was published in *Voprosy filosofii*, no. 3, 1990, pp. 134–48, with a critical rejoinder, pp. 148–55.

8 *Komsomol'skaya pravda*, 3 April 1996, p. 1.

9 *Izvestiya*, 1 June 1994, pp. 1, 7.

10 Quoted in *Sotsiologicheskii zhurnal*, no. 4, 1997, p. 73.

11 *Obshchaya gazeta*, no. 47, 1996, p. 3.

12 Hillel Ticktin, 'Permanent chaos without the market: the non-Latinamericanisation of the USSR', *Studies in Comparative Communism*, vol. 25, no. 3 (September 1992), pp. 242–56.

13 For a discussion of this characteristic pattern, see Theodore Taranovski, ed., *Reform in Modern Russian History: Progress or Cycle?* (Washington, DC: Woodrow Wilson Center Press, 1995).

14 Leonard Schapiro, *Rationalism and Nationalism in Russian Nineteenth-Century Political Thought* (New Haven, CT: Yale University Press, 1967), pp. 8–9.

15 Stephen White, *Political Culture and Soviet Politics* (London: Macmillan, 1979), pp. 36–7.

16 Hugh Seton-Watson, *The Russian Empire 1801–1917* (Oxford: Clarendon Press, 1967), p. 629.

17 Richard Pipes, *Russia Under the Old Regime* (London: Weidenfeld and Nicolson, 1974), pp. 293–4, 311.

18 *Izvestiya*, 19 August 1995, p. 1.

19 These and other characteristics, developed from the eighth century onwards, are identified in Samuel P. Huntington, *The Clash of Civilizations and the Remaking of World Order* (London: Simon and Schuster, 1997), pp. 68–72.

20 Samuel P. Huntington, 'Will more countries become democratic?', *Political Science Quarterly*, vol. 99, no. 2 (Summer 1984), p. 217.

21 Andrzej Korbonski in Marco Carnovale and William C. Potter, eds., *Continuity and Change in Soviet–East European Relations: Implications for the West* (Boulder, CO: Westview, 1989), p. 22.

22 Valerie Bunce in *PS: Political Science and Politics*, vol. 22, no. 2 (June 1989), p. 239.

23 Jerry F. Hough, 'Gorbachev's endgame', *World Policy Journal*, vol. 7, no. 4 (Fall 1990), pp. 642, 669.

24 Jerry F. Hough, 'Understanding Gorbachev: the importance of politics', *Soviet Economy*, vol. 7, no. 2 (April–June 1991), p. 106. Wider issues of interpretation are considered in Michael Cox, ed., *Rethinking the Soviet Collapse: Sovietology, the Death of Communism and the New Russia* (London: Pinter, 1999).

25 *Novaya i noveishaya istoriya*, no. 1, 1996, p. 113, in a telegram of February 1989; Matlock responded to some of the wider issues that had been raised ibid., no. 3, 1997, pp. 226–8.

26 Jack F. Matlock Jr, *Autopsy on an Empire: The American Ambassador's Account of the Collapse of the Soviet Union* (New York: Random House, 1995), p. 622.

27 See for instance P. J. D. Wiles and Stefan Markowski, 'Income distribution under communism and capitalism: some facts about Poland, the United Kingdom, the USA and the USSR', *Soviet Studies*, vol. 22, nos. 3 and 4 (January and April 1971), pp. 344–69 and 485–511.

28 According to UNESCO data, there were higher levels of enrolment in relation to population than in the United Kingdom and Germany, and only slightly lower levels than in France and Japan (*UNESCO Statistical Yearbook 1980* [Paris: UNESCO, 1980], table 3.10, pp. 423–31).

29 Seweryn Bialer, *Stalin's Successors: Leadership, Stability, and Change in the Soviet Union* (Cambridge: Cambridge University Press, 1980), p. 177.

30 See for instance Alexander J. Groth, 'Worker welfare systems in Marxist-Leninist states: a comparative perspective, c. 1975', *Coexistence*, vol. 19, no. 1 (April 1982), pp. 33–50; and L. L. Wade and Groth, 'Predicting educational outcomes by political regime: a global comparison', ibid., vol. 26, no. 2 (June 1989), pp. 147–59; both studies are based on GNP comparators.

31 See for instance F. V. Konstantinov, ed., *Filosofskaya entsiklopediya*, vol. IV (Moscow: Sovetskaya entsiklopediya, 1967), p. 237.

32 Richard Rose, *Governing Without Consensus* (London: Faber, 1971), p. 35.

33 Calculated from *Itogi Vsesoyuznoi perepisi naseleniya 1989 goda*, vol. II, part 1 (Minneapolis: EastView, 1992), pp. 13–14, based on the population aged seventy-three and over.

34 Albert Parry, *The New Class Divided: Russian Science and Technology Versus Communism* (New York: Macmillan, 1966).

35 Chalmers Johnson, ed., *Change in Communist Systems* (Stanford, CA: Stanford University Press, 1970).

36 Isaac Deutscher, *The Unfinished Revolution: Russia 1917–1967* (Oxford: Oxford University Press, 1967), pp. 59–60.

37 Marshall Goldman, *The USSR in Crisis* (New York: Norton, 1983).

38 Richard Pipes, 'Can the Soviet Union reform?', *Foreign Affairs*, vol. 63, no. 1 (Fall 1984), p. 50.

39 R. V. Burks, 'The coming crisis in the Soviet Union', *East European Quarterly*, vol. 18, no. 1 (Spring 1984), p. 71.

40 Martin Malia [Z], 'To the Stalin mausoleum', *Daedalus*, vol. 119, no. 1 (Winter 1990), p. 295.

41 Talcott Parsons, 'Evolutionary universals in society', *American Sociological Review*, vol. 29, no. 3 (June 1964), pp. 340–1. Parsons had already concluded that the single monolithic party would be obliged to 'relinquish its monopoly' (p. 356).

42 Talcott Parsons, 'Communism and the West: the sociology of the conflict', in Amitai Etzioni and Eva Etzioni, eds., *Social Change: Sources, Patterns and Consequences* (New York: Basic Books, 1964), pp. 396–8.

43 See Stephen White, 'Communist systems and the "iron law of plur-

alism"', *British Journal of Political Science*, vol. 8, no. 1 (January 1978), pp. 101–17.

44 Gabriel A. Almond, *Political Development* (Boston: Little, Brown, 1970), pp. 27, 318–19.

45 Robert C. Tucker, 'Swollen state, spent society: Stalin's legacy to Brezhnev's Russia', *Foreign Affairs*, vol. 60, no. 2 (Winter 1981), pp. 414–35.

46 Seweryn Bialer, *The Soviet Paradox: External Expansion, Internal Decline* (New York: Knopf, 1986).

47 *Newsnet: The Newsletter of the AAASS*, vol. 44, no. 1 (January 1994), p. 11.

48 On the environmental crisis, see Murray Feshbach and Alfred Friendly Jr, *Ecocide in the USSR: Health and Nature Under Siege* (New York: BasicBooks, 1992), and on social divisions Mervyn Matthews, *Poverty in the Soviet Union* (Cambridge: Cambridge University Press, 1986).

49 Konstantin Simis, *Secrets of a Corrupt Society* (London: Dent, 1982); Il'ya Zemtsov, *Partiya ili mafiya* (Paris: Editeurs réunis, 1976).

50 See respectively Lucian Pye, 'Political science and the crisis of authoritarianism', *American Political Science Review*, vol. 84, no. 1 (March 1990), pp. 6–9; and Moshe Lewin, *The Gorbachev Phenomenon* (Berkeley: University of California Press, 1988), p. 146.

51 See Adam Przeworski, et al., *Sustainable Democracy* (Cambridge: Cambridge University Press, 1995), p. 63.

52 Stephen Sestanovich, 'Gorbachev's foreign policy: a diplomacy of decline', *Problems of Communism*, vol. 38, no. 1 (January–February 1988), pp. 1–15.

53 M. S. Gorbachev, *Izbrannye rechi i stat'i*, 7 vols. (Moscow: Politizdat, 1987–90), vol. III, p. 199.

54 *Vedomosti S"ezda narodnykh deputatov SSSR i Verkhovnogo Soveta SSSR*, no. 26, 1990, art. 492, 12 June 1990.

55 Ibid., no. 11, 1990, art. 164, 6 March 1990, and no. 32, 1991, art. 904, 1 July 1991.

56 By early 1991 about twenty parties had come into existence at the national level, and about 500 in the republics (see respectively *Glasnost'*, no. 12, 1991, p. 2, and *Pravda*, 28 February 1991, p. 2). The new law was published in *Vedomosti S"ezda narodnykh deputatov SSSR i Verkhovnogo Soveta SSSR*, no. 42, 1990, art. 839, 9 October 1990.

57 Ibid., no. 37, 1991, art. 1083, 5 September 1991, and *Vedomosti S"ezda narodnykh deputatov RSFSR i Verkhovnogo Soveta RSFSR*, no. 52, 1991, art. 1865, 22 November 1991.

58 These events are reported in John Sweeney, *The Life and Evil Times of Nicolae Ceausescu* (London: Hutchinson, 1991), and Mark Almond, *The Rise and Fall of Nicolae and Elena Ceausescu* (London: Chapman, 1992).

59 *Argumenty i fakty*, no. 33, 1994, p. 1.

60 In the second case 43 per cent agreed, 45 per cent disagreed: *Izvestiya*, 20 August 1993, p. 4.

61 *Argumenty i fakty*, no. 34, 1997, p. 1.

62 *Sovetskaya Rossiya*, 20 August 1991, p. 2.

63 *Izvestiya*, 20 September 1991, p. 3.

64 Ibid., 27 August 1991, p. 3.

65 *Pravda*, 26 October 1991, p. 3.

66 *Izvestiya*, 31 August 1991, p. 3; there were also letters opposed to the coup.

67 Ibid., 21 October 1991, p. 3.

68 The vote in favour of a 'renewed federation' was 76 per cent, on a turnout of 80 per cent: *Izvestiya*, 28 March 1991, pp. 1, 3.

69 M. S. Gorbachev, *Dekabr'-91. Moya pozitsiya* (Moscow: Novosti, 1992), p. 9 (Yeltsin was speaking at a meeting of the State Council on 14 November 1991).

70 *Izvestiya*, 4 December 1991, p. 2.

71 *Daily Telegraph*, 30 January 1999, p. 16.

72 Olga Kryshtanovskaya and Stephen White, 'From Soviet nomenklatura to Russian elite', *Europe–Asia Studies*, vol. 48, no. 5 (July 1996), pp. 711–33. According to *Rossiiskaya gazeta*, up to 80 per cent of local functionaries were the same as in the Soviet period (4 March 1992, p. 2); local studies in Voronezh and Belgorod reached similar conclusions (*Dialog*, no. 8, 1996, p. 10).

73 *Izvestiya TsK KPSS*, no. 2, 1989, p. 243.

74 As Grigorii Yavlinsky put it, what had taken place was the 'conversion of the power that belonged to the old party *nomenklatura* into real property, and then its conversion back into power of an almost unlimited kind' (*Izvestiya*, 15 February 1997, p. 1).

75 John B. Dunlop, *The Rise of Russia and the Fall of the Soviet Empire* (Princeton, NJ: Princeton University Press, 1993), p. 223; contemporaries recorded a wide range of estimates, from 'scores of Muscovites' (Interfax) to 'many thousands' (*Pravda*) or even 'more than 1 million' (Budapest radio, all in FBIS: SOV 91-162, 21 August 1991, pp. 23, 67, 68). Later recollections are reported in *Izvestiya*, 17 August 1992, p. 3.

76 Bernard Wheaton and Zdenek Kavan, *The Velvet Revolution: Czechoslovakia, 1988–1991* (Boulder, CO: Westview, 1992), p. 95.

77 Of those elected, 86.3 per cent were Communist Party members or candidates: *I S"ezd narodnykh deputatov RSFSR 16 maya–22 iyunya 1990 goda. Stenograficheskii otchet*, 6 vols. (Moscow: Respublika, 1992–3), vol. I, p. 5. This was 10 per cent more than the highest proportion of party membership ever previously recorded: *Itogi vyborov i sostav deputatov verkhovnykh sovetov soyuznykh i avtonomnykh respublik (statisticheskii sbornik)* (Moscow: Izvestiya, 1980), pp. 88–9.

78 Gabriel A. Almond and Sidney Verba, *The Civic Culture: Political Attitudes and Democracy in Five Countries*, abridged edn (Boston: Little, Brown, 1965), pp. x, 339, 366.

79 See for instance Brian Barry, *Sociologists, Economists, and Democracy* (London: Collier-Macmillan, 1970); William L. Miller, *The Survey Method in the Social and Political Sciences* (New York: St Martin's, 1983), pp. 166–76; and Gabriel A. Almond and Sidney Verba, eds., *The Civic Culture Revisited* (Boston: Little, Brown, 1980). As Verba noted later, there were 'echoes of *The Civic Culture* in the discussions on the prospects for democracy in newly democratizing states' ('*The Civic Culture* and beyond: citizens, subjects and survey research in comparative politics', in Hans Daalder, ed., *Comparative European Politics: The Story of a Profession* [London: Pinter, 1997], p. 282).

80 See Kendall L. Baker, Russell J. Dalton, and Kai Hildebrant, *Germany Transformed: Political Culture and the New Politics* (Cambridge, MA: Harvard University Press, 1981).

81 See Stephen White, 'Political culture in communist states: some problems of theory and method', *Comparative Politics*, vol. 16, no. 3 (April 1984), pp. 351–65.

82 Seymour Martin Lipset, 'The social requisites of democracy revisited', *American Sociological Review*, vol. 59, no. 1 (February 1994), p. 3.

83 For a thoughtful review, see Frederic J. Fleron and Richard Alt, 'Does the public matter for democratization in Russia? What we have learned from "third wave" transitions and public opinion surveys', in Harry Eckstein, et al., *Can Democracy Take Root in Post-Soviet Russia? Explorations in State–Society Relations* (Lanham, MD: Rowman and Littlefield, 1998), pp. 287–327.

84 *Ekonomicheskie i sotsial'nye peremeny: monitoring obshchestvennogo mneniya*, no. 6, 1998, p. 52 (2.3 per cent thought the president deserved their 'entire confidence', 20 per cent had confidence in him 'to some extent', and 71.6 per cent had 'no confidence').

85 Ibid.

86 Ibid., pp. 52–3; for the comparison with investment funds, see Richard Rose, *Getting Things Done with Social Capital: New Russia Barometer VII* (Glasgow: University of Strathclyde, Centre for the Study of Public Policy, SPP 303, 1998), pp. 58–9.

87 Rose, *Getting Things Done*, pp. 35–6. These were not isolated findings: earlier New Russia Barometers had found, for instance, that 13 per cent thought it was 'easier' or 'much easier' to influence government, but that 32 per cent thought it was 'harder' or 'much harder' (Richard Rose, *New Russia Barometer V: Between Two Elections* [Glasgow: University of Strathclyde, Centre for the Study of Public Policy, SPP 260, 1996], p. 56). Other scholars found that Russians in 1990 were as likely as Americans to believe they were 'free' and more likely to do so than American blacks (James L. Gibson, 'Perceived political freedom in the Soviet Union', *Journal of Politics*, vol. 55, no. 4 [November 1993], pp. 964, 948), or that 'many Soviet citizens in the Brezhnev era did in fact trust other people and did value cooperative activity' (Donna Bahry and Brian D. Silver, 'Soviet citizen participation on the eve of democratization', *American Political Science Review*, vol. 84, no. 3 [September 1990], p. 841).

88 These results are based on a national representative survey conducted in December 1993 and January 1994 by Russian Public Opinion and Market Research (n=2141); a full report appears in William L. Miller, Stephen White, and Paul Heywood, *Values and Political Change in Postcommunist Europe* (London: Macmillan, 1998). Andrei Sakharov's widow Yelena Bonner complained that the state of human rights was 'worse than under Leonid Brezhnev', citing torture in prison, the persecution in Moscow of refugees from conflicts all over the former Soviet Union, and the political repression of environmental campaigners (*Guardian*, 22 May 1997, p. 13).

89 Miller, et al., *Values and Political Change*, p. 96.

90 *Central and Eastern European Barometer 7* (Brussels: European Commission,

1997), Annex Fig. 5 (Lithuanians were almost as dissatisfied as Ukrainians, but still less than Russians).

91 These findings are derived from our ROMIR survey (see n. 88 above).

92 *Ekonomicheskie i sotsial'nye peremeny*, no. 1, 1995, p. 10; similarly *Segodnya*, 24 January 1995, p. 10.

93 *USIA Opinion Analysis* M-70-97, 1 May 1997 (CESSI, n=1868).

94 *USIA Opinion Analysis* M-16-98, 9 February 1998 (ROMIR, n=1800); Jon H. Pammett and Joan DeBardeleben, 'The meaning of elections in transitional democracies: evidence from Russia and Ukraine', *Electoral Studies*, vol. 15, no. 3 (August 1996), p. 373; Pammett, 'Elections and democracy in Russia', *Communist and Post-Communist Studies*, vol. 32, no. 1 (March 1999), pp. 45–60.

95 Rose, *Getting Things Done*, pp. 47, 37.

96 Sarah Ashwin, '"There's no joy any more": the experience of reform in a Kuzbass mining settlement', *Europe–Asia Studies*, vol. 27, no. 8 (December 1995), pp. 1375–8.

97 Michael E. Urban, 'December 1993 as a replication of late-Soviet electoral practices', *Post-Soviet Affairs*, vol. 10, no. 2 (April–June 1994), pp. 127–58.

98 *Segodnya*, 12 January 1999, p. 2.

99 *Ekonomicheskie i sotsial'nye peremeny*, no. 1, 1995, p. 12; and for the comparison with the West, James L. Gibson and Raymond M. Duch, 'Political intolerance in the USSR: the distribution and etiology of mass opinion', *Comparative Political Studies*, vol. 26, no. 3 (October 1993), p. 300.

100 *Ekonomicheskie i sotsial'nye peremeny*, no. 2, 1995, pp. 59–60. Issues of this kind are considered further in James L. Gibson, 'A mile wide but an inch deep (?): the strength of democratic commitments in the former USSR', *American Journal of Political Science*, vol. 40, no. 2 (May 1996), pp. 396–420.

101 *Central and Eastern Eurobarometer*, no. 2 (Brussels: European Commission, 1992), Annex Fig. 8, and no. 7, Annex Fig. 4 (the 1996 results were in fact a slight improvement on those for 1995; none are available for subsequent years).

102 On pacts, see the studies collected in John Higley and Richard Gunther, eds., *Elites and Democratic Consolidation in Latin America and Southern Europe* (Cambridge: Cambridge University Press, 1992). Di Palma is quoted in Juan J. Linz and Albert Stepan, *Problems of Democratic Transition and Consolidation: Southern Europe, South America, and Post-Communist Europe* (Baltimore: Johns Hopkins University Press, 1996), p. 5.

103 Alexander Tsipko cited in Robert B. Sharlet, 'Transitional constitutionalism: politics and law in the Second Russian Republic', *Wisconsin International Law Journal*, vol. 14, no. 3 (Summer 1996), p. 496.

104 *Rossiya v tsifrakh. Kratkii statisticheskii yezhegodnik* (Moscow: Goskomstat Rossii, 1998), p. 108.

105 Rose, *Getting Things Done*, p. 32; 35 per cent, at the same time, read a regional or local paper on a regular basis.

106 Richard Rose, William Mishler, and Christian Haerpfer, *Democracy and Its*

Alternatives: Understanding Post-Communist Societies (Cambridge: Polity, 1998), p. 33.

107 Ibid., p. 32, and more generally ch. 2.

108 See Stuart Weir and David Beetham, *Political Power and Democratic Control in Britain* (London: Routledge, 1998), p. 10, drawing upon the work of Democratic Audit. Linz and Stepan emphasise other dimensions of a 'modern consolidated democracy' including 'rational-legal bureaucratic norms' and an 'institutionalized market': *Problems of Democratic Transition and Consolidation*, p. 14.

109 See for instance Abraham F. Lowenthal, ed., *Exporting Democracy: The United States and Latin America* (Baltimore: Johns Hopkins University Press, 1991), and Thomas Carothers, *In the Name of Democracy: US Policy Towards Latin America in the Reagan Years* (Berkeley: University of California Press, 1991); the quotation is on p. 243.

110 Samuel P. Huntington, 'After thirty years: the future of the third wave', *Journal of Democracy*, vol. 8, no. 4 (October 1997), p. 8.

111 Larry Diamond, 'Is the third wave over?', *Journal of Democracy*, vol. 7, no. 3 (July 1996), pp. 23–4. Some of these distinctions are considered in David Collier and Steven Levitsky, 'Democracy with adjectives: conceptual innovation in comparative research', *World Politics*, vol. 49, no. 3 (April 1997), pp. 430–51.

112 According to the European Institute for the Media, there was three times as much coverage for Yeltsin as for his nearest rival on national television and many other inequalities and irregularities: see *Media and the Russian Presidential Elections: Preliminary Report* (Dusseldorf: European Institute for the Media, 1996).

113 *OMRI Daily Digest*, no. 58, part 1, 22 March 1996.

114 David Remnick, 'The war for the Kremlin', *New Yorker*, 22 July 1996, p. 47.

115 Interview on Radio Liberty, 'Face to Face', 23 June 1996.

116 Remnick, 'The war', p. 47.

117 Samuel P. Huntington, *The Third Wave: Democratization in the Late Twentieth Century* (Norman: University of Oklahoma Press, 1991), p. 21. Others suggested a 'one-turnover test', but others still found all these tests 'too unidimensional and too vague' (Fritz Plasser, Peter A. Ulram, and Harald Waldrauch, *Democratic Consolidation in East-Central Europe* [London: Macmillan, 1998], p. 21).

118 *Rossiiskaya gazeta*, 27 August 1991, p. 3, and *Izvestiya*, 30 August 1991, p. 2.

119 *Komsomol'skaya pravda*, 12 April 1994, p. 3.

120 *Amnesty International Report 1994* (London: Amnesty, 1994), p. 250.

121 On asylum seekers, ibid. (the same problem was cited in subsequent reports); on arrests for evading the draft, *Amnesty International Report 1995* (London: Amnesty, 1995; hereafter *1995 Report*), p. 247, and *Amnesty International Report 1997* (London: Amnesty, 1997; hereafter *1997 Report*), p. 268.

122 *1995 Report*, p. 248; and for the report of deaths while awaiting trial, *Human Rights Watch World Report 1997* (New York: Human Rights Watch, 1996), p. 234.

123 *Amnesty International Report 1996* (London: Amnesty, 1996; hereafter *1996 Report*), p. 258. In a more detailed report, *Torture in Russia: 'This Man-Made Hell'* (April 1997, EUR 46/04/97), Amnesty found evidence of 'systematic and widespread use of torture and ill-treatment'.

124 *1997 Report*, p. 269; the parallel with Nazi Germany is reported in Svante E. Cornell, 'International reactions to massive human rights violations: the case of Chechnya', *Europe–Asia Studies*, vol. 51, no. 1 (January 1999), p. 90.

125 *1996 Report*, pp. 258–9, and *1997 Report*, p. 269.

126 *1996 Report*, p. 259; and on Sernovodsk, *1997 Report*, p. 269. In a more detailed report – *Russian Federation: Brief Summary of Concerns About Human Rights Violations in the Chechen Republic* (April 1996, EUR 46/20/96) – Amnesty reiterated its concern about 'massive human rights violations'.

127 *1997 Report*, pp. 268–70.

128 Human Rights Watch was established in 1978 as an 'independent, non-governmental organization, supported by contributions from private individuals and foundations worldwide'; it 'accepts no government funds, directly or indirectly': *Human Rights Watch World Report 1997*, p. vii.

129 *Human Rights Watch World Report 1999* (New York: Human Rights Watch, 1998; hereafter *1999 World Report*), pp. 280–1.

130 Ibid., pp. 282, 283.

131 Human Rights Watch Helsinki, *Russia/Chechnya: Report to the 1996 OSCE Review Conference*, November 1996, pp. 4, 8, 10.

132 *1999 World Report*, pp. 283–6.

133 *Country Reports on Human Rights Practices for 1997* (Washington, DC: US Government Printing Office, 1998), pp. 1244–5. The Country Reports were themselves scrutinised by the US Lawyers' Committee for Human Rights in an annual report: see for instance George Black, ed., *Critique: Review of the US Department of State's Country Reports on Human Rights Practices for 1996* (Philadelphia: University of Pennsylvania Press, 1997).

134 *Country Reports 1997*, pp. 1245, 1254–5.

135 Ibid., pp. 1246, 1264–5, 1253–4.

136 Freedom House is a 'national organization dedicated to strengthening democratic institutions'; the 'comparative survey' succeeded a year-end 'balance sheet of freedom' that had been initiated in 1955. The survey seeks to measure political rights (the 'extent that the people have a choice in determining the nature of the system and its leaders'), and civil liberties (which are the 'freedoms to develop views, institutions and personal autonomy apart from the state'): *Freedom Review*, vol. 28, no. 1 (January–February 1997), pp. 10, 193. For a review, see Youcef Bouandel and Stephen White, 'Measuring human rights: the Comparative Survey of Freedom', *Politics*, vol. 13, no. 1 (April 1993), pp. 17–21. For an overview of Freedom House's recent findings relating to the postcommunist world, see Adrian Karatnycky, et al., eds., *Nations in Transit: Civil Society, Democracy and Markets in East Central Europe and the Newly Independent States* (New Brunswick, NJ: Transaction, 1997). The quantitative assessment of human rights performance remains imperfect and controversial: see for instance Thomas B. Jabine and Richard P. Claude, eds., *Human*

Rights and Statistics: Getting the Record Straight (Philadelphia: University of Pennsylvania Press, 1992), and David Beetham, ed., *Defining and Measuring Democracy* (London: Sage, 1994).

137 *Freedom Review,* vol. 22, no. 1 (January–February 1991), p. 8.

138 Ibid., vol. 28, no. 1 (January–February 1997), p. 26.

139 Ibid., vol. 27, no. 1 (January–February 1996), p. 10.

140 Karatnycky, et al., *Nations in Transit,* p. 439.

141 *Freedom Review,* vol. 28, no. 1 (January–February 1997), pp. 9, 7, 15.

142 Roman Szporluk, 'The Soviet West – or Far Eastern Europe', *East European Politics and Society,* vol. 5, no. 3 (Fall 1991), pp. 466–82.

143 Robert D. Putnam with Roberto Leonardi and Raffaelle Y. Nanetti, *Making Democracy Work* (Princeton, NJ: Princeton University Press, 1993), pp. 183, 173.

144 *Freedom Review,* vol. 28, no. 1 (January–February 1997), p. 7.

145 The receding of the third wave is noted in Huntington, *The Third Wave,* pp. 17–21; reverses are also noted by K. S. Gadzhiev in *Voprosy filosofii,* no. 9, 1996, pp. 17–18 (democracy, for instance, had been repudiated three times in Turkey). In retrospect, 1991–2 appeared to represent a high-water mark; after 1991 the proportion of 'free states' fell slightly and the proportion of 'unfree' states increased sharply, showing the 'shallowness of democratization in the latter part of the third wave' (Diamond, 'Is the third wave over?', p. 28).

146 Christopher G. A. Bryant and Edmund Mokrzycki, eds., *The New Great Transformation? Change and Continuity in East-Central Europe* (London: Routledge, 1994), p. 3. The extent to which the transition in Russia and Eastern Europe was *sui generis* is considered in Philippe C. Schmitter with Terry Lynn Karl, 'The conceptual travels of transitologists and consolidologists', *Slavic Review,* vol. 53, no. 1 (Spring 1994), pp. 173–85; Sarah M. Terry, 'Thinking about postcommunist transitions: how different are they?', *Slavic Review,* vol. 52, no. 2 (Summer 1993), pp. 333–7; and Valerie Bunce, 'Should transitologists be grounded?', *Slavic Review,* vol. 54, no. 1 (Spring 1995), pp. 111–27. Wider issues of democratisation are considered in Robert D. Grey, ed., *Democratic Theory and Post-Communist Change* (Upper Saddle River, NJ: Prentice-Hall, 1997).

147 Barrington Moore Jr, *Liberal Prospects Under Soviet Socialism: A Comparative Historical Perspective* (New York: Harriman Institute, Columbia University, 1989), p. 20.

148 The role of the former communist *nomenklatura* was 'negligible' in the former Czech Republic, and also in the former GDR, although not in Slovakia (Thomas A. Baylis, 'Elite change after communism: Eastern Germany, the Czech Republic, and Slovakia', *East European Politics and Society,* vol. 12, no. 2 (Spring 1998), p. 276. Pareto's views are set out in his *Treatise on General Sociology* (New York: Harcourt, Brace, Jovanovitch, 1935).

149 Charles Tilly, *European Revolutions, 1492–1992* (Oxford: Blackwell, 1993), pp. 234, 233 (quoting Samuel Eisenstadt).

150 On 'power metamorphosis', see Bill Lomax in Gordon Wightman, ed., *Party Formation in East-Central Europe* (Aldershot: Edward Elgar, 1995),

p. 178; Andrei Grachev's assessment appears in his *Dal'she bez menya. Ukhod Prezidenta* (Moscow: Progress/Kul'tura, 1994), p. 9.

151 Leon Trotsky, *The Revolution Betrayed: What Is the Soviet Union and Where Is It Going?* (London: Faber and Faber, 1937), p. 240.

152 Samuel Huntington as quoted in the *New York Review of Books*, vol. 44, no. 1 (9 January 1997), p. 18.

153 Lipset, 'Social requisites', p. 5.

154 Fareed Zakaria, 'The rise of illiberal democracy', *Foreign Affairs*, vol. 76, no. 6 (November–December 1997), p. 29.

155 Huntington, *Clash of Civilizations*, p. 71.

156 Fedor Burlatsky in *Pravda*, 18 July 1987, p. 3.

Index